THE RADICAL EMPIRICISM OF WILLIAM JAMES

OTHER BOOKS BY JOHN WILD:

George Berkeley: A Study of His Life and Philosophy

Plato's Theory of Man

Introduction to Realistic Philosophy

Plato's Modern Enemies and the Theory of Natural Law

The Challenge of Existentialism

Human Freedom and the Social Order

Existence and the World of Freedom

The
Radical Empiricism
of
William James

John Wild

GREENWOOD PRESS, PUBLISHERS
WESTPORT, CONNECTICUT

Library of Congress Cataloging in Publication Data

Wild, John Daniel, 1902-1972.
  The radical empiricism of William James.

  Reprint of the ed. published by Doubleday, Garden
City, N.Y.
  Bibliography: p.
  Includes index.
  1. James, William, 1842-1910. 2. Empiricism.
I. Title.
[B945.J24W47 1980] 191   80-17547
ISBN 0-313-22641-5 (lib. bdg.)

This is a reprint of the first edition.

Reprinted by arrangement with Doubleday & Company, Inc.

Reprinted in 1980 by Greenwood Press,
A division of Congressional Information Service, Inc.
88 Post Road West, Westport, Connecticut 06881

Printed in the United States of America

10 9 8 7 6 5 4 3 2 1

I wish to thank the editors of the *Journal of Existentialism* for granting me permission to republish parts of my article on "William James and Existential Authenticity," which appeared in the Journal, V, 19 (1965), 243-56, in Chapter XII of this work.

PREFACE

Ever since I met Edmund Husserl personally in 1931 and studied with Heidegger at the University of Freiburg, I have been deeply interested in phenomenology and existential philosophy. The former is concerned with the clarification of patterns, the latter with human existence as we live it through, and I have been impressed by the uniting of these two approaches in Heidegger's *Sein und Zeit,* and the various works of Merleau-Ponty. It seems to me that such studies have already begun to lay the foundations for that central, humane discipline of which the philosopher Dilthey dreamed at the end of the last century. Once established, this discipline might greatly strengthen the human sciences, protect them against the reductive influences of scientism, and offer a firm basis for speculative philosophy.

Until the last six years, however, I have thought of this whole development as being exclusively European, and as having no significant American component. It was at this time that I first heard of Husserl's intensive reading of James' *Principles of Psychology* soon after it was published in 1890, and read the words of my friend, Gordon Allport at Harvard, who said that this work, if properly understood, might have inaugurated a native phenomenological movement in the United States. I was familiar with James' pragmatism and with his moral essays, but I had made no detailed study of his *Principles of Psychology.* I looked upon it as an early contribution to the new science of psychology, having little relevance to the patterns of existence as they are lived in the concrete. But when I began a careful study of the work, I soon saw the radical inadequacy of this point of view.

James is primarily interested not in science but in mental phenomena and their patterns as we are directly familiar with them and live them through. The *Principles* is full of concrete descriptions which can convey to the attentive reader a sense of the logos of the phenomena as they appear. We are thus entitled to think of James as an early member of that significant group of thinkers, scattered widely over the Western world, who became dissatisfied with the artificial abstractness of traditional systems of thought. In seeking not to construct but rather to find patterns in the world of existence, they were all phenomenologists, in a broad sense of this term. But in the case of James we can go even further.

From the beginning, he thought of himself as an empiricist, and in his early essay "The Sentiment of Rationality," he tried to work out the distinctive characteristics of this point of view, which he never regarded as a mere method, but always thought of as an integral philosophic attitude on a level with rationalism, scepticism, mysticism, etc. Later on, he used the phrase *radical empiricism* to avoid any confusion with British Empiricism. But at every stage of his career, his major aim was to avoid verbal construction, and to keep his thought in line with structures that could be found in the brute facts of experience. This guiding aim is present in his reflections on the most diverse topics, from the *Principles of Psychology* to his moral essays and *The Varieties of Religious Experience*. It does not impose a fixed order on these divergent ranges of fact. It can make new beginnings in accord with new facts. But in spite of this absence of finished order, there are constant glimpses of unity that open up new horizons and suggest new lines of inquiry.

In the present work I have tried to follow this open empirical inquiry in its major successive stages, in each of these, constantly singling out and dwelling on aspects of James' thought which are of special interest to phenomenologists. In Part I, I have focused his answers to certain questions concerning the world of sense and our knowledge of it, which he works out in the first volume of the *Principles of Psychology*. In Part II, I turn to the second volume of the *Principles* and the descriptive analyses we find there of "the three departments of the mind", perceptual facts, conceptual meanings, and finally, human choices and acts. Part III is devoted to the ethical and religious norms of action, and the pragmatic theory of truth to which they lead. In Part IV, I have first considered *The Essays in Radical Empiricism*, the last creative phase of James' development. Then I have tried to grasp this development as a whole, and to make judgments concerning its significance for our time.

Throughout Parts I to IV, I have constantly tried to let James speak for himself, so as to expose the reader directly to his extraordinary powers of finding stable patterns in the concrete, and of describing them as they are lived. In my comments, I have compared and contrasted them with later insights of phenomenology. Where James' descriptions are still too vague and confused, I have tried to clarify them; where they are sound but inchoate, I have sometimes tried to develop them further; where they are mistaken, I have criticized them.

I hope that this work may more solidly confirm a historical fact that others have suspected, namely that around the turn of the century, a native American philosopher began to think in an existential manner, and made important contributions to the phenomenological movement, in that broader sense which we are now beginning to recognize is required to understand it as a whole. But this is a relatively minor point. In my more optimistic moments I sometimes hope that by trying to see through the conventional tags and labels which have buried a great man of our past, I may have made some of his insights more accessible, and may thus indirectly help some of those who really read him not merely to think, but to think empirically in relation to our existence in the world, and thus to take philosophy seriously again.

I wish to express my thanks to Robert Ehman and to Hubert L. Dreyfus, who read important sections of the manuscript, and from whose criticisms I greatly benefited. I am grateful to members of seminars I have recently given at Yale with whom I have discussed some of the ideas presented here, and whose responses have been stimulating and suggestive. I am also grateful to the Philosophy Department of Yale University for grants covering secretarial expenses, to Mrs. Patricia Slatter for her general aid in preparing the manuscript, and to Mrs. Nancy Kaplan for her most effective and accurate overtime typing.

New Haven, Connecticut
January 2, 1968

CONTENTS

Part Three. Responsible Action and the Strenuous Life. How Beliefs Are Verified

Major works of James abbreviated in the text*

DOD "The Dilemma of Determinism," pp. 145–83 in both EFM and WBA

EFM *Essays on Faith and Morals,* Meridian Books, Cleveland, 1962

ERE *Essays in Radical Empiricism,* Longmans, New York, 1958

MPM "The Moral Philosopher and the Moral Life," pp. 184–215 in both EFM and WBA

MT *The Meaning of Truth: A Sequel to* Pragmatism, Longmans, New York, 1911

OSH "On some Hegelisms," pp. 263–98 in WBA

PR *The Principles of Psychology,* Vols. I and II, Dover Publications, New York, 1950

PRAG *Pragmatism,* Meridian Books, Cleveland, 1955

PU *A Pluralistic Universe,* Longmans, New York, 1958

RAAT "Reflex Action and Theism," pp. 111–44 in both EFM and WBA

SR "The Sentiment of Rationality," pp. 63–110 in both EFM and WBA

TT *Talks to Teachers on Psychology,* Dover Publications, New York, 1962

VA *The Varieties of Religious Experience,* Modern Library, New York, n.d.

WBA *The Will to Believe and Other Essays in Popular Philosophy,* Dover Publications, New York, 1956

* Page references in the text are to the editions listed. For a complete bibliography, see pp. 417–20.

THE RADICAL EMPIRICISM OF WILLIAM JAMES

Part One

❖

The World of Sense
and Its Patterns

Chapter One

❁

A Phenomenological Psychology

"Psychology is the Science of Mental Life, both of its phenomena and their conditions." This is the first sentence of James' classic text,[1] and in the first chapter, he carefully develops its meaning. It is important to note that first of all come *the phenomena*. These are what "we call feelings, desires, cognitions, reasonings, decisions and the like . . ." (PR, I, 1) The first task of psychology, as James conceives of it, is to describe these phenomena of mental life exactly as they are lived, so far as this is possible, and then to find out something concerning their relations and the patterns into which they fall.

There is no point in trying to explain the phenomena which actually appear by the construction of entities, like the soul substance of the scholastics and the unitary sensations of the

[1] All page references to *The Principles of Psychology* (PR) in the text will refer to Vols. I and II, Dover Publications, Inc., New York, 1950—an authorized republication, unabridged and unaltered, of the original 1890 edition.

associationists, which do not appear. In order to explain the phenomena of knowing past time as past, the spiritualist may conjure up a special "faculty" of memory, and the associationist certain special laws by which our ideas arrange themselves. But these constructive procedures only divert our attention from the actual phenomena of remembering as they are experienced by us. If they are ever to be explained, it is precisely these data, and not some others, that need to be explained. Our first duty, therefore, is to describe them as they appear, not to make them.

The attempt of the empiricists to reduce them to more ultimate data in terms of which they can be analytically explained is fictitious. For these are the ultimate data, and any attempt to reduce them will lead not to their explanation but rather to their destruction. "When, for instance, I recall my graduation-day, and drag all its incidents and emotions up from death's dateless night, no mechanical cause can explain this process, nor can any analysis reduce it to lower terms or make its nature seem other than an ultimate *datum*, which, whether we rebel or not at its mysteriousness, must simply be taken for granted if we are to psychologize at all" (p. 2). This phenomenological principle holds true for any humane discipline concerned with human phenomena. For such a discipline nothing can take the place of existence as it is lived through.

It is this existence, and not something else, that is to be clarified, or ultimately explained. Otherwise the discipline has completely failed to perform its peculiar task. Psychology is such a discipline. Hence its first responsibility is phenomenological— to describe these phenomena as they are lived, and as we are directly acquainted with them. The "we" here refers to all men everywhere, who are at least dimly familiar with the primary data of psychology, which are often, therefore, discounted as "obvious". But these obvious things are always the hardest to focus and clarify. The task of psychology is precisely that of bringing these obvious and familiar experiences into the light. As we shall see, this is an extremely complex and arduous task.

The Living Body

Let us now turn to the second part of James' definition, *the conditions* of these life phenomena with which we have so far been concerned. James refers here primarily to the brain and the bodily conditions of "mental" phenomena, which he thinks have been neglected or misunderstood by both empiricists and traditional defenders of a soul substance (pp. 3–5). Two points need to be noted in connection with these conditions. The first is that they stand for constant patterns found in experience. The brain that conditions our "mental" life is not an extra-experiential brain in itself. It is "experiences of the body" (not some body in itself), and even experiences of the brain (not some brain in itself) which contribute something essential to the total experience of memory (p. 4).

It is true that we may not be directly aware of this contribution in our lived experience. But we find this out by further observation and reflection, which show us that "if the brain be injured, consciousness is abolished or altered, even although every other organ in the body be ready to play its normal part" (p. 4). This brain is not the object which may later be dissected in an autopsy. It is the living brain in my head with whose position I am directly acquainted, and which I carry with me wherever I go. This subjective brain is not the cause of something else that I experience. It actually undergoes an "experience" of correlation, or integration, which even though never focused by me, nevertheless enters into my life-experience. As James puts it: "bodily experiences, therefore, and more particularly brain-experiences, must take a place amongst those conditions of the mental life of which Psychology need take account" (p. 4).

The second point is that these bodily conditions, while necessary, are not sufficient, and, therefore, not to be confused with causes. The brain contribution enters into the total experience, together with other contributions, as the "codeterminant" of a whole that is more than the sum of its parts. A third point deserves even greater emphasis. "Mental phenomena are not only conditioned *a parte ante* by bodily processes; but they lead to them *a parte post*" (p. 5). This is not a dualistic interaction between body and mind. James does not say that the mental phenomena cause bodily changes. The former rather "lead to" the latter and *vice versa*.

It is true that later on in the text James expresses the prevalent hope for an explanatory psychology that will be able to "control" psychic phenomena, and even speaks disparagingly of description as a primitive stage in science (*cf.* II, 448, 454). But in the text, it is the phenomena which come first, and with a few exceptions, it is only after they have been described that room is found for speculations concerning the brain. James had an extraordinary capacity for phenomenological description and analysis, and in spite of his self-depreciation, it is this primary part of his text that has kept it alive, and is of special interest at the present time. Hence we shall concentrate our attention upon it, and subordinate the rest.

It is clear in any case that James is struggling at the very beginning of his text to overcome the dualism that is still present in his thought. The living body contributes something to every mental experience, and these mental experiences contribute something to later bodily experiences. The two are involved with each other, and whether we can call a given experience "mental" or "physical" is really a matter of degree and emphasis. He is working here, and as we shall see later, in the text as a whole, towards the present phenomenological conception of the "conscious", living body[2] which moves and behaves as an integrated whole.

The mental life, in which the psychologist is interested, is not enclosed within a subjective container, nor is it conditioned solely by the experiences of its own body. This mental life has been thrown into a vast world-field of external things and persons with which it is directly acquainted. James makes it clear

2 *Cf.* M. Merleau-Ponty, *The Phenomenology of Perception,* tr. Smith, New York, 1962, pp. 138–39.

in this first chapter that he is rejecting the traditional notion of an isolated "mind" that can be understood apart from the external things with which it is constantly engaged. This mind has been thrown into the midst of these external things, and exists in the world with them. But it is not merely in the world as a chair is spatially contained in the room. It *inhabits* the world and dwells in the world, as a soldier is *in* the army or a doctor is *in* medicine as in a field of care. The living mind cannot be separated from its environment, and the new psychology must take this fact into account, thus departing radically from traditional versions. As James puts it in a pregnant sentence (I, 6): "because it takes into account the fact that minds inhabit environments which act on them, and on which they in turn react; because, in short, it takes mind in the midst of all its concrete relations, it is immensely more fertile than the old-fashioned 'rational psychology', which treated the soul as a detached existent, sufficient unto itself, and assumed to consider only its nature and properties."

If this is true, our mental life is not only conditioned by our bodily experiences. It is also conditioned by our direct experience of external things and persons, and the impressions they impose upon us, as well as by our own active impulses and desires. As James says (p. 6), the mental life "seems to intervene" in such a way as to make a radical difference between the whole pattern of human behavior and the causal interaction of inorganic things. James does not develop this idea in detail in the first chapter. Nevertheless he gives some important hints which need to be borne in mind as we read through the main body of the text.

Without any awareness of what they are doing, the iron filings are simply drawn to the surface of the magnet or, if prevented by obstacles, as close as they can come. In this case, the end is "a mere passive result" that is pushed into being from behind, "having had, so to speak, no voice in its own production" (p. 8). There is no mean between the cause and its effect. When a stick or a stone is moved by some external cause to a new position, it does not move for the sake of anything.

There is no intervention of a middle term to give the motion of such things any meaning. So as James says: "we unhesitatingly call them senseless" (p. 8).

But with the intervention of mental life, the whole pattern changes. First of all, there is an opening to the future which places the agent at a distance from his past and present. The causal result becomes an anticipated end, which can be maintained under varying conditions. The causes which automatically tend to the result now also gain a meaning, and become means for attaining the end. From the future vantage point where the agent now stands, they can be envisaged, taken into account, and altered to meet different situations. Thus Romeo is moved towards Juliet, as the filings are moved towards the magnet. But "with the filings, the path is fixed; whether it reaches the end depends on accidents. With the lover it is the end which is fixed, the path may be modified indefinitely" (p. 7). Also, though James does not specifically note this fact, a further future may be opened up, and the "fixed end" may gain a new meaning in the light of which it may be altered, or even eliminated to meet new conditions.

Such meaningful action, performed for the sake of an end, is the peculiar subject-matter of the new psychology (p. 11). This action is based on an elaborate substructure of causal action and interaction, which is only peripheral to the distinctive region of psychology. "Many nervous performances will, therefore, be unmentioned, as being purely physiological", though the functions of the cerebral hemispheres, "since they directly subserve consciousness", will be considered in Chapters II and III of the *Principles*. But it remains true for James that "*no actions but such as are done for an end, and show a choice of means, can be called indubitable expressions of Mind*" (p. 11, James' italics). It is important to note here the close connection between meaningful action and freedom of choice. Meaning and freedom are achieved together.

It is also important to recognize that, on the basis of this conception, with which we shall be constantly concerned throughout this work, causal connections are in no sense violated or abrogated by meaningful action. They are rather taken over, exactly as they stand, into a world of meaning. Without being broken or violated in any way, causes become means, and causal results become ends. Only a genuine cause can function as a reliable means to an anticipated end, so that in so far as causal laws cease to hold, meaningful action becomes impossible. This is no doubt the explanation for James' indifference in the *Psychology* to the traditional issue between freedom of the will and determination (PR, Chap. XXVI). The freedom that comes with meaning leaves causal laws intact, and, indeed, rests upon them. Nevertheless, meaning does transform the senseless sequences of nature into a human world, and makes a radical difference in what we call "free" behavior. Hence in his later works where he is more deeply concerned with ultimate questions, James more openly and clearly defends human freedom, though not in any sense that would involve a violation of natural laws.

Consciousness in the World

The psychologist is a student of meaningful action performed by human beings actually existing in the world. In the first chapter, James indicates the central conception which will govern his study, and sketches the general program he will follow. Now let us turn to the actual working out of this program in the text, with which he was occupied for a period of fourteen years. As we have seen, James is sceptical of any approach to mental life which would artificially isolate it from those conditions with which it is inextricably involved in our lived experience. The first of these is the living, "conscious" body without which meaningful action is never found. We shall pass over Chapters II and III where he deals with the human brain and summarizes the basic content of the brain physiology of his time. That the central nervous system makes an essential contribution to mental life is indirectly indicated by a vast number of well-authenticated facts, like the effects of concussion, drugs, etc. We shall now take these facts for granted, and turn to Chapter IV where James singles out a phenomenon in which a basic contribution of the living brain to our mental life is directly experienced by all men. This phenomenon is habit.

Man is a creature of habit, and as soon as our attention is focused upon it, we can see that it pervades every phase of our meaningful life. In this chapter, James traces it back to a basic characteristic of matter, which he calls *plasticity*. There are, of course, certain rigid structures of nature in which any marked change involves total destruction. In such cases, extreme change is correlated with inflexibility. But in a fluid, evolutionary world, they are the exception rather than the rule. Most patterns that survive for any length of time in such a world must possess a plasticity that enables them to adapt to changing circumstances. This is particularly true of living organisms endowed with hereditary organs that dictate "instinctive" patterns of action. But within certain limits, even these responses can be modified. In the higher animals, these changes become established as learned habits which vary from generation to generation and even from individual to individual.

In man, this plasticity of habit has reached its climax, which James finds expressed in the extraordinary complexity and flexibility of the nervous paths in the brain, where incoming perceptual currents are united with outgoing currents initiating muscular contractions and actions of various kinds. In such a system, where the different parts are maintained in different states of tension, but also tend to equalize themselves through paths of least resistance, new paths may readily occur (I, 109), and as James says, even in the absence of more exact knowledge, "nothing is easier than to imagine how, when a current once has traversed a certain path, it should traverse it more readily still a second time" (p. 109). These are the necessary conditions for the process of habit formation.

The point that is especially worthy of notice in this long discussion of the nervous background (pp. 104–12) is James' rejection of the traditional idea of a disembodied consciousness, and his constant attempt to emphasize the role of the living body in every phase of our "conscious" life. As nervous pathways become established, the action required to achieve a meaningful end is simplified and accomplished with less fatigue. Another result of habit formation is the diminishing of the conscious attention required for what come to be the instrumental phases of the act. Thus one who is learning to play the piano at the beginning must pay attention to the playing of a single chord, and then to a simple sequence of chords. At first, these simple operations are an end. But as habit formation advances, further horizons of meaning open up, and what were once ends, gradually become means which can be set off in large groups with only a very slight effort of attention.

Nevertheless James insists that these habitual sequences are not wholly automatic and unconscious, though such a condition is often approached, as in the case of the man who goes to his room to change his clothes before dining, and suddenly finds himself in bed. Such a man will be quickly aroused from his meditations if the lights suddenly go out, and the skilled musician will at once pay conscious attention to a single finger that has played a wrong note. Hence James concludes that, while consciousness has "diminished", it is not entirely eliminated. Throughout the whole discussion, it is noteworthy that he does not refer to consciousness as a separate effect of nervous changes. It is, rather, directly involved with them, and accompanies them in a diminished form even in their routine chains and sequences, which, as we say, go off of themselves. Thus (p. 118) "these immediate antecedents of each movement of the chain are at any rate *accompanied* by consciousness of some kind" (my italics). "They are *sensations* to which we are *usually inattentive*, but which immediately call our attention if they go *wrong*" (James' italics).

There can be little question that the nervous system and its laws make an essential contribution to the conscious process of habit formation. The basic fact we have noted—that as habit increases, consciousness diminishes—is one reason for our failure to follow Aristotle in recognizing that consciousness itself falls into habits, and for the modern doctrine of a separate consciousness, which James strongly opposed. This is no doubt why he begins his account of mental life by this chapter on habit, and why he is so anxious to call his reader's attention to the pervasive presence of habit in every aspect of human experience. This becomes especially clear in the last section (pp. 120–27), devoted to what he calls "the ethical implications of the law of habit".

These, he says, are "numerous and momentous", but he summarizes them in the form of three basic maxims. Unlike the other animals, man, within certain hereditary limits, is enabled by the plasticity of the human nervous system to make himself, and to some degree even to remake himself, not as Sartre would say by conscious choice alone, but by conscious choice of habit. If it is to be effective, this process of human self-making must begin at a very early age. This is the first maxim of habit formation that James considers. He begins by calling attention to the large-scale social and political effects of habit, "the enormous fly-wheel of society, its most precious conservative agent". It conserves not only the precious discoveries and advances of the past, but also its defects and limitations. Thus "men grown old in prison have asked to be readmitted after being once set free" (p. 121). Habit is the real defender of custom and law, as of their biases and weaknesses. It keeps the poor in order, prevents the most repulsive walks of life from being deserted, and keeps different classes and social strata from mixing. "It dooms us all to fight out the battle of life upon the lines of our nurture or our early choice, and to make the best of a pursuit that disagrees, because there is no other for which we are fitted, and it is too late to begin again" (p. 121). All this points to the major importance of early training.

We do not merely have a nervous system. We are our nervous systems, and we cannot ignore them without falling into enmity with ourselves. "The great thing, then, in all education, is to *make our nervous system our ally instead of our enemy,*" and *"for this we must make automatic and habitual, as early as possible, as many useful actions as we can,* and guard against the growing into ways that are likely to be disadvantageous to us, as we should guard against the plague" (p. 122). Needless to say, the importance of parental care and intelligent counselling is not to be minimized, but unless this process can be internalized, and a man can learn to counsel himself, he will be doomed to some form of slavery, even though it may be well-concealed. So the primary maxim of any counsellor must be the eliciting of self-counselling. But even this self-advice is bound to be futile, unless the child learns how to develop the necessary habits on his own. Hence the next four maxims are concerned with the formation of new habits.

The forming of a new habit involves the breaking of old habits, and ultimately the rearranging of a whole mode of life. The beginning is all-important. We must choose the most favorable circumstances for embarking on the new way, and arrange for situations that are incompatible with the old. This is the first maxim which needs to be followed to avoid a disastrous early breakdown, and to make a less fatal later one less likely. The second closely associated maxim is: *"never suffer an exception to occur till the new habit is securely rooted in your life"* (p. 123). In breaking firmly ingrained habits of long standing, a process of tapering off may be necessary. But this is dangerous, and may come to nothing. It is always advisable to make the transition as abrupt and uncompromising as possible.

The third is never to lose ourselves in good intentions but to embrace every possible opportunity for resolute action in line with the new way of life, for actions speak louder than words. James clearly recognizes that action begins with feeling. But he emphasizes the danger of indulging in "false" orgies of feeling and abstract ideas which never terminate in action. Truth in this context means actually leading us to authentic, meaningful action in the world. Hence if an idea, or a feeling, never leads us beyond itself, it loses its meaning and we call it false. As we shall see, James develops this idea further in his pragmatic theory of truth (*cf. infra,* Chapter XIII). A fourth and final maxim is concerned with the need for practice in the freedom of habit formation. *"Keep the faculty of effort alive in you by a little gratuitous exercise every day"* (I, 126). Effort lies at the heart of our human freedom. Asceticism, therefore, in the little things of everyday life is the best insurance against slavery. James ends this chapter on habit with a warning against the teaching of ethics in an abstract and intellectualistic manner, with no attention to the nervous system and other basic facts of life. Nothing we actually do is ever wiped out, and the young should be constantly reminded that the time is soon coming when they will become "mere walking bundles of habits" (p. 127).

Having mapped out his general program for a concrete psychology, close to the phenomena of lived experience, James now turns to a critical consideration of two influential and more abstract approaches, against which he is rebelling—epiphenomenalism and the mind-stuff theories as he calls them.

The Automaton Theory

The first is the view of consciousness as an inefficacious epiphenomenon which had been defended by Huxley, Clifford, James' friend, Shadworth Hodgson, and many others. According to this theory, consciousness is an inert spectator, a mere foam, or melody, that runs alongside of the brain events which determine each other according to causal laws. James suggests three reasons that make the theory attractive to scientifically oriented thinkers, and in his critical comments indicates their purely abstract and metaphysical character. The first is an argument from continuity. Thus it may be said that there is no cogent evidence for the presence of consciousness in the frog and in other lower animals. The intelligence of their actions can be accounted for, without making any appeal to such a mysterious factor, by nervous and physiological processes which are causally determined. Why then should we not suppose that the higher intelligence of men, though attended by consciousness, can be similarly explained?

But, as James points out, the facts here adduced are equally open to an opposite interpretation. It is no more legitimate to read the lower into the higher than to follow others, like Lewes, who read the higher into the lower. They maintain that since human intelligence is due to the consciousness we know to be there, so it is reasonable to explain the intelligence of the frog in terms of a consciousness of lower degree. The argument from continuity is inconclusive, since it works equally well in both directions.

The second is an argument from convenience. The scientific method is concerned with observable objects that can be measured and related together by quantitatively expressible, causal laws. Conscious phenomena cannot be exhaustively understood in this way, for they involve subjective factors that cannot be objectified and measured. Hence it is easy to see why scientists, from the nature of their task, should prefer a strict metaphysical dualism which would leave their physical field intact and excuse them from attending to strange factors not readily accessible to their methods. It is interesting to note that, contrary to certain interpretations of the "pragmatic method" which he later formulated but already had in mind, James sharply rejects this argument from convenience. He does this, moreover, as an empiricist, radically committed to following the phenomena as they appear, wherever they may lead. Why should we suppose that the universe has been constructed for the convenience of scientists? Their method has limits, and in approaching different phenomena, different methods should be used.

The third argument is based on the difficulty of imagining any way in which a conscious idea, or feeling, as traditionally understood, can physically influence and move the molecules of the brain. James replies to this argument in two ways. His first move is to point out that how persons influence other persons and things, which he calls psychic causation, is no more mysterious than how physical things produce their effects, material causation, as he calls it (p. 137). The whole subject is plunged into the darkest obscurity, and there is no ground for an invidious distinction between the two. We cannot justifiably accept the efficacy of physical causes which act without sense and then dogmatically rule out the possibility of any efficacy of meaning. We must be "impartially *naif* or impartially critical" (p. 137).

James' remarks here are very interesting. If we choose to be critical, we cannot stop short of a complete metaphysical interpretation of the world in which causation occurs. If we do this, we "will probably preserve the common-sense view that ideas (or meanings) are forces, in some translated form", that is, at this time, James believes that meanings, in connection with human activity, do exert some peculiar kind of efficacy, though not as "forces" in the traditional sense of these terms, and certainly not as physical causes. Then he goes on to say that, as a science, psychology, like physics, must be naïve in accepting certain basic terms, like causation, in their common usage without attempting to define them more exactly. It has nothing to gain by departing from common usage in describing the facts. ". . . In her very peculiar field of study ideas *seem* to be causes" and "she had better continue to talk of them as such" (p. 137).

James is well aware of the consequence that this must involve —a broadening of our conception of the living body, and especially of the brain. Thus the brain "will be, for us, a sort of vat in which feelings and motions somehow go on stewing together, and in which innumerable things happen of which we catch but the statistical result" (p. 138). In the living body, meanings are involved with attitudes and sets of various kinds of motions, and these bodily motions carry meaning. This stewing together of motions and meanings is certainly a mystery, but if the facts clearly indicate that this stewing is going on, as they do, we must follow ordinary language in accepting them, and seek for further light. But what facts indicate this? James is not content with merely showing the inadequacies of the automaton theory. He proceeds in the next pages (138–44) to sketch a positive theory of his own, which lies at the root of his pragmatic theory of truth as he later called it, and is a basic factor in the whole remainder of his writings.

In order to understand this decisive step in James' thinking, we must bear in mind his early contacts with Agassiz, and his training as a medical student. These experiences had familiarized him with the basic facts of evolution, and left a firm impression on his mind. From this time on, he was convinced that man had evolved from lower forms through a historical process in which the principle of natural selection must have played an essential role. With this principle in operation, there is clearly no place for the persistent survival of an inefficacious, useless consciousness. But our kind of consciousness has not only survived; it has also developed from simple levels, as in the frog and other lower animals, to much more complex and higher levels in man. It must possess some biological utility to account for this long survival and development. What can this utility be? Such is the background of James' theory of consciousness, which he starts to develop at this point in the *Principles*, and which leads to his pragmatic theory of truth.

James now returns to the theme of habit, and we can see why he begins his own systematic development of psychology (the study of consciousness) with a consideration of this topic. Habit is opposed to consciousness, for the two vary inversely. Where habit is fixed and firm, consciousness is at low ebb, where intense, habit is unstable. How is this instability expressed in structural terms? The answer is clear. It is found in the "high" nerve centers where many alternative currents are possible whose performance is therefore, "indeterminate and unforeseeable" (p. 139). If proper use can be made of these nerve centers, "this very vagueness constitutes their advantage", since "they allow their possessor to adapt his conduct to the minutest alterations in the environing circumstances, any one of which may be for him a sign, suggesting distant motives more powerful than any present solicitations of sense" (p. 139).

We may say, in fact, that consciousness is basically a systematic vagueness which places us at a distance from objects to which lower animals react with firmness and certainty. Their simpler nervous system allows them flexibility only with respect to minor, instrumental phases of their action. Its basic patterns are firmly fixed by instinct and habit and, therefore, unconscious. But, in man, this ambiguity extends much further, ultimately even to the underlying patterns of his existence. From these, too, he can gain a distance and imagine possible alternatives. To each thing to which a set response is normally given, an opposite mode of response can be prepared (imagined). Hence this hesitating consciousness is basically negative, or dialectical. But these paths proceed from a different center on another path which also has an alternative, and so on. The central source, from which these opposed alternatives may or may not proceed, is always present, but at a distance from them, and opposed to them as a "subject" to its objects. This is perhaps the source of what we call *self-consciousness.* Gaining a distance in this way not only from things but from himself, to whom he may respond in different ways, the human individual is placed in a field of ambiguity which, in our common language, is called *the world.*

But a consciousness hesitating before the object of an habitual response, and viewing it in the light of an opposed alternative, would be of no use unless it were completed by a selection of the better alternative. This is only a partial phase of a fully functioning consciousness. As James sees it, the trouble with the automaton theory, and other purely spectatorial views of this phenomenon, is that they end with this partial phase of hesitation before an object, without proceeding to its completion, an act of choice or selection. They deal with consciousness as though it were a vast cafeteria, offering us a variegated display of hot, and cold, and desultory viands, arousing our hunger, but never allowing us to choose a meal. Such a view is not only unintelligible; it is false to the phenomena. As James says, "the study of the phenomena of consciousness which we shall make throughout the rest of this book will show us that consciousness is at all times primarily *a selecting agency.* Whether we take it in the lowest sphere of sense, or in the highest of intellection, we find it always doing one thing, choosing one out of several of the materials so presented to its notice, emphasizing and accentuating that and suppressing as far as possible all the rest" (p. 139). The ambiguity provided by the complex, central nervous systems of the higher animals would be a hindrance rather than a help, unless it were completed by meaningful choice. In its integral manifestations, consciousness is essentially bound up with meaning. Physical things do not hesitate and vacillate between opposed alternatives. They act straightaway, and we call this action meaningless, since it may lead just as well to destruction as to survival. In the interval of hesitation, however, there is time for opposed currents to connect up with, or to signify, other patterns of response to more remote objects, and for a selection of that which fits a primary mode of response.

Thus a higher animal can maintain a stable course of action throughout a long period of time, during which various selective adjustments can be made to variable circumstances. But this flexibility is restricted. The primary patterns are set to go off with only a minimum of consciousness, and selection is concerned only with subordinate phases of the total act. In man, however, "where indecision is great . . . consciousness is agonizingly intense" (p. 142). Hence in times of reflection, or hesitation, he can bring whole patterns of action, and even existence itself, into question, which animals cannot do. Hence, for him alone, suicide is possible. This process, of course, is vastly expanded by the coming of language, which enables him to explore the meanings of absent situations, and to develop others which have never occurred before. In this way, as James points out, he is able to make, and to remake himself by the invention of new meanings, and the establishment of new systems of habit.

James finds this theory corroborated by a fact that had been emphasized by evolutionary writers not prone to defend the efficacy of consciousness. It is well known that pleasures generally arise from beneficial and pains from harmful actions. Healthful food and drink, unbroken bones, and rest when fatigued are usually pleasant, whereas privation of food and drink, the effects of poison, burning, wounds, and suffocation are usually painful, though there are exceptions. James notes that this fact implies a real efficacy of consciousness, since a totally unconscious pleasure or pain is impossible. Thus a person who found enough pleasure in not breathing to immerse his head indefinitely in water would not be apt to survive for any long period of time, if left to himself.

Let us now turn to James' criticism of what he calls the mind-stuff or dust theory. With this we may be more brief, since it does not involve such a deep break with traditional views.

The Mind-Stuff Theory

As against the automaton theory, James holds, as we have seen, that consciousness is an efficacious principle of ambiguity, which finds patterns of meaning in the world, and in the light of these, chooses to act in purposeful ways. If it is, therefore, something more than an inert spectator, that makes a difference in the flow of events, it is clear that James must also reject another related view, which he calls the mind-stuff theory. According to this theory, conscious experience may be reduced to ultimate atoms of consciousness, which associate together in different combinations to form higher and more complex experiences. The classical British empiricists called these atoms of consciousness *ideas,* or sense impressions, and thought of them as produced by the physical impact of physical influences on the sense organs.

In this chapter, VI, James is more directly concerned with certain of their followers, especially Spencer, who carried the reductive process one step further, holding that the different sense-data of sound, vision, touch, etc., could be analyzed into combinations of similar units, which he identified with nervous excitement or the sense of shock. On this view, each light vibration causes a nervous shock when received by the retina. If received at a more rapid rate, these shocks combine together in the mind to form the sensation of red; if at a slower rate, the sensation of green, and so on.

James here offers two general arguments against this reductive theory. The first is an empirical argument which points out the absence of any proof "that the physical processes get through air and ear, auditory nerve and medulla, lower brain and hemispheres, without their number being reduced" (p. 155). This is confirmed by the absence of any direct experience of these atoms of consciousness and their mixing. James refers to the experimental evidence showing that when green light and red light fall simultaneously on the retina, we have no experience of a conscious green and a conscious red together with a mixing of the two feelings, as the theory would demand (pp. 156–57). We immediately see only yellow, with no sense of any component atomic shocks. To break it down into these colorless elements would destroy the phenomenon of yellow as we experience it.

This leads James to a second "logical" argument in which he points to a fallacy committed by reductive explanations of this kind. No mere "association", or summing together of distinct elements, can fully explain the unique characteristics found in the "whole". If such a new whole really emerges from the combining of separate units, this whole, with its distinctive properties, cannot be reduced to the summing of the original elements as they were in separation. Thus a whole meaningful sentence cannot be reduced to the summing together of the component words (p. 160). This whole is a new being with unique properties of its own. The associationists, and other reductive analysts, really admit this in offering their analysis as an explanation of the phenomenon in terms of different elements. They then proceed to assert that what they have explained is nothing but the controllable summation of the independent units. But as James points out, this is a contradiction. The whole cannot be both a new being, with distinctive properties of its own, and a mere sum of units, each with different properties. James thinks that the Hegelians, in holding that each single thing is both a one and a many, have not only committed this fallacy, but have turned it into the methodological core of their dialectical system (p. 163).

James is here defending the notion of levels of phenomena. He is not denying that a lower level may be a necessary condition for a higher level, nor that units of the former may be found by analysis in the latter. But to say that the higher level phenomenon is totally explained in this way and is nothing but a summation of lower level units is usually to jump to a premature conclusion, which might be called the post-analytic fallacy. The only remedy is phenomenological description. We need to dwell on a given phenomenon, to grasp its peculiar characteristics, to understand what it is, before we attempt to explain it. In the light of such an examination, we may discover, as James says, that "the two sorts of fact are not identical: a higher state *is* not a lot of lower states: it is itself" (p. 162, note, James' italics).

The intellectualistic defenders of reductive explanations of conscious phenomena use another line of argument based on the conception of an unconscious mode of consciousness. James refers here (p. 164, note) to E. von Hartmann's *Philosophy of the Unconscious*, and seems to be thinking not so much of those who try to reduce all conscious phenomena to combinations of simple units as of idealistic monists who reduce personal thoughts and feelings to the manifestations of a single super-individual consciousness (*Bewusstsein*). Both share a common interest in maintaining that the phenomena of human life are not as they appear, but rather the products of an underlying unity which never appears. The distinction between the unconscious and the conscious being of a mental state is a very useful instrument for such a purpose. As James says, "it is the sovereign means for believing what one likes in psychology", and for turning it into a tumbling ground for speculative "whimsies" (p. 163).

James knew nothing of Freud at this time. But there is little doubt that he would have applied the same sort of criticism to the unobserved forces of Freud, which explain the inner life of man on a mechanical model. James was never anti-metaphysical, and he recognizes that in this chapter he is himself engaging in metaphysical criticism. But before engaging in disciplined speculation, it is well to become aware of our metaphysical frames, and to compare them with the facts. This is the object of the present chapter. It is the only way, as James saw it, to a responsible and grounded metaphysics of experience.

A Critique of the Unconscious

In examining the distinction between the conscious and the unconscious (pp. 164 ff.), as it appears primarily in idealistic thinkers, James goes through ten arguments for the notion of the unconscious found in the literature, and subjects each one of the ten to a cogent criticism as he goes along. We shall single out three of these, 1, 9, and 10, for a brief comment. The first is taken from Leibnitz' defence of his notion of insensible units of consciousness (*petites perceptions*). In his preface to the *Nouveaux Essais*, he illustrates this conception by the roaring of the waves near the seashore. Even though one would not notice it if it were alone, one must nevertheless actually hear the noise of each single wave. Otherwise one would not hear the roaring of 100,000 waves, since "of 100,000 zeros one can never make a quantity".

Certain mathematically minded psychologists have applied this quantitative idea to their conception of the minimum visible, the minimum audible, etc. James sharply rejects this argument as an example of the fallacy of "division", that is, "predicting what is true only of a collection, of each member of the collection distributively" (p. 164). There is no doubt that a conscious experience involves a total state of the brain, which can be analyzed into a number of nervous excitations. It may be said that each of these disposes the brain towards an experience of this kind. But to infer that it must possess a tiny unit of unconscious sensibility is to commit the analytic fallacy. The experience itself, with its total brain condition, is a new being with distinctive characteristics of its own.

A second argument is concerned with habitual responses that have become largely automatic and seemingly unconscious. These responses first require conscious planning and deliberation at each step. It is now known that in man, at least, some intelligence is at work even after they have been learned, and that the higher cortical centres are involved. But these acts can be accurately performed while our conscious attention is directed elsewhere. Hence they must be directed by unconscious perceptions, inferences, and volitions. James counters this argument by suggesting two alternative explanations that are closely related. The first involves his view of consciousness as essentially a selective activity. All selection involves rejecting as well as accepting, forgetting as well as remembering. Indeed, he will later say (I, 679) that "in the practical use of our intellect, forgetting is as important a function as recollecting", and his present suggestion concerning the supposed unconscious is in keeping with this line of thought. Automatic acts may be performed with a certain perceptual consciousness which, like that of dreams, is at once forgotten, thus preventing a clogging of the reflective mind with useless memories.

The second suggestion is closely related. The operations of our perceptual consciousness may not be completely forgotten, but rather "split off" into a separate compartment of experience, with which it is difficult for our conceptual thought to remain in intimate contact. This would be James' explanation of the great difficulty confronting phenomenologists in trying to bring the patterns of pre-reflective experience into the light, and of the remarkable way in which this world of perceptual experience has been neglected and lost sight of in the great conceptual systems of Western philosophy. The authors of these systems are like split personalities who live much of the time in a perceptual world which never enters into their sophisticated reflections.

These suggestions about forgetting and compartmentalizing are given further applications in James' refutations of arguments 3–8 for the notion of the unconscious. We will now pass over these, in order to consider his criticisms of 9 and 10. The ninth argument expresses an intellectualistic attitude which is found in many idealistic thinkers, and, in an exaggerated form, in von Hartmann and Schopenhauer. It thinks of sense experience as the presentation of bare "data" with little or no significance of their own. Meaning comes only with the formation of concepts, and the making of inferences by a subterranean and unconscious "reason". Thus as a result of such hidden logical processes, we interpret a small human shape on the visual field as a large man at a distance, and a gray patch is judged to be a white seen in dim light. When a wrong premise is chosen, we are led to illusory conclusions. A favorite move in this style of argument is to ask whether blank sense-data are ever found, or whether they can ever be described without the tacit use of intellectual categories and patterns of judgment. The suggested inference is that unconscious, or at least semi-conscious concepts and reasoning processes are always at work.

The basic error here lies in the assumption that the only meaningful patterns to which we have access are those of conceptual thought. James must have been familiar with this discounting of experience as mere "data" by his idealistic friends, and he sharply opposes it near the beginning of his *Psychology*. As he says, "color- and light-contrast are purely sensational affairs, in which inference plays no part" (I, 169). There is an active, conscious agent who is involved in sense experience which is filled with meaningful patterns, like size, shape, and distance. These patterns may be grasped by an active gaze without ever being conceptualized. They are sensed through "conscious percepts" (p. 169) by an active agent in pursuing his meaningful projects in the world.

Men first become acquainted with this world not by conceptualizing it but by actively living in it, and, as James will show, there is a logic of life quite distinct from that of conceptual understanding. Both are, of course, essential for different purposes, but it is a fatal mistake to reduce the former to an unconscious version of the latter. Its results may be similar but not the same, and they are achieved in a very different way. As James says: "results *like* those of reasoning may accrue without any actual reasoning process unconsciously taking place" (p. 169). In thus pointing out the meaningful autonomy of so-called sense experience, James is anticipating some of the most firmly established results of recent phenomenology.[3]

The tenth argument expresses basic reasons which still seem

[3] *Cf.* Merleau-Ponty, *Phenomenology of Perception,* esp. Part II.

to require the notion of the unconscious, and which are harder
to refute. Hence James considers them in greater detail (pp.
170–76). They are connected with a large and important class
of experiences in which we learn something about ourselves.
In such experiences, some subjective feeling, or condition, turns
out to be quite different from what we had at first supposed
it to be. Thus I may at first like a certain person, and then later
find that I am in love. Or I may, at first, feel myself guided by
purely friendly motives and then, in careful self-analysis after a
moment of forgetfulness or a slip of the tongue, I may discover
motives of cupidity or jealousy of which I had never been fully
aware. In fact any new knowledge about the real nature of
vocal sounds, visceral feelings, and muscular tensions would fall
into this class of self-learning experiences. Thus for a long time
I may have been able practically to distinguish in a crude way
between the *sonants* D, B, Z, G, V and the so-called *surd*
consonants T, P, S, K, and F. But it is only later, after a careful
analysis, that I learn the real difference. The sonants are
nothing but the surds with a new element added—the laryngeal
sound with which they are uttered.

Now it is easy to interpret all these cases in terms of the so-
called unconscious. Thus I may have supposed that I only
liked the person, but vaguely and unconsciously I was in love
all the time, for this is what it turned out to be. Similarly I
thought I felt only sympathy and benevolence towards my
"friend". But as subsequent analysis showed, I was really jealous,
though I had this jealousy only in a vague and unconscious way,
and it was not until later that I became clearly conscious of the
feeling. Finally, in the case of the surds and sonants, I must
have been aware all along of the compound nature of the latter.
Otherwise how could I have distinguished them? But I must
have had this awareness unconsciously, since it became clear
and distinct only after a later analysis.

Now several points need to be noted concerning this interpretation of analysis. First, consciousness, as such, is identified
with that theoretical awareness which simply repeats certain
determinate characteristics as they already exist in the object.

It has no other function than to achieve this merging with the thing. In the second place, no clear distinction is made between awareness and the object of which it is aware. Thus my former state of liking, which is the object of a later analysis, must be identical with the state of love which is the point of view of this analysis. In the third place, consciousness as such must be clear and distinct (the ideal of pure theory). The vague and the indeterminate are identified with the unconscious. Practical awareness, always partially vague, is dismissed as a mere unconscious *having*, which loses any identity of its own. Hence any result of later analysis may be read back into it as having been unconsciously present. Finally, fourth, there is only one way in which consciousness can develop or advance. This is from a condition of the unconscious, where any number of determinate things may be present though unrevealed, to a condition of consciousness where these things, in their full determinacy, are clearly and distinctly revealed. No other mode of advance, no other mode of consciousness is possible.

James calls these reasonings "one tissue of confusion" (p. 172), and rejects each of the conclusions we have just considered. First of all, the practical mode of awareness which guides our action is quite different from that of a purely theoretical attention. Thus I can roughly distinguish the sonants B and V from the surds P and F in the act of conversing with a friend. But this experience is basically different from that which results from theoretical analysis in a detached attitude of voluntary attention. It is simply not true that the former is an unconscious version of the latter. There is a basic difference in psychic attitude, though the objects are abstractly the same letters, B and V on the one hand, and P and F on the other. "It is an absolute psychic difference . . ." (p. 173).

There are other modes of awareness connected with projects, quite different from that of theoretical analysis. Hence, in the second place, it must be recognized that these different modes of awareness are intentional, to use a phenomenological term. That is, the conscious operation of loving, desiring, hating, and knowing must be distinguished from their objects, that which

I love, desire, hate, or know. Thus before 1890, and probably before 1885, James clearly recognized that human consciousness is not enclosed within a subjective container, but is rather stretched out towards objects of various kinds in the manner called *intentional* by later phenomenologists.[4]

When this distinction is clearly borne in mind, the fallacy of the unconscious in many cases becomes evident. Thus I may first like and then fall in love with the same person. But the fact that the object, in this case the person, remains the same, does not require me to hold that the intentional attitudes towards this person were the same, or that my liking was merely an unconscious version of the latter attitude. The liking may have developed into loving, but the two attitudes towards the same person were quite different, and the phrase, *falling in love*, may be retained as referring to a genuine change of conscious intention.

Furthermore, in the third place, it is simply not true that every genuine mode of consciousness is clear and distinct, and that all vague and peripheral awareness is to be reduced to the unconscious. This is merely the expression of a theoretical ideal which has its place but cannot be generalized. Every distinct object of perception is surrounded by vague fringes, to use James' term, and many objects and attitudes, of which we are dimly aware, are permanently condemned to these fringes by other dominant interests. But though certain feelings are only dimly felt, this does not mean that they are unconscious, merely *had* but not felt at all. As James says, "they may be faint and weak; they may be very vague cognizers of the same realities which other conscious states cognize and name exactly; they may be unconscious of much in the reality which the other states are conscious of". But this does not make them unconscious, or rule them out of existence. "They *are* eternally as they feel when they exist, and can, neither actually nor

---

[4] *Cf.* E. Husserl, *Ideen zu einer reinen Phänomenologie und phänomenologischen Philosophie*, Halle, 1928, pp. 167–71—or *Ideas* . . . , tr. Gibson, Collier Books, 1967, pp. 222–26.

potentially, be identified with anything else than their own faint selves" (p. 174).

Thus my jealousy may be present only in the outermost fringes of my conscious behavior towards my friend which is now dominated, with increasing difficulty, by a forced benevolence. On these outer fringes, it may be growing and organizing a set of allied negative feelings around itself, until at last it may find expression in a moment of forgetfulness, or a slip of the tongue, which may attract attention and lead to careful analysis. Out of this may emerge a clear understanding of what has been going on. But this does not mean that the present clarity must be read back into the past vague awareness, as though it were preceded by an unconscious version of itself. The earlier state was certainly conscious, and had a conscious autonomy of its own. The later state of clear focusing is quite different. A real transition has occurred which is only confused and partially masked by the use of "the unconscious".

Respect for the Phenomena

James ends the section by indicating the connection between this conception of the unconscious and other versions of what he calls the mind-stuff theory. It holds that different manifestations of consciousness are derived from a neutral stuff, the unconscious, in ways that can be calculated and anticipated. He makes it clear that a major reason for his rejection of this theory is his sense of the distinctive nature of different conscious experiences. The identity of each of these experiences must be respected. Each of these is what it is, and must be described as such, if we are to understand it. No such "mental fact can be two things at once" (p. 175). He also makes it clear that in rejecting the mind-dust theory, he is rejecting the notion of any automatic parallelism between a particular unit of consciousness and a particular part of the brain. There are no psychic atoms which may be added together to form complex modes of consciousness.

His own view takes "the entire thought (even of a complex object) as the minimum with which it deals on the mental side . . .", and "the entire brain-process as its minimal fact on the material side" (p. 177). It would have been better if he had said "an entire meaningful course of action", first as felt from within, and then as carried out by the living, conscious body, in which case he would have recognized more clearly the identity of the two expressions. But his thought is moving prophetically in this direction. He rejects the conception of a "central or pontifical" arch-cell (pp. 179–80), which integrates the conscious experiences of other cells, on empirical grounds. There is no physiological evidence supporting such a theory. If we engage in such pure speculation we "therewith leave physiology behind us and dive into regions inaccessible to experience and verification" (p. 180).

As we have already noted, James was aiming at an empirically grounded philosophy, and never abandoned this aim. He admits that the scholastic notion of a separate soul substance which is "influenced in some mysterious way by the brain-states and responding to them by conscious affections of its own, seems to me the line of least logical resistance, so far as we yet have attained" (p. 181). It is not subject to some of the difficulties pertaining to the mind-dust and the material monad views. But it is a speculative theory supported by no direct empirical evidence, for we experience successive thoughts and feelings, not a soul substance (cf. pp. 3–4). So James himself rejects the theory of the soul, for this and other reasons to be presented in Chapter X.

This is why he says at the end (p. 182), of Chapter VI "that nature in her unfathomable designs has mixed us of clay and flame, of brain and mind, that the two things hang indubitably together and determine each other's being, but how or why, no mortal may ever know". James still does not know how to escape from the use of dualistic language. But he is going as far as he can in this direction. The living mind of man is incarnate in a living body which is itself conscious. They "hang indubitably together" and work together as one.

The body is more than a mere instrument of the soul. He is constantly aware of the brain and its determining influence on our conscious life. He even hopes for an explanatory psychology that will be able to control much of this life through its knowledge of causal laws. But from the beginning James rejects materialism and the epiphenomenalism to which it leads.

Later commentators have complained about this tension between description and explanation which runs through the whole of his text. Why does he not choose one or the other instead of remaining confused? But James preferred rather to remain confused, for he distrusted one-sided, systematic solutions. And this contributed to the strange vitality of his work, which still strikes the reader as being close to the world of life where there seems to be room for explanation as well as description, for body as well as mind. In and through his various "inconsistencies", he was feeling his way towards a new point of view, a new kind of phenomenological psychology, as we shall call it, which might do justice to both conscious states and their bodily conditions.

Chapter Two

※

The Psychologist's
Fallacy and the
Existential A Priori

Having considered the physiological conditions of mental life, and certain metaphysical prejudices (the automaton and the mind-stuff theories) that might stand in the way of an impartial investigation, James, now in Chapter VII, turns to the mental phenomena which are the primary objects of psychological study. But before this, he makes some interesting remarks about the relation of psychology to philosophy which are worthy of attention. James speaks of psychology as a natural science, and he made significant contributions to its establishment as an autonomous discipline which was then under way. To the psychologist as a scientist "the minds he studies are *objects*, in a world of other objects", which is simply presupposed (p. 183). This is true even of his own mind when he studies it in a scientific way.

But after making these statements, James makes it clear that he doubts whether this science can ever completely free itself

from all involvement in philosophical and especially epistemological problems. "Now the psychologist," he says, "necessarily
becomes . . . an *Erkenntnisstheoretiker*" (p. 184). James' explanation of this statement is somewhat ambiguous. But in the
light of his actual procedure, which we shall note as we go
along, the position towards which he is moving may be summarized as follows. The embodied mind, which is the special
concern of the psychologist, is certainly a being in the world
which may be studied as objectively as other objects. The term
object here means simply an entity of some kind which is found
in the world, which possesses distinctive characteristics, and
can be studied by disciplined methods. In this sense the subjectivity of a given person is an object.

But as we shall see, this object also involves a whole version
of the world, and some of its activities, like selective attention,
choice, and cognition, have something to do with the ordering
of this world. Hence in any thorough study of such activities
within his proper province, the psychologist becomes involved
in questions concerning the structure and origin of the whole
human life-world. It is true that any science at its foundational
levels becomes philosophical. But this is peculiarly true of
psychology whose basic levels are concerned not merely with
fundamental structures of the world but with its very center,
man, and the ways by which it is constituted. As we follow his
text, we shall see that James does not evade this task, and at
the proper points where basic issues arise, does not hesitate to
engage in philosophical investigation, without ever abandoning
his view that psychology is also a natural science, concerned with
the disciplined study of mental states and their conditions.

In a table on page 184, James emphasizes the peculiar intentional nature of these phenomena, which are never enclosed
within themselves, like atoms or impressions, but always
stretched out to their objects. Thus in his scientific observations,
the psychologist (1) must recognize first of all his own existence
(4), then the intentional thought, desire, or feeling he is studying (2), and finally "the thought's object" (3). That we are

directly acquainted with mental phenomena of this sort is for
James indubitable, or, as he puts it, "the *inconcussum* in a world
most of whose other facts have at some time tottered in the
breath of philosophic doubt" (p. 185; *cf.* II, 297). When left in
this blank form, the Cartesian argument is sound. But as soon
as we begin to fill in the blank with more definite content, we
become fallible, and the certainty of the *cogito* ceases to hold.
It is fair to say, however, that the sheer existence of mental
phenomena, the facts of psychology, is more certain than that
of other types of fact. To this degree, the argument of the
cogito can be accepted.

James finds no single term in common use adequate to cover
the vast range of these psychic facts. As we have seen, to call
them *mental* fails to do justice to the way in which they involve
motions of the living body, while to call them physical fails to
do justice to the sense in which they are conscious. To use
either term means simply to fall back into that traditional
dualism which James is trying to overcome. We often refer to
them as psychic states, but this term has no verbal form, and is
too static to indicate the dynamism that pervades our conscious
life. We might use the term *thought*. But this is too intellectual,
and ignores the wide range of non-conceptual feelings and
perceptions which guide our everyday activities. We might use
the term *feeling*. But this fails to do justice to the life of the
mind. He finally decides to use both of the latter terms, depending on the context.

He turns next to the topic of introspection, which, he says,
is the method of strictly psychological investigation. Present-
day phenomenologists object to the use of this term, since it
suggests the *post mortem* looking at an inner activity as an
object rather than reflective grasp of it as it is going on. It
probably would have been closer to his real meaning if James
had used a term like *reflection*, coming from the French tradition which influenced him deeply in these matters. But if we
read carefully his detailed discussion (I, 185–92), we can see
that his thought is moving in this direction. As we have just

indicated, he is clearly aware of the fact that our feelings and thoughts are not enclosed within a mental container, and that in the bare having of them, there is a certain consciousness which he is soon to call *knowledge by acquaintance*. The aim of psychology is to gain a conceptual understanding of these phenomena, as they are actually lived through, by a special development of this direct awareness.

But James is unclear as to the nature of this development. He is bothered by the views of Comte and others who maintain, in line with an ancient Aristotelian tradition, that the only precise mode of consciousness is that of detached observation, which is incompatible with the having of any strong feeling or passion. Comte even went so far as to say concerning the observing of any mental phenomena "at the time of their actual presence, that is a manifest impossibility" (quoted, p. 188). James does not accept this view, and agrees rather with Mill that we know our intentions, which are never instantaneous, "either at the very time, or by memory the moment after; in either case, by direct knowledge, and not (like things done by us in a state of somnambulism) merely by their results" (quoted, p. 189). Thus an act, still held fresh in the memory of a momentary past, can still be known directly in the very act, and not merely as an object observed from the outside. James concludes this long discussion by the following statement: "in cases like this, where the state outlasts the act of naming it, exists before it, and recurs when it is past, we probably run little practical risk of error when we talk as if the state knew itself. The state of feeling and the state of naming the feeling are continuous, and the infallibility of such prompt introspective judgments is probably great" (p. 190, note).

To achieve sound results by this reflective development of self-consciousness, both memory and imagination must be strictly disciplined, and even then, the psychologist may go astray. This is especially true when he concerns himself with "weaker feelings" and "the *relations to each other* of all feelings" (p. 191). His classifications of feelings and motives, and his judgment of their exact component elements are always subject to error, for it is impossible to say just where the phenomenon ends and the element of interpretation begins. But when there is a real communication between the two, when each seems to answer back and to assimilate something of the other, we may have confidence that we are on the right track. In this way, by careful study, plausible hypotheses concerning a given phenomenon may be gradually formulated and checked by other observers until an informed opinion concerning related phenomena may be reached. As James puts it (p. 192), "the only safeguard is in the final *consensus* of our farther knowledge of the thing in question, later views correcting earlier ones, until at last the harmony of a consistent system is reached". So he hopes for the development of a cooperative discipline concerned with the clarification of our existence in the world as we live it. James never abandoned this hope which was shared, with certain qualifications, by Husserl and expressed by him in certain statements about phenomenology as a cooperative discipline concerned with the concrete experience of men in the *Lebenswelt*.[1]

In addition to this descriptive and comparative discipline, there is the experimental psychology which James was helping to get started in America by his support of the Psychological Laboratory at Harvard. He studied the works of its German founders very thoroughly, and though often disagreeing with them, always speaks of them with respect. He is disappointed that the facts so far achieved have not as yet led to more significant theoretical results. But he recognized from the beginning that any sound theory, either in psychology or in philosophy, must be based upon facts. Hence the accumulation of facts that may be relevant is worth while. As he says, "facts are facts, and if we only get enough of them they are sure to combine" (p. 193). But it is clear that he regards the role of experiment and the reduction of its results to a quantitative form as subordinate to the main task—the description and interpretation of the phenomena of lived experience.

---

[1] *Die Krisis der europäischen Wissenschaften und die transzendentale Phänomenologie*, The Hague, 1954, pp. 123–35.

The Psychologist's Fallacy

In this early chapter (VII), James mentions a basic danger which confronts the psychologist as he embarks on this task. He calls this "the psychologist's fallacy", and defines it as "the *confusion of his own standpoint with that of the mental fact* about which he is making his report" (p. 196). This might also be called the fallacy of not listening, or the subjectivistic fallacy. This danger confronts the psychologist in every region of his concern. If he is trying to understand the experience of a child or a disturbed person, he must be able to bracket his own adult, normal attitudes for the time being, and then use his imagination, and, indeed, all his cognitive powers to follow the alien thoughts that are presented to him. The failure to do this takes two forms, which follow from the intentional structure of experience as falling between a subjective and an objective pole.

Thus the psychologist may suppose that the child he is trying to understand knows the woods near his home in the same detached and objective way that he knows them—as a dense grove of pines and oaks on a windy hill. Our thoughts are predominantly directed outwards towards the objects with which we deal, and as James notes, language follows this objectivity of thought in developing a far richer and more finely shaded vocabulary for objects than for our feelings towards them. Thus we have many ordinary words for different kinds and shapes of tree, and for different kinds of light and degrees of shade. For both of these we also have an elaborate technical and semi-technical vocabulary, botanical and artistic. But James points out, this is not true of our thoughts and feelings, which we usually have to lump together as our feelings about the woods, and for which we are only beginning to have a refined and semi-technical vocabulary.

We tend to regard thought in general as a sort of replica of the object in the mind. This also tempts the psychologist in all of us to assume that the child must be thinking of the woods in the same objective manner in which we think of them. But as is now well known, this may be far from the truth. He probably does not know these trees in a theoretical manner, but rather as a region of life which he must pass through on certain errands. As a result of some frightening experience at twilight or in the dark, the child may think of the woods as a region of terrible, moving shapes where demonic forces reach out at him from the dark. This idea is in no sense a replica of the trees; it is a response of fear and terror, bearing only the most superficial resemblance to the "object" of a detached observation. Unless the psychologist brackets this theoretical attitude for the time being, and feels his way into the lived experience of the child, he will fall into the first form of the psychologist's fallacy, believing that all objects are known in the same way by concepts and judgmental intermediaries in the mind.

As James points out (p. 196), this has led to the creation of "fictitious puzzles" in the history of philosophy, like the issue between presentative and representative theories of perception. Those defending the latter point of view have insisted that, since objects can be known in only one way, the child also must know the fearful, moving shapes by sense-data, image things, and other intermediaries in his mind. But this is false. In perceptual experience, the objects are *directly* known as they are for us, without any intermediaries "in the mind", though this does not mean that logical knowledge is impossible. The nominalist is right in holding that the child's experience in the woods is an individual response to an individual situation. But he is wrong in inferring that, since knowledge is of only one kind, universal concepts are impossible. Objects may be known in different ways, and when these different ways are rightly described and understood, many artificial problems may be resolved.

But there is also a second form of the psychologist's fallacy. He may assume that the mental state he is studying must be aware of itself in the same way in which he is aware of it. For him, not only its object but the thought he is studying is an object. This makes it still easier for him to fall into a representative theory of consciousness and to think of the person he is observing as knowing the contents of his own mind as objects that intervene between him and the things outside. But this involves other mistakes as well. As James says, "the mental state is aware of itself only from within" (p. 197), not from the outside as an object of any kind. Furthermore, "what the thought sees is only its own object".

The psychologist may know much more about the trees, the winds, and branches. He may see "the thought's object, plus the thought itself, plus possibly all the rest of the world" (p. 197). In the light of this wider and more accurate *knowledge about* the object and its relations to other things, he may judge that the child's experience is false, that it will not really lead him away from any real danger. He may, therefore, try to guide him away from the having of such experiences. But if he is to succeed in doing this, he must never discount the illusory experience of the child as unreal. On the contrary, he must come to understand it exactly as it occurred to the child, and not read his own attitudes into it. Otherwise, he will be committing the second form of the psychologist's fallacy. This passage is interesting in showing that James clearly recognized the intentional structure of consciousness at this time (before 1882), and many diverse modes of awareness, of which theoretical understanding is only one.

In the next pages (Chap. VIII), after reminding us again that "for psychology, a mind is an object in a world of other objects" (p. 199), James considers the relation of this mind to these other things. Is this relation constant through time? He first considers the Cartesian view that the mind is always thinking, and admits that there are important reasons which can be offered in support of this opinion. One of these is that we often remember dreams for a few minutes after waking, and then completely forget them. Also when awake and absent-minded, we experience thoughts and images which the next minute we cannot recall. This phenomenon of immediate forgetting deeply impressed James, and he admits that there may be an element of consciousness in states of seemingly complete unconsciousness.

Thus when exhausted, we can sleep during loud sounds, extreme cold, and the presence of other sensations which previously prevented sleep. It would seem probable that in such cases we refuse to recognize certain impressions of which we are at least dimly aware, for we cannot refuse what we do not know at all. This is illustrated by the experience of mothers and nurses who refuse many noises, but awaken at once at the slightest cry of the patient or child they are tending. Other people have an amazing capacity to register the passage of time, and are able to rouse themselves at unusual hours agreed upon the night before. All these facts provide evidence for mental activities of which the mind is unconscious. But the strongest evidence comes from the studies by Janet and others of "unconsciousness" in hysterics (pp. 202 ff.).

In such cases, which impressed James deeply, one part of a conscious life becomes separated from the rest, and the two or more personalities perform their own projects and develop their own memories independently of the others. In other less extreme cases, a subject will become blind or refuse to see certain patterns belonging to a suppressed system which is still basically conscious. In post-hypnotic suggestion, the subject will obey detailed commands of which he is now completely unaware. James admits that on the basis of such evidence we can no longer accept as conclusive the statement of a person that he was experiencing nothing. But to the question as to whether a mind is continually conscious throughout the whole time of its existence, he refuses to give a definite answer though inclining to the negative (p. 213).

With respect to where the soul is (the seat of the soul), James has no ready-made answer. He is sceptical of the traditional doctrine of the unextended soul, as we have already indicated (*supra*, pp. 28–29), though he sometimes (I, 215, 219–20) uses its terminology in a sympathetic manner. This is because he is equally sceptical of any "materialistic" theory which would limit the presence of consciousness merely to the brain or even the whole body. Any such restriction is "false", for "cognitively its presence extends far beyond the body" (p. 215). His introduction of the notion of *presence* here is significant. Two things may be lying side by side; they may be in physical contact and yet not present to each other, for this requires a center of consciousness and meaning. As James says (p. 214), "in some manner our consciousness is 'present' to everything with which it is in relation".

In a minimal cognitive sense, we become present to a distant object by perceiving it. Thus "I am *cognitively* present to Orion whenever I perceive that constellation, but I am not *dynamically* present there, I work no effects" (p. 214). I become dynamically present only through the conscious field I carry with me, and within the limits of which I can exert active effects. This requires the conscious body, which can coexist with other things and persons, can take a position with reference to them, and act on them in different ways. A disembodied soul, or mind, could never be present in this way. As James puts it: "a thing not perceived at all, such as the inextended soul must be, cannot coexist with any perceived objects in this way. No lines can be felt stretching from it to the other objects. It can form no terminus to any space-interval. It can therefore in no intelligible sense enjoy position. Its relations cannot be spatial. . . . So far as they are dynamic, to talk of the soul being 'present' is only a figure of speech" (p. 215). This is what we mean when we say that he was present at the meeting, that is, he was physically there, of course, but more than this, he was consciously at a place in the situation and able to operate, whether he did or not. Thus we may say he was present but did not participate.

Without the body and its bodily awareness, this presence is impossible. Thus if someone is lost in meditation or in a fainting spell, we speak of him as absent or "not there". This presence is not only actively exercised; it is also recognized and directly felt. Thus we speak of a person's presence, meaning his whole field of meaning and style of action in this field, and of feeling his presence as he joined in a social gathering or suddenly entered the room. If James had developed this pregnant suggestion further, he might have speculated on the meaning of such phrases. We do not see the presence of another person; we hear what he says, not his presence; nor do we touch it, though what we see, and hear, and touch may be special manifestations of it. But what of the global presence of an alien, or of a friendly person?

How do we become aware of these?

Is it through the mere reception of a sensory signal coming from the outside which we must then laboriously reconstruct into a foreign world from our own notions? No, for how would I possess the conceptual tools to construct a whole world that is other than my own? And yet from the very beginning, I feel this world as other. I feel it directly in the hostile gaze which invades my world, objectifies my dearest meanings, and takes them over as trivia into an alien frame. I feel it directly in a single friendly word from a stranger, which, without physical assistance of any kind, may reverberate with my basic meanings, and help me on my way.

These gestures bear a whole foreign world of meaning in their fringes which I feel in the same way as I feel the fringes of meaning hovering over my own gestures and the different words that I say. Sometimes a foreign presence can be sensed seemingly with no impression at all, as when a very sick man feels the presence of a close friend in his room. If he had reflected further on this notion of presence, James might have become even more critical of the notion of a separate mind, or soul, with no windows, which leads inevitably towards the idealism of Bowne whom he quotes sympathetically at the end of this passage (pp. 219–20). James' thought at this time had not reached a fixed conclusion on these issues, but it was moving in a non-idealistic direction, as we can see from his remarks on the nature of knowledge in general (pp. 216–18).

In these pages, he says that, as a psychologist, he must accept the knowing relation, which makes things present, as an ultimate fact. He exists in a world of independent beings which, under certain conditions, he may know as they are. He exists in this world with others who know these things in the same finite and fallible manner as he. Knowledge has no meaning except over against falsehood. Hence in our sense of the word, an absolute mind would have no *knowledge*. It would simply have *thoughts*. There would be no external realities with which they could be compared. But the psychologist deals only with finite minds whose thoughts may be true or false in relation to what exists beyond them. In terms of what he knows of these objects, the psychologist must often judge the truth or falsity of these thoughts. What is the test? Here James makes a point that is in line with his later pragmatic theory of truth.

Being is not necessarily relational, and does not have to lead us anywhere. It simply is. But truth is concerned with meaning. A meaning becomes true in so far as it is related to other meanings in such a way as to lead us to a definite, perceivable being. How can we find out if it will lead us in this way? Only by action with the bodily organs (p. 217). A disembodied mind, or even an inactive spectator, would never be able to distinguish the true from the false. Any experience, like a dream, for example, would be just as real as any other, since without action, the distinction between true and false would be irrelevant. It is only by relating the dream to other events in the waking state (death, *e.g.* p. 218), and then by acting on the basis of this meaningful relation that we can find out its truth or falsity. Isolated, atomic events may be real. They cannot be true or false.

Hence if the idea he is considering resembles a true idea of his own that has already been tested, the psychologist will judge it to be true. But the ultimate test lies in action. Hence James' summary formula (p. 217): "if . . . the mental state under examination neither resembles nor operates on any of the realities known to the psychologist, he calls it a subjective state pure and simple, possessed of no cognitive worth." On this view, which James will develop further later on, truth is sharply distinguished from being. Something may very well be without being true. There are no eternal truths, unless there are eternal meanings, for truth depends on meaning. Beings become true in so far as they are gathered together in such a way as to guide meaningful action. Truth happens to things that already are, and has a history.

The psychologist, therefore, must sharply distinguish meaning from being. "The *psychologist's attitude towards cognition* [namely his own] . . . *is a thoroughgoing dualism.*" This also follows from the intentional structure of consciousness, which is always divided into the knowing intention and the thing known. As James goes on to say: "neither gets out of itself or into the other, neither in any way *is* the other, neither *makes* the other. They just stand face to face in a common world, and one simply knows, or is known unto, its counterpart" (p. 218). On the next page, he emphasizes the fact that "the thing remains the same whether known or not", which is reinforced by a footnote that sounds like traditional realism. When we remember how strongly James has emphasized his view that consciousness makes a difference (*supra,* pp. 15 ff.), we must suspect that his position is more refined. But for the present we must leave this basic question, and turn to the next few pages where he introduces a distinction that was destined to play a very basic role in his thought, as well as in the phenomenology of the future.

Knowledge of Acquaintance *versus* Knowledge About

James explains that this distinction between what we know by sheer acquaintance and what we know about it through the use of concepts was first suggested to him by reading a passage in John Grote's *Exploratio Philosophica.* But he at once took it up into his pattern of thought, widened its scope, and found new meanings in it as his ideas developed. As we shall see, it lies at the root of his pragmatic theory of meaning and the pragmatic theory of truth grew out of this. The first thing to notice is the vast number of objects covered by this knowledge of acquaintance, the width of its range. It is through this direct "intuition" that we know not only space and time but also the presence and absence of "people and things", sensory qualities, like the color blue and the taste of a pear, my own activities, like an effort of attention, "all the elementary natures of the world, its highest genera. . . . together with the kinds of relation that subsist between them" (I, 221).

In every field of exact knowledge (about), James is saying that there are certain ultimate terms which cannot be conceptually defined. All logical thought, for example, involves what we call comparison, the finding of likenesses and differences. In terms of these notions, many other more complex findings can be understood. But if someone asks us what difference is, no purely conceptual answer can be given. Here we must simply refer to direct experience. "At most", James says, "I can say to my friends, Go to certain places and act in certain ways, and these objects will probably come" (p. 221). Once they have become familiar through perception, they can be clarified by conceptual analysis. But the experience itself is prior to all analysis.

Such experience is an empirical *a priori*, presupposed by all exact analysis and disciplined reflection. It is not, like the Kantian *a priori*, concerned with formal structure alone, though it involves many patterns. It includes "content" as well, like sounds and colors, and indeed, all the highest *genera* of things. These must first be intuitively perceived before they can be conceptually understood and related. It is prior even to "the universal and necessary" in the Kantian sense, for, according to James, these meanings also rest ultimately on experiences of direct familiarity. If the universal is what holds not merely of one case, or of several, but of all, can we imagine that such a clarification would have any meaning for one who had never intuitively confronted a single thing, never let his imagination wander through other examples, and never had the feeling of the all? If the necessary is that which cannot not be, will such a conceptual formula have any real meaning for one who is totally unfamiliar with the notion of negativity, and in facing the future has never lived through the feeling of can and cannot? These formulae may be helpful in clarifying our lived experience. But if they try to replace it, they fall into empty verbalism.

All our conceptual meanings refer back finally to what James calls "this dumb way of acquaintance" (p. 221), that goes with our existence. Nothing can replace it. What sense would our conceptual systems and philosophies have to a non-existing one? All such systems are about a prior world that is already dimly felt by our lived existence in it. From the comprehensive nature of what is known in this way, it is clear that James thinks of acquaintance as giving us a vague grasp of the whole world together with all its basic structures in a dim and hazy way that is prior to reflective clarification.

No scientist or philosopher ever begins to think *de novo*. He begins to think in a world that is already known to him by acquaintance, and whose basic perceptual meanings are, for the most part, taken for granted. But if he is to achieve reality as well as clarity, he must not take them for granted. He must come to understand something of them as they are lived through in the original. This is the aim of what James came to call *radical empiricism*, but it lies already implicit in this distinction. It is radical in that it tries to shed light on these ultimate meanings, such as being, world, consciousness, body, and truth. It is empirical in that it tries to penetrate back to the meanings of these terms as they are lived through originally in our existence.

As we have tried to show, James' terminology shows a definite order of priority in these two kinds of knowledge. Knowledge by acquaintance is the more original. What we come to know *about* this is secondary and derived. Does it add something new or merely repeat what was already there? The idealist would give the former kind of answer, the realist the latter. James makes it clear that he would give a divided answer that is neither the one nor the other. Our perceptual knowledge by acquaintance, he says (p. 259), is focused on a "bare impression" like a middle C sound, or the passage of time. "Of most of its relations we are only aware in the penumbral nascent way of a 'fringe' of unarticulated affinities about it." Thus in our feeling of time, that it is different from space, that it somehow involves past, present, and future, that it somehow pervades the whole of our experience—all these facts and relations are dimly apprehended on its fringes, without being clearly distinguished and spelled out.

"Knowledge *about* a thing is knowledge of its relations", or as we may say, spelling out what lies on its "fringes". This passage from a state of ambiguity and confusion to one of definiteness and distinctness is not a mere copying of what was already there, since new facts and unsuspected relations may emerge from the previous obscurity. On the other hand, this is not a creation *ex nihilo*. As the investigation proceeds, it must keep in constant touch with the original experience to see if the barely felt facts respond to the new interpretation by opening up new fringes in line with it, and if the new meanings fit together with these new facts. If they are sound, there will be such a growing inter-communion and inter-assimilation between the two.

A new discovery must be stimulated by a new idea from a new point of view which may take account of the fringes. But it must be supported by the facts. It is only in this way that the implicit becomes explicit by the development of real meaning. The new system which brings the facts together and sheds light is never a mere copy, nor a pure creation. It may be radically new, and yet it must be, at the same time, in touch with the original facts, and able to account for them, as well as for others at first far off on the fringes.

It is important to recognize that this process of inter-communion and inter-assimilation between feeling and thought works both ways. It is not only possible for the vaguely felt fringes of an object to be clearly worked out by conceptual analysis; the opposite mode of assimilation also takes place. A sound analysis, which really reverberates with the inarticulate experience, may be taken over again by a higher level feeling. This is, no doubt, what we mean when we speak of a person who has gained conceptual mastery over any field as now *getting the feeling of the thing*. In an interesting passage concerned with reasoning (II, 370), James comments on this total mastery of a field which comes only with feeling, and makes laborious analysis no longer necessary. "When two minds of a high order, interested in kindred subjects, come together", he says, "their conversation is chiefly remarkable for the summariness of its allusions and the rapidity of its transitions. Before one of them is half through a sentence the other knows his meaning and replies. Such genial play with such massive materials, such an easy flashing of light over far perspectives, such careless indifference to the dust and apparatus that ordinarily surround the subject and seem to pertain to its essence, make these conversations seem true feasts for gods to a listener who is educated enough to follow them at all."

A few lines further, after commenting on feelings, like wonder and tediousness, which attend our conversations, he remarks that "the charm of conversation is in direct proportion to the possibility of abridgment and elision, and in inverse ratio to the need of explicit statement. With old friends a word stands for a whole story or set of opinions. With new-comers, everything must be gone over in detail." But when an analyzed field is taken over in this way and felt together as a single whole, new fringes of vagueness come into view which require further clarification and analysis. So the process is a relative one. The very same field that we first know only by acquaintance can come to be known about and then assimilated by a higher level of acquaintance. But, in general, the less exactly we analyze an object, and the less clearly we focus its relations to other objects on its fringes, the more our familiarity with it is of the acquaintance type. But in almost all cases, our knowledge of an object includes at least something from both, and the judgment as to whether it is to be called one or the other is a relative one. As James remarks (I, 221), "the same thought of a thing may be called knowledge about it in comparison with a simpler thought, or acquaintance with it in comparison with a thought of it that is more articulate and explicit still".

If this distinction is as basic as James thinks it is, it should be found in linguistic usage, and, in fact, James does find it there. On page 222 he makes some characteristically suggestive but brief comments on the matter. As he sees it, the distinction between knowledge by acquaintance and knowledge about is found in the structure of any meaningful sentence in ordinary language. As he states it, "the grammatical sentence expresses this". The subject stands for something with which we are already acquainted, including its surrounding fringes. When I say *Paul is frightened*, the word *Paul* stands for the individual youth with whom I am acquainted, not, however, in isolation, but surrounded by a whole halo of vaguely felt fringes, including his parents, the regions he frequents, his relations with me, his present situation, his difficulties and, indeed, the world that we share in common. This whole perceptual field is presupposed, and must be sensed if the sentence is to convey its real meaning to me.

This is also true of interjections like lo and behold, articles, personal and demonstrative pronouns, which simply point to something that is directly perceived, or felt, together with its fringes. "Such a word", James says (p. 222), "is the interjection, as *lo! there! ecco! voilà!* or the article or demonstrative pronoun introducing the sentence, as *the, it, that.*" Thus in the much discussed phrase *it is raining*, the term *it* refers expressively, as by a verbal gesture, to the whole situation surrounding the speaker, as it is felt in its entirety. The predicate *is raining* then gives us a certain clearly focused knowledge about this total situation, arising from conceptual analysis. But without the perceptual background, it would have no real meaning. *Is raining*, or *rain*, is a sheer abstraction that can happen only in an existential situation which is presupposed. Any exact analysis of science, any conceptual scheme, any philosophical system arises out of such a perceived background, even though it be rejected and even subconscious.

In playing an abstract conceptual game which may be useful for certain purposes, we may define a concept as we please, and forget the background. But in actual use, the background must be taken into account. And even when we forget it or ignore it, this background is still there, or it would not have to be forgotten. It is important to notice that in spite of its inadequacies, which he often stresses, as in this passage, and its need for conceptual fulfillment, James recognizes it as a kind of knowledge—"knowledge of acquaintance" as he calls it here. This knowledge is pre-reflective and pre-predicative, to use Husserl's term. It must be present before all conceptual explanations and theories which presuppose it. I myself, as an existing subject directly known to myself, and the world of fringes around me as they are perceived are prior to all exact, conceptual reflection. Back of all determinate predicates lies the indeterminate subject, and ultimately the indeterminate subject of the speaker as he speaks, and his surrounding fringes as he feels them.

The Existential A Priori

We have called this the *existential a priori,* and it might be interesting to dwell on the significance of this new conception, and to contrast it with others that are closely related. We have already noted that James derived the distinction, through Grote, from Kantian sources. Kant thinks of sensation as a chaotic manifold coming into the mind from unknown sources until it is ordered by the forms of intuition and the categories. But without sensation, these are empty forms with no actual content. Hence the Kantian saying: concepts without intuitions are empty; intuitions without concepts are blind. James would accept the first half of the statement but not the second. Concepts with no reference to the experience are empty, verbal forms. In this part of his philosophy, James is thoroughly Kantian and most of the criticisms of the self-flagellations of an empty reason he would accept. But the second part he would deny, together with the whole intellectualist aspect of the Kantian doctrine.

In comparison with perception clarified by conceptual analysis, pure perception is blind. But it is far from being totally blind, and is certainly not a mere manifold. It is a world in which an intentionally polarized perception knows itself, though hazily, together with objects, relations, and patterns of meaning, though dimly, in relation to what it can achieve with the aid of concepts. James would agree with Kant that a fulfilled knowledge of objects involves conceptual as well as sensory elements. But instead of associating the spontaneous imagination with concepts, and regarding these as prior to perception, he associates the imagination with perception, and regards these and their objects as prior to conception. These perceptual patterns do not exist as fixed forms in a worldless mind. They exist rather as a world of figures, surrounded by fringes, that is centered in existing men. It is the world in which I exist, as I feel it, that is prior to every particular experience, and every specific judgment I make, whether I am fully aware of it or not.

This is the vague *a priori* element, so hard to put our fingers on exactly and conceptually, which philosophers, as well as ordinary men, have felt in the background of all their fully conscious reflections and acts. This is the hazy horizon which we already know before we begin to think or act on one of its objects. It is from this background that our thought emerges and then in which, no matter what we may think, it somehow remains. In other words, this is the *a priori* factor in our experience which is presupposed by and necessarily conditions all that we say and do. Of course this background is contingent, for the human world and the self around which it is ordered are neither logically nor ontologically necessary. It is, furthermore, in constant change.

We can say, however, that it is prior to any logical or ontological necessities, if there be such, that may be found within it. For the meaning of these terms, logic, being, and necessity are derived from this world, which surrounds them with its fringes and conditions them. They are found and developed by existing men, and in so far as they become true, it is the real world which verifies them. Furthermore, though logically contingent, it is existentially necessary, in the sense that if I am to exist, I must exist in this world, and if I am to exist with understanding, I must take account of it. We cannot get outside this world to discover what makes it possible. Even if we could, it would already have determined what we mean by *possible*, for it is prior to all our categories. But this priority is not one of rational necessity. We cannot say that it must be as it is. What we can say is only *it is*. This is an *existential a priori* from which all real necessities and possibilities are derived. Unless they could be understood by men who exist in this real world, they would be really meaningless.

The Kantian notion of *a priori*, critical thinking retains its importance, but with a change of meaning. To think critically no longer means to turn away from the world of sense and feeling to its logical conditions. This whole direction is now reversed. To think critically, or self-consciously, now means rather to return towards the sources of our categories and meanings, whether in science or common sense, in the real world of our existence, with which we are originally and prereflectively acquainted. To return to the first sources, or, as Husserl said, to the things themselves—this is to be self-conscious and critical in our thinking. There is a basic difference between a mode of investigation, or even an individual statement, which simply accepts the given world as it seems, and develops its own thought on the basis of this large and questionable assumption, and on the other hand, one which asks questions and seeks to clarify in some special or general way, this vast region of the *a priori*. A large part of James' psychology is devoted to tasks of this kind, and one can say the same of present-day phenomenology.

By making this distinction between what we know by perceptive familiarity and what we know rationally by concepts, James is also taking a stand on another question that has long concerned philosophers. This is the relation between sense experience, where we come into direct contact with independent beings, and the patterns of meaning we work out through conceptual thought and "reason". The sceptic holds that these are separated by an unbridgable chasm. James accepts the notion of a real chasm between the two. The two levels are not the same. The distinction is real and important, as we shall see more clearly when we turn to his analysis of conception and reasoning (*infra*, Chapters V, IX). But James holds on empirical grounds that the chasm may be bridged. Conceptual thought may clarify and extend the range of the meanings that are present in perception. This is not guaranteed, however, by any *a priori* status of reason. It is a hope that may be approximated by historical effort and struggle. To this degree James would agree with the sceptic.

The Kantian rationalist, on the other hand, believes that the mastery of reason over experience is guaranteed, at least epistemologically, in the field of phenomena, which are determined *a priori* by a noumenal mind that is prior to them. We have already noted James' disagreements with this conception, which prepared the way for the post-Kantian rationalists. By abolishing the thing in itself they assumed that reason was not only epistemologically but ontologically prior to the concrete experiences of history. This led them to the view that experience must be meaningful *a priori*, and encouraged them to make interpretations of historical experience that were often fruitful and suggestive, but also warped by fantasy and speculative hubris. By identifying perceptual experience as the *a priori*, James was led to very different conclusions. By turning to this experience more carefully, he saw that it is not a mere chaotic manifold, as the rationalists had supposed. It already contains the germs of meaningful patterns which later appear in disciplined thought. By careful study, these shadowy patterns, lying on the fringes of what we perceive, may be conceptually clarified. There is no absolute guarantee of success. The venture involves uncertainty and risk.

The rational *a priori* of traditional thought is protected by logical sanctions. If it is neglected or denied, we fall into necessary contradictions and antinomies. The existential *a priori* involves sanctions of a different kind. If we ignore it, or deny it, our words become empty, or if we mean what we say, they contradict not other propositions but patterns of our own existence, and attitudes of life. We fall into contradiction with ourselves, and in such cases it is not only our thought but our existence that is disintegrating. The words expressed are fully conscious, but they conflict with a living attitude presupposed by the expression, or the mode of expression, that is semi-conscious. For example, a man, when aroused, may express lofty sentiments concerning freedom in a browbeating, dictatorial manner which unconsciously conflicts with what he says. This conflict may. be concealed from him, but very evident to his hearers. Statements which contradict their own existential conditions fall into similar difficulties. For example, *no proposition is true* and *all thought is relative*. No one would actually make a statement if he actually felt that it could not be true. Hence such a statement is in conflict with the actual, though unconscious, attitude that is presupposed by its own assertion. It expresses not a logical, but a deeper type of existential contradiction.

Chapter Three

The Stream
of Consciousness

James now begins his study of human experience as it is lived through by the existing agent, or as James says, "from within" (I, 197). But first he warns us against the still prevalent notion, inherited from British Empiricism, that this experience is made up of ultimate units or sensations. James emphatically rejects any such assumption, and says that those who accept it are "abandoning the empirical method of investigation", for "no one ever had a simple sensation by itself" (p. 224). In his opinion, British Empiricism is not a form of genuine empiricism at all, but a form of analytic rationalism, putting itself forth in an empirical disguise. "Consciousness, from our natal day, is of a teeming multiplicity of objects and relations, and what we call simple sensations are results of discriminative attention, pushed often to a very high degree" (p. 224).

His use of the term *relation* in this passage shows that he had made a careful study, before 1890, of the classical British authors and was well aware of those areas in which they fell short and which, if empiricism was to survive, required a new

approach that he was later to call *radical empiricism*. He also
warns us of another dangerous assumption which prevented
Descartes and Kant from penetrating to what Bergson was
later to call *les données immédiates de la conscience*. This is the
assumption that our experience must, from the very beginning,
involve a substantial self, or a subjective unifying principle of
some kind. This may, or may not, turn out to be true. But we
have no right to take it for granted before a disciplined examination of the facts.

Indeed, James goes further. He wishes that it were possible
in English to say "it thinks" instead of "I think," (p. 224), in order to avoid questionable assumptions about the self, and to
come closer to the indisputable facts of experience. As we have
already suggested (*supra*, pp. 49 ff.), James holds at this time
that neither the categories nor the self is prior to experience. His
view is precisely the opposite. Experience is prior to both. If the
self is a basic factor in experience, this must be shown on empirical grounds. It cannot be demonstrated *a priori* in the Kantian
manner without making questionable assumptions that have not
been justified in the light of the empirical evidence. There
are thoughts and feelings going on—this is all we have a right
to say at the start. Our task is first to describe them exactly as
they appear in the basic stream of consciousness. James now
turns to five basic "characters" (p. 225) which he finds in this
stream. His consideration of them makes up the body of Chapter IX.

The stream tends to a personal form

The first is that all conscious phenomena "tend to a personal
form", or more specifically, that "every thought" is "part of a
personal consciousness" (p. 225). Having rejected the notion of
a centre of consciousness to be demonstrated *a priori*, James
now accepts the notion of personality, as long as it is kept in an
indeterminate form, on empirical grounds. Speaking to his
students in a lecture room, he says that no one of them will

ever find "a mere thought, which is nobody's thought". We never have such an experience. "The only states of consciousness that we naturally deal with are found in personal consciousnesses, minds, selves, concrete particular I's and you's" (p. 226). It is important to notice again the way in which James here emphasizes the indeterminacy of this notion with reference to possible philosophical interpretations. This does not imply that we should not attempt to find such an interpretation. In fact, James does attempt to do this in Chapter XI, as we shall see.

But what we want is a sound interpretation that actually fits the facts, not one which forces something alien on them, or reduces them to something else. If we are to avoid mistakes of this kind, the empiricist must not try to go too fast. At first, he must bracket all such interpretations, and recapture the feeling of the original experience as he is directly acquainted with it. In so far as he reaches this, he is on solid ground, and has arrived at something that "everyone will recognize . . . to be true" (p. 226). Noetic certainty seems to vary indirectly with the clarity of definiteness, at least in common discourse. The more definite and clear my statements are, the more uncertain they usually become, whereas the things of which I am most certain seem to be vague. As James notes, following St. Augustine on time, this seems to be true of the term "personal consciousness", for "its meaning we know so long as no one asks us to define it, but to give an accurate account of it is the most difficult of philosophical tasks" (p. 225).

In reminding the reader of how thoughts and feelings do not float around by themselves, but are owned by different personal minds, he is trying to get back to a very broad, very vague, and yet very certain fact of this kind. "It seems", he says, "as if the elementary psychic fact were not *thought* or *this thought* or *that thought,* but *my thought,* every thought being *owned*" (p. 226). This is not, of course, true of the objects of these thoughts. These may be shared. But the thoughts belong to different selves. This is something known directly by acquaintance, and then simply translated into a verbal formula of ordinary use. If the reader will allow these words to stand in their ordinary vagueness, without trying to read a more exact meaning into "selves" and "owned", he should be able to recapture the breadth and certainty which belongs to such primordial knowledge.

James' method of radical empiricism demands that he begin with such prereflective knowledge in all its vast breadth and vagueness. Then, after freeing his mind, so far as possible, from prevailing theories and prejudices, he will proceed slowly and carefully to examine the phenomena, trying to give an accurate formulation of the patterns that are already evident, and to make explicit those that are still vague. Finally he will try to gather them together in a meaningful way that will not destroy or replace the original feeling of the whole situation, but will be accepted as a clarification of its original sense.

What emerges from this process of *knowing about* will be different in certain respects from what was originally felt. The self will be seen to have many distinct aspects only vaguely present in the original perceptions. The same will be true of ownership in which many elements, at first only implicit, will now be brought into the light. The relation of the self to the not-self will be clarified. Furthermore, this self will be compared with other things that it is not, but might be and has been held to be, in ways that will extend the whole horizon of understanding, and place it in a wider field of meaning. But even though these differences will pertain to the new concept, the general pattern of what was originally felt by acquaintance may still stand. It will still remain true that thoughts and feelings belong to a self that differs radically from others. In this respect what emerges from the conceptual analysis remains the same.

James will attempt such an analysis in Chapter XI, but for the present, he is content to summarize his view of the basic feeling by stating "that the thoughts which psychology studies do continually tend to appear as parts of personal selves" (p. 227). This qualification is necessary, in order to take care of hysteric cases in which special systems of thought and feeling become separated off from the main center of personality. But, as James suggests, these secondary systems develop memories of their own, and certain types of unity resembling that of normal persons. So even these fragmentary thoughts and feelings follow the general law, and tend to become parts of a personal self (p. 229).

Thought is in constant change

A second basic characteristic of conscious phenomena is their constant flux. No conscious "state" ever exactly repeats itself. James makes it clear that he is referring here to the total unit of consciousness, namely the intentional activity of feeling, thinking, desiring, etc., which always belongs to a personal self, and its object, that which is felt, thought about, or desired. These objects can certainly be repeated. "We hear the same note over again; we see the same quality of green, or smell the same objective perfume, or experience the same species of pain" (p. 231). Our attention is normally directed outwards towards these objects rather than to our conscious intentions. Hence when the same object is repeated, we tend to suppose that the whole mental phenomenon is similarly repeated.

But this is a mistake which results from the neglect of the intentional structure of experience. It has led to the assumption of British empiricists, following Locke, that our mental life is constituted by ever-varying combinations of "simple ideas", or sensations, that remain "unchanged amid the flow" (p. 230). But both the premiss and the conclusion of this inference are mistaken. While the same objects may be felt or desired, the feelings and the desires are not the same. There are no mental atoms, or "simple ideas", out of which these intentions are compounded.

James uses two types of empirical argument to justify this conclusion. The first is an appeal to our direct experience of constant change in our perception and thought. Thus we never doubt that we are constantly perceiving the very same things in

a world that is one and the same. Nevertheless, we realize that
our perceptions and thoughts are ceaselessly changing. "We feel
things differently according as we are sleepy or awake, hungry
or full, fresh or tired; differently at night and in the morning,
differently in summer and in winter, and, above all, differently
in childhood, manhood, and old age" (p. 232). It is impossible
for us to maintain exactly the same attitude towards the same
thing through a protracted interval of time. Even though it may
have become familiar and even obvious, we come to place it in
a different point of view. Thus the things which once aroused
our interest become dull and commonplace; the persons who
fascinated us lose their appeal. And the opposite also occurs.
New horizons open up for us in those "duties" to which we
really devote ourselves, and they are touched by a gleam of
adventure. As James puts it: "more zestful than ever is the
work, the work; and fuller and deeper the import of common
duties and of common goods" (pp. 233–34).

In his second argument, James refers to the living body and
the brain changes which are certainly involved in any psycho-
physical experience. If we are to suppose that such an experience is repeated after an interval of time, this will imply that
the changes which have occurred in this interval will have
disappeared without a trace, and will make no difference to the
second identical experience. But this is both physically and ex-
perientially against the facts. Any response of a physical organ
will be at least partly determined by what has preceded it. Thus
"one color, succeeding another, is modified by the contrast,
silence sounds delicious after noise, and a note when the scale is
sung up, sounds unlike itself when the scale is sung down"
(p. 234). It is, therefore, unreasonable to believe that either the
physical or the psychical factors, or both taken together in a
psycho-physical change, should ever repeat themselves in the
identical form. Our total consciousness is constantly in transition,
and whatever may happen, it never returns in its totality to the
self-same condition. This is one reason why James refers to it as a
stream of thought. At any given moment, the field of conscious-

ness is too manifold to be clearly conceived. This total field is felt rather than thought and conceived. Of this "river of elementary feeling it would be certainly true to say, with Heraclitus, that we never descend twice into the same stream" (p. 233).

The stream is sensibly continuous

James next considers the sensible continuity of conscious thought, and devotes more space to it than to any of the other four. It is, in fact, the main reason why he decides to call our conscious life *a stream*. Also it needs to be dwelt on because it is so often passed over, by both the empiricist and the intellectualist schools of thought. Thus the empiricists have tended to follow Hume in defending the view that experience is made up of isolated units succeeding one another. The intellectualists (idealists) are misled by the absence of any accepted names for these experiences to deny that there *are* feelings of relation. But seeing that the world is not a disordered manifold, they arrive at a very different conclusion. In order to account for the orderly aspect of experience, the intellectualists assume a transcendental mind, a pure act of reason which is, in some sense, above experience, and from on high establishes and knows its relations.

Against both these views and in accordance with his radical empiricism, James holds, as we have seen, that our lived experience comes to us originally as related and organized. We know its relational aspects by direct acquaintance as well as conceptually, just as we know its substantive parts. It is true that these permanent factors in which we are practically interested, as the stable ends we are constantly seeking, attract our attention. Hence the transitional, or relational, aspects lack names. It is also true that these transitional stages of experience, in which we are moving from one permanent standing point to another, are hard to observe. As James says, they are like snow crystals which melt in our hand as soon as we touch them. Hence he devotes all his powers of insight and imagination to describing these unnamed but still familiar experiences, and in these pages (237–71) he makes several extremely perceptive phenomenological descriptions.

James is here concerned primarily with the temporal continuity of conscious life, which often seems to be interrupted by discontinuities and gaps of various kinds. Thus there are the unfelt gaps of anaesthesia and of fainting spells when we drift off into unconsciousness, and return again without knowing what has happened in between. These are distinct from periods of sleep, of which we are clearly aware and whose duration we judge by interpreting various signs. We have no difficulty in bridging these gaps and in making the broken edges of sentient life "meet and merge over the gap, much as the feelings of space of the opposite margins of the 'blind spot' meet and merge over that objective interruption to the sensitiveness of the eye" (p. 238). On both sides of the blind spot, there are the same horizontal and vertical directions in the spatial field which at once complete themselves subjectively over the gap, even though no object is seen there. When Peter and Paul wake up in the same bed and each reaches back to make a connection with his own past through memory, a similar explanation may be given. I directly feel my own past purposes and meanings. They come to me with the very same "warmth and intimacy" that attaches to my present projects. Just as the lines and directions around the blind spot belong to a single common space, so the meanings and purposes on both sides of the sleep gap belong to a single, common self. Hence, though nothing objective may have been experienced during that interval, the time gap is subjectively bridged. The past memories are taken over by the present self "and accepted as belonging together with it in a common self" (p. 239).

But even granted that the self, together with his living body, gives a basic continuity to our temporal experience, this still does not account for many sudden breaks which appear in our experience, and which have led to the type of atomistic analysis James is attacking. Thus when one object is succeeded by another in strong contrast, we notice only this objective contrast, and pass over the continuity of the intentional perceptions. When we are stunned by a clap of thunder, we believe that it has utterly abolished the silence. But this is a false and overhasty analysis. "What we hear when the thunder crashes is not thunder *pure*, but thunder-breaking-upon-silence-and-contrasting-with-it." Thunder as an abstract object is quite opposed to silence "but the feeling of the thunder is also a feeling of the silence as just gone; and it would be difficult to find in the actual concrete consciousness of man a feeling so limited to the present as not to have an inkling of anything that went before" (p. 241).

Here James stresses again the outward orientation of language, which usually passes over our intentions to focus only their objects. This has led to atomistic analyses, and to the neglect of a vast array of transition feelings which James now calls to our attention. Indeed, he claims that they are as much a part of our consciousness "as the joint is a part of the bamboo" (p. 240). These feelings of relation are found not only in the lived existence, which we know directly by acquaintance. They are also found in our conceptual *knowledge about*. In our discussion here, we shall reverse James' order and deal first with the former. We shall then turn to the latter, adding some comments on the general significance of his pioneering efforts in this field.

James is here developing his notion of *fringes*, which we have already considered in connection with what he calls knowledge by acquaintance (*supra*, pp. 43–49). This kind of perception, like conceptual thought, is able to focus its attention on specific objects which seem to exclude all else. But this is false. Every such object is set in a world-field, or in James' language, surrounded by *a halo of fringes* which gives it an original place and meaning in the world. In a remarkable passage (I, 255), he says that the traditional analytic psychology is "like one who should say a river consists of nothing but pailsful, spoonsful, quartpotsful, barrelsful, and other molded forms of water". But even if these pails and pots were all standing in the stream "still between them the free water would continue to flow". This moving field of meaning, this "free water" has been neglected by traditional psychology and philosophy. But every definite usage, or object, that ever appears is "steeped and dyed in the free water that flows around it". The meaning and value of the object, or image, is derived from this ever-moving field. As James puts it: "the significance, the value, of the image is all in this halo, or penumbra, that surrounds and escorts it,—or rather that is fused and one with it, and has become bone of its bone and flesh of its flesh. . .". The thing cannot be separated from its meaning. It *is* what it means.

But even though its patterns of change may be fixed, this field, like the human brain, is constantly arranging and rearranging itself in response to constant change. When the rate of change is slow, we feel this as a condition of rest which we identify with a static thing, or as James puts it, a "substantive state of consciousness". These are named and recognized, but the more rapidly moving, transitional feelings are neglected and usually unnamed. James is especially anxious to call two types of these to our attention. The first are outwardly directed towards objective relations, such as those holding between displeasing and pleasing things, or between ugly and beautiful objects. We tend to interpret such contrasts as a complete annihilation of the former and its replacement by the latter. But as in the case of the clap of thunder to which we have just referred (*supra*, pp. 62–63), this analysis is too simple, since it misses the actual transition. What we experience is the ugly giving way to the beautiful, not simply the position of the ball at A, and then its position at B, as in Zeno's intellectualist analysis, but rather the motion of the ball from A towards B. It is clear that no state of the brain ever instantly disappears. Similarly in the stream of conscious experience, there is a "consciousness of the *whence* and *whither* that always accompanies its flows" (I, 242). This whence and whither are often ignored. But they belong necessarily to the fringe of any sensory object.

At the conceptual level of language, we refer to these relations of transition by prepositions, adverbial phrases, and inflections of the voice. James stresses two important facts about these relations. The first is that they are primordially known by direct acquaintance, or feeling. ". . . So surely as relations between objects exist in *rerum natura*, so surely, and more surely, do feelings exist to which these relations are known." They are, in fact, "numberless", and "no existing language is capable of doing justice to all their shades" (p. 245). Many of these feelings of meaning are taken up into our ordinary language, and some of them express its basic syntactic structure. Thus as James says, there is "a feeling of *and*, and a feeling of *if*, a feeling of *but*, and a feeling of *by*" (p. 245). We often think of learning a foreign language as a pure conceptual exercise. But this is not the case. Something more is going on than the association of static concepts with new sounds. Relations of transition are also invoked which must be felt, and thus brought into direct relation with our non-conceptual experience. If we are to learn how to think and to speak in a foreign tongue, we must get a sense of its directions, how to move around in it. This is what we mean when we speak of acquiring the *feeling of the language*.

These patterns of meaning are basically dynamic, not static. This is the second point that James emphasizes. We are apt to interpret phrases like *nothing but, either one or the other, a is b but, although x is true, nevertheless* as fixed logical forms under which an indefinite number of specific instances may be subsumed. James does not deny this. But he is interested in examining them, not *ex post facto* after the thought is finished, but in the actual speaking of the speaker as he speaks. From this point of view, as he points out, they are "signs of direction" in a living, moving thought. They do not call up fixed images at which we may gaze as long as we like. But neither are they adequately analyzed as changeless relational forms. This applies to them only after they have been finished. In living thought, as James says: "these bare images of logical movement, on the contrary, are psychic transitions, always on the wing, so to speak, and not to be glimpsed except in flight." Their function is not merely to subsume a number of instances under a single mold which is always valid, but rather "to lead from one set of images to another" (p. 253).

These relations of transition start from a definite *terminus a quo* and proceed to another definite *terminus ad quem*, as in the case of the moving ball. When the motion is finished, it may be interpreted as a timeless relation between two fixed positions, as the spatial distance between two points, or the number of degrees between a cold and a warm temperature. There is another type, which James calls *relations of tendency*. These terminate in something specific, like a specific sound, or vision, of some kind. But they begin with an intentional attitude that is vague and indeterminate and, therefore, neglected and passed over by the objectively oriented mind. James is especially anxious to call our attention to the positive factors in these vague attitudes, to their vast number, and to the importance of the role that they play in our mental life. As he says, "it is, in short, the re-instatement of the vague to its proper place in our mental life which I am so anxious to press on the attention" (p. 254).

Take the terms *wait! hark! look!* They refer to no definite object before the senses or the mind. Hence we are apt to merge them and dismiss them as referring to a mere absence. Nevertheless if we reflect upon the concrete situations in which these terms are used, it is clear that "our consciousness is thrown into three quite different attitudes of expectancy . . .", and that each conveys to us "a sense of the direction from which an impression is about to come, although no positive impression is yet there" (p. 251). The same is true of the interrogatives *who? when? where?* They refer to no definite objects. But this does not mean that their "felt meaning" is purely negative.

Each of them conveys a positive "feeling of direction" (pp. 252–53) towards a person, a time, and a place. Our tendency "to assume that they are all emptinesses of consciousness, and so in the same state" is completely mistaken. As James points out, it is basically due to a failure to recognize the intentional structure of consciousness, that is, the difference between my feeling and the emptiness that I feel, for "the feeling of an absence is *toto caelo* other than the absence of a feeling" (p. 252). The two must not be confused, for the former may indeed be "an intense feeling" that is very positive, as, for example, the feeling of blindness (the absence of sight) which strikes a man when the bandages are taken from his eyes and, in opening them and facing the world, he first positively and even violently feels that he cannot see. Here again our attention is outwardly directed to the object, in this case blindness, the absence of sight. But we have no separate name for the feeling. As James says: "there are innumerable consciousnesses of emptiness, no one of which taken in itself has a name but all different from each other" (pp. 251–52).

James gives an example (p. 251) which brings out with unusual cogency the positive aspect of such a vague feeling of tendency. "Suppose we try to recall a forgotten name. The state of our consciousness is peculiar. There is a gap therein; but no mere gap. It is a gap that is intensely active. A part of the name is in it, beckoning as in a given direction, making us at moments tingle with the sense of our closeness, and then letting us sink back without the longed for term. If wrong names are proposed to us, this singularly definite gap acts immediately so as to negate them. They do not fit into its mould. And the gap of our word does not feel like the gap of another, all empty of content as both might seem necessarily to be when described as gaps. . . ." In cases like this, it may be truly said that not the word, but the halo of the word (its "mould") is present to our feeling.

As was true of feelings of transition, James finds that these "feelings of tendency" also play an important role in our conceptual thought. He offers as an example for the reader "his *intention of saying a thing* before he has said it" (p. 253). This has no conceptual content, nor any definite images of either words or things. "But as the words that replace it arrive, it welcomes them successively and calls them right if they agree with it, it rejects them and calls them wrong if they do not" (p. 253). What is it that is active here in making this separation? James' answer is clear. Once again, it is a vast complex of meaningful relations spreading out from the general topic or interest we are pursuing. They are pre-linguistic. But they are vaguely sensed and held together by a feeling. Later on (Chapter VII, pp. 188 ff.) we shall point out the significance of this observation for the study of language and the vague, preconceptual meanings it first expresses.

Our language is constantly guided in our speaking by feelings which always surround it on the fringes. "Relation, then, to our topic, or interest, is constantly felt in the fringe, and particularly the relation of harmony and discord, of furtherance or hindrance of the topic. When the sense of furtherance is there, we are 'all right'. With the sense of hindrance we are dissatisfied and perplexed, and cast about us for other thoughts" (I, 259). It is not merely our topic that has fringes. Every word, and every specific object we focus, swims in a dim halo of fringes that stretch out from it to the limits of its world. This is true of each thought that comes up as we pursue the topic of our choice. "Now any thought the quality of whose fringe lets us feel ourselves 'all right', is an acceptable member of our thinking, whatever kind of thought it may otherwise be. Provided we only feel it to have a place in the scheme of relations in which the interesting topic also lies, that is quite sufficient to make of it a relevant and appropriate portion of our train of ideas" (pp. 259–60).

What makes two concepts relevant to each other? It is not any coincidence of their logical implications when taken alone, for two terms whose meanings are utterly different may still be relevant. Yet difference alone is not sufficient, for two different terms like triangle and musical harmony, may be quite irrelevant. Relevance is not decided by any logical analysis of the single terms and phrases. They may radically differ or agree. But the question of relevance must be decided in a different way. Do the concepts belong to the same basic world or region? If so, a careful logical analysis may shed some light. If not, such an analysis will be beside the point, for any differences or similarities in meaning will simply be irrelevant. How then is this kind of question decided? As James would say, by feeling, or more particularly by a feeling of the overlapping of the fringes.

How is it that we get a total impression of a picture, a play, a philosophy, of its whole meaning, and its place in the world? In a creative project of thinking, what is it that gives us a sense of whither our thought is moving before we have arrived, and on the basis of which we judge our work when it is done? James gives the following answer. "It is a feeling like any other, a feeling of what thoughts are next to arise before they have arisen" (p. 256). He calls this the "field view of consciousness", and holds that it is primarily through feeling, not through precise concepts, that we grasp this field as a whole, as the background on which every precise concept and object is focused.

This discussion of the continuity of human experience is remarkable for its emphasis on the role of perception, or *feeling* as James calls it. As against both the traditional empiricists and idealists, he shows that this experience possesses many features which they supposed to be exclusively conceptual. It is not purely "subjective", but may be stretched out intentionally towards objects of purposive concern. It is pervaded with meaning and value. It is not a chaotic manifold of impressions but is held together in a temporal horizon that surrounds them and places them in a field of meaning that limits our perspective but at the same time lures us on. Even at the level of pure conceptual experience, these fringes of meaning are dimly felt, and it is through them that we gain our sense of transition and tendency, and our total orientation in the world. The direction in which we are moving is felt rather than methodically thought through by clearly defined concepts. And even in the processes of conceptual thinking, the sense of what we are about to say, but have not yet said, is provided by feeling.

Yet in spite of the emphasis on feeling, it would be profoundly mistaken to interpret this chapter (IX) as an expression of anti-intellectualism. James is not arguing for an exclusive reliance on feeling, which would contradict his own procedure in this chapter. He constantly evokes familiar feelings, like that of searching for a forgotten name. But at the same time this experience is subjected to a clear conceptual analysis. Both types of knowledge are required for any sound understanding of experience as we live it. This is made quite clear in a passage (p. 259) which we have already quoted. Our feeling for a thing, our direct acquaintance with it is limited "to the bare impression it makes" together with a dim awareness "in the penumbral, nascent way of a fringe of unarticulated affinities about it". These "affinities" must first be felt, but to be understood they must be clearly spelled out and articulated as "relations" of a certain kind to X, Y, and Z. This articulation of relations, which we call the "meaning" of a thing, is provided only by the conceptual analysis which James calls *knowledge about*. As he says, "knowledge *about* a thing is knowledge of its relations". Both are required for adequate understanding.

Feeling without conceptual clarity is vague and inarticulate. This is why clarity is often equated with insight. But this is a mistake. Conceptual articulation without direct acquaintance is artificial and lacks general orientation. It turns into a groundless game without that "warmth and intimacy to which no object of mere conception ever attains" (p. 239). Hence we call those whose thinking is compartmentalized in this way "cold" and "heartless". On the other hand, those who are dominated by their feeling for a single object, surrounded by a haze of fringes, become narrow and provincial. Each provides something needed by the other. When properly grounded, conceptual thinking can clarify the meanings of a certain region of experience and can open up new vistas. But only feeling can then take it over and give it a place in a world that is total and continuous. This is the ideal towards which James' thought is moving. It is his version of the modern ideal of phenomenological insight, or grasp of experienced meaning.

The stream is cognitive; that is, it manifests itself as dealing with beings independent of itself

The stream of consciousness is centered in an embodied person, and the first two characteristics which James considers are concerned with this "subjective centering". Thus, (1) it "tends" to a personal form, and (2) it is in constant flux which is correlated with the continuous changes of the brain and the central nervous system. We have just seen how, under (3), the continuity of consciousness, James introduces his notion of "fringes". They hold these changes together in a more or less constant temporal horizon, always preserving something of the past and anticipating something of the future in an ever-moving present. Now under (4), he develops this notion of fringes even further, and calls our attention to its basic cognitive function. The background of fringes not only keeps us in touch with the immediate past and future (*cf. infra*, Chapter VII, pp. 175 ff.); it establishes a field which opens up cognitive relations not only with the past and future, but in general with "extra-mental" beings, existing in their own right, altogether "independent" of our stream of thought.

According to James, the idealist denies this phenomenon of independent being. In his view, the very thinking of an object by the absolute mind constitutes its being. For such a mind there would be no sense in distinguishing between its meanings and the beings fulfilling or negating them. Meaning and being would necessarily coincide. But our experience follows a more complex pattern, which requires us to distinguish between appearances that are only mental and others that are not only mentally intended but also exist independently of the mind (*cf. infra*, Chapter VI). Thus the friend, standing behind me, reading over my shoulder what I have just written, is now only for me as I imagine him, but the table that I perceive here before me also has an independent existence of its own, which is directly perceived as I touch it.

James does not attribute this to my sense of its resistance to the pressure of my fingers. He claims that it is due rather to my recognition of it as the same object that I saw a few moments ago when I gazed at a scratch on its surface, and perceived on the preceding day from a different point of view. An object which remains the same through varying experiences in the stream must be distinguished from these ever-shifting experiences. Our sense of independent existence develops from this recognition of sameness. We shall return to these themes later on when we take up the subject of conceptual thinking (*infra,* Chapter V). For the moment, we shall let it drop to pursue the subject of idealism.

We have noted James' sharp rejection of absolute idealism, which confuses the being of the thinking with that of what is thought, and, therefore, fails to make a clear distinction between imagination and perception. But there is another qualified form of idealism that does not go so far. According to this view, which originated with Kant (I, 274, note) a "reflective consciousness of the self is essential to the cognitive function of thought" (p. 274).

This view leads to two important consequences, with both of which James strongly disagrees. The first is that I can never simply reveal an object as it is. In revealing it, I must at the same time bring it into relation with a transcendental self and the conditions of its knowing, of which I am already aware, and with which I must contrast it as an object. The second is that this self must be supposed to stand outside the whole world of objects. Hence it can never be known as a being, or object, among other objects in the world. James rejects both of these phases of the transcendental point of view.

As against this, he denies categorically that in becoming aware of an object of any kind, I must also be aware of my awareness. Thus in experiencing a new taste in the throat, I do not at first think of myself as feeling it. I do not at once place it under

either a subjective or an objective category. It is simply felt as a
new being that has entered into the world (p. 272). It is only
later on, after a doctor has brought out certain elements on the
fringes of this experience, has compared it and contrasted it with
others, and has said to me, "now you know what heartburn is",
that I find two different ways of regarding it in two different
frames.

On the one hand, I can look at it objectively as an indis-
position with physiological grounds, which is not peculiar to me
but shared with other men. Or on the other hand, I can emphasize those warm and intimate aspects which make me call
it my own, and thus bring it into the context of my individual
autobiography. One can see here, as elsewhere in the *Principles*,
the roots of what, at the end of his life, James was to call his
radical empiricism (*cf. infra*, Chapter XIV). After self-consciousness has developed, any personal experience can be regarded
legitimately in either of these two ways, and placed in a subjective or an objective context. But there is a wider world
horizon which encompasses both. James calls this *the field of
experience* in which things appear "as simple *beings* neither in
nor out of thought" (I, 272).

It is important to understand that he also uses the term
"object" in this general way, for any being, whether subjective
or objective, that is focused and manifested in the world. This
usage has led certain readers to suppose that James is denying
the subjective, or playing it down in favor of an objectivistic or
behavioristic approach. But this is a misunderstanding. He is
certainly not denying that I have my own intimate, personal
experience of heartburn. He is rather emphasizing this fact by
calling it an object. That is, it is as objective (real) as any
objective, scientific fact. Furthermore, he is at this point engaged
in a basic criticism of Kantian idealism, and its thesis that all
human experience is transcendentally subjective.

As against this, he is asserting, first of all, that objects (beings
of all kinds) can simply be revealed as they are in the world,
without being brought into relation with a transcendental subject with which they must be contrasted, and thereby determined

to some degree. In my primordial experience I may perfectly well become aware of an "object" without knowing anything of my awareness of it, or even without having any centralized self to be aware. This is probably true of the experiences of children. James finds this thesis confirmed by the reports of persons undergoing incipient anaesthesia who refer to an almost complete lapse of subjectivity "while objects are still cognized" (p. 273). In the second place, in opposition to the Kantian theory, he is also denying that the human self includes a transcendental factor apart from the world. Let us now briefly summarize this phase of his thinking, without anticipating the whole of his argument in the next chapter on *The Consciousness of Self*.

As we have already noted, this Kantian theory rests on an assumption, also accepted by "empiricist" philosophers and psychologists, that experience comes to us originally as a "chaotic manifold" (*supra*, pp. 49 ff.). This is reduced by rational analysis to atomic ideas, or impressions. Ignoring the intentional structure of consciousness, the "empiricists" suppose "that whenever an object of thought contains many elements, the thought itself must be made up of just as many ideas, one idea for each element, and all fused together in appearance, but really separate" (I, 277). Their Kantian opponents, on the other hand, have little difficulty in showing "that such a bundle of separate ideas would never form one thought at all". Hence they argue that a transcendental ego must be introduced to "bring the various ideas into relation with each other" (p. 277).

In rejecting the common assumptions on which these opposed but related positions are based, James is working out a view of his own which differs sharply from both of them, and which is similar, in many basic respects, to that of recent phenomenologists. First of all, he lays great emphasis once again, on the intentional structure of consciousness. Our thought of something must be sharply distinguised from that of which it is thinking. To know a thing is not merely to build a replica of it in the mind. It is to grasp its meaning—to place it in an organized pattern of relations. Hence even if we were to suppose (which James would doubt) that some object, like a pack of cards on the table, could be reduced to the fifty-two individual cards in the deck, it would not follow that our thought of this is nothing but "an assemblage or pack of ideas, each answering to some element of what it knows" (p. 278). James now devotes several pages (278–83) to showing the falsity of this atomistic conception.

This thought: *the pack of cards is on the table* is not a mere assemblage of separate units. It is a unitary whole which is present not only before and after the sentence is pronounced, "but also whilst each word is being uttered" (p. 281). These words "melt into each other like dissolving views, and no two of them feel the object just alike, but each feels the total object in a unitary undivided way" (p. 279). This total meaning is first present as a bare intention. Then as further words are expressed, it becomes more nearly articulated, until, finally, it is expressed. But in different ways, with different modulations, the whole meaning is present in every word which, in its own particular way, is "suffused with the whole idea" (p. 282). Hence as James says, "there is no manifold of coexisting ideas; the notion of such a thing is a chimera". Whatever things we think in a meaningful way "are thought from the outset in a single pulse of subjectivity . . ." (p. 278).

This is a discerning piece of phenomenological description which few readers, I believe, will find contrary to their own experience. If we examine ourselves as we pronounce a meaningful sentence, we will find this to be true. But if this is so, there is no need to suppose that the sentence results from a synthetic act performed by a transcendental agent, working from a position beyond experience. On the contrary, we find this activity going on *in* our experience. Furthermore, we can examine it and describe it with some accuracy as it goes on in the world. No transcendental ego is required. I can perfectly well know something about an object, O, without being aware that I am knowing it. "If in addition to thinking O, I also think that I exist, and that I know O, well and good; I then know one more thing. . . . O *per se*, or O plus P are as good objects of knowledge as O plus me is" (p. 274). Thus the subjective act of knowing is an event that goes on in the world. It can be accurately (objectively) described, like other modes of action with which it can be compared and contrasted.

In this sense, the act of knowing and the empirical self that knows are objects among other objects in the world. They can be objectively known and described, together with the fringes that always surround them, and fade off to the ultimate limits of the human world. James is here rejecting both absolute and Kantian idealism. But does this empirical self, this object existing among other objects in the world, then, have nothing to do with ordering or constituting the world in which it exists? James deals with this question in considering the next selective characteristic of consciousness. In this section it becomes clear that he is also rejecting traditional realism as well.

The stream is "always interested", either welcoming or rejecting all the while it thinks

According to the realistic theory, the human mind, in so far as it functions properly, is forming copies of objective structures exactly as they are. In so far as this mind becomes spontaneously active on its own account, it falls into error by subjectively distorting the natures of things as they are outside the mind. As against this theory, James now stresses the selective activity of consciousness as one of its constant characteristics. Thus, "accentuation and emphasis" are present in all perception. Our selective emphasis on here or there, now or then, this or that, underlies conscious activities in space and time. But our selective attention goes even further. It is constantly eliminating wide ranges of possible objects by simply passing them over or ignoring them. Thus the structure of each sense organ makes it sensitive only to motions and pressures of a certain range.

Other vast ranges are simply passed by. But enough filters through to enable us to perceive the things, or objects, with which we must deal in order to live. Among the possible objects of perception, our "habits of attention" are constantly selecting those which are of immediate concern. "We are all seeing flies, moths, and beetles by the thousand, but to whom, save an entomologist, do they say anything distinct?" (p. 286). Rational clarification (knowledge *about*) also involves a selection governed by interest and the nature of the problem at hand, whether it be theoretical or practical. There are always different ways of reflecting about the object, and, in the process of selection among them, new meanings may be developed which are relevant to the emergency. The same is true in the field of aesthetics where "the artist notoriously selects his items, rejecting all tones, colors, shapes which do not harmonize with each other, and with the main purpose of his work" (p. 287). It is important to note that James places "Ethics" at the top of his hierarchy of conscious levels. Here, where the whole way of human life is at stake, decisions must be made concerning the subordination, or elimination, of interests, and "choice reigns supreme".

It is clear from these pages that James is not only rejecting traditional forms of idealism, but traditional forms of realism as well. The function of consciousness, as he conceives it, is not merely to inscribe copies of structures, that already exist outside, on the tablets of the mind. Consciousness, as we have already seen (*supra*, pp. 16 ff.), is always active and engaged. It selects, pays attention, strives, and chooses. Even the search for pure understanding is a project that must be selected and chosen as against other possible alternatives. In so far as it satisfies this need, it makes a difference. We may even say a tremendous difference, for this engaged awareness is not only an event, an object among other objects in the world, that may be objectively examined. It is also involved in the meaningful ordering and constituting of the world in which it exists. This paradox lies at the heart of James' philosophy (*cf. infra*, Chapter IV). Our telic consciousness appears as a finite, empirical being in the world. But at the same time, it has something to do with the moulding of the very same world it is already in. This consciousness is surrounded by independent beings which exist in their own right, and constrain us to accept them as they are. But with respect to their meaning, it exercises a selective and creative function. To bring this out more strongly, we can do no better than to quote James' own words (I, 288–89).

"The mind, in short, works on the data it receives very much as a sculptor works on his block of stone. In a sense, the statue stood there from eternity. But there were a thousand different ones beside it, and the sculptor alone is to thank for having extricated this one from the rest. . . . We may if we like, by our reasonings, unwind things back to that black and jointless continuity of space and moving clouds of swarming atoms which science calls the only real world. But all the while, the world *we* feel and live in will be that which our ancestors and we, by slowly cumulative strokes of choice, have extricated out of this, like sculptors, by simply rejecting certain portions of the given stuff. Other sculptors, other statues from the same stone! . . . My world is but one in a million, alike embedded, alike real, to those who may abstract them. How different must be the worlds in the consciousness of ant, cuttle-fish, or crab!"

Of course this analogy must not be pressed too far, as James does in the sentences we have omitted where he speaks of knowing in Kantian terms, as though it were literally the moulding of a raw "matter". Knowing, as the realists say, is not the same as making. It exerts no force, or pressure, on the facts. It leaves them exactly as they were. Here the metaphor breaks down. But by finding a sense in them, by gathering them together in a meaningful context, it sees them in a new light, and this makes a difference. Here the metaphor holds. The contrast between the "black and jointless" realm of science and "the world we feel and live in" will remain basic to James' thought. But the very words that are used in stating it are incompatible with the notion of forming the latter by mere abstraction and whittling away. The life-world is not less but more than the abstract regions of the special sciences, and *the* world must have a place for both. We shall see how James later corrected this deficiency in his statue metaphor by which he is, at this time, too much carried away. But his sense of the vast diversity of different worlds of meaning ordered around the projects of different empirical centres, each existing with the others as objects in the world, will remain to the end.

But if there is no transcendental self beyond the world, if this function of world-formation is performed by an empirical self which is only an object in the world, we must now ask further questions about the nature of this self. It is to these questions that James now turns in the next chapter.

Chapter Four

❀

The Self and
Self-consciousness

Chapter X is a long chapter consisting of many intricate arguments falling under many diverse headings. We shall not attempt to follow each of these arguments in their full detail and in the precise order in which they are presented. We shall, however, follow this order roughly, and divide our comments under three headings which cover the main steps of James' general argument. These are: 1, a phenomenological description of three major aspects of what is called the "self" and of the phenomenon of self-love as they are directly experienced (pp. 82–99); 2, the formulation of a theory of the self that can take account of these facts—of the self, that is, as a finite being in time which is nevertheless able to interpret itself and the world in which it lives (pp. 99–106); and finally 3, the clarification of this view through a careful criticism of opposed theories, scholastic, empirical, and transcendental (pp. 106–14).

The Self as a Field

At the beginning of the chapter, James presents us with some penetrating descriptions of self-phenomena which are very wide in range, highly original, and rich in content. He makes it clear immediately that he is concerned with "the empirical self" which can be observed as an object, or being, existing with other beings in the world. This self has a subjective centre with which he will be concerned later. But first of all, he will consider its peripheral aspects, that is, everything that I can call *me*. The living body has been traditionally regarded as an instrument which belongs to me, but is not really me. James at once expresses his basic doubt of this view by asking concerning our bodies: "are they simply ours, or are they *us?*" (I, 291). It is often hard to draw the line between myself and what belongs to me. "In its widest possible sense, however, a man's Self is the sum total of all that he *can* call his. . . . All these things give him the same emotions. If they wax and prosper, he feels triumphant; if they dwindle and die away, he feels cast down,— not necessarily in the same degree for each thing, but in much the same way for all."

In adopting this broader conception of the self, he finds three distinct "constituents" in what we commonly refer to as the self: the material self, the social self, and the spiritual self, which he then describes in this order. I can see no strong reason for doubting that, in these descriptions, James is not only following then current linguistic usages but is at the same time outlining genuine phenomena which actually appear in different cultures.

One of the most original aspects of James' discussion of the self is his refusal to separate it from the body in accordance with the traditional theory of psycho-physical dualism. My self is a material self, and "the body is the innermost part of *the material self* in each of us" (p. 292). From the beginning to the end of human life, we are all instinctively concerned with our body, with other living bodies related to it, and with the manifold variety of things that they require. "We all have a blind impulse to watch over our body, to deck it with clothing of an ornamental sort, to cherish parents, wife and babes, and to find for ourselves a home of our own which we may live in and 'improve'" (p. 292). In different degrees, these objects become identified with the empirical self, or me. This is also true of the possessions I gather around me, even those which have no direct connection with the maintenance of my bodily life. This is peculiarly true of objects "saturated with our labor", like a manuscript on which I have worked for years. It is true that we value such objects in part because of further benefits to which we expect them to lead. But our relation to them is more intimate than this. We actually identify ourselves with them, and when they are lost, we feel a certain shrinkage of our being, "a partial conversion of ourselves to nothingness" (p. 293).

These facts are sufficient to show that the human self is not a purely immaterial, nor spiritual, nor even a purely subjective being. As James suggests in these penetrating descriptions, I am the body that I am living through and feeling, the other living bodies related by kinship to me, and in various degrees of intimacy, the clothing I wear, the possessions I own, and the physical works I have produced. Traditional thought has taught us to believe that over and above all these objective instruments, there is a pure principle of subjectivity, an inner self that can never be objectified. James does not reject this notion of an innermost citadel of selfhood. But as we shall see, even this is inseparably intertwined with the living body and its internal self-motions.

Before we come to this, however, we must consider a higher level of objects in which the self is not only interested but with which he becomes actually identified. These are the attitudes, or as James puts it, "the images" of ourselves in the minds of our friends and acquaintances, and in the various groups to which we belong. This section is very brief, but is filled with fertile suggestions. A man plays a different role in the various groups to which he belongs, "and shows a different side of himself to each of these different groups" (p. 294). Underlying these various roles is the self, conceived not as an isolated substance, but as a field, always stretched out towards others, and always open to their approbation or disapproval. James makes this clear at the beginning of his discussion. "We are not only gregarious animals, liking to be noticed by our fellows", he says, "but we have an innate propensity to get ourselves noticed and noticed favorably by our kind" (p. 293).

Man is here being regarded not as a substance, but as a centre of active intentions reaching out to constitute objects of various kinds, as in Husserl and many of his followers. He is also the receiver of double-intentions, as we may call them, coming back to him from others who approve, or hate, or scorn him. These intentions of others towards us are not mere accidents but belong to our innermost being. Thus in his consideration of the feeling of shame, James asks whether the change experienced with the coming of this emotion is not wholly internal to me, and whether the proper object of my self-regard "is not the condition of this thing inside of me"? A moment ago this opinion of myself was "big and strong and lusty, but now weak, contracted, and collapsed" (p. 322).

James answers these questions with an emphatic negative. In what capacity, as a being of what kind, do I claim a respectful greeting rather than one of disdain? "It is not as a bare I that I claim it." It is rather as an I stretched out towards other beings from the start, "as being an I . . . who has certain powers, possessions, and public functions, sensibilities, duties and purposes, and merits and deserts". It is this being-with-others, which I am, that your scorn negates. "This is the thing inside of me whose changed treatment I feel the shame about; this is what was lusty and now, in consequence of your conduct, is collapsed . . ." (p. 322).

In other words, this thing inside of me is not a thing at all. It is rather a relational phase of my being which reaches out towards things and attitudes that are wholly external to me in a spatial sense, and, indeed, independent of me in their existence. And yet my inner being is involved with them, and is dependent on them in many respects. Thus "no more fiendish punishment could be devised . . . than that one should be turned loose in society, and remain absolutely unnoticed by all the members thereof" (p. 293). Indifference would not be felt in this way, if the human person were an isolated substance, or a pure ego with no essential relations to empirical objects. Nor would the constant appeal which James believes to be universal in some degree (pp. 316–17), to ideal associates, or an ideal observer of some kind, be readily explained. Thus the lonely innovator struggling for a lost cause imagines ideal associates who, somewhere at some remote time, will understand what he is doing. And when he, or, indeed, the rest of us, falls into complete despair, we tend to pray. James puts it even more strongly: "we cannot *help* praying" (p. 316). We are led by the social nature of our being to appeal to an ideal spectator, who will grant us some credit for our failing aspirations.

This field conception of the human self, as being necessarily involved with empirical objects, is central to James' whole phenomenological psychology. In its social aspect, it means that, in some one of many possible modes, man is always existing with others. It is clear, therefore, that he would accept Heidegger's dictum[1] that being alone is a privative manifestation of being with others, or, as he would put it, the frustration of "a native propensity" of man. It is for this reason that the problem of solipsism, which plagues Husserl and other phenomenologists, never seriously troubled James.

Since the individual exists in his social relations, "he has as many different social selves as there are distinct *groups* of persons about whose opinion he cares" (p. 294). He is the different roles he plays in his family, his profession, and the different institutions to which he belongs. In a pluralistic society, this may result in a discordant splitting of the man into several selves, each with its special standards for behavior. What we call a

---

[1] *Sein und Zeit*, 7th ed., Tübingen, 1957, p. 120. *Cf. Being and Time*, tr. MacQuarrie/Robinson, London, 1962, pp. 156–57.

man's reputation, or honor, is his social self, or role, in a particular group of special importance. He exists in the minds of these others, and his honor or dishonor is his acceptance or rejection by them. As James says, "it is his image in the eyes of his own set" (p. 294). As this image waxes and wanes, his reputation is expanded or contracted.

Most of the selves that we meet are social selves of this kind. But in a free society, it is possible for the individual to achieve a certain integrity of his own, and a certain relation of his whole being to that of another person. Since the "whole" self is here involved, these are social selves in the strictest sense. James seems to recognize this when he says (p. 294) that "properly speaking, a man has as many social selves as there are individuals who recognize him and carry an image of him in their mind". He literally exists in the minds of these others, so that "to wound any of these, his images, is to wound him". James does not clearly develop this conception here, but he does refer to the distinctive character of love between two individual persons. "The most peculiar social self which one is apt to have is in the mind of the person one is in love with" (p. 294).

It is important to note that James here uses the term *person,* not *individual.* For him, this means the attainment of a total or "organic" integrity of existence, which the mere principle of individual separateness does not imply. Thus he goes on to say that the good or bad fortunes of this self, which exists in the person of the beloved, brings forth "the most intense elation and dejection—unreasonable enough as measured by every other standard than that of the organic feeling of the individual. To his own consciousness he *is* not, so long as this particular social self fails to get recognition . . ." (p. 294). Here we find a concrete illustration of what James means by taking relations seriously—a cardinal principle of his radical empiricism. My existence is not enclosed within the limits of an atomic self or substance. I exist in the groups to which I belong, and in the "relation" of love, my entire "organic" being exists in the person of the beloved.

The Inner Citadel of Selfhood

Nevertheless, we must not infer from this that the self is nothing but these relations. I may exist in them, even totally, but I am not necessarily lost in them. A relational being requires not only a terminus but an ultimate source. This ultimate source is what James calls *the spiritual self*, to which we shall now turn. This is the I-myself to which all objects are opposed (pp. 296–97). Indeed, without this inner citadel of selfhood, the term *object* would lose its meaning. Even the material self, and the social selves, are objective in this sense, for they can be observed from the outside, and their functions can be objectively described and analyzed. Hence I refer to them and to the objects of their care as my objective self, or *me*. As we shall see, this is even true of the principle of subjectivity itself when its action is over, and it has slipped into the past where it can be regarded as an object and either accepted or rejected. This "self of all other selves" (p. 297) is not an object referred *to*. It is *expressed by* the personal pronoun I.

We cannot think about this I as something that is already there, for by this time it is no longer active and has become merely *me*. We must catch it in the very act by "a reflective process", in the French sense of this term, which is able to grasp the act as it is actually proceeding or actively imagined. It is only in this way that we may learn to think not merely about ourselves as we have been, but "to think ourselves as thinkers" (p. 296). What is this innermost citadel of selfhood?

James calls it "the active element in all consciousness" (p. 297). The various things and qualities which we perceive come into the field of consciousness from the outside. But there is something in me "which seems to go out to meet these qualities and contents", to gather them, and to contain them within its fringes. "It is what welcomes or rejects" as "the home of interest", for it is I who must decide whether I really care or not. "It is the source of effort and attention, and the place from which appear to emanate the fiats of the will" (p. 298). It is I who must pay attention to a new or unwelcome thing if it is to be really noticed, and who must strain my last effort to keep it focused. The physiologist, reflecting about this self-experience in the first person, will no doubt connect it more or less vaguely with the central nervous system where incoming sensations and ideas terminate, from which motor impulses proceed, and where there is a linkage between the two. "Being more incessantly there than any other single element of the mental life, the other elements end by seeming to accrete round it and to belong to it" (p. 298).

James finds this analysis confirmed by his reflections on his own thinking, where he finds a variegated complex of obstacles and releases arising from the constant interplay of tendencies running with his own desires, and others coming in from the outside. Becoming more specific, he then describes the feelings of motion he finds in his own acts of attention, assent, negation, and finally, effort. In attending to an object, even when it is not present, he feels himself, in an abbreviated form, going through those ocular and bodily movements by which he usually prepares himself to receive the visible thing. In shifting his attention to objects of different sensory spheres, he feels what seems like a shifting of direction in his brain.

The feelings of consenting and negating are more complex and harder to describe. James finds that in his own case the opening and closing of the glottis plays an important role in these operations. At every hesitation and aversion, there is an interception of the breath which is released when the tension is over. "The feeling of the movement of this air is, in me, one strong ingredient of the feeling of assent" (p. 301). In effort of any sort, there are contractions of the muscles of the jaw and those of respiration, if the exertion is intense. At this point, many bodily parts become involved, and the head feelings are swallowed up in the total bodily expression of emotion.

James admits that there are "dim portions" in his own self-feeling, which he "cannot yet define" (p. 301). But the conclusion to which his investigations point is "that our entire feeling of spiritual activity, or what commonly passes by that name, is really a feeling of bodily activities . . ." (pp. 301–2). These feelings come from the brain where incoming nervous impressions terminate and outgoing motor impulses begin. They express our "primary reactions", our acceptance or rejection of what is perceived. Hence James says they "are like the opening or the closing of the door" (p. 302). Since they are involved in all sensation and action, and are, indeed, the central link between the two, it is not surprising that they seem "central and interior" in comparison with all foreign objects. It is here that these objects are first selected for attention, and here that our active responses begin. Hence it is no wonder that they appear as "the 'sanctuary within the citadel' of our personal life" (p. 303).

These well-known statements opened James to the charge of materialism and behaviorism which have often been urged against him. But in the light of recent phenomenological investigations, especially those of Merleau-Ponty in his *Phénoménologie de la perception*, we can now see that these charges, never admitted by James, are unjustified. It is not the body of traditional dualistic thought, the mere mass of matter extended in space. It is the moving, living, conscious body which expresses our emotions and is the non-objective centre of my world. It is this self-moving body, never fully placed before us as an object, which is the pure subjective centre of our lived experience. In its primal activity this living body cannot be thought about as a conceptual object without reduction. This is one reason why the intellectualist is so easily led into transcendentalism. If we cannot think about it as an object, we must deduce it as an empty but necessary condition for experience.

But we do not have to deduce it. Conceptual thinking is not the only, nor even the primary source of our knowledge. We know it first of all by "direct sensible acquaintance". As James says, "when it is found, it is felt" (p. 299). We may develop its meaning by reflection and imagination, but never without the support of that primary feeling which catches the self in its very act. We must remember, however, as James reminds us (p. 299), that this living body is never felt as an isolated substance, or thinking thing, in the Cartesian sense. "Never is the body felt all alone, but always together with other things." Thus the pure centre of consciousness, the principle of subjectivity, is never experienced apart from the world, but always together with other objects and things in the world. How can this body be both an object and a "subjective" centre? It is no wonder that James does not wish to seem dogmatic in defending what was for his time a novel and radical conclusion. Perhaps the empirical self, or selves, is a mere cluster of objects with no subjective center of its own. The body has been traditionally regarded as an object. This fits in with the Kantian view that supposes the empirical self to be an object thought about, incapable of thinking.

Hence before any further elaboration and defence, James briefly develops this transcendental theory as though it were his own (p. 304). It is, he believes, the most formidable opponent of his empirical theory. The text here has been misunderstood, but the general sense is clear. So far the evidence is ambiguous, and can be interpreted in two ways. Before proceeding with his argument, James wishes to contrast the two theories in their general outlines: the transcendental on the one hand, and the empirical view he has presented on the other. This will help the reader to understand the basic issues between them, and to judge the further evidence that will be produced. So he now gives a sketch of the transcendental theory. As we have noted, James admits that there is an obscure "something more" than the bodily feelings he finds in his sense of intimate selfhood. A psychologist, like Wundt, therefore, may claim "that the completely abstract ego as pure activity, although suggested by the natural development of our consciousness, is never actually found therein" (p. 303, note).

The consequences of this Kantian view are now spelled out for us on page 304. Experience will not be understood as a world in which independent beings are confronted, cared for, and interpreted by a self which is directly known as existing, together with them, in this world. It is rather taken to be "a stream of consciousness pure and simple" in which only objects are directly known. These objects are divided into two classes, those which are not-me, and others, the empirical selves, which are me. But the thinker of these objects is never directly known, neither by conceptual thinking, nor, of course, by feeling, which has little or no cognitive value.

This thinker has to be inferred by a deduction from the objects found in experience, and is, therefore, known only "in an abstract, hypothetic or conceptual way" as their indispensable condition. It is not a "direct inner perception of spiritual activity", but a logical postulate required to account for experience in general, and having no specific content of its own. Matter also, as something having its own existence independent of our consciousness, is not found in the world of experience. It, too, is a postulate of the same kind. Between this postulated matter and the postulated thinker, the curtain of phenomena swings, partly dependent on both. But these two postulates are empty forms, and in answer to the questions as to what the matter is, or as to who or how many the thinkers are, no empirical evidence is relevant. These are all "subjects for an ultimate metaphysical inquiry" (p. 304).

As over against this metaphysical view, James now begins to develop his own empirical, or as we should now say, phenomenological position in detail. This requires the remainder of the chapter. But before commenting on the main steps of this elaborate argument, let us first summarize the empirical position, so that we can contrast it with the Kantian view. Experience is not "a stream of consciousness" in which objects are simply synthesized and known by a pure transcendental thinker. It is a world in which independent beings are encountered and, to some degree, known as they are. The self which encounters these beings, however, not only knows them. He struggles with them, cares for them, and responds to them in a variety of different ways. Furthermore, this self is not an empty form of *I think* which has to be postulated on the basis of no direct evidence. He is known directly by feelings, which, in spite of their initial vagueness, can be clarified by disciplined reflection. The task of understanding the basic patterns of this world,

therefore, is not primarily metaphysical in the sense of speculation without the support of relevant evidence. It is rather a
hermeneutic task of interpreting an evidence that is extremely
far-ranging and vague, but nevertheless directly relevant. James
grants that the evidence so far presented is insufficient to demon-
strate his theory of an empirical principle of subjectivity that
is directly known. So he now proceeds to adduce further evidence from the phenomena of self-love.

Self-love

In working out this argument, James first says a few words
about the feelings of self-complacency, self-dissatisfaction, and
their associates, pride, conceit, vanity, self-esteem, on the one
hand, modesty, humility, confusion, and shame on the other. He
rejects the hedonist view that these feelings result from a compu-
tation of the prospects of one's situation in terms of pleasure and
pain (p. 306). This is only a secondary aspect of the phenomenon
which, aside from morbid cases, is concerned rather with the
expansion and contraction of empirical selves. "The normal pro-
vocative of self feeling", he says, "is one's actual success or failure,
and the good or bad position one holds in the world" (p. 306).

He next turns to self-seeking and self-preservation, and makes
the same general point. What we are seeking here is not something purely subjective, like pleasure or pain, nor a pure inner
self which is separated from all objects. It is rather the material,
the social, or the spiritual self we are trying to enlarge by giving
them a more effective control over their proper objects, which
are always things located in space and time. Even "the places
and things I know enlarge my Self in a sort of metaphoric social
way" (p. 308). In the popular Mohammedan and Christian
views of heaven, the material nature of the goods involved is
"undisguised". And even in more refined conceptions of heaven,
"many of its goods, the fellowship of the saints and of our dead
ones, and the presence of God are but social goods of the most

exalted kind" (p. 309). The self that we actually seek to preserve and enlarge is always a self concerned with objects of some kind.

If we are to reach a man and communicate with him, we must "touch" his actual self, and find out that for which he really cares. This actual self has to be arrived at through selective choice between different conflicting selves. Otherwise the potential person will remain floating in a haze of possibilities. When such a choice is made, one self becomes actual and the others become "unreal" (p. 310). In so far as the purpose of this chosen self are realized, his very being is expanded. In so far as they are maimed and frustrated, "he is to his own regard as if he were not, indeed he is not". But this success or failure, and the self-feeling dependent upon it, is to some degree within our control. It is determined by a fraction of which our success is the numerator and our pretensions the denominator. Thus "self-esteem$=\dfrac{\text{success}}{\text{pretensions}}$" (p. 310), and the fraction may be increased either by increasing the numerator or lessening the denominator in the Stoic manner.

James recognizes the nobility in the early Stoic attitude, but he attacks the negative manifestations of early Stoicism for their tendency to bring forth "narrow and unsympathetic character". He also notes the connection between such a negative attitude and the phenomena of resentment studied by Nietzsche and others. Thus as he says (p. 312), "all narrow people *intrench* their Me, they *retract* it from the region of what they cannot securely possess. People who don't resemble them, or who treat them with indifference, people over whom they gain no influence are people on whose existence, however meritorious it may intrinsically be, they look with chill negation, if not with positive hate." For the goods that they cannot appropriate are not only not their goods; they are readily regarded as positive evils. James makes it clear that he prefers the "sympathetic" way, which proceeds by expansion and inclusion, and finds it illustrated in a saying of the Emperor Marcus Aurelius, whose position he rightly distinguishes from that of early Stoicism.

As to other moral principles which may give us sound guidance in the choice between different selves, James accepts what he calls "tolerably unanimous opinion" that there is a hierarchical order "with the bodily Self at the bottom, the spiritual Self at the top, and the extracorporeal material selves and the various social selves between" (p. 313). He is sceptical about the possibility of eliminating all that may be called *selfish*. Too much attention to the material self is generally condemned by this term. This inordinate desire for things is exemplified especially in the young child, the egoist *par excellence* (p. 321), and is usually suppressed by social constraint, which becomes a virtue of necessity. But this "virtue" is often strengthened by an independent judgment arising from seeing my own lusts mirrored in the lusts of others. This may lead me to think about them in a way which modifies my original feeling for the better (p. 314). The only way to eliminate all care for the self is through suicide, and such a frenzy towards non-being is, of course, possible. But as long as we remain alive, we are governed by some sort of self-concern. What is the nature of the self that is loved in self-love? The answer is given in the section bearing this title (pp. 317–29), where the whole argument comes to a head.

We generally think of the self in spatial terms as a substance, or thing, cut off from other external things, and even from the world itself. This leads us to think of self-love as concern for a purely subjective principle, the soul or transcendental ego, the principle of individuation in me, which makes me I as against all other objects. James makes it clear that he regards this as a basic mistake of traditional thought that began with the Greek view of the self as a substance, and which, with many variations, has continued to exert its influence until the present time. He now proceeds to show that it cannot be reconciled with the evidence he has called to the attention of the reader. If we are to keep our thinking in line with these facts of the active life of man, we must abandon the old notion for another conception he here suggests. We may call this the field-conception of the self.

Whatever else it may be, the living body is not a transcendental principle. Neither is it a separate substance that can be isolated from its environment and the objects it needs to sustain it. This living body is an object in the sense that it is felt or perceived "in our objective field" (p. 320), with other objects for which it cares in a positive or negative way. Unless it resists noxious influences and seeks for what it needs, it cannot stay alive. Thus it must have clothing, utensils, a home for shelter, and a minimum of material possessions. This whole field of objects constitutes my material self, the most basic portion of my being.

Furthermore, a man loves his family and his possessions, so far as he really loves them, for their own sake, not merely because they are his, as a mother loves her child. Thus the man who grabs a seat on the train and cuts out his neighbor, desires *it,* the comfortable seat. The most selfish acts are not concerned with an internal principle of identity, but rather with external objects. The self is then built up around these things which are desired for their own sake. As we have already noticed in the case of the child, the egoist *par excellence,* his interest is not in himself as an internal principle which may be altogether lacking. He wants the food or the plaything, and the self that he later develops is ordered around these primitive and even instinctive objects of desire.

The same is true of the living body itself, which is the centre of this field of desire. A man loves this body which he directly remembers and feels, not because it belongs to an inner principle, but for itself. Hence James says (pp. 319–20) "that he identifies himself with this body because he loves *it,* and that he does not love it because he finds it to be identified with himself." What happens to our bodies "excites in us emotions and tendencies to action more energetic and habitual than any which are excited by other portions of the field" (p. 320). The material self, therefore, is not an internal principle, or substance. It is a whole "field" of objects centered in the living body, stretched out around it, and before and behind it in space and time. I literally *am* this whole field, bound together and ordered by desire.

The same is true of the social self which is concerned with images of me which exist in the minds of other persons, and the intentions reflecting back from these images. We still say that I myself, as an inner principle, am susceptible or impervious to these intentions. But James is here questioning the assumptions lying back of this remark. The attitudes of others towards me are constantly fluctuating. They are sometimes more and sometimes less favorable. But I am literally stretched out into these images and attitudes of others, and it is true to say that my being expands or contracts with them. If I am impervious, this means, as we have seen, that I identify myself with other ideal spectators in the past or future, or with an eternal spectator beyond all time. This self, which can be empirically felt and studied, is a field of social relations held together now not merely by instinctive desire but by a selective choice.

Finally this is also true of the spiritual self, which exists at the top of the hierarchy. This self involves my powers of perceiving, understanding, and willing, which have their source in cephalic movements I dimly feel. But such feelings of initiation must be analyzed out of a richer context. In the concrete, they are joined with acts of perceiving, understanding, and willing which have objects. I cannot perceive without perceiving something; I cannot love or hate without loving or hating something. These objects are ordered around a subjective centre, but a centre loses its meaning apart from its circumference. So once again, we are confronted with the field phenomenon. In so far as I love this spiritual self, what I really care for is certainly not a separated thinker or transcendental Ego, but rather "my more phenomenal and perishable powers, my loves and hates, willingnesses and sensibilities and the like" (p. 323). Not only are these activities inseparably bound up with transitory objects; they themselves "come and go" as objects in time. So in this case also, our love for the spiritual self, which is manifested in experience, leads us not to a formal, timeless principle, but to a trans-subjective objective field that expands and contracts in time.

Thus the material, social, and spiritual selves that are manifested in the phenomena of self-love have nothing to do with a separate, transcendental ego. They are concrete, objective appearances in the world of space and time. James summarized the conclusion to which these phenomena point in the following words (p. 323): "its own body, then, first of all, its friends next, and finally its spiritual dispositions, MUST be the supremely interesting OBJECTS for each human mind." It is not merely that these forms of self-love are manifested in our actual experience. An existing mind which took no care of its body, its associates, or its meaningful purposes would soon be eliminated by the processes of natural selection that are ever at work in this evolving world. It is James' thoroughgoing acceptance of this "zoological psychology", as he calls it (p. 323), which justifies the term MUST in this statement.

He recognizes that against the account of the self he has given, the following objection may still be raised. There is a wide range of phenomena, it may be said, which show that any self takes a peculiar interest in its own talents and possessions rather than in those of others. How can these facts be explained apart from a prior interest in the separate self as such? James does not deny the fact. It is true that I take a special interest in the music I play, that my own jokes seem funnier than those of others, and the wine that I own the best that can be had, at least for the price (p. 326). But he does deny the explanation in terms of an exclusive regard for a self that is isolated and fixed for all time.

Of course I take a special interest in the objects of my own desires. There is no issue here. The question is rather do I love them in a special way merely because they are mine, as the traditionalists assert, or do they become mine because I love them in a special way, for themselves alone? James prefers this latter explanation for two reasons. First, it requires us to conceive of the self as a dynamic, growing entity rather than as a timeless form, which is more in harmony with the data of experience. In the second place, if the I is deprived of all objective content and is reduced to a bare principle of synthesis, it is hard to see why being related to such a formal principle should bring about any special form of preference or knowledge, which is the fact to be explained.

Objects of indifference, or hate, which are excluded from the self, are conceptually known just as clearly as the objects of intense desire which belong to me. The real explanation is to be found not in conceptual knowledge, but rather in direct feeling and acquaintance. The reason I take a special interest in the pieces I play is because I know them in exact detail by direct acquaintance, in actually producing them, and living them through, as the German author Horwicz has suggested (pp. 325–28). They call up many poignant memories of the past and anticipations of the future. They are thus woven into the context of my actual existence as I live it through.

The self that I love in all its levels is certainly not a bare principle of identity, nor a formal *I think*. It not only knows its objects, but loves them and hates them as well. It is a self that is engaged. If there is a transcendental principle, it may be the condition without which this living, caring self cannot be known. But it is not the self that is manifested in our experience. James still recognizes that further argument is necessary to dispose of this transcendental conception, for which he has a deep respect.

When Chapter X is read as a whole, it is clear that he rejects this theory. James is engaging in a complex argument, leading him to the final conclusion that the empirical self is the only self that there is. This is a basic thesis of what he later called his radical empiricism. At the present point, he has shown that three distinct levels of self-hood, which certainly belong to the self, are perceived and known as objects which come into being, exist, and pass away in the time of world history. He has also shown that the objects of self-love are transitory phenomena of this kind.

But though the transcendental theory has been weakened, it would still be possible for a Kantian defender to assert that an *a priori* synthetic principle, completely divorced from any empirical manifestations, is still necessary to explain our knowledge both of the self and of other objects. This will be true as long as no plausible empirical explanation is suggested. Can it be shown, in the light of the facts already revealed, that this empirical self, a mere finite being in the world, can maintain its identity throughout the changes of time? Can it know the world as a whole, and hold it together in a meaningful frame? Or, in other words, can it be shown, with any degree of plausibility, that this fragile and ephemeral object in experience can also function as an ultimate subject of this experience? Until this can be done, the case for radical empiricism will be radically incomplete. So it is to this task that James turns his attention in the next section entitled "The Pure Ego".

Self-identity and Appropriation

The ultimate subject of experience must remain the same. Otherwise it would not be able to hold the manifold aspects of the stream of consciousness together, and to call them *mine*. The name for this sameness in difference is *identity*. Now the empirical self, in its variable manifestations, certainly shows differences. In what sense can it be the same? This is the question with which James deals in the following pages (pp. 329–42), which are of central importance for his whole work. In order to understand the original answer he suggests, it is necessary to understand why he cannot accept the traditional answers of the empiricists and rationalists.

The empiricists have rightly called our attention to the diverse manifestations of the empirical self. "It is to the imperishable glory of Hume and Herbart and their successors to have taken so much of the meaning of personal identity out of the clouds, and made of the self an empirical and verifiable thing" (p. 336). But instead of one thing, they have left us with a mere "sum of passing things", somehow glued or associated together. They have given us no intelligible account of this unity. What is it in a past experience that leads me to call it mine? The spiritualists and transcendentalists, on the other hand, have given us an answer that seems to pacify the sense of mankind. But this is a metaphysical answer in the clouds with no distinct content, and unsupported by any observable evidence.

After noting these difficulties, James now adds a further criticism of the Kantian theory (pp. 331–32). The transcendental principle of synthesis is too broad to account for personal self-identity. It applies to any thought, whether it be of a connected or a disconnected set of objects. Whichever it be, certain objects must be brought together in an intellectual synthesis. But in the case of self-identity something more than this "subjective synthesis" is involved. Why is it that the self of yesterday, a month ago, and a year ago are judged objectively to be the same? A subjective synthesis would be involved, even if they were judged to be entirely different. As James maintains (pp. 331–32, note), the Kantians have here fallen into a confusion of a subjective with an objective synthesis. What is it in our experiences that leads us to judge different selves not only as subjectively but also as objectively the same?

In answering this question, which the Kantians have really evaded, James turns to the region of feeling. The basis for our "sense of personal identity" (p. 330) is to be found not in conceptual thought but in what we feel and know directly by acquaintance. Thus we directly feel "the whole cubic mass of our body all the while", and "some degree of organic emotion in the shape of quickened heart-beats, oppressed breathing, or some other alteration, even though it be a slight one, in the general bodily tone". These feelings bring a warmth and intimacy to the activity of our present action as it is going on, which constitute "the inner 'nucleus of the spiritual self'" (p. 333). James does not specifically say that these bodily feelings give us the sense of conscious activity as it is now proceeding. The traditional dualism, which he never overcame, makes him mention them as distinct. But he sees them as very closely connected, and as constituting together that "warmth and intimacy" which give me a sense of myself.

This sense, he says, "reduces itself to either of two things,— something in the feeling which we have of thought itself, as thinking, or else the feeling of the body's actual existence at the moment,—or finally to both" (p. 333). In the mind of the careful reader, there can be little doubt that his thought is moving towards an identification of the two. My sense of mental activity is the feeling of nascent bodily activities coming into being. Thus James can say that "*the central adjustments* which accompany the act of thinking in the head . . . *are the real nucleus of our personal identity*" (p. 341). Here the two are being thought of as one. But even when he thinks of them as two, it is the two together which bring us the "warmth" that belongs to activities of the self. Thus "any other fact which brings these two things with it into consciousness will be thought of with a warmth and an intimacy like those which cling to the present self" (p. 333).

We must add to this similarity in the feelings of warmth the sense of continuous change between them. I am aware of these changes as running on with no break for hours, and between very different experiences my memory can supply intermediaries which bring the two extremes together in a continuous flow. If I see before me a physical object like a piece of molten steel slowly changing its shape, I recognize it as the same. Similarly the temporal continuity of my own experiences brings forth this recognition of a sameness in myself. "Resemblance *among* the parts of a continuum of feelings (especially bodily feelings) experienced along with things widely different in all other regards, thus constitutes the real and verifiable 'personal identity' which we feel. . . . Its parts differ, but under all their differences, they are knit in these two ways (warmth of bodily self-feeling and continuity); and if either way of knitting disappears, the sense of unity departs" (p. 336).

James then illustrates this by well-known pathological cases where, for example, a man remembers his past experiences in an abstract way merely as things that once occurred with no sense of warmth, or where his habits undergo a radical change so that each of his organs gives a different tone, and he becomes aware of himself in a different way. In such cases, he will feel and he will say that he is a different person. The same is true of the anecdotes told by our parents about our childhood. Ridiculous or appealing as they may be, they arouse in our maturity no embarrassment or complacency, because of the absence of the factors of warmth and continuity. This little creature is foreign to me as I now am. I know what he did and said, but I can regain no sense of his small body and its strivings as they felt to him. Also we cannot return to these experiences by any continuous flow of memory. So the sense of identity is lost.

But these similarities and continuities must not only be there, as in the molten steel; they must also be recognized. When does this recognition occur? Who performs it? And what is its nature? In answering these questions, James develops his theory of appropriation.

According to him, it is not necessary to postulate a substance, or ego, back of the phenomena to perform these functions. The recognition occurs in the present pulsation of thought with its own warm feelings of bodily activity. As it passes away, it is replaced by another which, among the things it knows, also knows its immediate predecessor, and recognizes in it the same warmth of self-activity it feels in itself. On the basis of this similarity and felt continuity, it then takes over, or "appropriates", this past self with its various objects and predecessors as its own. "Each later thought, knowing and thus including the thoughts which went before, is the final receptacle—and appropriating them, is the final owner—of all that they contain and own" (p. 339).

This empirical concept of the self comes as the climax of a long argument and, as we have pointed out, is central to James' descriptive psychology. So it is worthy of some critical comment. He emphasizes the fact that I cannot appropriate, or adopt, what is already completely my own. Thus I cannot adopt my own child, but only the child of others. Nevertheless, if I really adopt him, this relation of externality may be transformed, and he may become my own. This does justice, James believes, to the ambiguity and dynamism of the process of self-development, or self-disintegration, as it appears in experience. The self that I am at present is not the same as I was yesterday, or a year ago. There is a real diversity. But by the process of adoption, either this diversity may be overcome and taken up into a higher unity, or disintegration may occur.

This interpretation certainly takes account of the precarious nature of self-identity, and the phenomena of hysteria and mental breakdown, by which, as we know, James was deeply impressed. Does it do justice to the common opinion of mankind, which tells us that my past self is already mine, and that these different selves are possessed by an arch-self which is in some sense superior to them all? James believes that his theory does do justice to these common feelings without introducing a soul substance, or a transcendental entity of any kind. The past self that I appropriate, in its time, took over its predecessors and represented them in its own way. So there is a very real sense in which it was then I, and that when I now appropriate it, I am taking over something that is already mine.

James also reminds us that there is a significant sense in which the present self, which does the appropriating, is superior to the rest, which are now only objects of knowledge and memory. It is only this self of the present which can act and insert its being into the world here and now. The past selves are like incapacitated agents who can no longer act. They can operate only in so far as their true interests can be taken over by that one of their members who can *represent* them by his acts in the present. Can this theory do justice to the absolute unity which the term *self-identity* seems to suggest? Here the answer is perhaps more controversial. But James would question whether this extreme interpretation of identity is correct. Thus we speak of identical twins, where there is clearly an element of diversity. It is true that we speak of self-identity in the singular. But this emphasis may be due to the sense of a threat from a constant diversity that always needs to be overcome. The unity of the empirical self, which James describes, is certainly not absolute. It is a precarious unity, which "coexists with generic differences just as real as the unity" (p. 335). But do the facts warrant us in assuming any unity more absolute than this?

One may agree that James has suggested a plausible alternative to the transcendentalist theories. But his notion of *ap-propriation* is still only vaguely sketched out, and many questions may be raised concerning its nature. For the most part, in defending his theory against its transcendental alternatives, he seems to think of adoption as an almost automatic process in which a felt similarity in warmth and continuity with the past would lead at once to a feeling of identity. This might well apply to persons living under conditions of social and cultural stability, facing no violent upheavals and challenges to their integrity. For them, the world of the past selves they assimilate may be dimly felt to have the same warmth and familiarity that belongs to the bodily feelings of which they constitute the fringes. In such cases, the two may be taken over together in a routine manner, without any sense of crisis or critical reflection. The same is no doubt true of narrow selves who carve out a quiet niche for themselves even in times of social change and revolution.

But this does not apply to those who have to face violent changes of circumstance or who, even in quiet times, are endowed with a spark of creative fire. Some of them will think about the dim fringes of the selves they have lived through in the past, and will spell them out into meaningful worlds. For them, the achievement of self-identity will no longer be a routine matter of mere feeling. It will be lifted to the level of conceptual consciousness, and will confront these open growing selves with critical problems of acceptance or rejection which are hard to bear. It is, no doubt, with such persons in mind that James speaks of the appropriating self as "the present judging thought" (p. 339). But he does not explain its contrast with the feeling self, nor comment on the special problems of meaning it faces.

He does say that this "thought is a vehicle of choice as well as of cognition" (p. 340). We should expect this in view of his understanding of consciousness as engaged. But he offers no further words of explanation. He speaks of the self in this section as though it were only a being in the world, having some connections with other beings. Thus in taking over a past self, the present I "owns some of the past facts which it surveys, and disowns the rest" (p. 338). Of course, the self is a limited object of this kind. But it is also something more. It cannot be separated from the objects with which it is concerned, their fringes, and, therefore, the whole world in which it lives.

As James puts it (p. 340), the self that appropriates the other self also appropriates "the object which the other appropriated", and, of course, its world fringes. Hence in rejecting a past self, a whole world is being rejected, not a mere set of objects. The self originates in the empirical world, maintains itself or collapses, and then passes away. A narrow, rigid self can be readily achieved with the aid of stable circumstances. But a wide ranging, growing self cannot be developed and maintained without strain and struggle. This raises several questions which James does not consider. One of these is: how can a self remain the same after undergoing a transformation of this kind, in which he comes to live in a different world? If he had considered it, he would have had to bring in the future, which is strangely absent from these reflections in the *Principles*. It is only by opening myself to a future world, transcending my past and my present, that I may survive such a radical transition.

James' new notion of appropriation is left undeveloped in many respects. He leaves it primarily at the level of semi-conscious feeling, and does not analyze it carefully at the level of conscious choice and rejection, where it involves the taking over of a whole situation into a new world of meaning in which responsible action can be justified. But it is a highly original and fertile conception, open to this and other interpretations. It provides us with the notion of a unified, but open, self that is able to grow and break down. As James says, this conception is able to take full account of all the empirical facts without the postulation of questionable transempirical entities. But to confirm this affirmative conclusion, it is essential to compare this theory with its main rivals. And it is to this task that James turns in the concluding pages of this chapter (342–73).

The Theory of the Soul

This is the scholastic theory that goes back to Plato and Aristotle. It holds that there is something more than the observed phenomena which, as accidents, must inhere in a substance that inheres in nothing, but exists in itself. According to the Aristotelian tradition, this soul is a compound of a material and an immaterial part. The former is the source of physical faculties, like generation and nutrition; the latter of immaterial faculties, like those of thought and will. It is the operation of these faculties, in relation to the environment, that produces the stream of phenomena we observe. Since the will is immaterial, it is not determined by physical causes, but makes free and spontaneous choices. Since we think by means of immaterial, universal concepts, this thinking cannot be explained by the physical brain, which is compounded of material parts and cannot get outside itself, to know anything else.

This soul theory seems to support our desire for immortality, and this has certainly helped it to survive—as has its connection with Christian doctrines of divine retribution in an afterlife. Such retribution would lose all meaning unless there were a substantial core of personality that could remain the same in surviving death. Similar arguments are often applied to our experience in this world. Here, too, the meaning of life would be diluted and the sense of responsibility weakened, if they were not supported by a substantial centre that remains identically the same throughout the whole of life. Only such a centre can guarantee the separate individuality of my own experience against that of others, and my unique responsibility for what I alone can do. Such are the most convincing arguments still used to defend the theory of a substantial soul.

James counters them in a brief passage which gives us a clear summary of his attitude towards traditional thought on the self. He is acutely aware of the dangers of falling into logically exact and intricate modes of argument, which are purely verbal and tell us nothing new. They merely give us more complex and elaborate verbal formulations of what we know already, with the supposition that these must correspond with peculiar, unexperienced entities. The soul is an entity of this kind. To say that my stream of experience inheres in an unobserved substance tells me nothing new about this stream. I can deduce nothing from this conception of inherence. It is an empty verbalism which explains nothing. I am left with the very stream that I knew before, which now merely repeats itself in a transcendental setting. James hated verbal proliferations of this sort, and felt that they were a major obstacle in the way of sound philosophy.

As to the free will argument, to say that this freedom comes from a separate soul substance will convince no one who is not convinced already by the empirical evidence. It may, however, blind one who adopts this verbalism to the evidence which must be decisive for all sound argument. An immaterial soul substance might be free. But what is the use of arguing over this? What we need to know more about are the empirical selves we already know by acquaintance and really care for. Why do we turn away from these? There is no empirical reason to suppose that a passing, temporary thought cannot be as free as a simple, immaterial substance.

Is it necessary to believe in an immaterial soul substance to escape from materialism? In his brief discussion of this question (pp. 346–47), James gives a negative answer, and also, at the same time, clearly rejects the charge of materialism that has often been raised against his own position. It is no doubt true that the brain, as a mere extended mass, cannot think. But James says he has never asserted that it can. He has tried to describe the phenomena of thought, which are as they appear to be. If the phenomena show (as they do) that they are self-conscious, and able to cognize in terms of universal concepts, then these facts must be accepted, whatever our ultimate explanation may be. It is on these facts that he is "relying".

But the facts show also that these thoughts are "connected" with changes and activities of the living brain. When we come to explain the facts of cognition, once we understand them, why should we not think of the living, active brain as a likely candidate for being responsible for them, since we know it is connected with them? To call that which cognizes a *soul* does not get us into a more favorable position. It is merely the name for an unknown something which is responsible for the phenomena of thought, which we should know already. It explains nothing. We deduce nothing from it. The major difficulty is how we know anything at all. With respect to this, we have merely a new name. We have made no further advance.

In answer to the practical arguments, James expresses a similar scepticism. Any immortality that would mean anything to us would involve a conscious stream, continuous with what we have experienced in this life. But the survival of a simple soul substance can give us no assurance of this. Hence the practical significance of this abstract concept may be based upon a delusion. In reply to the orthodox doctrines of future rewards and punishments, James expresses the doubts that must occur to anyone familiar with modern thought and science. In place of this indiscriminate survival, he suggests a "teleological" theory, according to which survival is restricted to those whose continuance belongs to the developing meaning of the world, and who are, therefore, in some sense worthy of it.

It is true that the theory of a simple soul substance, owning all our self-experiences from the beginning, takes account of a factor working for unity in our lives. But it not only accounts for this unity; it gives it an automatic guarantee in a way that goes far beyond the facts, which, as we have seen, include those of mental breakdown and disintegration. These phenomena indicate rather a passing principle of unity, working itself out, with many degrees of success and failure, in a historical development. It is true, no doubt, that the notion of a fixed soul substance guarantees a greater degree of unity, but a lesser degree of freedom and responsibility. In fact, a negative answer to that theory is indicated, for, in the empirical conception, the person becomes not only responsible for his accidental deeds, he becomes responsible for himself, which seems to agree with our experience and the ordinary language by which it is more or less expressed.

The Associationist Theory

With James' detailed criticism of the associationist, or empirical, theory of the self (pp. 350–60) we can be more brief, for we have already considered it, at least in its general outlines. It is interesting to note, however, that in these pages, which are certainly worth reading, he praises Locke, in spite of his acceptance of the doctrine of soul substance, for having called the reader's attention to the greater importance of the "verifiable and felt unity" of consciousness (p. 351). Hume is criticized as a disappointed metaphysician, for whom "there is no *tertium quid* between pure unity and pure separateness". Having rightly dismissed the metaphysical notion of substance, therefore, he could see no other view of consciousness than that of a succession of ideas. This failure to see relational patterns in experience made it impossible for Hume to see any *I* at all, and led his successors into over-simplified descriptions of experience that perversely distort the facts.

Many of these, according to James, involve a commission of what he has called the psychologist's fallacy (*cf. supra,* pp. 36 ff.). Thus the psychologist can think of two ideas, one of A followed by another idea of B. But because in his knowing of them, he remembers the former in thinking of the latter, it is easy for him to transform this into the very different single idea of B after A (I, 353). Similarly in their strange attempts to build a complex experience from supposedly simple units, Hume's descendants have transmuted an idea of last year returning now, into an idea of last year, and two similar ideas into a single idea of similarity. This kind of empiricist explanation "both assumes to explain them [the facts] and in the same breath falsifies them, and for each reason stands condemned" (p. 354).

Working out an explanation for a non-existent fact takes us further from the truth than no explanation at all. These passages are important in showing how, in writing the *Principles,* James conceived of his task primarily in terms of describing the phenomena, and how great an emphasis he placed on the accuracy of these descriptions. In their failure to achieve such accuracy, the so-called "empiricists" have ignored the basic responsibility of any genuine empiricism. They have ignored the warmth of bodily feelings, their continuity, and the appropriative activities, which are all involved in personal self-consciousness. As a result, they have managed to work out no cogent and cohesive theory of the self at all.

The Transcendentalist Theory

In this section (pp. 360–71), we can also be brief, since James gives a summary of general criticisms with which we are already familiar. But some new negative points are added, and certain differences from his own theory are further clarified. On the Kantian view, the transcendental unity of apperception is a necessary condition of our phenomenal experience, which never knows itself directly in its act of thinking. Hence it remains as an empty postulate from which nothing specific can be deduced. It is not responsible for any definite thought, or action, but merely for the synthetic activity required for all objects in general. As we know already, James is suspicious of empty constructs of this kind that are isolated from any concrete, empirical manifestations. The soul at least is an active agent. It is responsible and permanent in its own way. But this transcendental ego is a barren form of consciousness with "no properties", so that we cannot tell "whether it be substantial, nor whether it be immaterial, nor whether it be simple, nor whether it be permanent" (p. 362).

No wonder that James refers to it as "simply nothing", and calls it "as ineffectual and windy an abortion as philosophy can show" (p. 365). But there are other difficulties of a more specific kind. According to Kant, "the only self that I know anything positive about is the empirical *me*, not the pure I; the self which is an object among other objects, and the constituents of which we ourselves have seen and recognized to be phenomenal things appearing in the form of space as well as time" (p. 362). Between this self and the transcendental ego which knows it, there is a seemingly impassable gulf, for the latter is a timeless principle outside the forms of space and time.

How, then, are the phenomena of self-knowledge, so carefully described by James, to be accounted for—the feeling of my bodily self in the very act of knowing and choosing, and in the act of taking over past selves, which I now know to have known and chosen? In accordance with these facts, James holds the seemingly paradoxical view that it is precisely the bodily self, as an object among others in experience, that also knows and finds meaning in the world. It is precisely the objective self that is directly felt to be the subject of experience. But in the Kantian scheme, there seems to be no place for any direct self-consciousness of this kind. The objective self never knows itself as a subject, and the transcendental subject never becomes a real object by inserting itself in the world. This is the most basic difference between the two theories, and it underlies the other criticisms that James mentions here.

According to radical empiricism, the objective self is a real subject in its own right, struggling with a multiplicity of real beings, and both can be known as they are. On the Kantian view, both the empirical self, and the beings with which it is engaged, are mere phenomena which never appear as they really are. "The Reality becomes a mere empty *locus* or unknowable, the so-called Noumenon . . ." (p. 363). This imaginizing of perception makes it hard to account for the distinction between the real and the imaginary. But our sense of this difference, while not infallible, guides us in all our purposive activities, and is certainly intrinsic to experience.

By bringing a multiplicity of data to be known *inside* the mind, Kant has confused the unitary act of knowing with the plurality of objects to be known, and has thus ignored the intentional structure of all objective knowledge. "If we are to have a dualism of Thought and Reality at all, the multiplicity should be lodged in the latter and not in the former member of the couple of related terms" (p. 364). Finally, the unnecessary "complication" of language and architectonic machinery in the Kantian system were offensive to James, who refers to them as "an inborn infirmity enhanced by the musty academicism of his Königsberg existence" (pp. 365–66).

"With Hegel", he says, "it was a raging fever". Kant's idealistic followers tried to bridge the chasm between the empirical and the transcendental knowing self by uniting the two. But the result bears little resemblance to the finite empirical self who is self-conscious, and also aware of world meanings in time. It is a transcendental self that inserts itself into history, indeed, but while also remaining out of time. With the destruction of the thing in itself, the sense of independent beings disappears from the scene, even as an ideal, or limiting, conception, and we are left with a panorama of mere objects that are posited, negated, and resynthesized by the creative activity of an absolute Mind.

James admits that these thinkers have corrected some of the mistakes of the atomistic empiricists. But this is an over-correction, in which the careful study of the appearances, as they appear, is sacrificed in favor of an imaginary construction "invented" a priori by the Mind (p. 370). After this critical discussion, it is clear that James is in no sense a transcendentalist. As he puts it in his own conclusion, these "deliverances" of the idealistic thinkers "in no wise oblige us to revise our own formulation of the Stream of Thought" (p. 370). The empirical person, known as an object in the world, is the same as the subjective, thinking person who represents him in the moving present. There is no transcendental self beyond time. There is rather "an objective person, known by a passing, subjective thought, and recognized as continuing in time" (p. 371).

In order to give further evidence for this conception of a fragile "identity on the whole" which may be won by a struggle for integrity or lost through lack of purpose, James devotes the last pages of this central chapter (pp. 373–401) to an examination of cases of aphasia and hysteria, where various degrees of personal disintegration actually occur. The personal self that is here threatened, or breaks down, is certainly not that of a fixed soul substance, or of a transcendental self in some sense beyond time. It is a temporal, bodily self that catches itself in its acts of knowing and struggling with other beings. It is this temporal self that knows and struggles with past selves it seeks to take over and place in a pattern of meaning which may make responsible action possible.

We shall not review here the content of these informative pages; we shall only quote James' conclusion to remind us again of the radically empirical conception of the human self to which he is led by his careful descriptions of observable facts. After speaking again of the objective me, James says (p. 400), "this me is an empirical aggregate of things objectively known. The I which knows them cannot itself be an aggregate. . . . It is a *Thought* at each moment different from that of the last moment, but *appropriative* of the latter, together with all that the latter called its own. All the experiential facts find their place in this description, unencumbered with any hypothesis save that of the existence of passing thoughts or states of mind. The same brain may subserve many conscious selves, either alternate or coexisting. . .".

Here is James' theory of the self in a nutshell. The last sentence refers to the cases of aphasia and multiple personality he has dealt with in this section. But in the comment which directly follows (p. 401), James lays special emphasis on one feature of his view which, as we have already suggested, lies at the root of his difference from transcendentalist theories. For him, the passing, present thought knows itself directly by acquaintance in the very act of knowing and choosing. For the transcendentalist, there is no such self-knowledge by direct acquaintance. My knowing and choosing can be known only as objects, or appearances, by a transcendental self that is never united with them. Hence as James says: "the only pathway that I can discover for bringing in a more transcendental thinker would be to *deny* that we have any *direct* knowledge of the thought as such. The latter existence would then be reduced to a postulate, an assertion that there *must be* a *knower* correlative to all this *known;* and the problem *who that knower is* would have become a metaphysical problem" (p. 401).

The issue between radical empiricism and transcendentalism, therefore, comes down to this. Do I ever directly feel my living, thinking body in the act of thinking and choosing objects, accepting or rejecting some phase of a past self? If I answer in the negative with the idealists, and also with Husserl in his Middle Period, I will be forced to transcendentalism, and to some phase of what he called the *transcendental reduction,* in so far as phenomenology is possible. If I answer in the affirmative, with James, Merleau-Ponty, and others, a transcendental ego will be unnecessary.

The self can be known not metaphysically but descriptively, and a phenomenology of the self and its active operations will be possible. These include not only the fully formed acts which finally emerge (*cf: infra,* Chapter X), but the "intellectual" acts of thinking and meaning, which prepare the way for these. A large part of the *Principles* is devoted to these operations of what James called the "second department of the mind" (*cf.* RAAT, pp. 123–29, and *infra,* pp. 215–16). We shall consider some of the more complex patterns that are found in these operations in Chapters VIII and IX. But we shall turn now to certain basic types of activity, attention and inattention, conception, and analysis, which, according to James, lie at the root of the life of the mind.

Chapter Five

❀

Phenomenology and the
Life of the Mind

So far we have followed James' argument step by step as he lays the foundations for a phenomenological psychology. This discipline is based not on metaphysical postulates nor on the quantitative results of special experiments, though these are often relevant, but rather on a description of the phenomena as they actually appear. These phenomena are known, first of all, by direct acquaintance, or feeling, and the world that is revealed in this way is presupposed by all later conceptual analysis. Nothing can take the place of this existing world, but it can be more clearly revealed by the use of conceptual description. We have seen how, as a result of the application of such methods, this world emerges as a stream of consciousness, always belonging to a personal self, in constant and unbroken flux, stretched out towards independent objects which are known and cared for by the active being at its centre.

We have noted the peculiar dangers confronting the psychologist in performing his clarifying and descriptive functions, especially that of the "psychologist's fallacy"—reading his own experiences and interpretations into the phenomena he is describing. We have seen how James opposes both the empiricists and the idealists in developing his conception of the self as an object in experience which is, at the same time, able to order a world around its projects.

From this point on, we shall have to be more selective in our account. We shall pass over those sections which are concerned with experimental data collected before 1890 when the *Principles* was published. In most cases, they have been superseded by later work, and are hence of little interest. We shall confine our attention to other sections in which James is concerned with the description and interpretation of the most basic mental phenomena. These parts are still phenomenologically interesting and suggestive, and in my summaries and critical comments I shall try to show the reader that this is so. Let us start, first of all, with James' account of attention in Chapter XI.

Attention

He begins by referring to the serious neglect of the phenomena of attention by the so-called empiricists, who think of experience as "something simply given" (I, 402). As over against this, James points out that millions of items are presented to the senses which never enter into experience at all, because they are of no interest to the experiencer. My experience is not made up of what is merely given to me. It is rather "what I agree to attend to" (p. 402). It is this interest alone which gives "accent and emphasis, light and shade, background and foreground" by singling out this object, or this aspect of an object, from the perceptual field. In order to bring out these general features of attention, James begins with a striking description of the opposite state, lack of concentration, or distraction, from which we are awakened, or aroused, when we come to pay attention. This receptive attitude of merely staring, or gaping at something given is precisely that of vacancy, or seeing nothing.

"The eyes are fixed on vacancy, the sounds of the world melt into confused unity, the attention is dispersed so that the whole body is felt, as it were, at once, and the foreground of consciousness is filled, if by anything, by a sort of solemn sense of surrender to the empty passing of time. . . . Every moment we expect the spell to break, for we know no reason why it should continue. But it does continue, pulse after pulse, and we float along with it, until—also without reason that we can discover—an energy is given, something—we know not what—enables us to gather ourselves together, we wink our eyes, we shake our heads, the background-ideas become effective, and the wheels of life go round again" (p. 404). When we are aroused in this way from distraction, which is not the state of sleep, we are able to concentrate on one object which emerges from that dim background which is the necessary condition for any experience of any kind.

The object, with its background of fringes, is always complex. But the pulse of thought, which attends to it, is one. James attributes the widespread neglect of this intentional structure of experience to either "fantastic metaphysics", or "the ambiguity of the word *idea*" (p. 406). In so far as the different parts, or aspects of an object, fit together into a total system, we can attend to them all at once. But if the object breaks down into separate parts, or systems, we lose our sense of the whole as we attend to these components, one at a time. Hence in answer to the question: how many things can we attend to at once? James answers "not easily more than one, unless the processes are very habitual; but then two or three, without very much oscillation of the attention" (p. 409). He then considers the phenomena of expectant attention, and the striking effects it may have on our perception of different events ordered in time. We shall omit his detailed consideration of Wundt's experiments in this field, mentioning only one example of this subjective quickening, or reversal of an objective time order, due to the "ripening" of preparatory responses in the brain: the smith who becomes aware of the sparks before he strikes the iron.

After a review of experimental facts, James gives a classification of the different types of attention into which they fall. The things which interest us, and to which we attend, are either present objects of sense (sensory attention), or ideal objects which are absent and represented (intellectual attention). James distinguishes between attention which is immediate, when the object is interesting in itself, and derived, when it is interesting only because of its association in some way with another object that is immediately interesting. Passive or effortless attention is also different from that which is active and voluntary.

Voluntary attention, since it requires effort, is always derived. But both sensory and intellectual attention may be either passive or voluntary. In the passive sensory type, the stimulus is normally intense, or moderate if it fits with some instinctive need. The element of surprise, which attends a sudden or unexpected occurrence, always attracts attention. Intense or sudden sights, sounds, blows, and pains are stimuli of this kind, to which the child, and even more the animal, is peculiarly sensitive. As James says, the child is outwardly directed and full of active energy. Hence he flows along with the sensory stream and, belonging less to himself, is taken over by every successive object. As we grow older, and gain possession of a stable self, our interests become organized, and our attention is more active and selective. In our conceptual thinking, great numbers of things become connected together as meaningful objects in which there is little or no difference between the immediate and the derived. This gives us an indifference to all but the most sudden and surprising stimuli, the rest being at once absorbed into a system of meaning. This existence in a selected world of our own sets us apart from others, and when carried to certain extremes, gives the impression of absent-mindedness.

The sense of effort belongs to active, or voluntary, attention. We experience this at the sensory level when we try to discriminate a very faint impression, or to resist more potent or more welcome stimuli, as when we resolutely try to listen to the faint and boring words of our neighbor at a dinner table, while all around us there is loud laughter and exciting talk. We feel this effort at the intellectual level when we try to clarify a dim idea, to distinguish delicate shades of meaning in a supposedly single term, or to pay attention to a difficult and unfamiliar thought that is usually on the fringes of our conscious field. Since our thoughts are for the most part directed to outer objects, the self-consciousness attending them is an experience of this kind, usually relegated to the fringes, and very hard to focus as it occurs in the act. On James' view, this would explain the appeal of transcendental theories of consciousness, which pass over the direct but dim feeling of self-awareness, and substitute for it a remote ego, which cognizes ourselves as objects from a non-situated point of view.

He has great respect for this phenomenon of voluntary effort, or attention, to which we refer by such words as trying, seeking, and struggling to attain. He recognizes that it plays a central role in the life of the mind, and considers it at some length, making several observations concerning it which are worthy of further development. At the sensory level, we see an object by facing it, gazing at it, and then moving towards it to feel its surface, and to finger it in certain ways. Similar bodily motions are involved in the case of the other senses. This brings forth a massive raising of bodily tone that is more intense when the object is ambiguous, or obscure. This organic feeling is contrasted with the objects before us as our own activity. At the intellectual level, analogous feelings occur which have been described by Fechner, whom James quotes on page 436.

In our sensory attention to real objects, he says, "the strain is plainly forwards, and when the attention changes from one sense to another, only alters its direction between the several external sense organs, leaving the rest of the head free from strain. The case is different in memory or fancy, for here the feeling withdraws entirely from the external sense organs, and seems rather to take refuge in that part of the head which the brain fills; if I wish, for example, to recall a place, or a person, it will arise before me with vividness, not according as I strain my attention forwards, but rather in proportion as I, so to speak, retract it backwards". These remarks are interesting in that they recognize an opposite turning backward and inward as characteristic of intellectual effort. We are apt to close our eyes as we concentrate on our inward thoughts and words. We feel a heightened tone in the bodily muscles, and our verbal expressions, whether overt or silent, are marked by gaps and hesitations, as we try to focus a single object and to articulate our thought.

James notes that there are certain unwelcome objects that we find it hard to focus, and tend to shy away from, as a spendthrift in full career puts from him the thought of ebbing assets. "How long", James asks, "O healthy reader, can you now continue thinking of your tomb"? (p. 421). To the fanatic, whose passion is directed to restricted objects in a world of very narrow range, the thought of any interests or ideas opposed to his own is anathema. "To every man actuated by passion the thought of interests which negate the passion can hardly, for more than a fleeting instant, stay before the mind" (p. 421). But according to James, such fanaticism has its roots in a "stagnant" intellect that is unable to attend to unfamiliar and difficult ideas. This leads to a narrowing and hardening of the world of meaning which can no longer grow. When it moves beyond the narrow range of its fixed interests, the mind of such a person will wander to ever new distractions, on which it cannot dwell for any length of time. And even in the familiar region of its passion, it merely repeats the same ideas and attitudes, since everything else is lost in the fringes and never clarified. "An intellect unfurnished with materials, stagnant, unoriginal, will hardly be likely to consider any subject long" (p. 423). Hence those with weaker feelings merely fall into rigidity, while those with passion become bigoted and fanatical.

In order to avoid these dangers, the child must be supplied with a rich stock of ideas not thrown at him haphazard, but connected together in patterns of meaning, related to his initial interests. Then he must be encouraged to think of the fringes of these patterns, and to clarify them by the revealing of some new thing in relation to what he already knows. This can be done while interest and curiosity are maintained in such a way "that the new thing shall seem to come as an answer, or part of an answer, to a question pre-existing in his mind" (p. 424). With this kind of education, and sometimes without it, the child may be able to control his attention, and to keep the topic of his meditation "the same" (p. 424). In this connection, we cannot help but think of Callicles' remark to Socrates that he was repeating the same thing, and of Socrates' reply "Yes, and not only that, Callicles, but on the same subject too".[1]

But James develops this answer in his own way. "There is no such thing", he says, "as voluntary attention sustained for more than a few seconds at a time" (p. 420). Thinking the same does not mean a monotonous concentration on one idea. It means a development of this idea, seeing it in new relations and new perspectives, and then returning to it again and again with these in mind. For this, the three things we have mentioned in connection with education are essential: a sustaining of interest, a rich store of meanings, and a sense of their possible connections. Without these, the inner control of attention is impossible. With them, we may become able to think the same. This "faculty of voluntarily bringing back a wandering attention over and over again is the very root of judgment, character, and will". It is also the root of freedom and responsibility, as we shall see. "No one is *compos sui* if he have it not" (p. 424).

The effects of attention are multitudinous, and ultimately, they form the patterns of the worlds which we inhabit. First of all, the relative intensity of two sensations may be changed if we attend to one rather than the other. "Every artist knows how he can make a scene before his eyes appear warmer or colder in color, according to the way he sets his attention. If for warm, he soon begins to *see* the red color start out of everything; if for cold, the blue. Similarly in listening for certain notes in a chord, or overtones in a musical sound, the one we attend to sounds probably a little more loud as well as more emphatic than it did before. When we mentally break a series of monotonous strokes into a rhythm by accentuating every second or

---

[1] *Gorgias* 490E–491.

third one, etc., the stroke on which the stress of attention is laid seems to become stronger as well as more emphatic" (p. 425).

It is, of course, the perceptual and intellectual operations of discrimination, comparison, and analysis that make things clear. But attention is a necessary condition for such activity. Nothing will be clarified unless it is sharply focused and attended to. This is also a condition for the remembering of an object, for an experience to which we pay no attention will simply pass by, and leave no vestiges for recollection. Finally, James stresses again what he is later to call *Pre-perception*—the way in which a concentration of expectant attention may facilitate and accelerate perception which is first confused and retarded by distractions (p. 429). He thinks of this internal preparation and reinforcement in terms of excitations in relevant regions of the brain, which are "continuous subjectively" (p. 429) with the response. Thus when a subject is told in advance the general sphere in which a question is to be asked, "those brain-processes in him which were connected with this entire 'sphere' were kept sub-excited, and the question could then discharge with a minimum amount of lost time that particular answer out of the 'sphere' which belonged especially to it" (p. 433).

These preparatory excitations of attention, as James believes, are to some degree under our internal control, and the different directions to which they point determine the general way in which our different worlds are ordered. The adult person carries the general pattern of his world with him in his body and nervous system, and the selective attention through which he builds it up is choosing the world that is about to be. Hence James can say (p. 424) that "each of us literally *chooses*, by his ways of attending to things, what sort of a universe he shall appear to himself to inhabit", that is, the one in which he shall live.

Now attention not only precedes and prepares the way for perception; it goes on in the form of inner activities of various kinds during perception itself. In the first place, there are the movements of accommodation on the part of the sense organs.

In seeing and hearing, the eyes and ears are automatically adjusted to the object, but motions of the head and body also occur. In feeling an angular object, we finger it in a suitable way. Furthermore, in making these movements, we inhibit others that might interfere. Thus in listening to a faint sound, we hold our breath, and in tasting, we close our eyes. "The result", as James says, "is a more or less massive organic feeling that attention is going on" (p. 435). In addition to these, James maintains that there are also, at the perceptual level, internal activities of memory, imagination, and discrimination.

In watching a rapidly moving animal in the country at dusk, the impression is uncertain. I am not sure whether it is a cat or a neighbor's dog. I remember seeing the cat before under similar conditions, and recall its moving shape in the dark. I then imagine its total form, how it ought to look at this moment, and compare this with what I see. I finally perceive it as the cat coming home, and I also feel the strain of my attention as it momentarily goes through these operations. Similar operations are carried out when we try to clarify a vague patch on the fringes of the visual field, or a vague, ambiguous object of any kind. Here too, not only external stimuli but internal factors are involved, and we feel them in the straining of attention.

James conceives of this in bodily terms as a brain cell being played upon from two directions (p. 441) at once. "Whilst the object excites it from without, other brain cells, or perhaps spiritual forces, arouse it from within. The latter influence is the adaptation of the attention. *The plenary energy of the brain cell demands the cooperation of both factors:* not when merely present but when both present and attended to, is the object fully perceived." As we have noted, James held that it is only in facing obstacles and obscurities that the full activities of consciousness are elicited. But these inner factors are also constantly at work, though to a lesser degree of intensity, even in the perception of familiar objects. We prepare ourselves inwardly for them, and preperceive them before they are externally perceived. "When watching for the distant clock to strike, our mind is so filled with its image that at every moment we think we hear the longed-for or dreaded sound. So of an awaited footstep. Every stir in the wood is for the hunter his game; for the fugitive his pursuers. Every bonnet in the street is momentarily taken by the lover to enshroud the head of his idol. The image in the mind *is* the attention; the preperception . . . is half of the perception of the looked-for thing" (p. 442).

This is why men perceive only what they are already prepared to see, and why it is so difficult for them to change their perspective and to notice something new. "It is for this reason that men have no eyes but for those aspects of things which they have already been taught to discern. Any one of us can notice a phenomenon after it has once been pointed out, which not one in ten thousand could ever have discovered for himself" (p. 443). This is the tyranny of the obvious, for the obvious is what we are prepared to see. If we are to avoid mental stagnation and bigotry, we must learn how to shift our attention in new perspectives, and to experiment with different worlds. This is the message James is attempting to convey in these pages. It should be a major aim of the discipline of philosophy.

Perception always belongs to a project of the active agent. The gaze that we send out to the distant object is a shaft of purpose sent from a point of view. But then in order to grasp it, we must reenact it from the inside. Only when this inner reproduction fits what comes in from without can we know it as it is. This theory has important implications for human communication. In grasping the meaning of another person, it is not sufficient merely to listen passively to his words. If we attend to him only in this way, our minds are apt to wander. We must learn rather to listen actively by echoing his words and reenacting his meanings for ourselves. This is what we mean when we speak of *following the thought of another*, and James recognized the need for this in a remarkable passage (p. 447). "If attention be the reproduction of the sensation from within, the habit of reading not merely with the eye, and of listening not merely with the ear, but of articulating to oneself the words seen or heard ought to deepen one's attention to the latter.

Experience shows that this is the case. I can keep my wandering mind a great deal more closely upon a conversation or a lecture if I actively re-echo to myself the words than if I simply hear them. . . ."

Attention, of course, is not the whole story. If it is to be perceived, the thing must also send forth influences and impressions of its own. But attention is involved at every stage of the process. We must first select the object of our care and prepare for it. Then we must approach the thing, and open ourselves to incoming impressions. As this goes on, with the aid of memory and imagination we must reenact the thing from the inside, and, finally, when a maximum grasp has been attained, give it its proper place in the world, and fit it to our purposes. All this is the work of attention, a basic aspect of our lived experience, the nucleus of our innermost self, and the first source of our freedom and responsibility.

Inattention and Noetic Freedom

At the end of the chapter, James turns to the important phenomenon of inattention. As we have already learned, one of his cardinal doctrines is that we experience a vast range of impressions to which we never attend because of their irrelevance to our practical projects. So they are relegated to the fringes, and we pass them by. One of the major aims of psychology, or as we should say now, *phenomenology*, is to focus them and to bring them into the light. It is important to remember this in connection with his later pragmatic theory of truth. Attention itself, which we have just been examining, is a phenomenon of this kind.

James begins his discussion of inattention by mentioning a number of other unnoticed phenomena, such as the odors which belong to the characteristic tastes of certain substances like fish, cheese, butter, and meat, and the muscular feelings which enter into the perception of attributes like wet, elastic, and doughy.

We are exclusively interested in the objects, and have no names for the feelings by which we know them. Of course, we may doubt whether we have any actual feelings of this kind and, therefore, consign them to the subterranean region of the unconscious. This is contrary to James' theory of fringes. So he offers several examples of unnoticed occurrences which are nevertheless experienced in some way for protracted intervals of time, since we notice them when they come to an end. One example is the man who wakes up in church when the sermon ends, and the miller, busy with his other work, who notices when the mill-wheel stops. This certainly shows that there was, on the fringes, some unfocused experience of the sermon, and the turning of the wheel. How is this to be explained?

Thinking again in bodily terms and, in particular, of nervous paths, James analyzes the situation in the following way. Preoccupation with a given task involves nervous activity along certain pathways in certain regions of the brain. This activity will interfere with competing currents in the same region, and will force them to discharge along other lines. At first, such resistance to distractions, as we may say in conscious terms, will require great effort, and the intensification of activity in the task of our concern. But in time, regular habits of secondary discharge will be learned, and it will be said that we now know how to concentrate. Fingering a rosary during prayer, playing with beads during meditation may be offered as examples of secondary activities of this kind, which may protect us against distraction. In any case, it is clear that we cannot learn how to attend without developing habits of inattention which are an essential aspect of the whole phenomenon.

At the end of his account of attention, James discusses the issue as to whether it is indeterminate or determined. He goes out of his way to be fair to the deterministic theory which is really a general, metaphysical view. We may then say that the conscious feeling of effort is a mere accompaniment of physical motions that would happen anyway in an all-inclusive network of causes and effects. This is certainly metaphysics, and not science, as it often claims to be. Furthermore, it is bad meta-physics, because it ignores the direct evidence of the phenomena as they appear. Once we start to ignore direct evidence of this sort, we may ask where we can find sounder evidence on which to base a theory of determinism, and even any sound evidence at all. If we are to proceed in an empirical manner, it is safer for us not to ignore our "whole feeling of reality, the whole sting and excitement of our voluntary life . . . our sense that in it things are *really being decided* from one moment to another, and that it is not the dull rattling off of a chain that was forged innumer-able ages ago" (p. 453).

It is important to note the crucial role played by feeling in this argument, which does not rest primarily on conceptual analysis. It rests primarily on the direct sense of conscious effort in choosing and deciding. We feel that this conscious effort makes a difference, and that it is real, not a mere delusion. If it is dismissed as unreal, where, we may ask, do we ever more directly and certainly find what is real? This is what James means here by "the feeling of reality". As he sees it, it is the inner activity of my moving body that I know most directly and most certainly. If this is doubted, there would seem to be no consistent way of avoiding a universal scepticism that will stifle the impulse for any further serious thought. As an empiricist, James believes that this evidence must be accepted.

By attending to this rather than that, especially by attending to unusual and difficult objects, and by dwelling on them until they become more clear, we can avoid intellectual stagnation, and keep our minds open to new truth. By first gaining some control over our thoughts, we can then gain control over our acts. Thus, as James sees it, our moral freedom is rooted in our noetic freedom of mind. If we attend to one idea slightly more than another, a different motion will result. As James says: "when we come to the chapter on the will, we shall see that the whole drama of the voluntary life hinges on the amount of attention, slightly more or slightly less, which rival motor ideas may receive" (p. 453).

Conception

In approaching the topic of conception, as James calls it
(I, Chap. XII), we must remember his account of the stream
of consciousness as in constant flux and never repeating itself
(*cf. supra*, pp. 59–61). Life is an ongoing process which can
never return to what it has already passed through. This does
not necessarily mean a constant advance, for there is also
decline. But every successive total experience brings with it
something different from what has happened before. Novelty is
a necessity of nature, and in this sense we can say that nothing
is so old as the new. The surprising thing is the phenomenon of
sameness which emerges at the level of perception with what
James calls *conception*, and is further developed in what we call
the higher mental life of man. But if no natural cycle ever
exactly repeats itself, how is this possible?

Only because of the intentional structure of experience which
is always divided into intentional acts of perceiving, desiring,
hoping, and fearing, and the objects of these intentions. Thus
by several acts of desire, each differing from the rest, I can desire
an object that is one and the same. Or by several acts of conceiving, or meaning, I can mean one and the same thing. Thus
even though my act of conceiving, and its fringes, may be
different, I can nevertheless mean the same object. This sameness of meaning is always partial. It always occurs in a shifting
world context that is never the same. But within this moving,
historical world, we can return again and again to the very same
object, and mean what we meant before. Later on, Husserl, who
read James' *Principles* with great care, recognized the central
importance of this mental capacity to return to the same[2] and
identified it as an essential feature of what he called the intentional structure of consciousness. This is the heart and core of
the life of the mind. Without it we would not be able to think.

---

[2] *Ideen*, pp. 73 ff. and 180 ff. *Cf. Ideas*, tr. Gibson, pp. 117 ff. and 237 ff.

James makes it clear (I, 463) that this kind of identification can happen at the level of perception, and even in the experience of "creatures extremely low in the intellectual scale", which may be able to recognize an object that has been felt before. Thus he says that "a polyp would be a conceptual thinker if a feeling of 'Hollo! thingumbob again!' ever flitted through its mind". Since we have no direct access to the experience of these animals, such a statement can be only hypothetical. But there is no question that, in our human perception, we recognize the partial perspectives we acquire in seeing and feeling a nearby object as pertaining to something that is one and the same, even though it may never be verbalized. Thus the child knows that it is sucking the same lollypop, and playing with the same doll. But these are total concrete things which are involved in our instinctive appetites for food and play. It is only when they are broken down into their manifold parts and properties, and when these are gathered together with the similar parts and properties of other things that the conceptual life comes into its own. As we shall see later when we come to deal with reasoning (*infra*, pp. 197–201), this extension of conceptual thinking, which leads to a total reconstruction of the life-world, comes only with language and the quickening of imaginative power that this makes possible. But in the sense of grasping the same thing in and through different perspectives, "conception" is already present in perception (I, 462–63).

James has already noted the basic similarity of the functions performed by the so-called imagination and those of language. Thus it is by imagination that we refer to absent objects as though they were present, and disregard present objects as though they were absent, which, in extreme cases, can bring forth the phenomenon of absent-mindedness. It is also by imagination that we can conjure up new objects, like mermaids, centaurs, golden mountains, and utopias, which never appear except before the eye of fancy. Finally, it is through this power of reference to the absent, as we may call it, that we gain a certain distance from the objects which at first obsess our attention, and a certain freedom from the tyranny of the actual. In fact, it is first of all through this power that possibilities come before the mind.

These three functions are also found in language where it is just as easy to speak of absent as of present objects, where new combinations of basic meanings, and completions of those which are imperfect, are readily formed, and where possibility and futurity are as heavily weighted as actuality and the presence of the past. All this must be understood as the background of James' important statement (pp. 265–66) that "if the words 'coffee', 'bacon', 'muffins', and 'eggs' lead a man to speak to his cook, to pay his bills, and to take measures for the morrow's meal, exactly as visual and gustatory memories would, why are they not, for all practical intents and purposes, as good a kind of material in which to think? In fact, we may suspect them to be for most purposes better than terms with a richer imaginative coloring".

Nevertheless there is an important way in which these two activities, imagination on the one hand, and linguistic conception on the other, differ from each other. This concerns the vagueness and clarity of their respective objects. As James explains in his chapter on reasoning (XXII), we imagine a thing, or event, in its concrete totality as we experienced it, without breaking it up into its component elements and aspects. Thus the child remembers her whole doll, without separating it from the sunshine gleaming in the golden hair and her own feelings of affection as she held it in her arms. Such objects of direct perception and imagination are "vague", because they are neither separated from the situation in which they occur, nor analyzed into their component parts. Hence it is questionable whether they are ever imagined as precisely the same, though vague similarities in the total experiences are sufficient to justify the use of what we call a single name. But it is only when the object is sharply separated from the environing situation and its essential parts focused that it is linguistically conceived as the same.

Linguistic Analysis

Of course in the mature adult, the activities of imagination and conception work hand in hand. But as James notes, the preponderance of one or the other factor justifies the distinction between two different types of thinking (pp. 487–88; cf. II, 360 ff.): the intuitive which refers directly to the concrete objects of perception and imagination and sees analogies between them, and the analytic which refers to the results of separation and abstraction and is able to return again and again to what is precisely the same meaning. "Each act of conception", he says, "results from our attention singling out some one part of the mass of matter for thought which the world presents, and holding fast to it, without confusion. . . . The mind may change its states, and its meanings, at different times; may drop one conception and take up another, but the dropped conception can in no intelligible sense be said to *change into* its successor. The paper, a moment ago white, I may now see to have been scorched black. But my conception 'white' does not change into my conception 'black'" (I, 461–62). James calls this *"the principle of constancy in the mind's meanings"* (p. 459).

As we have seen, it is presupposed by the sense of personal identity. It is, in fact, the most basic characteristic of conceptual meaning, and James refers to it as "the very keel and backbone of our thinking" (p. 459). This thinking has its roots in the world of perception where we can perceive the same thing as before. But in virtue of its abstractive capacity, it is distinguished from perception. Let us now dwell for a moment on these two modes of understanding and their distinctive operations. This may enable us later on to gain an over-all view of James' account of the mental life, and what distinguishes it from traditional, intellectualistic and empirical theories.

Our perceptual experience comes to us in the form of complex objects vaguely concreted together and apprehended as wholes. "The 'simple impressions' of Hume, the 'simple idea' of Locke, are both abstractions never realized in the concrete. Experience, from the very first, presents us with concreted objects vaguely continuous with the rest of the world which envelops them in space and time, and potentially divisible into inward elements and parts" (p. 487). Intellectual understanding involves both breaking these complex objects into their component parts and aspects, and reuniting them in a world order that has been conceptually clarified. "We must treat them in both ways for our knowledge of them to grow . . ." (p. 487). So James begins with a consideration of discrimination which is involved in any process of analysis.

"The noticing of any *part* whatever of our object is an act of discrimination" (p. 487). After we have analyzed a concrete object by discriminating many of its parts, we are apt to think that these parts must have been implicitly, or unconsciously, present in our original perception, which must now be discarded, or replaced, by the more detailed conceptual analysis. But as James points out, "this is nothing but the fatal 'psychologist's fallacy' of treating an inferior state of mind as if it must somehow know implicitly all that is explicitly known about the same topic by superior states of mind" (pp. 488–89). The later thoughts are "superior" from a purely objective point of view. "It is only *as mirrors of things*" that the earlier total perception is inferior. "And when the omitted things are discovered, and the unnoticed differences laid bare, it is not that the old *thoughts* split up, but that *new thoughts supersede* which make new judgments about the same objective world" (p. 489). But the older judgments have their rights which must not be ignored, and the new judgments must take account of them, if one-sided reduction is to be avoided.

Those who have defended the mind-stuff theory (*cf. supra,* pp. 18 ff.) have maintained that the qualitative difference between two qualities can be explained by the presence in one of something lacking in the other, and thus reduced to addition and subtraction (I, 491–92). James rejects this speculative theory on phenomenological grounds (pp. 493–94), and concludes that, while quantitative differences do exist, "differences of simple kind form an irreducible sort of relation between some of the elements of our experience". Blue, for example, is simply different from yellow; it is not yellow plus something. And the same is true of the difference between left and right (p. 493).

James is sympathetic to the view that experience in the world is first felt as a confused continuum which becomes gradually differentiated as understanding develops (pp. 495–96). He holds that the original perception of difference always involves a temporal succession in which we first attend to the one quality and then, after a certain interval, to the other. The temporal shift conveys a basic feeling of transition which brings out the difference between the two terms, whatever they may be. Once we have become acquainted with such a difference between two terms and are ready for it, we may perceive it as holding between the two objects simultaneously. But originally it is felt only between objects that succeed each other in time.

As the time interval becomes longer, our sense of difference becomes vaguer, and the more we must rely on secondary knowledge about the different terms. "Thus I know that the sunshine today is less bright than on a certain day last week, because I then said it was quite dazzling, a remark I should not now care to make" (p. 497). My act of remembering a past pleasure or pain is not a mere repetition, or copy, of that experience, as the associationists erroneously have supposed. I remember the past experience by a new act with a different setting and unity of its own. Thus the idea of a past pleasure is not necessarily pleasant, nor is that of a past pain necessarily painful. Contrary to this over-simplified and non-intentional view, we agree with Homer, who tells us that our memory of past griefs may give us an intense joy, and with Dante, who speaks of the deep sorrow that comes to us in our misery when we remember joys of the past (p. 497).

Empiricists have supposed that two ideas being different is the same as a recognition of their difference. But this is a serious error based on a widespread tendency to confuse being with meaning. The two ideas that are different may not be related at all. But the recognition of their difference is a relation between a term that precedes and another that succeeds it. This relation, however, does not necessarily involve a timeless soul, or ego, which holds the two terms together by being or containing both. As James says, "this last thought need, however, not *be* these terms, with their difference, nor contain them" (p. 501). All we need to suppose is a specious present (*cf. supra*, pp. 61–62), in which the vanishing of the first term will still be present as the second term is perceived. It will then not be perceived as a pure atomic N, but rather as N-preceded-by-the-vanishing-of-M-that-is-different-from-it.

If the elements of a total impression are never experienced apart, this impression is unanalyzable, and the "elements" are not really distinct. An example of this is "the contraction of the diaphragm and the expansion of the lungs" (I, 502). Another example is the supposed difference between the feeling of an emotion and its bodily expression. We are led by certain theories to regard these as quite distinct. But since "they" are always experienced together, James believes that the experience is really one, and that the traditional theories need to be revised as in the case of the mind-body "problem". When our expectations have been distorted by erroneous theories and images, they may lead us into misinterpretations of our experience, and sometimes into perceptual error. But in any case, separate imagination is "the condition of analysis" (p. 503), whether it be true or false, and unless we are imaginatively prepared, we cannot discriminate any element in a total sense impression. "The image seems to welcome its own mate from out of the compound, and to heighten the feeling thereof" (p. 504).

Very few elements of reality are experienced by us in complete isolation, but rather in union with other components. It may happen, however, in a compound *abcd* that the element *a* varies in intensity as the *b, c,* and *d* remain constant, or that *a* may occur with other associates *efg*. In such cases, we can perceptually single out the component *a*, not absolutely, because it will always appear with certain fringes, "but approximately". This is the perceptual source of what we call abstraction, and the element that is singled out is an abstract (p. 505). But these abstracts are never perfect, since they are never given to us alone. By watching their various fluctuations and permutations with differing associates, we get a feeling "of the *direction* in which each element differs from the rest" (p. 508). We then form the notion of it as the ideal terminus of this direction. But this terminus is never directly perceived or imagined. It is rather the object of conception, which is able to go beyond the various tendencies and directions which we perceive. All abstract notions according to James are ideal extrapolations of this kind (p. 508).

When they are first abstracted, these elements, like the absolute predicaments, or natures, of scholastic philosophy, are neither universal nor individual. Thus we may think, "if I abstract *white* from the rest of the wintry landscape this morning, it is a perfectly definite conception, a self-identical quality which I can mean again; but, as I have not yet individualized it by expressly meaning to restrict it to this particular snow, nor thought at all of the possibility of other things to which it may be applicable, it is so far nothing but . . . a topic broken out from the rest of the world," . . . "singular" only in the sense that "I have 'singled it out'". If I then decide to singularize, or to universalize its reference, "I am in reality meaning two new things and forming two new conceptions" (p. 473). In either case, the act of conceiving will be an individual pulse of thought, which differs each time that it is repeated. But the reference will be either to a universal class of similars, or to a single individual.

This is fairly close to the Aristotelian point of view. But there are two significant differences. One involves the status of classes. Since they are based on ideal conceptions which are never found in perception, but can only be approximated in various degrees, their boundary lines are vague, and they never do full justice to the shades and variations of real things. The other concerns the traditional dogma that all knowledge is universal, and that the individual, though sensible, can never be clearly known. James rejects this emphatically. "Our meanings", he says, "are of singulars, indefinites, and universals mixed together in every way. A singular individual is as much *conceived* when he is isolated and identified away from the rest of the world in my mind, as is the most rarified and universally applicable quality he may possess, *being*, for example, when treated in the same way" (p. 479). An individual being can, therefore, be not only perceived but conceived, analyzed, and understood, though with more difficulty than a less complex quality. Such knowledge of the individual, of myself, for example, though harder to obtain, is far more precious than that of ideal classes. As James puts it, "the only value of universal characters is that they help us, by reasoning, to know new truths about individual things" (pp. 479–80).

To arrive at a level beyond that of perceptual discrimination and comparison, language is necessary. James offers phenomenological evidence for this thesis, namely that giving a name to something helps us to distinguish and, therefore, to analyze it. "I went out, for instance, the other day, and found that the snow just fallen had a very odd look, different from the common appearance of snow. I presently called it a 'micacious' look; and it seemed to me as if the moment I did so, the difference grew more distinct and fixed than it was before. The other connotations of the word 'micacious' dragged the snow farther away from ordinary snow, and seemed even to aggravate the peculiar look in question" (p. 512). This also suggests the vital role of language in not only bearing, but creating new meanings. James never says this in so many words, but his thinking certainly points clearly in this direction.

He holds that the perception of similarity is inseparably bound up with the perception of difference. He has been criticized for failing to see that "before we can make significant comparisons, we must ourselves find relevant third terms that will prove both fruitful and illuminating".[3] He is supposed to have thought that "when we perceive a brown object and a blue one in close

---

[3] J. E. Smith, "Radical Empiricism," *Proceedings of the Aristotelian Society*, March 22, 1965, p. 217.

proximity and say that they differ, we are merely seeing a fact that is expressed in a comparative judgment".[4] This is, however, a mistake. James is aware of the fact that there are certain basic differences which are unmediated, like that between being and nothing, for example. But he states specifically that any act of comparison requires us "to define wherein the difference and wherein the resemblance respectively consists". This means that "to be found different, things must, as a rule, have some commensurability, some aspect in common . . ." (I, 528). In most cases, things differ only in this or that respect. As James put it (p. 529), "difference, commonly so-called, is thus between species of a genus".

Those who are interested in understanding James' total view of the intellectual life of man, including his theories of reasoning and abstract thinking in general, should turn to Chapters VIII and IX, *infra.*, where these subjects are considered in further detail. As we are here concerned in Part I only with the most basic patterns of existence, such as the stream of consciousness and the self, and with the methods of revealing them, we must now turn to another one of these, the world of sense, which is the ultimate horizon of our lived existence.

After we have discovered in what respects a strange thing is different from, and in what respects it is similar to other things already known, we become ready to place it in the meaningful horizon of the life-world, or the world of sense as James calls it. This is the spatio-temporal field which encompasses the real things and events we encounter, and from which they derive their real meaning. It is the broadest pattern of our lived experience, which is presupposed by all those narrower in scope. James deals with it in Chapter XXI of his *Principles,* and it is to this highly significant discussion that we must now turn.

[4] *Ibid.*

Chapter Six

❧

The Perception of Reality

Empirically oriented philosophers at the present time are concerned with a basic issue that now divides the whole phenomenological movement in Europe and the United States. On the one hand, there are those who follow Husserl in holding that the whole of human experience, including all its various regions and realms, can be intentionally described and analyzed from a transcendental point of view by *bracketing* the question of existence. On the other hand, there are the existential phenomenologists who hold that the question of existence cannot be bracketed in this way, and that the transcendental reduction cannot be fully achieved. Chapter XXI of James' *Principles* is now of peculiar interest because he faces this issue here in his own way, and takes a definite stand for reasons that are very relevant to contemporary discussions. In accordance with our general program, we shall try to single out what he says about this issue, and to bring in the other material in this chapter only in so far as it is relevant.

The Nature of Belief

James begins by referring to "two ways of studying every psychic state . . . first, the way of analysis . . . second, the way of history" (II, 283). This distinction is not described too clearly in the text. But by the former James seems to mean a static analysis— What is the nature of the phenomenon apart from other things? What does it consist in? The second is a dynamic approach which considers "its connection with other facts", and how it arises and passes away. Thus in dealing with our recognition of reality, it wants to know "under what circumstances do we think things real?" (p. 287). James makes it clear that he is more interested in this second type of analysis, and devotes much more space to it in the text. He begins, however, with the former.

What then is the nature of belief, and how does it differ from other cognate phenomena? Belief involves not merely an apprehension of the object by the mind but something more, holding it "to have reality" (p. 283). This element of acceptance is closely related to our volitional nature. So James says: "it resembles more than anything what in the psychology of volition we know as consent" (p. 283). Nevertheless the two are distinct. At the level of conceptual thinking, both involve the cessation of theoretic agitation and the coming of a stable idea which "fills the mind solidly", and excludes what contradicts it. This is the nature of belief. But when this happens, action tends to follow automatically, and we are in the region of consent, which includes at least a tendency to act.

We are apt to think of disbelief as the true opposite of belief, but according to James this is not the case. Since we cannot disbelieve in X without believing in something else, Y, disbelief is only "an incidental complication to belief" (p. 284), and not its true opposite. This tendency to look for the generic similarities underlying "opposites", which is found in Greek thought, is characteristic not only of James but of more recent phenomenology.[1] The generic opposite of belief and disbelief is the mental unrest which we express by such terms as "doubt and inquiry, not disbelief" (p. 284). In this condition of instability, the mind finds no firm percept, or idea, in which it can rest. As soon as one object appears, it conjures up the picture of its opposite. In certain extreme forms it becomes the questioning mania which the Germans call *Grübelsucht* (p. 284). In this condition, the mind is unable "to rest in any conception", and seeks for theoretical confirmation and explanation even of waking percepts such as *this is a glass*. Carrying James' analysis out a step further, we may say that in less extreme forms, this instability is expressed practically in the carping attitude which disagrees with everything and everyone, and theoretically in the different types of scepticism.

The opposite attitude of firm belief also has its pathological extremes, as in drunkenness, where the sense of reality and truth becomes abnormally intensified. "In whatever light things may then appear to us, they seem more utterly what they are, more 'utterly utter' than when we are sober." James then indicates that one of the charms of certain forms of drug intoxication is the reaching of a "fully unutterable extreme" of belief, "in which a man's very soul will sweat with conviction, and he be all the while unable to tell what he is convinced of at all" (p. 284). We may add that without artificial stimulants, this attitude is often expressed practically in the form of what we call bigotry and fanaticism, and theoretically in what we know as dogmatism. James is, of course, implying here that sound belief is attended by some degree of doubt.

There is a third attitude often confused with hesitation and doubt, but really quite distinct from both doubt and belief where conviction is either hoped for or achieved. This is a more radical condition in which the sense of meaning and reality is lost. In its

[1] *Cf.* Heidegger, *Sein und Zeit*, 7th ed., pp. 120–21 and 296; *Being and Time*, tr. Macquarrie/Robinson, pp. 156–57 and 342–43.

extreme and pathological forms, we find this in those "melancholic patients" who complain "that nothing is believed in by them as it used to be, and that all sense of reality is fled from life. They are sheathed in india-rubber; nothing penetrates to the quick or draws blood, as it were" (p. 298). Adding again, we may say that in less extreme forms this is expressed concretely in those non-pathological forms of boredom and anxiety where the world fades away into clouds of indifference, and theoretically in those forms of relativism and scientism which recognize ranges of gaping facts but no meaning.

James' reference to Brentano's *Psychologie* (p. 286) is worthy of some comment. He alludes to the generally accepted view of judgment as a mere logical union of subject and predicate in a proposition, and gives Brentano credit for clearly revealing the inadequacy of this intellectualistic conception. It is inadequate because it slurs over the important difference between merely thinking of an object, as expressed in a proposition, and believing it or denying it. We cannot believe in any object without first thinking of it in some way. But the two operations are quite distinct. As Brentano says, "it is then twice present in consciousness, as thought of, and as held for real or denied".[2] James agrees with this distinction and emphasizes it in his own thought, as we shall see.

But he disagrees with Brentano's use of the term *judgment* for the act of acceptance and rejection, which he prefers to call *belief*. Why? James gives no reasons, but on the ground of his general theory and the actual content of this chapter, I believe that it lies in the intellectualistic associations of the term judgment, which suggests a logical operation of some kind. He does not wish to deny that there are theoretical beliefs in conceptualized objects. But by his use of the term *belief*, he wishes to suggest something more concrete and earthy. As he is going to show, our firmest beliefs are in the self and in perceptual objects

[2] F. Brentano, *Psychologie vom empirischen Standpunkte*, I, Leipzig, 1874, p. 266. Quoted in PR, II, 286.

which may be only partially conceptualized, or, perhaps, not at all. Furthermore, our belief, even in conceptual objects and theories, always involves factors of feeling and desire, in addition to reason and judgment.

As others have pointed out, it is not without significance that to express our basic "cognition of reality" James consciously chooses a term *belief* (*doksa*) that was used disparagingly by Plato, and the whole tradition following him, as never knowing reality at all, but only becoming. For James, of course, becoming is reality. So, for him, belief is a basic act, not of reason alone, but of the whole man, including reason, feeling, and desire. By this act of consent, he accepts himself, the beings that appear to him directly, and others that may not appear but may be conceptually connected therewith. It is important to note that Husserl, at the end of his life, also used the term *doksa* in an analogous way, and *Urdoksa* for our primary belief in the world of life (*Lebenswelt*), which is presupposed by science and theoretical knowledge in general.

Mental Being and the Phenomenological Reduction

Having given a static analysis of belief, and having distinguished it from mere presence before the mind, James now turns to the historical analysis, which is of more interest to him. How does the sense of reality arise in our experience? "Under what circumstances do we think things real?" (p. 287). What are the first realities in which we believe? What are the secondary objects, and how are these related to the former? He begins this basic discussion with a consideration of what he calls "the various orders of reality" (p. 287). Suppose a new-born or pre-natal mind, entirely blank and waiting for experience to begin. Then suppose that this comes with the appearance of a lighted candle. Since nothing can be perceived without a ground, we must suppose that it will appear "against a dark background" (p. 287).

If a psychologist could gain some access to this experience by noticing an opening of the eyes and ocular attention, he would say that this is a hallucination, since there is no real candle in the real world which he knows. But will this candle be believed in by the child? James answers with a decisive affirmative. We must not confuse our own situation with that of the other, and thus commit the psychological fallacy. For the child, the candle "is *that; it is there*", and his "entire faculty of attention is absorbed by it". He has no memories of other candles with which to compare this one. "So how can the mind help believing the candle real?" (p. 288). The psychologist may call it a *hallucination*. But a hallucination "is a sort of existing fact", and the child "has no knowledge of *other* facts". So he will believe in the candle-fact though he has no word to express it.

The same point may be made with reference to any other mental object, like the winged horse, Pegasus. It has its own peculiar properties and its own peculiar being in its peculiar space, and in this world of imagination, there is no point in denying it the being that it has. "That horse exists no otherwise than as winged, and is moreover really there, for that place exists no otherwise than as the place of that horse, and claims as yet no connection with the other places of the world" (p. 289). But if I make an inroad with this horse into the real world "otherwise known", the situation is different. If I say, for example, "that is my old mare, Maggie, having grown a pair of wings where she stands in her stall, the whole case is altered; for now the horse and place are identified with a horse and place otherwise known . . ." (p. 289).

Two different worlds, each known in a different way, are being confused. "Maggie in her stall with wings! Never! The wings are unreal, then, visionary" (p. 289). The point that James is making is very clear. The objects of delusion and hallucination have a real being in their respective worlds. This being needs to be recognized and respected as long as these worlds are not confused with each other, nor with the real world whose being is not only very different but known in a different way. In fact, it is only by a disciplined comparative study of some kind that such confusion is to be avoided. What, then, are these different worlds or universes? And how are we to think of the wider world to which they belong? James turns to these fundamental questions in the next section of his *Principles*, which he calls "The Many Worlds" (pp. 291 ff.). In these pages, he suggests the possibility of something closely resembling what was later to be called the *"transcendental phenomenological reduction".*[3]

James begins by speaking of the practical attitude which dominates our everyday life. In this "natural attitude", as it was soon to be called, existence means the objects which resist us or help us in our struggle for life. Little attention is paid to the self, which is carrying on this struggle, and its meanings or intentions. For the most part, it too is an object in the world. Dreams, fantasies, and illusions simply do not count. They are disregarded and dismissed as non-existent. "*Vae victis*" is the law in the "popular philosophy" which dominates this natural attitude. These mental objects "are not even treated as appearances; they are treated as if they were mere waste, equivalent to nothing at all" (p. 291).

James then contrasts this "popular philosophy" with the attitude of "the genuinely philosophic mind" which holds to a much wider view of being, and thus withdraws from the practical notions that guide our practical life. The philosopher does not deny the former attitude. He recognizes that it plays a necessary role in his own existence. As a philosopher, he does not go along with it. He holds it in suspense so that he may examine it more carefully. For he sees that there are many other regions and realms of fancy, illusion, collective belief, abstract reality, ideal relations, and many others, each with its own special mode

[3] *Cf.* Husserl, *Ideas*, tr. Gibson, secs. 75–76, pp. 191–97; *Cartesian Meditations*, tr. Cairns, The Hague, 1960, *Med.* II, secs. 12–15.

of being. All of these need to be taken account of, if we are to gain a sound understanding of "the total world which is" (p. 291).

Hence neither asserting nor denying the natural attitude and its practical conception of existence, the philosopher will detach himself from this as from all special attitudes. Then from this transcendental position, he will describe and analyze each sub-world, together with its various regions and objects, in order to compare and contrast it with others, and thus to find its true position in the whole. Thus "the complete philosopher", or phenomenologist, "is he who seeks not only to assign to every given object of his thought its right place in one or other of these sub-worlds, but he also seeks to determine the relation of each sub-world to the others in the total world which is" (p. 291).

Two points especially need to be emphasized about this remarkable statement. The first is that the natural attitude, as we have said, is neither asserted nor denied. It simply becomes an object of scrutiny in the hope that its nature and history may be more clearly understood in relation to the many other sub-worlds. Its special notion of existence is also to be studied in this way, so that its origin and its relation to those of other regions may be properly analyzed. But the philosopher no longer uses this practical notion of existence, which he abandons for one that is much wider and more abstract. It includes not only practical existence, but mathematical, aesthetic, normative, and dream existence as well. Through this wider view of being, that of any appearance, or object, that comes before the mind, he may detach himself from his own existence and, indeed, from that of every special sub-world. From this detached, or transcendental, position he may then examine all the sub-universes and regions as they roll out before him for his observation and review. By painstaking analysis of these sub-universes, one by one, he may hope to approach a final understanding of all of them together, and, therefore, of the "total world which is" (p. 291).

Seven Worlds

James then presents a list of these various "sub-universes". He does not claim that it is exhaustive. He is prepared to recognize many more. But these are "the most important sub-universes commonly discriminated from each other and recognized by most of us" (p. 291), though "more or less disconnectedly" in the natural attitude where practicality and objectivity are the rule.

James mentions seven sub-worlds on this list (pp. 292–93). First comes the world of the natural attitude, or "the world of sense", as James calls it. He says that this is the world of "physical things", including the human body, as we directly or "instinctively apprehend them" (p. 292). This is not the dark midnight world of the physical sciences. It is fully endowed with light, color, and sound, exactly as we perceive them. It is also filled with real forces, like gravity and electricity as they are directly experienced, which were excluded from the scientific universe as anthropomorphic fictions. But these forces exist in the life-world where they resist us and finally shatter us, or at other times, when brought under control, yield their power to us. James recognizes that there is room in this life-world for the realm of fancy and, indeed, for all the other regions. "The popular mind conceives of all these sub-worlds more or less disconnectedly; and when dealing with one of them, forgets for the time being its relation to the rest" (p. 291). Also when finished with one, the popular philosophy easily forgets it, and discards it as "unreal", since the objective attitude dominates. It is important to recognize, however, that the life-world is here listed among the other sub-universes, though in the first position, thus giving us a hint of what is to come.

Second, comes the world of science, in James' time, as in our own, the life-world's chief competitor for the position of supremacy. This world, as James points out, has no place for sounds, colors, and the other so-called secondary qualities. "The molecules and ether-waves of the scientific world", he says, "simply kick the object's warmth and color out, they refuse to have any relations with them" (p. 293). And while James does not say so specifically, the *living* body, as we directly feel it moving, perceiving, and thinking from within, is dismissed as something *subjective*, for the objective methods of science have no access to this region of our lived experience. The great powers of fire, storm, and disease as we feel them looming up in our vicinity and sometimes overwhelming us are also excluded as subjective. The objects of this scientific world are not related by patterns of human meaning and value, but rather by relations of quantitative variables or, as James says, by "laws" (p. 292).

These perceived aspects of the life-world are dismissed as the effects of scientific causes and, therefore, as *appearances*. In this way, they are "reduced to relative unreality when their causes come to view", though these same appearances are "the things on which our knowledge of the causes rests" (p. 301). But how can a delusion conduct us to the truth? James' comment on this paradoxical situation is interesting, and shows how deeply he felt the need for a more adequate phenomenology which would do justice to diverse perspectives. "Strange mutual dependence this", he says, "in which the appearance needs the reality in order to exist, but the reality needs the appearance in order to be known!" (p. 301).

In the third place on the list, comes "the world of ideal relations, or abstract truths believed, or believable by all" (p. 292). These ideal relations are based originally on concepts that are sheer inventions of the mind, not having any necessary relevance to concrete experience. Once such concepts are found, their relations of similarity, dissimilarity, and implication will be believed as real by anyone who will take the trouble to examine them, as in the case of mathematics. On the basis of these relations, consistent systems may be elaborated in fields like logic, aesthetics, ethics, and metaphysics, and then applied to experience in the hope that some agreement may be found. In the case of mathematics, and certain parts of logic, such agreements have been discovered in areas where nature actually seems to work in accordance with conceptual schemes. The practical results have been tremendous, and in the other fields similar hopes are entertained, but in their case, no systematic agreements with empirical facts have yet been found. So we are left with a vast array of divergent aesthetic, ethical, and metaphysical systems, many of which continue to be elaborated with little or no reference to experience as it is.

James felt that such elaboration was of little use without a prior attempt to clarify the areas of experience where these systems might be relevant. But even so, as a radical empiricist, he was from the very beginning a "logical realist". These concepts and conceptual systems cannot be dismissed as unreal. They have a "mental being" of their own which must be respected, and if formulated with some reference to experience, they are capable of shedding light on the sensory world where realities become present to us as in the flesh. James never abandoned this logical realism, and we shall see (Chapter VIII, *infra*) how he worked it out in greater detail in the last chapter of the *Principles* (Chap. XXVIII), and maintained it to the very end of his life. There is a world of conceptual norms and systems with many regions and sub-regions of its own.

In the fourth place, James mentions "the world of 'idols of the tribe'", that is, "illusions or prejudices common to the race". The examples he gives are of isolated appearances, like the motion of the sky around the earth, and of supposed delusions like the existence of matter, so called by certain philosophers. But under the other headings in his list, he seems to have whole versions of the world in mind, like the world of everyday life, the universe of science, and a complete metaphysical system. So it is hard to know just what he means. If he is thinking of public versions of the world, collectively held by certain races, peoples, and national groups, these certainly deserve a place in his scheme. No group of this kind can exist without some shared version of the world which is expressed in the basic structure of its language, and filled with many illusions and prejudices concerning both itself and alien groups. James may have been misled by too quickly adopting the phrase "idols of the tribe", which, as conceived by Bacon, does not fit in with his general plan. Nevertheless he may have had these collective worlds in mind, and, in any case, they do deserve to be included in his scheme.

Next, in the fifth place, come the worlds of religious mythology and fiction. Each of these is a complete world system "with definite relations among its own parts" which, like those of a logical or metaphysical system, hold true *in* it whether or not they are true to the facts of experience. This also holds of the worlds created by the literary artist. Such worlds must be understood in their entirety, or not at all, to give the impression of absolute reality. "Whilst absorbed in the novel, we turn our backs on all other worlds, and, for the time, the Ivanhoe-world remains our absolute reality. When we wake from the spell, however, we find a still more real world, which reduces Ivanhoe, and all things connected with him, to the fictive status . . ." (pp. 292–93, note). In creating his characters, the novelist must create such integral worlds encompassing them, for man is inseparable from the world in which he lives.

In the sixth place, we find "the various worlds of individual opinion, as numerous as men are" (p. 293). James is using the term *opinion* here not in the pejorative sense of classical thought, but as a synonym for belief. He is speaking primarily not of the world that an individual may profess theoretically but of the world in which he acts, and on the basis of which he stakes the meaning of his life. In the last part of his statement, James seems to be over-estimating the creative capacities of the "ordinary man", who, for the most part, accepts the public world of his community without requiring any profound alterations. The achievement of distinctive originality which, according to James, is the source of social change and history[4] is very rare. But he wishes to be generous, and if the various peculiarities of circumstances are taken into account, there is no doubt that each individual in a modern free society lives in a world of

---

[4] *Cf.* "Great Men and Their Environment," WBA, pp. 216 ff.

his own. Certainly he cannot be understood without understanding his world.

This is also true of what falls under the last and seventh heading. These are "the worlds of sheer madness and vagary, also indefinitely numerous". As modern psycho-therapy has learned, one cannot understand a disturbed person as a mere objective case in a common world that is taken for granted. The person who is really disturbed lives in a disturbed world, and it is impossible to understand the former without the latter. Hence the therapist must listen. The investigation of these disturbed worlds has been intensively pursued since James' time, and something has been learned of the strange contractions and distortions to which these worlds are subject.

This vital section of the *Principles* is marked by James' characteristic sense of the vast richness and variety of human experience which H. M. Kallen brought out so clearly in his book.[5] In the natural attitude of daily life which takes the public world of our community for granted, we pay only a momentary and disordered attention to most of these worlds. Many of them are turned over to specialists, and many of those with which we are not concerned are merely dismissed as unreal. But every object and region in every one of these diverse universes is existent in the most ultimate or abstract sense of this term. As James says (p. 294), "in the strict and ultimate sense of the word existence, everything which can be thought of at all exists as *some* sort of object, whether mythical object, individual thinker's object, or object in outer space and for intelligence at large. Errors, fictions, tribal beliefs are parts of the whole great Universe . . .". They must all be taken account of, if we are to gain an understanding of experience which is unbiased and impartial. One would expect, therefore, that James would get on with this task of transcendental exploration. Having made the phenomenological reduction which unrolls all the manifold objects and worlds before the detached consciousness, he should then proceed to explore them. Taking up these dif-

[5] *The Philosophy of William James*, New York, 1925.

ferent worlds one by one, he should subject each of them to a careful objective examination, discovering its basic patterns, assigning to "every given object . . . its right place", and then determining "the relation of each sub-world to the others in the total world which *is*" (p. 291). This is the task of transcendental phenomenology as it was conceived by Husserl in his middle period.[6]

Those who have read James' *Principles*, or even the earlier chapters of this work, know that he did not pursue this path. Why not? Because of the peculiar position he was forced to assign to the life-world, number one on his list. That world does not exist in the same manner as the other worlds and realms of being. Furthermore, it cannot be understood in the same way. Hence the whole phenomenological enterprise, as James understands it, has to be basically altered in a direction which would be called today *existential*. He presents his reasons for assigning this special status to the world of life in the remainder of this chapter (pp. 293–322). In terms of contemporary discussion, these may also be taken as James' reasons for abandoning transcendental phenomenology and its reduction. We shall make further comments on this critical aspect of his thought later on (*infra*, pp. 159 ff.).

The Peculiar Status
of the World of Life

The first reason why the life-world does not fit into the transcendental scheme is the presence in it of "subjective" factors to which the intentional methods of transcendental phenomenology have no access. Thus James says "the mere fact of appearing as an object at all is not enough to constitute reality" (II, 295). My grasp of reality in this eminent sense is gained from my non-objective self-awareness in the very act of pursuing

---

[6] *Cf. Ideas*, tr. Gibson, secs. 50–51, pp. 139–42.

my various projects in the world. This world is centered in selves, and, therefore, all the objects of the various realms and regions we have been considering involve the self of which I am directly and immediately aware. James refers to the Cartesian *cogito* in this connection, and to "the indubitable reality" of that experience of self-awareness where thought and being coincide. As soon as I think about myself as an object, I have fallen into the past and have slipped through my own fingers. But this self is involved here and now in every object that I perceive in any way. Hence it is no wonder that James asserts categorically that *"the fons et origo of all reality . . . is thus subjective, is ourselves"* (pp. 296–97). The appearing of an object before me may be "ultimate" in the direction of abstractness. But *"our own reality, that sense of our own life . . . is the ultimate of ultimates for our belief"* (p. 297).

In the second place, the point of indubitability which we have just mentioned is worthy of further examination. It is true that I cannot doubt any object which appears before me. So far as it appears, it has a minimum of reality. But, for James, reality means an independent being which exists in its own right, (*supra*, pp. 71 ff. and I, 218–19). And in the case of a conceived, or imagined, object, this can always be doubted. Is this object more than a creation of my mind? Does it have real, independent existence in itself? Even when further evidence shows me that this is so, and I perceive the thing, or something connected with it, I am still at a distance from it. I am detached from it and perceiving it from a point of view. But in the experience of self-awareness, I am not at a distance from myself. Here being and knowing are not separated. This knowing belongs to my being and in this act, my being becomes a self-knowing. As Descartes noted, here being and knowing coincide. Hence as James says (II, 297): "'As sure as I exist!'— this is our uttermost warrant for the being of all other things". The world of life (the sense-world) possesses this uttermost warrant, and is thus distinguished from the other realms and universes.

And now we must bring up an aspect of James' account

which differs radically from that of Descartes. As we have seen (*supra*, pp. 106 ff.), the self is no soul substance or thinking thing, enclosed within itself. By its cares and concerns, the self reaches out to other independent things and persons. It is intimately and really related to them in many ways other than the knowing relation. It seeks after them and struggles with them. It loves them and hates them. It conquers them and controls them, is shattered by them, or somehow gets along with them. These things and persons, with whom I am engaged in the world, are bound up with my being, and they partake of the same indubitability with which I am and know myself. *"Whatever things have intimate and continuous connection with my life are things of whose reality I cannot doubt"* (II, 298). This is far from the Cartesian thinking substance. The human person is stretched out into an external world of independent beings, and he knows them in the same manner, and with the same mode of certainty, with which he knows himself.

We have noted the sense in which our lived experience is indubitable. But, as James now notes emphatically, it is also inescapable. And this marks it off sharply from all the realms and regions of objective thought and imagination. We possess a sense of our own life "at every moment" here and now (p. 297). Even though I may lose myself for periods of time in imaginative flights and speculative adventures, the fringes of the real world (p. 320) always surround them in the background, and its objects soon return as the focus of our attention. After reading a novel, like Ivanhoe, we may be lost in the "Ivanhoe-world" for a time (pp. 292–93), but when we wake from the spell, we find ourselves in a still more real world which has been around us all the time, and which reduces Ivanhoe to the fictive status. Even when we are witnessing the most exciting drama, we are vaguely aware of the real building in which it is taking place, and of the faint but real sounds of the street outside. The fringes of the real world are always around us. Other objects and ideas may be in some sense real for specialists. We may from time to time concern ourselves with other realms and regions. But they are not inescapable. We can live without them. As James puts it: "other things, to be sure, may be real for this man or for that—things of science, abstract moral relations, things of the Christian theology, or what not. But even for the special man, these things are usually real with a less real reality than that of the things of sense. They are taken less seriously; and the very utmost that can be said for anyone's belief in them is that it is as strong as his 'belief in his own senses'" (p. 294). This world of life is as inescapable as the death to which it inexorably leads us. We may try to forget it or lose ourselves in other things. But the sense-world is always there waiting for us when we return. Its very being is different from that of the other worlds, and the things of sense are "more really real" than they are.

We are now led to another basic point of difference between this world of life and the other universes which are real only in a minimum sense. "As bare logical thinkers, without emotional reaction, we give reality to whatever objects we think of, for they are really phenomena, or objects of our passing thought, if nothing more. But, *as thinkers with emotional reaction, we give what seems to us a still higher degree of reality to whatever things we select, and emphasize and turn to* WITH A WILL. These are our *living* realities; and not only these, but all the other things which are connected with these" (p. 297). James is saying here that our lived existence must be distinguished from the abstract reality which belongs to any mental object. This existence has subjective features and opaque depths which are lacking in mental appearances. Furthermore, it brings along with it a whole world of active engagement that is reduced and distorted if placed in the frame of a purely detached and transcendental consciousness. It can be described and analyzed as it is lived from within by another type of phenomenology developed especially in France, which James himself employed, and which he sometimes called sympathetic imagination.[7] Instead of appealing to a transcendental consciousness, it turns rather to the direct self-consciousness that is possessed by every

[7] *Cf.* "What Makes a Life Significant," EFM, pp. 306-7.

man, and tries to develop and clarify it by reflective description and analysis. James was familiar with this literature, which probably influenced him in working out his own reflective method. "The world of living realities as contrasted with unrealities [James might have said *unreal realities*] is thus anchored in the Ego, considered as an active and emotional term" (p. 297).

This brings up another point which runs through James' whole description of the distinctive features of the world of life. I participate in this world not with some part or parts of myself, not as a "man of science", a Christian theologian, or a "bare logical thinker", but with the whole of my rational, emotional, and active being. This is clear in the case of abstract, intellectual meditation. It is not so clear in the case of reading a moving story or witnessing a drama where my feelings as well as my intellectual powers become involved. I am being moved by the images and thoughts of the author, by the words and the acts of the actors. But I am listening, taking it in, not acting myself on my own responsibility. I may learn much, and be imaginatively enriched by experiences of this kind, which may enter into the very texture of my existence. But I am not thinking and speaking for myself with the whole of my being, on my own, as I must when I think, feel, imagine, and live in the life-world.

The need which is felt, even by abstract thinkers and metaphysicians, to find some verification for their conceptions in some bodily, sensible form is another indication of the "paramount reality of sensations" (p. 299). Thus the child is not content with a wholly imaginary playmate. She needs to identify her playmate "with some doll or other material object, and this evidently solidifies belief, little as it may resemble what it is held to stand for" (p. 303). A disembodied person will not do. It is not *fully* real. And even adults share in this sense of the greater reality of what is like ourselves in being embodied. "Who does not 'realize' more", James asks, "the fact of a dead or distant friend's existence, at the moment when a portrait, letter, garment, or other material reminder of him is found?" (p. 303). Our own lives are inseparable from our living bodies and, therefore, "all our inward images tend invincibly to attach themselves to something sensible, so as to gain in corporeity and life" (p. 305).

Imaginative and conceptual references have a certain reality of their own. But this is inadequate. They seek to have their full reality verified by embodied, perceptual experience. This experience needs nothing more. It is fully real. It requires no further verification from either fantasies or concepts, for these are insufficient. To become truly real *they* need something more. "A conception, to prevail, must *terminate* in the world of orderly sense experience" (p. 301). This is evidently true of the sciences whose histories are "strewn with wrecks and ruins of theory—essences and principles, fluids and forces—once fondly clung to, but found to hang together with no facts of sense" (p. 301). James knows very well that experience is not a mere array of disconnected sensations (*cf. supra*, pp. 49–50). The objects of perception are pervaded by meanings "filling the gaps between them, and weaving their interrupted chaos into order" (II, 311) to make this experience into "the world of orderly sense experience".

The worlds of different groups and individuals are ordered in different ways. Such systems must convey a meaning to us. But in so far as they are subjected to a test of verification, their ability or inability to take account of actual sensory facts will play the most critical role. "*The conceived system, to pass for true, must at least include the reality of the sensible objects in it. . . . The system which includes the most of them, will, ceteris paribus, prevail*" (p. 312). Thus, according to James, the objects of sensory perception are real in a "paramount" sense, and they also constitute the crucial test for our supposed conceptual realities. "Sensible objects are thus either our realities or the tests of our realities" (p. 301).

The last distinguishing feature of lived reality is perhaps the most important of them all. But James does not talk about it in a special section of this central chapter, so it must be picked up from scattered suggestions. Indeed, it cannot be talked *about* without objectifying and reducing it. For it is concerned with that feeling of an irreplaceable existence which is found in existing and in no other way. Hence it must be elicited from the reader himself by hints and suggestions, which will have no meaning for a non-existing being, nor in a purely detached and objective discourse. This feeling attaches to my own actions, and to *"whatever things have intimate and continuous connection with my life"* (p. 298). It belongs to tangible things rather than to the objects of the distance senses, since the former are "most intimately connected with our weal or woe" (p. 306). Thus a dagger hurts us only when it penetrates our skin, and a poison only when we take it into our mouths. Objects which touch me and call forth internal bodily feelings carry with them a "pungent" tang of reality. As James says, "the reason of the belief is undoubtedly the bodily commotion which the exciting idea sets up" (p. 308).

I feel such objects directly without the mediation of any concept or sign of any kind, since I "have immediate practical relations" with them (p. 296). These are *"ipso facto* real relations, and confer reality upon their objective term". Such feelings belong to me, and I have them only by living them through. James stresses this again and again. Thus he speaks of those "living realities" to which we give a "higher degree of reality", "that sense of our own life which we at every moment possess" in the here and now, and even of "the world of living realities" (p. 297; *cf.* pp. 300, 305, 321). This direct feeling of existence is irreplaceable. It can be supplied only by direct acquaintance with the feeling itself, which must fringe all authentic discussion of what is really real.

This chapter of the *Principles* bears a basic significance for James' psychology and, indeed, for his whole philosophy. He is making a sharp distinction between a minimal meaning of reality which belongs to any object coming before the mind, and another "higher" sense which is "richer", "paramount", and "more really real". This is the argument of the chapter, and everything that he says in it bears on this central theme. There are two modes of being to which we have access in our experience. That of the world of sense is marked by certain special traits.

Understanding these distinctive traits of the world of life requires a distinctive method which James loosely refers to by such phrases as "sympathetic imagination" and a "sense for the concrete", and which is quite different from any purely conceptual analysis. Hence in the central portions of the *Principles*, which are concerned with the stream of consciousness, the self, feeling, perception, and the perceptual world, James employs this method, and relies very largely on direct acquaintance. We must note, however, that any object coming before the mind has a minimal mental being that must be recognized. In spite of his primary interest in lived existence, James never denies this. The various mental worlds of myth, fiction, and conceptual construction are all real in the minimal sense, and must be taken account of. But to verify them fully, to find out what they really are, we must understand them in relation to the life-world, which is more real. They have no room for it, but it has room for them. In his chapters on imagination and reasoning, to which we shall soon turn, he is doing precisely this, finding their place in the world of life. Concepts are also needed to clarify the vague meaning of feelings and perceptions, and to bring them into relation. But this involves a very special use of concepts, which is never content with their fixed objects but constantly refers them back to what is known through direct acquaintance. In this way, a firm existential foundation may be laid. Once this has been done, the other realms and ranges of mental being may be related to this central "nucleus", and progress may be made in finding their true positions in the world that is "really real".

The Rejection of the Reduction

This is the main argument of James' chapter on "The Perception of Reality". Of course, written before 1890, it is not directed against transcendental phenomenology and its reduction. Nevertheless it is very relevant to the present issues between this type of empirical approach and the existential phenomenology that is beginning to develop in our time. In fact, every one of the distinctive features of the life-world that he mentions may be used as an argument to show why the transcendental reduction, as first described by Husserl, cannot be carried through. The most critical phase of this reduction, as we have seen, is the bracketing of existence. We are not to doubt the existence which the natural attitude attributes to certain of its objects. But neither are we to assert it. We simply detach ourselves from this attitude in order to observe it along with all other intentions and objects that come before the transcendental observer. This leads us into that vast universe of fields and regions which possess the minimal reality to which James refers. This includes hallucinations, dreams, fictions, illusions, logical operations, and their objects, together with our experiences in the life-world. Without raising any questions concerning their real existence, all these experiences can be described and analyzed exactly as they appear before the mind. If these appearances are carefully described exactly as they appear, the results cannot be questioned, and an apodictic certainty can be attained. For no one can seriously question that a mind means what it means.

In every case, the object of examination is an act of meaning of some kind (*noesis*) and what it means (*noema*). The mind itself constitutes these meanings and has a privileged access to them, for surely the mind can discover the nature of what it has itself originated. This is true also of the natural attitude, its various intentions and their objects. The mind's own existence, *as it is meant*, can be impartially described, together with its thoughts, feelings, and actions, and their existent objects as they are meant. Their relations to one another can be precisely analyzed, and the whole existential field compared and contrasted with other fields. Here too an apodictic certainty can be achieved.

This is the vast universe of meanings opened up by the transcendental reduction. It is a world of meanings. This is granted. As James says, these objects possess a mental being. In Husserl's language they are constituted by the transcendental consciousness. But for Husserl it is all-inclusive, for the vague, the ineffable, and even existence itself are only meanings that are meant.

Such is the grand conception of the transcendental reduction, which has stimulated many revealing investigations that have shown the grave limitations of traditional forms of empiricism, and have shed a much needed light on many obscure and neglected fields of human experience. As we have noted, James was aware of this field of mental being, as he called it, and often explored certain parts of it in his own way. But he was also aware of its limits, and of the need for a radically different method to explore the world of existence. He did not, of course, directly criticize the transcendental reduction, which was not yet formulated. But as we have seen, he did sharply distinguish the two realms of mental and existential being to the advantage of the latter. Every one of the differences which he pointed out can be used as an argument against these all inclusive claims, as we shall now see.

The empirical self is embodied, and as such it is subject to external observation and measurement, as James well knew. But this self is directly acquainted with its own bodily movements and feelings from the inside. And this direct self-awareness can never be observed as an object without reduction and distortion. Phenomenologists who think they are observing these subjective phenomena from the outside, and carefully probing into intimate thoughts and feelings are mistaken. Even though they may be unaware of it, they are directly following these self-revelations as they are expressed in gesture and language, or interpreting them in the light of their own self-consciousness, with which they are directly acquainted. In neither case are they merely observing them as objects. The self does not originally know itself intentionally in this way. It feels itself by a direct acquaintance to which the intentional method of Husserl, in the strict sense, has no access.[8] The existing self, its self-awareness, and its acquaintance with primary objects cannot be known

[8] *Cf.* L. Landgrebe, "Husserl und Cartesianismus," *Philosophische Rundschau*, 1961.

objectively in this way. The natural attitude and its world have a being that is more than mental being. They really exist, and, therefore, cannot be brought, in their entirety, within the field of the transcendental reduction.

It is true that the mind can be certain of its meaning and of *what* is meant. When these are really present, they cannot be doubted. But then, as James points out, a further question can be raised. Is this meaning (and what is meant) a mere supposition? Or does it have an independent existence of its own? Of course I may be meaning actual existence. But is this existence really there? The whole vast field of transcendental phenomenology is open to this question. And it cannot be settled by any mode of supposition or by conceptual argument of any kind. It can be settled only in one way, by direct acquaintance and feeling. Only the life-world can become existentially certain. At this level of complete reality the *transcendental* reduction cannot be performed. It is existentially uncertain. It presupposes another *existential* reduction which has a distinctive factual certainty of its own.

Furthermore, this whole universe, together with its manifold realms and regions, is not inescapable. I may attend to one or all of these realms for a while. But then I may forget them and turn to other tasks. For all I know, they may completely disappear, since they leave no ever-present fringes. I need never return to them, for they are not really real. I am not sure that they possess an independent being of their own with depths that resist my efforts to know. But my empirical self and the life-world are always with me as long as I exist in a waking state. Even though I may lose myself in a novel or in a system of meaning of some kind, and even though I may do my best to forget them and suppress them, their fringes are always around me in the background waiting for me to return. The field of the transcendental reduction can be forgotten and escaped. But the life-world is ever-present and inescapable. It remains.

In the world of life, I am not merely supposing that I am engaged. I am really engaged, even if my project is to avoid all serious commitment, or to do transcendental phenomenology. I

am staking my time and, therefore, my life on some aim. But
when I observe this active engagement from an objective point
of view, something is missing. I see motions and hear words,
and I may get a sense of some inner purpose. But I cannot tell
whether the engagement is genuine or only supposed. This is
true even of the enterprise of phenomenology itself. In observing
himself as an object, the thinker may know that he has done
this and that, that he now thinks X or Y or Z. But is he really
devoting himself to this task with the whole of his being? Is it
authentic or only supposed? He cannot say. Perhaps he never
will be able to say. But such knowledge, if it ever comes, will
come from only one source—that is, feeling and direct acquaintance either with himself, or with the self-revealing communications of another. Actual engagement in meaningful action is
reduced, if it is observed as an object. It can be adequately
grasped and understood only with the aid of direct acquaintance.

In his consideration of the realms of mental being, James, as
we have seen, stresses the fact that it is not the whole man but
only man as an observer who participates in these realms. It is
only in the richer horizon of the life-world where everything
happens, often in the strangest and most bewildering combinations, that I participate with *the whole* of my being, which
involves memories, projects, desires, feelings, and passions, as
well as thoughts. It may be argued, however, that even though
this may be so, a disciplined observation may be able to probe
into all these facets of our being, and thus to reveal the existing
person as a whole. Now a further point needs to be suggested,
for this is not true.

Looking at us objectively in this way, the observer may single
out certain surface phases of our being and subject them to an
exact analysis one by one. But he cannot gather them all together as they are gathered in our existence, because to this
existence he is blind. Nor can he gather together the various
objects, regions, and other world fragments he may observe into
the one world in which we actually exist. He tears this world to
pieces, into the worlds of this tribe and that people, of X, and Y
and Z, and reifies them into separate world-objects without

glimpsing those vague and oscillating fringes of the one world into which they open, and which encompasses them all. The self is neither an object nor a substance enclosed within itself. It is a lived opening into the world. And this world must first be felt to be understood, for it is neither an object nor any set of objects. It is rather a background on which objects appear, and this too must first be perceived before it is understood. Neither the whole man nor the whole world which he inhabits will appear on the magnifying screen of the transcendental observer. His observations of special objects presuppose a wider frame. In order to observe, he must first exist.

If the mind-constituted meanings of the mental universe were self-sufficient, they would require no further verification. They would verify themselves. But they are not self-sufficient, and the mental being they possess, while real, is not really real. The real world is not luminous meaning alone, nor opaque being alone, but the two together in one, an order of meaning *in* the hard resistant facts that challenge us, and give us something to do. What we mean, though real in itself, is not self-sufficient. It must be confirmed by the independent beings which we *ultimately* mean. As an intention it must be fulfilled. Otherwise the vast universe of the reduction may be nothing more than a transcendental dream.

This is not a realistic theory. Meanings are not passively received from a world that is fixed and finished. They are first invented, and then confirmed or disconfirmed by the resistant realities with which we struggle in our human history. In so far as they become really true, they are verified in "the world of pure experience", as James came to call it. This is the gist of his pragmatic theory (*infra*, Chapter XIII). Our lived experiences are not verified in the first place by any system of pure ideas. This is a one-sided view which runs against the hesitant senses of history. It is rather our systems of ideas that are verified, so far as they are verified at all, in the real world of pure experience. It is in this world that we encounter independent and resistant beings. And in and through our meanings, it is these beings that we ultimately mean.

Our conceptual *knowledge about* something can always be replaced by becoming directly acquainted with it. Thus the description of a man as having red hair and a deep bass voice may enable me to find him, though other references may do as well. But when I become directly acquainted with him, I no longer need any of these. Furthermore, such a description will not help anyone who is not already acquainted with red hair or vocal sounds. My knowledge of existing and its basic patterns is like this. Objective concepts will not help without the direct acquaintance which they presuppose. The only way to find out what life is like is by actually living. No observation and no amount of conceptual analysis can take the place of it. In any report of observations on lived existence, we are constantly presented with terms like *being, feeling,* and *understanding* whose meaning has to be taken for granted. The observer is apt to suppose that these terms stand for objects whose meanings are as yet vague, and which may be clarified by further observations. But this is not true.

These terms do not stand for objects. They stand for living experiences that are known, always vaguely, by direct acquaintance. Their meaning may be to some degree clarified by the special use of concepts, not working alone, but always in cooperation with perception and feeling. These experiences have depths of opacity and mystery which resist our meanings, and, therefore, make it impossible to bring them into any systematic mental field. We may mean them, it is true. But without the dim guidance of preconceptual experience, we do not know what we mean. Hence they resist our conceptual nets, like living fish which escape through the openings in the mesh and vanish to their lairs in the depths of the sea. The *exhaustive* claims made for the phenomenological reduction are without foundation. These living beings resist it and escape. If they are to be caught, they must be caught by another net, another method of approach, now known as existential phenomenology.

In this chapter, we have tried to show the reader why James pursued a method of this kind, and avoided the techniques of transcendental phenomenology whose possibility he recognized.

There is a sense in which the transcendental method is closed. In explaining the meanings that it has itself constituted, it needs no help from other sources. In its detached position it is self-sufficient and confident. It can perform the task that it has laid down for itself. James' method is quite different. He is trying to reveal the meaning of a real existence which was not laid down by him, and which has depths of unfathomed opacity. Hence his tone is tentative and hesitant. He is dealing not with mental beings to which he has, in some transcendental capacity, a special access. He is dealing rather with real, independent beings with which the reader is already familiar, though not exclusively through concepts or conceptual argument. Hence he is constantly appealing to the lived experience of the reader, and one who does not actively respond to these appeals with the full force of his memory and imagination will miss the main thrust of his argument.

The patterns of life which he is attempting to reveal are not postulated by reason. They are *found* in the experience of living men where they are not merely conceptually understood but directly felt and perceived with or without the help of concepts. Hence he is constantly appealing to this pre-reflective experience of the reader—the sickening feeling of dread he may have felt while walking along a precipice's edge with its "sense of reality" and imminent fall (II, 307)—or that "nameless *Unheimlichkeit*" that comes over us when the absence of lasting meaning begins to loom in the world (p. 313). All this is foreign to the transcendental method when employed in its strict and most consistent manner.

As against this method, James held that the first task was to reveal the life-world and its basic patterns by an existential study, relying on both feeling and conceptual clarification working hand in hand. But then we must remember that he never denied the manifold realms of madness, hallucination, illusion, fiction, logic, and pure conceptual systems. All these regions have an indubitable meaning that must be respected. They need to be investigated, especially those that have been passed over as mere subjective aberrations by the traditions of intellectualism, but not as though their being were the highest level of reality, and this method the only way to truth.

The life world alone is *really* real, and if it is to be illumined, it must be explored by different methods. Once this foundation has been laid, however, there is room for the great vision of traditional phenomenology. These realms and universes are not nothing. They all have a being of some kind, each in its own way. Their meanings need to be explored and clarified, not by themselves alone but in relation to the life-world. For it is this world which has room for them all, and it is in this world of the *really real* that their ultimate meaning is to be found.

Part Two

❈

The Three Departments
of the Mind:
Perception, Reasoning,
and Action

Chapter Seven

❀

The World of Sense

In Part I we have considered certain basic topics which underlie the whole ènterprise that James is undertaking in his *Principles*, the nature of a phenomenological psychology, certain peculiar difficulties confronting it, the stream of thought, the self, selective attention, and the total world horizon of our lived experience. In the next four chapters, Part II, we shall follow James in considering in further detail the three major divisions into which this lived experience falls, the perception of facts (this chapter), the development of patterns of meaning (Chapters VIII and IX), and action (Chapter X). James refers to this as "the reflex-arc cycle", and the second volume of the *Principles* is organized on the basis of this conception. We shall consider this more thoroughly in Chapter VIII (pp. 214–16).

But we shall now turn to the perception of facts, the "first department of the mind", as James calls it. He deals with this in the last two chapters of Volume I of the *Principles* (XV and XVI) and in the first four chapters of Volume II (XVII–XX). We shall follow his own order, dealing first with time and memory, then with sensation, imagination, the perception of things, and finally the perception of space. In accordance with the method we have so far followed, we shall not attempt to give a complete summary and paraphrase of everything that James says on each of these topics. We shall rather single out certain themes which are of special interest from a phenomenological point of view, and then, while placing them in the context of James' general theory, we shall comment on them critically.

Time

The aim of the true empiricist, according to James, is to avoid theoretical constructions and to recover a sense of our original experiences as we live them through. In the case of time, he finds a common tendency to think of it in terms of a derived conception by which we represent or measure time. His major aim, therefore, is to describe the original pre-reflective phenomenon. It is only by first doing this that we may then gain a proper understanding of the conceptual representation with which it is for the most part confused. Thus we generally think of the present as an indivisible moment, or "knife-edge", and of time itself as a mere succession of momentary nows; one coming after another. The length of time is then measured by the space covered by the hands of a clock. "Our only way of knowing it accurately is by counting, or noticing the clock, or through some other symbolic conception" (I, 622). It is true that a longer interval, like a century, suggests to us more events and more dates on a calendar than a period of ten years. This leads us to think that we "directly perceive" their difference in length. But this is false. As James says, "there is properly no comparative time *intuition* in these cases at all. It is but dates and events *representing* time" (p. 623). But what is the original time that these clocks and calendars enable us to measure and represent? This is the question which leads James to his famous discovery of what he calls "the specious present".

The present moment is "an altogether ideal abstraction" (p. 608) that is never realized in the world of sense where we live and act. "In short, the practically cognized present is no knife-edge" . . . (p. 609). This is a theoretical construction. "The unit of composition of our perception of time is a *duration*, with a bow and a stern, as it were—a rearward- and a forward-looking end" (p. 609). Furthermore, time itself, this present, must not be confused with the successive events in time. "Its *content* is in a constant flux, events dawning into its forward end as fast as they fade out of its rearward one. . . . Meanwhile, the specious present, the intuited duration, stands permanent, like the rainbow on the waterfall . . ." (p. 630).

The British empiricists, who thought of time as a mere succession of ideas, were confusing lived time with clock time. But "a succession of feelings, in and of itself, is not a feeling of succession" (p. 628). So in this respect, their Kantian critics are right. But the specious present is also passing in its own peculiar way into its coming future, and fading into its past. Hence James points out how in the experiences of *"taedium, ennui, Langweile,* boredom . . . from the relative emptiness of content of a tract of time, we grow attentive to the passage of the time itself" (p. 626).

He is referring here, I believe, to the passage of the whole world-field that is centered in our existence. This "tract of time" may become meaningful or empty, depending to some degree on our constancy of purpose. In any case, we are not contained as an object in an "objective time" that is held together by a transcendental consciousness. Hence "Kant's notion of an intuition of objective time as an infinite necessary continuum has nothing to support it" (p. 642). We have a certain control over our meanings and projects, and James' recognition of this fact leads him to another important and original insight.

The specious present varies in its length of duration. In periods of intense purposive activity, it expands; in those of fatigue and "long illnesses" (p. 640), it contracts. With no active project to hold the recent past together with the present, the former rapidly fades away and "express acts of memory" are required to remember it (p. 640). Thus the same interval, as measured by the clock, will in the first case pass more rapidly and in the second more slowly. This shows that, in addition to the clock, we may develop another way of measuring time in terms of its meaning for us. *"In general"*, James says, *"a time filled with varied and interesting experiences seems short in passing, but long as we look back. On the other hand, a tract of time empty of experiences seems long in passing, but in retrospect short"* (p. 624).

The intervals of clock time—minutes, hours, and days, into which clock time is divided, are empty of content, and so may be equal in length. This provides us with an objective measure that is indispensable for social cooperation. But the intervals that we live through are not necessarily equal in length. They expand or contract with their varying content. Hence in retrospect they are open to a different kind of measurement in terms of their meaning. A life that is short chronologically may be rich and long in meaningful content.

But whatever measure we may use, we must not confuse it with the lived time that is measured. This is a specious present, directly perceived as a whole "block", but then divided into successive parts, fading off at one end into the closed but recoverable past, and developing at the other end into the foreseeable future. James suggests that this specious present is to be correlated with *"a cumulation of brain-processes overlapping each other, of which the fainter ones are the dying phases of processes which but shortly previous were active in a maximal degree"* (p. 635). As we shall see, his sense of man as an embodied being constantly led him into speculations of this kind. In this instance, it is important to note that he first turns to experience as it is directly perceived to find out what time is. After this, he then turns to physiology to see if he cannot find something roughly equivalent in the brain. Fortunately this is his usual procedure. In certain rare cases, however, where he starts from the supposed situation in the brain, and then looks for the experiential equivalent, he goes astray. But we must next turn to the related phenomenon of memory.

Memory

The stream of consciousness constantly flows on, and the specious present is the very heart of this continuity, since it embraces both dying echoes of the past as well as premonitions of the coming future. Part of the past, therefore, is still with us in the specious present. But what lies back of this has faded into a vague halo of fringes from which it can be recovered only by a special act of memory. According to James, this retention is a physical phenomenon based on that plasticity of matter which is responsible for habit in general. Thus if certain brain paths between certain centres, correlated with sets of experiences, have once been established by experiences that are long or intense, they will be retained and be liable to recall. If one path can be excited by some associated stimulus or operation in the present, its associates will also be excited. This is certainly a necessary condition. Many authors, and among them well-known empiricists, including Herbert Spencer, have held that this is also sufficient to account for all the phenomena of memory. When something leads me to remember my friend, who died a year ago, the brain paths involved in my encounters with him are reactivated, and images, or copies of these events, are called up in my mind.

But by a discerning piece of phenomenological analysis, James then shows (pp. 649 ff.) that this cannot be so. In the first place, memory is something more than the mere repetition of an event, whether it be regarded as physical or psychical. Thus the hall clock, at midnight, repeats a similar stroke eleven times after the original. But this does not mean that any of these later beats remembers the first. Similarly, eleven editions of the same feeling are independent events, "each snug in its own skin" (p. 650). There is no memory of one by another. For this, at least two further conditions must be met.

First, the fact must be *"expressly referred to the past"* (p. 650). To remember my dead friend is not to see a present replica. It is to refer to him directly as I encountered him, as he was. There is no copy of him in my mind. As James says, this supposed "image", or "copy", is "really not there at all in that simple shape, as a separate 'idea'. Or at least, if it be there as a separate idea, no memory will go with it" (p. 650). Such a copy is not required, for my original encounters with this friend are still with me. They are not with me as the primary past which is included within my specious present. But they are with me in the remote, temporal fringes of this present, which I call *my past*. From these obscure fringes they must be recaptured, as now absent and past, by a present act of memory. This is the only way in which the experience can be described without reduction.

But what is meant by my past?

Here a second condition must be recognized. Events of a thousand years ago, or those of any remote past, must first be imagined and then dated. This is a conceptual or linguistic operation. As James says, "remoter dates are conceived, not perceived." We *know about* them without direct acquaintance. They are "known symbolically by names" (p. 650). Even this, if it is to have anything more than a purely theoretical meaning, presupposes a memory of my past. But what is this?

It involves the two factors of self-identity that we have considered before (*cf. supra*, pp. 100-1). First, I must be able to join my past experience with my specious present by a set of continuous transitions. Second, this feeling of my past "must have that 'warmth and intimacy' which were so often spoken of in the chapter on the Self, as characterizing all experiences 'appropriated' by the thinker as his own" (I, 650). These encounters with my friend were mine. The self that had them has been taken over by the self that I now am, and so they belong to me. They are now present to me as absent, but absent in my past. It is this past that belongs to me, which gives me a sense of a past direction in time, and makes remote history something more than a mere imaginative construction. No matter how distant these remote events may be, they stretch continuously through historical records and traditions to the past that I remember, and to the present that I am living through and directly know.

Two points are worthy of special attention in this account of memory. The first is James' attack on the traditional theory of memory as based on a present image, or copy, which is similar to something in the past. In the light of his description of the phenomenon, he sees very clearly the weaknesses of this view. The phenomenon shows that memory is rather the direct recovery of a past experience as past. But his sense of obligation to brain physiology introduces an alien element that stands in the way of this conclusion to which his whole argument clearly points. A series of brain paths can follow their previous course in the present. But it is hard to see how they can bear any intentional reference to the past. Hence against the main drift of his argument from experience, James keeps speaking of referring some present image to the past, and of "a very complex representation" as going with memory (p. 651).

Nevertheless in a footnote (p. 649) he brings up telling negative examples, my memory of not winding my watch, or not locking the door, against the copy theory. He says, as we have noted, that retention is purely physical, but "recollection, on the other hand, is a *psycho-physical* phenomenon" (p. 655). The human body is both open to the whole world field, and yet at the same time a thing in the world, subject to objective scrutiny. This is responsible for one of those "productive paradoxes", as Gordon Allport has called them, which runs through the whole of James' psychology. Here, as elsewhere, it leads him into eclectic confusion and even contradiction. But sometimes it guides him towards novel insights. We can only regret that instead of the objective brain, James did not focus earlier on the notion of the living, conscious body as a whole (*cf. infra*, pp. 375 ff.).

The second noteworthy point in James' analysis is his subordination of what he calls "desultory memory"—the sheer retentiveness which enables us to recall isolated names and other details when the situation demands, to two other types. One of these is the theoretical memory which has thought about the facts and woven them together into a coherent system, so that one part suggests the rest, and short of total forgetfulness, no one is lost in isolation. Thus "*the one who* THINKS *over his experiences most, and weaves them into systematic relations with each other, will be the one with the best memory*" (I, 662). The other, which we may call memory proper, is the recalling of a past experience with all its fringes of thought and feeling as forming one whole "object" (p. 651), exactly as it was lived through in the past. As James says (p. 276), such memories are rare, but they can be approximated in what the French psychologists have come to call "affective memory".[1]

These higher types of memory require forgetting which, as James says, "is as important a function as recollecting" (p. 679). He notes that "as a rule, a man's memory is good in the departments in which his interest is strong" (p. 684). As our projects develop and change, our memories are reformed. In the light of this analysis, it is fair to say that a man is what he remembers, and is not what he forgets. A desultory memory means a disintegrated man.

Sensation and Perception

Let us now turn to the first three chapters of Volume II, in which James deals with sensation, imagination, and perception, or what we may call pre-predicative, pre-linguistic experience. Aside from some critical comments, we shall be concerned with three basic theses which are of major importance from a phenomenological point of view. First, he subjects certain subjectivist doctrines of British Empiricism to a penetrating criticism. Second, he expresses well-founded doubts concerning the empiricist theory of imagination. And finally, he suggests a non-representational view of perception as open to a pre-linguistic world of discriminated meanings, with which we shall be especially concerned.

[1] *Cf.* G. Gusdorf, *Mémoire et personne*, I, Paris, 1957, pp. 51 ff.

Locke and his followers held that human experience could be analyzed into simple units, or "ideas", like blue, hard, and middle C sound. The complex objects of experience are formed by the association of these simple elements, which retain their identity in these new mental combinations. Imagination gives us the power to combine simple elements together in new ways which may or may not correspond to existing things in the external world. But the same holds true of the supposedly real objects that are given in normal experience. We project these clusters of impressions outside of the mind, and assume that they are real. But since what we are directly aware of in either case is only an associated set of ideas, or sense-data in the mind, there is no guarantee. There is no sharp, qualitative difference between an imaginary moon and the real moon. The difference becomes merely one of degree, according to Hume a degree of faintness. The real moon is more vivid and lively than one that is only imagined.

These notions were taken over by the scientific psychology of the nineteenth century and are still far from dead. Thus according to the German psychologist Wundt, we can discover sensations, like the color blue, as the simplest elements in the complex objects of perception. These elements are caused by external, physical stimuli, and remain the same in different combinations. Thus a certain wave length will produce a certain color in consciousness and if this wave length is changed, a different color will be produced. If we ask how these elements come to be combined, the answer is some principle of automatic association. Thus if a set of sensations has occurred simultaneously, or in succession, the separate occurrences of one or more members of the original group will call up the others. Furthermore, there is general agreement that these sensations and perceptions are correlated directly with internal changes in the brain and central nervous system. Thus according to J. Muller in his *Handbuch der Physiologie des Menschen*, which appeared in 1838 and to which James refers, sensation does not point directly to an external thing but rather to changes in the nervous system of the perceiver. This author also follows Berkeley in holding that the third dimension of space is not directly perceived by sight, but only by associated touch sensations. Hence, the optical picture of space is an external projection, caused by associated tactual associations.

We can break this general causal theory of perception down into three distinct theories. First, our experience can be analyzed into simple units that remain the same in different combinations. Second, they are compounded by automatic laws of association. And third, our perceptual knowledge of external things is representational, or indirect. We are directly aware of subjective impressions, or sense-data, and must then somehow pass from these to the real objects we seem to know. In the chapters now before us, James subjects these traditional theories to a radical questioning which leads him to a total rejection of the first and third, and to a radical revision of the second, as we shall now see.

Let us begin with the third, the representational theory of knowledge. In its most extreme form in such authors as Taine, Schopenhauer, and Helmholtz (cf. II, 33), it holds that our sensations are originally situated in our own body, and mainly in the central nervous system. Thus according to Taine, the red color is not on the surface of my couch where I see it. No! It is "in the sensory centers of the encephalon" (p. 33, note). What I see is a mistaken appearance. This shows the lengths to which a theoretical mind can go in distorting the direct data of perception. Originally, that is, according to the theory, I see my couch in my brain, and then according to a "common law" (the theory again) I project it outside of me into the room.

How can one attack such a twisted theory? Not by theoretical argument of any kind. To argue with the absurd will only lead to further absurdities. The answer is to return to the facts of experience, to look, and to think about what you actually see, to give examples, and then to reflect on their meaning. This is James' procedure, and one that must be followed by any empirically oriented philosophy. "The supposition that a sensation primitively *feels either itself or its object to be in the same place with the brain* is absolutely groundless, and neither *a priori* probability nor facts from experience can be adduced to show that such a deliverance forms any part of the original cognitive function of our sensibility" (p. 34). The space in which we move and exist is not an intellectual construct. It is something sensed. The place where something is cannot be settled by argument. It can be settled finally only by looking or feeling. Spatial locations are conveyed to us by our sensations. "They *bring* space and all its places to our intellect, and do not derive it thence" (p. 35).

With respect to the less extreme and still very influential view of representational perception, James adopts a similar strategy. Is it true that I am directly aware of subjective representations, sense-data in the mind, and that I must then pass from them to the real things outside the mind? Let us take my red covered couch, or let the reader take some large object that he can now perceive. Let us turn to this object, look at it, feel it, and then dwell on this for a moment, while listening to James. "I cannot frame to myself an idea, however imaginary, of any feeling which I could ever possibly have got from it except the feeling of the same big extended sort of outward fact which I now perceive" (pp. 31–32). I do not see a sense-datum in me or in my mind. I see a large object outside of me in its place against the wall. "So far is it from being true that our first way of feeling things is the feeling of them as subjective or mental, that the exact opposite seems rather to be the truth" (p. 32).

The child's original experiences are objective. It is only later that he develops an awareness of himself as a self. The child is aware of its mother and of external objects before it knows its own name. So as James says, "our earliest, most instinctive, least developed kind of consciousness is the objective kind; and only as reflection becomes developed do we become aware of an inner world at all" (p. 32). The representational theory of perception is false. But while James' criticism of this view and the even more extreme "projection" theory is well taken, certain traces of it still remain in the *Principles*. From "one point of view *we* may say that a sensation is in the same place with the brain" (p. 34). In spite of the new direction in which his thought is moving, he does not yet reject the notion of "thoughts and memories" as "copies of sensations with their intensity greatly reduced" (p. 74, quotation from Münsterberg). It was not until the *Essays in Radical Empiricism*, as we shall see, (*cf. infra*, pp. 375 ff.), that he arrived at a clear and decisive formulation of a non-representational theory.

Let us now turn to the first theory, that of simple ideas. Here it must be granted that there is a certain truth in the empiricist contention that we may find elements in our perception, like hot, red, noise, and hard, which are ultimate and irreplaceable. I can know these only by becoming directly acquainted with them, and no kind of theory, or explanation, can take their place. No one can explain to a blind man the sensory meaning of light. But several other aspects of the theory of simple ideas are quite mistaken.

First, as we have seen, these simple sensations are not ideas in the mind. Either they are qualities present in certain objects—and James argues that even pain is an object of this kind—or they are the states of mind through which we become acquainted with these qualities more or less alone, with a minimum *knowledge about* their relations to other qualities and things. But this is a limit which can never be achieved. As James says, "*a pure sensation is an abstraction*" (II, 3). In adult life, we never find it alone, but always as a part of a more complex perception—a hot teakettle on the stove, a roaring thunder in the sky. These objects are perceived in relation to other things, in or out of their places in the world. They are "classed, located, measured, compared, assigned to a function, etc., etc." (p. 1) not by reason, but primarily by perception, with or without the aid of language.

Since we cannot classify and compare something that is not known already, we may follow the empiricists in inferring a primitive state of knowledge by acquaintance alone. But such knowledge is not of a single quality, nor of a mere set of such qualities, for even the simplest form of sensation requires not only a figure but a ground. The first infantile experience, before anything is clearly focused and before any categories are explicitly present, will nevertheless involve the fringes of a world ground. Or as James puts it, *"the first sensation which an infant gets is for him the Universe"* (p. 8). In this experience which might "be better expressed by the bare interjection 'lo!', . . . all the 'categories of the understanding' [objectivity, unity, substantiality, causality] are contained"—*implicitly,* as we may add. All his later experiences, whether they be perceptual, linguistic, practical, or theoretical, develop continuously out of this. As James says, "here the young knower meets and greets his world". There is no world ground in the intellectualist and analytic doctrines of the traditional empiricists.

And here we may note another error of this tradition. As the primitive knowledge by acquaintance develops into a perception which classifies and places the thing in the world, the original units of sensation do not remain the same. The red of my couch cover is not the same as the red of the cloud in the sunset (p. 27). The color itself is affected by its contrast with other colors (pp. 13 ff.). Sensations are not "immutable psychic things which coexist with higher mental functions". When perceived together in an ordered world, they are found to be different. My red covered couch is more than a combination of immutable visual and tactile ideas. The perceived thing has a unity which pervades its several qualities.

None of this is found in the reductive empiricist analysis into the elements of what is analyzed. Furthermore, it ignores the fringes of the world-field, and the new meanings discovered by perceptual discrimination and comparison. These are facts which may be revealed and verified by phenomenological description. Hence the traditional theory is mistaken. The objects of perception are not reducible to simple elements which remain the same in their various combinations.

This brings us now to the second theory, that of automatic association. Here James' fascination with brain processes leads him to make too many concessions. He accepts the habitual retention of brain-path connections, and still uses the word *association* in its traditional sense. But it is clear that his understanding of perception is moving in another direction to which this brain physiology is subordinate. What we perceive is always a *thing* which is identified, distinguished from other things, and assigned a place in the sensible world by the processes of discrimination and comparison (pp. 76–81). It is important to recognize that these processes go on, at least in a germinal form, at the pre-linguistic level of perception, and that they are not automatic. Thus, there is nothing in the thought of one shade of blue which requires us to think of another similar shade. Such comparisons are not produced without "some general purpose" in mind (I, 579). "There is no elementary tendency of pure qualities to awaken their similars" (p. 579). Brain processes are, no doubt, involved. But in James' terminology, they are not merely physical, but psycho-physical in character. Here also the causal theory, derived from traditional empiricism, is oversimple and reductive.

Imagination

This brings us to the topic of imagination. James sharply rejects Hume's view that centrally aroused images are only fainter copies of perceptions. This doctrine, he says, is "an exquisite example of the way in which a man will be blinded by *a priori* theories to the most flagrant facts" (II, 46). The object that I perceive is physically present. It "has a plastic reality and outwardness which the imagined object wholly lacks" (p. 70). My attention is directed outward from the sense organ, whereas in imagination it "feels as if drawn backwards to the brain" (p. 70). If there were no qualitative differences between the two experiences, there should be a border area where we could not tell whether we were hearing a faint sound, or imagining a strong one. But such is not the case. Furthermore, I can imaginatively refer to a sound much louder than the faint one I am actually hearing. Of course, our perceptions may be deceived, as when musicians, after the *pianissimo* has been reached, continue to bow as if still playing. But such mistakes can be corrected by a concentration of attention. They involve a failure to grasp a qualitative difference which can be clarified by phenomenological analysis, but which must be felt directly to be understood.

James calls our attention with special care to another aspect of what we may call the copy theory of imagination. If an image is a mental replica of a perception, we should be able to see in it every aspect of its original in full detail. But this is not the case. "Hume surely had images of his own works without seeing distinctly every word and letter upon the pages which floated before his mind's eye" (p. 46). Or as Sartre and Merleau-Ponty have pointed out,[2] one cannot count the pillars of the Pantheon while imagining it in Bordeaux. In his examination of the reports of different individuals, James brings out this vagueness, as well as the radical differences in habits of imagining (pp. 49, 53, 57). He also calls attention to the ease with which verbal references are confused with visual pictures (pp. 57–58). There is a basic similarity between the functions of so-called imagery and those of language. Much that we attribute to sensory imagery is probably semi-articulate, verbal reference of some kind.

Space and Motion

James was profoundly interested in space, and his chapter (XX) on this topic is the longest in his text. We shall have to single out those points which are of special interest in the light of later phenomenological research. A vague feeling of volume is found in every original sensation. "We call the reverberations of a thunderstorm more voluminous than the squeaking of a slate-pencil; the entrance into a warm bath gives our skin a more massive feeling than the prick of a pin; a little neuralgic pain, fine as a cobweb, in the face, seems less extensive than the heavy soreness of a boil or the vast discomfort of a colic or a

---

[2] *Cf.* M. Merleau-Ponty, *The Primacy of Perception and Other Essays*, tr. W. Cobb *et al.*, Northwestern University Press, 1964, p. 74.

lumbago; and a solitary star looks smaller than the noonday sky" (p. 134). A direct feeling of volume is also found in the sensations derived from our inner organs. Thus the whole body is spatially sensed in nausea, fever, and heavy fatigue. "Our entire cubic content seems then sensibly manifest to us as such, and feels much larger than any local pulsation, pressure, or discomfort" (p. 135). Since this spatial feeling is an aspect of all sensory experience, James does not hesitate to call it "the original sensation of space" (p. 135). It is, at first, vague and indeterminate. It is only later on, with the aid of "imagination, association, attention, and selection", that these volumes are subdivided and ordered (p. 145).

At first, each distinct sense has its own world of space, and to some degree each of these continues to retain its own autonomy. But by the felt motions of the living body in dealing with stable things, I come to correlate these different spaces together (pp. 182, 188). Thus I can see my fingers touching the visual surface of this pencil in my hand, and feel that the tactual and visual volumes coincide. Through experiences of this kind, we order the different spaces of the different senses into the all-encompassing but loosely organized single space in which we move and live. As over against the pure extensions of geometry, this is space oriented with respect to the different directions of in front and behind, up and down, right and left.

Kant denies that these orientations are derived from categories of the understanding. So he refers them to direct intuition (Anschauung), and speaks of them as sensations (Empfindungen).[3] So far James is in thorough agreement. But he cannot follow Kant in supposing that these differing directions can be explained by an "extrinsic total space". They refer rather to the mobile orientation of the living body. The direction towards which it faces is in front; what lies in back behind. As we have seen, what is to the right and left become generalized on our maps as East and West. There is no need of supposing

[3] Prolegomena, sec. 12.

a total objective space in the manner of Kant. As James says, (II, 151, note) "relation to our own body is enough".

He radically rejects Berkeley's idea that visual space is originally only two-dimensional, and that the third dimension is a projection based on tactual sensations. "It is impossible to lie on one's back on a hill, to let the empty abyss of blue fill one's whole visual field, and to sink deeper and deeper into the merely sensational mode of consciousness regarding it, without feeling that an indeterminate, palpitating, circling depth is as indefeasibly one of its attributes as its breadth" (pp. 212–13). He even suggests that of the three dimensions, depth is the most original and even the measure of the others (pp. 213–14), a notion which is also found in Merleau-Ponty.[4]

We can only mention briefly James' criticism of the intellectualistic view that before we can perceive motion, we must first know the *terminus a quo*, the *terminus ad quem*, and the distance between the two. He calls this an example of the psychologist's fallacy, and rejects it on phenomenological grounds (pp. 171 ff.). It may hold true of very slow motions, like that of the sun through the sky. First seeing it to the East in the morning, and then to the West at sunset, I may infer that, in the meantime, it must have passed over my head. But I cannot infer something with which I am not in some sense already familiar. So James defends the notion, also held by other psychologists, that motion is directly perceived, and describes many examples supported by experimental evidence and disciplined interpretation. He also calls our attention to the importance of the sensory feeling that dwells in certain moving parts of the body, in exploring the shapes and sizes of things (pp. 175 ff.). We do not discover these sizes and shapes as passive spectators, but as active, moving bodies, who explore things by covering them with our gaze, and by fingering, thumbing, and manipulating them. This suggestion has recently been developed with noteworthy results by Dr. Erwin Straus.[5]

[4] *Phenomenology of Perception*, tr. Smith, p. 256.
[5] *Cf.* "The Upright Posture," *Psychiatric Quarterly*, 26 (1952), 529 ff.

The Pre-reflective World

James unfortunately was not able to stimulate his philosophical colleagues in America to look around them and to see. They preferred to argue and to speculate. But as he pointed out, it is only sensation and perception that end such argument (I, 221). He himself had a remarkable talent for discernment, and at the same time a great gift for saying what he saw in penetrating descriptions. Once we read one of these, the thing becomes so clear that it often seems obvious, and the theoretically trained mind especially will tend to pass it by as being unworthy of disciplined reflection. This, however, is a tragic mistake, for many of the basic problems of epistemology and metaphysics are concerned with the nature of experience. If any verifiable answers, or even partial answers are to be found, they will come only from a careful reflection on experience as we live it through. In the chapters we have just reviewed, James arrived at certain tentative conclusions, based on observation, with a very wide import. If his observation is to be trusted, what then is the nature of the pre-reflective world of sense? We may perhaps summarize these results as follows.

From the very beginning, this world is ordered around a hard core of external and internal sensation. These sensations of light, sound, pain, etc., are directed to isolated spatial centers, whose relations are not brought out. They come to us as bald facts which simply occur. We feel them to be real and independent of our desires. While we have them, they are simply there in a naked facticity that we can do nothing to alter. They are never experienced alone, but always as figures on a ground. The first such fact that the child can focus, whatever it may be, is centered on a field of fringes that vaguely encompasses the germs of all that he will ever come to feel and know. His living body is the centre of this field, and the two are in constant flux. The living body never returns to a state it was in before, and no condition of the field ever exactly repeats itself. What we call *experience* is a history in which the desires of the child become purposes, and the field becomes more or less organized into a world of things.

The child's attention is outwardly directed towards the sources of sensations that appear in the spatial volumes that he hears, and sees, and tastes. They attract his desires, and he believes in their reality with a primitive belief (*Urdoksa*) that leads him to act and to explore them. This belief remains with him as long as he lives, and underlies everything that he later thinks and does, including his most radical questioning of them, even of the belief itself. As he fumbles with these sources of sensation, gazes at them, fingers them, tastes them, and feels them, he finds that certain feelings continue to come from certain voluminous regions, and that these regions are occupied by things with sensible properties. He learns to seek for these things when he needs them, and to derive their several satisfactions from them.

This process of perceiving things is constantly revised, and is never totally finished. What at first looks like an orange will turn out to be a ball, and what seems to be a small potato will turn out to be an egg (II, 110). The plasticity of the nervous system and the law of habit formation play an essential role in this learning process, but it is not altogether automatic. It is not ideas in the brain, or the mind, that are associated, but the real sources of sensation in the spaces within him and around him. These germinal things are always individual and changing. Nevertheless they are vaguely discriminated and compared. Pricking pins are similar and to be avoided. They are different from the rattle or the soft hair of a doll. One sensation arouses the expectation of others, and some sense of regular order is developed. In his specious present, the child sees a meaningful event, like the coming of his mother, or feels himself alone, and gives a wailing response.

Thus the vague horizon of fringes is partially clarified into different regions of bed, playroom, and kitchen, each filled with particular things that are at least partially identified at different times. This world is not subjective, for no personal self has yet arisen, and the child does not yet know exactly who he is. But neither is it objective, for language is only beginning, and the objective things are not yet clearly identified. It is a fluid, shifting world of bodily feelings, incipient things, and places. This horizon of meaning is the background for all purposive action and thought. It is taken for granted by science, and by the most radical philosophical questioning. We believe it with a trust that attaches to our life as long as we feel ourselves living. It is based on a sheer facticity, or feeling of thatness, from which the objective world of language grows. This feeling of alien being is close to the child and constantly encountered. It is expressed in his earliest cries of surprise and bewilderment, and in his first questioning of the obvious. He is continually stumbling over half-formed things which appear in no clearly outlined horizon of meaning. But as this order develops and articulates, with the coming of language, such experiences become more rare, and things appear with fringes of meaning from which they can hardly be separated.

Nevertheless the sensory core of facticity still remains, and in certain unusual situations, when things are torn from their contexts and cease for a time to be things, sheer being, or what we know as *the absurd,* is brought into the light. Sartre has given us descriptions of this feeling of bare being in his book *La Nausée.*[6] But in the *Principles,* James also has described these experiences where meaning is lost, and we are confronted with the naked sensation of an isolated facticity. As we have seen (*supra,* p. 68), a single word is surrounded by a halo of meaning that pervades the sentence as a whole and all of its parts. But if we tear this word from its context, the meaning is lost. As James says (II, 80–81): "if we look at an isolated printed word and repeat it long enough, it ends by assuming an entirely unnatural aspect. Let the reader try this with any word on this page. He will soon begin to wonder if it can possibly be the word he has been using all his life with that meaning. It stares at him from the page like a glass eye, with no speculation

---

[6] *Cf. Nausea,* tr. Alexander, Norfolk, Conn., 1949, pp. 170–82.

in it. Its body is indeed there, but its soul has fled. It is reduced, by this new way of attending to it, to its sensational nudity". A similar effect is achieved if we look at a landscape with our heads upside down. Many children love to do this, since their sensibility is still fresh and open to pure quality. According to James' account, "perception is to a certain extent baffled by this manoeuvre; gradations of distance and other space-determinations are made uncertain; the reproductive or associative processes, in short, decline; and, simultaneously with their diminution, the colors grow richer and more varied, and the contrasts of light and shade more marked" (p. 81). The same thing happens when we turn a picture upside down. "We lose much of its meaning, but, to compensate for the loss, we feel more freshly the value of the mere tints and shadings, . . ." James then gives a final and more striking example. If we lie on the floor and look up at the mouth of a person talking above us, a remarkable change occurs. "His lower lip here takes the habitual place of the upper one upon our retina, and seems animated by the most extraordinary and unnatural mobility, a mobility which now strikes us because . . . we get it as a naked sensation and not as part of a familiar object perceived" (p. 81).

These sensations, which give us a direct acquaintance with the alien beings inside and outside of us, are the central points around which the field of perception is organized by our unverbalized activities. James does not hesitate to call it a world, "the world of sense" (p. 292). This field is composed of various spatial volumes loosely organized into a single space. All the things in this field, including our bodies, are in a continuous flux through the specious present, though once they have passed by, some of them can be remembered, and others in the future can be anticipated before they arrive. These things are roughly compared and contrasted. But in their constant flow, nothing is absolutely fixed. All of them are individual, and before language, the universal has not appeared. Hence their boundaries are vague, and the classifications confused, and shifting from one situation to another.

These meanings are in the sensible world. They are attached

to concrete things and activities from which they cannot be separated. There is no universe of discourse where they can be verbally fixed and clarified. Perceptual meanings are centered in an individual body, and colored by the accidents of its private history. While abstraction and universality are only implicit, precise communication is impossible. Throughout his waking life, the individual is concerned with himself and surrounding things, and it is only through imagination that he can get at any distance from them. He is struggling in a vast confusion of unformed and half-formed meanings, attached to things which are perceived as similar, but which are never precisely cognized and identified as the same.

We have noted James' view that this sensory knowledge which we attain by direct acquaintance can never be replaced, and never even adequately expressed by any amount of verbal or conceptual knowledge about the fact. Later on when he read Bergson, he felt a profound sympathy for the French philosopher's thesis that the given data of consciousness are completely opaque to the static concepts of language. James could accept a large part of this theory. Our abstract thinking slurs over the individual differences with which we are acquainted in the concrete. Our fixed concepts reduce the flux of life to a series of motionless snapshots. Language arises from this flowing world of perception, and translates it into its fixed meanings that can be repeatedly recognized as the same. As we shall see, James calls this the *conceptual world*. But the *primordial world* of perception remains in the background. Every sentence begins with a denomination (a subject, name, or pronoun) that is already understood. Whatever we succeed in saying emerges from a horizon that is already known but remains unsaid. So James cannot go the whole way with Bergson.

The two worlds are not completely opposed. The world of sense is not wholly structureless and ineffable. It contains half-formed schemes and patterns that are ready to be expressed. It is only in this way that we can understand those strange intentions *to-say-so-and-so* which arise from the perceptual realm (I, 253). We do not know precisely what we mean as yet. But neither are we wholly ignorant. When the words come, we know, in the mode of feeling, which ones to accept and which to reject (p. 253). This hazy, flowing world is already half-human. But after we find the words, if we are at all critical, we feel their helplessness. We know there are things we have not expressed.

How do we know this?

Only by a mode of perceptual feeling that in its own dim way reflects upon itself. But this reflection is bound to the concrete situation, and is swept along in its constant flux. It is vague, inarticulate, and never returns to the same. So it calls for the gaining of distance, for the objective, for an escape from its isolation in the concrete, for perfect abstraction, universality, and communication. All these *functions,* as James calls them, are achieved, within certain limits, in language and the higher mental functions which language makes possible. So it is to these functions that we must now turn in the next chapters.

Chapter Eight

❀

Reasoning[1]

I think that we can best gain a clear view of James' analysis of reasoning, or thinking, as he sometimes calls it (*cf.* II, 325, 333) by contrasting it with those commoner forms which usually go by the same names and with which the authentic modes are often confused. Reasoning always proceeds from a definite interest, or purpose of some kind, which may be simply the purpose of understanding some object, or region, of the world. Whatever this purpose may be, it is never forgotten, but constantly held in mind as guiding the process from beginning to end. Popular thinking, on the other hand, may take the form of an idle daydreaming which has no set purpose, or it may wander incoherently from one purpose to another.

A second difference concerns the distinction between essence and accident, to which James devotes considerable attention. Popular thinking focuses now this and now that prominent aspect of an object without separating what is essential from the accidental. Disciplined thinking, on the other hand, con-

---

[1] We have already considered *conceptions* and *linguistic analysis* in Chapter V, pp. 128 ff. These pages should be read as part of the essential background for this chapter.

stantly rejects what is only incidental and circumstantial, in order to focus that aspect of the object in question which is essential for the purpose in hand. Any object may be regarded from a great variety of differing points of view, and what is essential for one purpose may be only incidental, or quite irrelevant, for another. "The essence of a thing is that one of its properties which is so *important for my interests* that, in comparison with it I may neglect the rest" (p. 335).

James makes many statements of this sort which have usually been interpreted as a complete relativism which would deny any final or total truth. This, I believe, is a misinterpretation. For any given purpose, certain aspects of the thing are really essential and others not. James is keenly aware of the vast variety of partial purposes, each of which takes itself so seriously as to be ready to wipe out the rest as inessential. But what if my purpose is simply to understand the whole world as it actually is? James never rules this out. In fact, in his important footnote to Volume II, page 336, he definitely speaks of it. If we could ever approximate such an understanding, we would find that what was really essential was what agreed with the purpose of the world as a whole.

If we could arrive at such understanding, we might see that one purpose, and one conception, might be truer than another. James is sceptical of ever achieving such knowledge except in fleeting glimpses. But he never abandons it. He is very much aware of the danger of exalting some partial purpose, with its partial conceptions, to an absolute status. Such an absolute is beyond us. But some of our partial views may come closer to it than others. In our struggles to attain such closer approximations, it is needful for us to bear this total truth in mind. Otherwise our efforts may falter. "The only real truth about the world, apart from particular purposes, is the *total* truth" (p. 336, note). This is James' last word on the subject in his *Psychology*.

In popular thinking, we do not distinguish clearly between the essential and the accidental. But according to James, we can go further than this. We can also say that abstract elements are lacking. We tell stories, and recite incidents that are associated with the immediate situation. The terms which are "coupled together" in this "irresponsible" way are "empirical concretes, not abstractions" (p. 325). A sunset may call up the vessel's deck from which I saw one last summer, the companions of my voyage, my arrival in port, etc. After recalling one such incident, we soon find ourselves "thinking of another, to which we have been lifted along, we hardly know how" (p. 325). The distinguishing feature of responsible reasoning is its capacity to focus abstract similarities between concrete objects which are not habitually associated. Thus "if habitual contiguities predominate, we have a prosaic mind; if rare contiguities, or similarities, have free play, we call the person fanciful, poetic, or witty" (p. 315). If he learns to proceed by abstraction in a disciplined way, paying constant attention to the facts, he will be able to reason.

It is important to recognize that this does not imply the loss of all sense for the concrete. For James, poetry and philosophy are not opposed, as in the Platonic tradition. They are closely related, but divergent, enterprises, each of which, in its own way, escapes from the tyranny of accidental association. The reasoner, however, grasps the exact respects (similarities) which bind disparate phenomena together. He does not, therefore, merely bring the two together. He knows the reason *why*. This makes him a reasoner, and marks him off from the popular thinker, who never frees himself from the accidents of contiguity.

This ability to give reasons, instead of analogous examples, marks off disciplined from childish and primitive thinking. Thus "in all primitive literature, in all savage oratory, we find persuasion carried on exclusively by parables and similes . . ." (p. 363). Instead of giving an abstract reason, the undeveloped mind will simply give another concrete instance. As the Platonic dialogues make so clearly evident, we all share in this tendency towards unspecified association. When thinking in this way, "we answer the question: *'Why is snow white?'* by saying, *'For the same reason that soap-suds or whipped eggs are white'"*. As James puts it, "instead of giving the *reason* for a fact, we give another *example* of the same fact" (pp. 363–64). It is this inability to abstract which leads the primitive man to think primarily in terms of "entire things" rather than abstract characters and structures. Hence "the primeval man will say, not 'the bread is hard,' but 'the bread is stone': not 'the face is round,' but 'the face is moon'; not 'the fruit is sweet,' but 'the fruit is sugar cane'" (p. 364).

The first words are neither particular nor general, but *vaguely* concrete, in the sense that the adjectival quality is not yet abstracted as such, but is thought of as merging with the total thing, and is still referred to as a noun. Nevertheless some degree of abstraction does occur in such human thinking, as in its base, perception, for a vague similarity of *round* is recognized. James suggests that in animals this degree of abstraction may be absent. The dog may be able to associate two concrete situations that happen to occur together, like the master with his hat on, and the master going out. If a single quality stands out alone, like a sound or a smell, it is always something instinctively exciting and in line with the animal's needs (p. 360). But the noting of abstract similarities between objects which are neutral, or remote, is beyond its capabilities. Such abstraction, which frees man from the domination of external contingencies, "must in the brute always remain drowned, swamped in the total phenomenon . . ." (p. 360). Rational analysis is superior to intuitive thinking, and certainly "*represents* the higher stage" (p. 363).

But this does not justify us in separating the two. If abstraction is to become fruitful and illuminating, it must rest on a fertile imagination and a sense for the concrete facts. "Furnishing parallel cases is the necessary first step towards abstracting the reason imbedded in them all" (p. 364). Without this, abstract reasoning may become either fantastic, or a dry and tedious verbalizing of the obvious. Neither reasoning alone nor intuition alone is apt to be fruitful. It is the patterns lying in what at first seem to be disjointed facts that the phenomenologist needs to recognize. And for this, both types of thinking are required, a feeling for the concrete cases, and a grasp of the abstract structures by which they may be fitted together.

A balancing of the two is very hard to achieve and, as James remarks, "rarely are both sorts of intellect . . . found in conjunction" (p. 362). He then cites Plato as one who, as a literary artist, combined both talents in his greatest works.

We have already noted James' view that our first experiences are outwardly directed towards the object, while our intentions are reduced to vague surrounding fringes. In the animal, attention is fixed and focused on certain objects by hereditary needs. In both cases, the freedom of action is restricted, because no distance from the object is achieved. The animal is like a man who is constantly obsessed, first with this and then with that, but never establishes a distance between himself and the objects with which he is exclusively concerned. These objects dominate his attention, and leave little room for his own acts.

Man, on the other hand, as we have seen, is a hesitating animal (cf. supra, pp. 16–17). "His character is still gelatinous, uncertain what shape to assume, 'trying it on' in every direction" (II, 369), as successive objects fade off into the fringes, and the sign functions in which they originate. The animal also uses signs. He yelps and begs. But "each sign is drowned in its import, and never awakens other signs and other imports in juxtaposition" (p. 357). He cannot gain sufficient distance to become aware of them as signs. Hence he is incapable of language, though in certain cases, "the particular sign may be consciously noticed by the animal, as distinct from the particular thing signified, and will thus, so far as it goes, be a true manifestation of language" (p. 356).

But in man we find a remarkable difference. "He has a deliberate intention to apply a sign to everything." Because he can abstract the notion of sign as such, "the linguistic impulse is with him generalized and systematic". He expects every object to have a name, which will apply to it, whether it be present or absent. Even when the object is present, the linguistic sign will enable him to imagine or conceive it as absent. At this distance, he can brood and hesitate over the object, whatever it may be. In the animal's mind, there is not only an absence of language in the strict sense, but an "utter absence of fancy" as well.

What, then, is the ultimate meaning of reasoning in the life of man? James is not a good summarizer, and at the end of the chapter, instead of giving a clear summary of his complex analysis, he seems to do the very opposite by laying emphasis again on the importance of feeling in the life of reason. We have already commented on this. But now let us attempt to give our own summary. It is through selective attention to the very same meanings in the phenomena that we escape, within certain limits, from the bondage of habit, which binds us to sequences of external objects merely as they happen to occur. Selective attention, the return to a meaning that is one and the same by different acts of conceiving, the analysis of concrete objects into their component elements, and the discovery of differences and similarities in them—these are the essential aspects of reasoning. These activities are not performed by a separate, spiritual principle, or soul. As James sees it, they are performed by the living brain. But in any case, their existence is unquestionable.

They actually appear in every instance of rational thought. They are subject to many distortions and misuses. But in so far as they are carefully worked out in relation to the concrete phenomena, they offer us the possibility of escaping, to some degree, from our natural bondage to external manipulation and the accidents of history. Without them, our habits are conditioned by the unanalyzed objects set before us, and their incidental associations. But with them, we are able to analyze these vague objects, and to discover the patterns which really relate them, and the contrasts which really divide them. Instead of associating them in ways that are forced on us from the outside, we can now "associate" them by real similarities and differences, which we ourselves can see from the inside.

Many writers think of such a seen similarity as though it were a causal agent "able to push objects before the mind". But as James says, "this is quite unintelligible" in the light of the facts (I, 591). Beings, no doubt, may exist without being perceived. But their similarities and differences do not exist before they are seen. They are not fictions. They are *entia rationis,* as James says (p. 461), which come into existence only after the fact of their being seen. As he puts it, "the similarity of two things does not exist till both things are there [before the mind], —it is meaningless to talk of it as an *agent of production* of anything. . . . It is a relation which the mind perceives after the fact . . ." (p. 591). Does this mean that the things were dissimilar before the mind brought them into the light? The answer is no! In this condition, we now know that they "were" similar. Before being singled out and compared, they were enveloped in a darkness which protected them from any recognition of either sameness or diversity.

It is this gathering of things together, this bringing them into the light, which enables us to give them meaning, and to see them as they are in the world. It is through this finding of meaning that we may hope to order these indifferent beings into a human world, and to transform a senseless succession of accidents into a meaningful history. As James says specifically (p. 424), it is through reasoning that a man becomes *compos sui* (responsible), that is, able to act and to think on his own behalf in a world that is his own. And in so far as we become responsible, we become free. As we shall see, James never abandoned this view of human freedom as being basically rooted not in an indeterminacy of the will, but in a freedom of the mind.

The Feeling of Rationality

Having now considered various aspects of the intellectual life, the construction of ideal objects and systems, the ultimate existential *a priori,* and the close connection between reasoning and freedom, the time has now come for us to see how James gathered these component elements together in a total conception of thinking. What is the path that may lead us to such an integral conception? And what is its nature, once we have arrived? The answer to these questions will be found in an early essay, "The Sentiment of Rationality" (SR), part of which was written in 1877–79 while he was working on the *Principles*. In this essay, as in so many of the others, he reconsiders the detailed descriptions of his major work, and attempts to bring them together in a meaningful interpretation of the whole. As we have seen, James recognizes that the facts have already been selected on the basis of an implicit interpretation which, in turn, must be tested in the light of the empirical facts. Hence, in order to gain a proper understanding of James' thought, it is essential to hold both in mind. So now, having examined certain salient facts about reasoning, let us turn to the total interpretation which is given in the essay as read to the Harvard Philosophical Club in 1880.

The title is significant. James is not concerned with arriving at a conceptual definition of rationality, *knowledge about* from a detached point of view, for this would not get to the root of the matter. It would presuppose the actual experience which we are trying to define. What is this original experience, as we live it through? How do we first sense that there is something running through a wide range of phenomena; describing, speculating, thinking, that can be conceptually defined? How do we first recognize this common factor? James' answer is clear. It is by direct acquaintance, the feeling of being rational, that we first get an inkling of what *it* means. Nothing can take the place of this existential feeling. As James says, "the entire man, who feels all needs by turns, will take nothing as an equivalent for life but the fulness of living itself" (SR, p. 69). And he is right. If no one had ever actually felt himself thinking rationally, these words would be empty of meaning, and all disputes concerning them would be without a ground.

This feeling of direct acquaintance covers a vast range of phenomena. It covers them all with an implicit meaning. But this meaning is vague, and calls for further clarification. Can we break it down into intelligible elements? What are its marks?

With what is it contrasted? These questions are the beginning of a conceptual discrimination and comparison. They can be answered only by conceptual thought, not working alone, however, but only in constant touch with the lived experience, in the manner of that concrete thinking of which we have just been speaking. James now gives such an analysis. Does it really lead us to the experience as we live it? Do these phenomena really reverberate and answer back? Are they really clarified? Does the analysis have a real ground, or is it merely verbal? This is for the reader to say after he has tried to free his mind of prejudice, and recaptured some examples of his own original experiences.

Here is the analysis James presents. The feeling of rationality is "a strong feeling of ease, peace, rest . . ." (p. 63). This attends a command of the subject which enables us to pass from one topic to another relevant topic with an uninhibited "fluency". As James puts it, "as soon, in short, as we are enabled from any cause whatever to think with perfect fluency, the thing we think of seems to us *pro tanto* rational. Whatever modes of conceiving the cosmos facilitate this fluency, produce the sentiment of rationality" (p. 64). But another mark is also essential. The fluent reeling off of a pattern of meaning is not sufficient. There must be a congruence of meaning and being, with no forcing or constraint. In so far as we have to insist that the meaning is there by proofs, derived from sources external to the thing itself, we are not wholly rational. Our formulations must simply show the thing as it is, and let it speak for itself. So James says, "conceived in such modes, being vouches for itself and needs no further philosophic formulation" (p. 64).

But one or more beings, or regions, are insufficient. "Universality or extensiveness" is another, third mark (p. 65). Rational meaning requires unity. "The facts of the world in their sensible diversity are always before us, but our theoretic need is that they should be conceived in a way that reduces their manifoldness to simplicity" (p. 65). James uses the word *gather* in this description. Rationality is a gathering process which brings beings together, and gives them a place in a meaningful world. Fluency in the development of a pattern of meaning, vouched for by being itself as present in the flesh, and worked out on the most extensive scale, are the three common marks of rational thought.

But now we must take note of a point of contrast that is essential to this feeling of rationality. The "uninhibited" ease and "fluency", which belongs to rational thought, is a feeling of "relief" from doubt and hesitation. In its most distinctive manifestations, it is, in fact, a feeling of "transition from a state of puzzle and perplexity to rational comprehension . . ." (p. 63). As is true of all activities, they become most intensively conscious when they are obstructed. It is then "that we can be said to strive, to crave, or to aspire" (p. 64). When fluency is recovered, conscious feeling becomes less intense. But even in the uninhibited flow of meaningful thought, a sense of contrast still remains. Hence there are good grounds for holding that the feeling of rationality is constituted "by the absence of any feeling of irrationality" (pp. 63–64). This is consistent with James' respect for dialectic as a way of describing real transitions that are found in experience.

But concepts do not move and turn into their opposites, unless they become confused. It is their function to bring clarity, and in order to do this, they must maintain their distance, and continue to mean the same. We cannot assume, once and for all, that ideal constructions of reason coincide with the real beings we confront in experience. Such extravagant claims will lead only to a blind imperialism of the mind. James makes this very clear in his essay "On some Hegelisms" (OSH, cf. pp. 271–73, 291–93), which he wrote at this same time. Reason is not the original architect of the world in which we live. There is a prior world of existence with which we are directly acquainted. Reason may take over this foundation, reform it, and build upon it. But in order to do this effectively, it must first accept it, and understand it as it is. As James says, " 'facts' are the bounds of human knowledge, set for it, not by it" (p. 271).

The Limits of Reason

A radically empirical philosophy which recognizes the pre-reflective sources of reason must also recognize its limits. And in the following pages (SR, pp. 66–75), he shows why no genuine empiricism can be unreservedly rationalistic. His argument proceeds along Kantian lines, and we might call this the Kantian, or critical, aspects of James' philosophy which he never abandoned. Reason is not fully free and autonomous. It cannot establish its own beginning, for it comes to itself in a world that is already formed. It cannot lay down the structures of existence *a priori*, for it must first exist before it lays down anything at all. As we have seen (*supra*, pp. 42 ff.), being is not the same as meaning, and being, in the sense of hard, recalcitrant facts, comes first. So the genuine philosopher must pay attention to them. He must look before he speculates, to gain a sense of its sources and limits.

The first of these limits is the defect of abstraction. The theoretical mind is constantly reaching out for similarities, and brings things together under essences, or laws. Who has not, to some degree, felt the delight "of knowing respiration and combustion to be one; of understanding that the balloon rises by the same law whereby the stone sinks . . ." (SR, p. 66). But there are also differences. The balloon is not a stone. Our laws and essences are always abstract and partial, "the rest of the living fact being for the time ignored by the classifier. This means that none of our explanations are complete" (p. 67). Furthermore, these essences are static and fixed. In our philosophic moments we may gain a certain peace "by a look at the immutable natures". But this point of view is also only partial. It necessarily misses "the teeming and dramatic richness of the concrete world" (p. 69).

A more basic way of bringing things together is through a unity of purpose, or value, as we call it. Back of every scheme of classification lies "some particular purpose", even though it be the achievement of a unity and simplicity of understanding. But this is only "one of a thousand human purposes" (p. 70). It gives us a theoretic, a philosophic version of the world. But there are also other practical versions of a moral and religious nature, which bring out other aspects of being, relevant to different purposes. Where are we to find the purpose that will suppress nothing and reveal the full richness of the concrete world? No matter which way it turns, when reason becomes self-conscious, it finds itself confronting an irrational element, which it knows it does not assimilate.

The rationalist, of course, will not be satisfied. What then will he say? At this point, James gives a quotation from Bain, who thinks of himself as a scientific empiricist. According to him, "mystery is isolation, exception, or it may be apparent contradiction: the resolution of the mystery is found in assimilation, identity, fraternity. . . . The path of science as exhibited in modern ages is toward generality, wider and wider, until we reach the highest, the widest laws of every department of things; there explanation is finished, mystery ends, perfect vision is gained" (p. 71). In his cogent critique of this conception (pp. 71–75), James develops his own conception of the meaning of empiricism, which is not merely a method of observation to be taken for granted, but a philosophic attitude of a distinctive kind.

Let us suppose, with a rationalist, like Bain, that *per impossibile*, the theoretical mind might succeed in gathering together all the disparate data of experience under a single principle, or law, and so as to present us with a single totality of being. Would such a system be complete? Could the free mind be included within it? Would it, then, give up its seeking, and come to a final rest? James gives a negative answer to these questions.

In the first place, such a system of being cannot be all-inclusive. There is always a beyond that is omitted, but nevertheless surrounds the system, in the form of a nothingness which is radically other, and not included within it. Even though the system be pervaded with the most total necessity, we may still glimpse a nothingness lying beyond, which presents us with a viable alternative. It is this nothingness which enables us to ask, "Why was there anything but nonentity; why just this universal datum and not another?" (p. 72). It thus reduces the most general principles, and the most necessary relations to an underlying, existential contingency. As Schopenhauer has said, "the non-existence of this world is just as possible as its existence" (p. 72). With respect to the act of being, in its act, the question *why* cannot receive a final, theoretical answer. James calls this "the ontological wonder-sickness", and remarks, in comment, that "the notion of nonentity may thus be called the parent of the philosophic craving in its subtilest and profoundest sense" (p. 72).

Hegel made a great attempt to bring nothingness into a unitary system of being. He tried to show "that nonentity and concrete being are linked together by a series of identities of a synthetic kind", which bind "everything conceivable into a unity, with no outlying notion to disturb the free, rotary circulation of the mind within its bounds" (p. 72). This unchecked motion of the endless dialectic bears a certain resemblance to the meaningful fluency of reason. But this is a delusion, for the dialectic lacks a sufficient grounding in particular facts, in beings *as they are*. If we bring James' remarks in "The Sentiment of Rationality" together with his essay "On some Hegelisms" (WBA, pp. 297 ff.), we can state his basic argument against Hegel in the form of a dilemma.

On the one hand, if we really bring something like negativity into the system, then the dialectic, "far from being the self-developing process which Hegel supposes, is really a self-consuming process" (OSH, p. 298, note). No sooner is any actual assertion made, than it is negated, and we pass on to another which is, in turn, negated. This is a mere mixture of being and nothing which bears no real meaning, and points in no determinate direction. It leads us towards an ultimate relativism in which being can no longer be clearly distinguished from nothing, and no one attitude, or position, is less arbitrary than any other. As James says, the only outcome of such a theory is "indifferentism" (p. 298). If he had been able to read Sartre's *Being and Nothingness,* where nothingness is identified with consciousness in the Hegelian manner, he would not have been surprised at the indifferentism in which it culminates. Being no longer "vouches" for any meaning, since such meaning is negated as soon as it appears on the scene. Hence life is a useless passion. This is one horn of the dilemma.

If, on the other hand, as Hegel seems to have maintained, being is manifested in a synthetic advance, and points to a real absolute end, then we are confronted with the original difficulty. Nothingness still lies beyond the system, and mystery remains. We are prompted to ask why this, and not nothing, or otherwise? No answer is forthcoming, except an acceptance of the ultimate datum, which is not essentially "secure from the blighting breath of the ultimate Why?" (SR, p. 73). So we are reduced to contingency again. Mystery is not eliminated. It is merely postponed, and Bain is wrong.

If reason then discovers its own limits, should we then abandon all "theoretic grubbing and brooding" (p. 74)? Is mysticism the answer? Should we seek for those moments of rapture which give some of us, at least, "the peace and knowledge that pass all the argument of the earth"? While he makes no claim to have had such experiences, James does not deny this possibility for others, and always speaks of it with respect.[2] But it suffers from seemingly incurable defects. First, it lacks universality, being available only "for few persons and at few times" (SR, p. 74). And even for those who attain it on rare occasions, it lacks stability, being followed "by fits of reaction and dryness" (p. 75). It has never been formed into a stable procedure, capable of yielding defensible and sharable results. So for most men, at least, we cannot think of it as a substitute for reasoning.

But are these the only two alternatives? Must we choose either an unrestricted rationalism which claims to include all being, and, indeed, everything conceivable within a theoretic system, or a mystical union with being which is beyond all

[2] *Cf. The Varieties of Religious Experience* (VA), Chaps. XVI and XVII.

clarity and intelligible expression? James believes that neither view is really tenable. There is a third alternative that is neither the one nor the other, nor any mere "synthesis" of the two. In "The Sentiment of Rationality", James calls this third position "empiricism", and refers to it not as a mere method but as "the ultimate philosophy" (p. 75). What does this mean?

First of all, it means the need for making distinctions and qualified judgments. The concept of being points to acts of existence which we find both in ourselves and in the stubborn beings, or brute facts, that confront us, which we never completely comprehend. As James puts it, "existence then will be a brute fact to which as a whole the emotion of ontologic wonder shall rightfully cleave, but remain eternally unsatisfied" (p. 75). This element of mystery is not a single whole of unqualified unintelligibility, for singleness and wholeness are rational categories, which we cannot take for granted. It is rather spread out into all the distinct beings which we find in our experience.

When we penetrate into the depths of any one of these "things", we find further facts which we do not understand. Why are they? Why this way and not some other? We do not know! This truth has been seen by the Jobs, and the Hamlets, the sceptics of all the ages. "Then wonderfulness or mysteriousness will be an essential attribute of the nature of things" (p. 75). Does this mean that scepticism-mysticism is the final answer, and that all reasoning is futile? We may get a better sense of James' negative answer to this question, if we now turn to certain passages in his essay "On some Hegelisms".

At the very beginning of the essay, James makes the following basic statement. "To show that the real is identical with the ideal may roughly be set down as the mainspring of philosophic activity" (OSH, p. 264). The "ideal" here stands for a coherent system of meaning and value. The basic aim of all philosophical reflection of whatever variety, rationalism, mysticism, or empiricism, is to do justice to the real facts, but at the same time to fit them together into a pattern that makes sense to us. Some philosophies break down because they fail to fit the particular, brute facts. As we have seen, this is James' most basic criticism of Hegelianism, and of idealism in general. Others break down primarily because, like scepticism and materialism, they give no real place to human aspirations, and make no sense to us. Truth, as we have noted, is the coincidence of meaning with being. James' position is that, among the various philosophical attitudes so far worked out or suggested, radical empiricism is best fitted to achieve this coincidence.

Being must be first lived through, and directly experienced, before it can be conceived. But once the concept has been formed, we tend to think of it as referring to certain basic traits, or properties, possessed in common by all things. This, however, is a mistake which underlies many versions of rationalism. The life-world includes properties and relations. But it cannot be reduced to these. It also includes independent beings which resist our cognitive efforts, and impose themselves upon us stubbornly, without any regard for our concepts or our desires. We are first acquainted with them as hard "brute facts" which simply happen, with no sense of their own. And yet this gives us no right to assume a priori either that they bear an ultimate meaning, or that they are completely irrational, and without sense. As James puts it, they strike us as "arbitrary, foreign, jolting, discontinuous. . . . And yet from out the bosom of it a partial ideality constantly arises which keeps alive our aspiration that the whole may some day be construed in ideal form" (p. 264). They are not a sheer chaos, for, from the first, they are bound together and separated by the orders of space and time, and other patterns. We can truly say that they are open to meaning. But whether they are ultimately meaningful, and how, will not be decided until the end of human history.

On this view, the field of possibility must be sharply distinguished from that of actuality. For example, the former is much wider in range. Divergent possibilities can be readily held together in great synthetic patterns. Thus it is possible for me both to have my cake and eat it, both to enjoy the delights of selfishness and the luxury of altruism at the same time. But as James points out, following Kierkegaard, "the real offers us these terms in the shape of mutually exclusive alternatives of which only one can be true at once; so that we must choose, and in choosing murder one possibility. The wrench is absolute: 'Either —Or!'" (WBA, p. 269). In the world of existence, the law of contradiction must be taken seriously.

And there is no way in which this world of existence can be taken over and subsumed as a possibility among many others, for after a real process begins, it grounds new "logically indeterminate possibilities", which could not have been anticipated. They "forbid there being any equivalent for the happening of it all but the happening itself" (p. 270). Thus the realizing of a possibility always involves more than this possibility: others as well. Hence the finished work is never the same as the blueprint, nor the work of art the same as the first conception of it in the mind of the artist. *Knowledge about* life, no matter how extensive it may be, cannot take the place of one instant of existence, as it is directly lived and felt. So as James says (p. 270), there is "no substitute, in short, for life but the living itself in all its long-drawn weary length and breadth and thickness".

Brute facts, being, comes first. This stubborn, resistant being is given to us as altogether independent of our desires and concepts. "Real being comes, moreover, and goes from any concept at its own sweet will, with no permission asked of the conceiver" (p. 273). This respect for the given facts is a realistic moment in James' thought that goes back to its first origins. It lies at the root of his empiricism, for it is because of this stubbornness of being, this bruteness of the facts that speculation in philosophy is not enough. The real philosopher must also constantly observe and look. Unless he does this at every step of his way, he will end up only by building systems and playing games. He may be agile, clever, and fluent in developing his patterns of meaning. But if he sees nothing, being will not "vouch" for anything he says. As James sees it, Hegel did not look carefully enough at the stubborn facts.

But though Hegel did not often succeed, he was looking for meaning not imposed on the facts, but to be found in the facts. This creative finding is also the aim of James' radical empiricism.

The life-world is not a chaotic manifold. It is given to us originally in the form of certain patterns, like space and time. But as directly perceived, they are vague and confused and desperately in need of conceptual clarification, which is a first task of philosophy. But it faces the danger of working out explanations that are more paradoxical and confused than the original experiences. James finds this in the Hegelian principle of dialectical contradiction, which is supposed to explain the dynamism of history. If we ask Hegel to show us, in detail, how this principle works, he refers us back to some original experience and says "Lo, thus". It is correct to refer us back to experience, in order to show that a genuine clarification has been achieved. But we cannot be helped by a clarification that is more obscure than what it is trying to explain. As James says, "surely such a system of explaining *notum per ignotum,* of making the *explicans* borrow credentials from the *explicand,* and of creating paradoxes and impossibilities where none were suspected, is a strange candidate for the honor of being a complete rationalizer of the world" (pp. 276–77).

This, then, is James' conception of the basic beliefs of empirical philosophy. The most basic of these is negative. The empirical philosopher does not believe that he is the lord and master of the being he is trying to understand. Nevertheless, he is devoting his full energies and capacities to the attempt to understand it as it is. But he does not feel that his success must be guaranteed from the beginning. He does not find his understanding to be completely autonomous, nor capable of making an absolute beginning by itself and out of itself alone. The beginning has already been made; the world is already there before he starts to think about it; and he finds himself already existing in it. He knows that this existence is irreplaceable, and can never be exhaustively comprehended by conceptual meaning. Nevertheless it bears meaning here and there, and the empirical thinker trusts that more meaning can be found. So he devotes himself to the slow and patient process of interpretation—the finding of meaning. But though meanings need to be elaborated for themselves, the ultimate test lies in being. So he is constantly looking back and observing to find if his meanings are real. Being comes first. This is the essential core of empirical procedure as James understands it.

Meaning is not enough. It must be found in something beyond, in life, in existence, in brute facts which resist us, but at the same time lead us on. So we may now return to "The Sentiment of Rationality", and the summary statement concerning mysticism with which our investigation of empirical philosophy began. There is a surd factor, a mystical element in the beings with seen, this wonderfulness or mysteriousness will be for him an essential attribute of the nature of things (*supra*, p. 190, 208). Hence, as Gabriel Marcel has said, the empirical philosopher, concerned with being, is not trying to solve problems once and for all. These involve meanings which lie on the surface of things.

He is facing mysteries which can never be solved in this way. And yet this does not mean that no light can be shed, no advance can be made. Being belongs to a different order from that of meaning, and gives rise to a different dialectic tension. It is neither fully intelligible, nor fully irrational and absurd. We find rather that it is open to our meanings, both resisting them, and at the same time luring us on. Thus as soon as we find a real meaning in existence, further vistas open up beyond, and the task remains unfinished. So empirical philosophers must "remain eternally unsatisfied" (SR, p. 75). And yet, guided by a certain trust, they still go on, responding to the lure of the mystery in being. What is the nature of this trust, and what are its sources?

The Need for an Integral Functioning
of the Mind

In our discussion of the limits of reason, we have so far been concerned primarily with two factors in the objective world confronting us. First of all, there is a surd factor of sheer being or brute fact, and in the second place, relational patterns of meaning that make sense to us. But among these, we must now take note of a special kind of meaning. These are the primary meanings which dominate the others, and determine the different ways in which the worlds of different groups and individuals are ordered. So we usually refer to them in the plural by such normative terms as goods, ends, purposes, and values. Of any object of experience, therefore, we may ask three questions. What is its factual foundation? What is it, or what is its meaning? And, finally, what is its central meaning for us, its value?

If these three factors can be found in every object, we should expect to find, correlated with them, three types of human intention. James believes that human mental life does fall into a threefold intentional pattern and he calls this "the reflex-action theory of mind" (RAAT, p. 122), often referring to the "three departments of the mind" (p. 125). The first attends to the factual element in things, the second to the finding of meaning, which prepares the way for the final stage—the active response. The whole latter part of the *Principles* is organized in accordance with this scheme (Chaps. XVII–XXVI), and it plays a prominent role in "The Sentiment of Rationality" (*cf.* esp. SR, pp. 84–85) and is the dominant theme of the essay "Reflex Action and Theism" (RAAT), which was written 1880–81 when James was starting to work on the *Principles*.

He was convinced that the pattern rests on firm physiological foundations, for "there is no one of those complicated performances in the convolutions of the brain to which our trains of thought correspond, which is not a mere middle term interposed between an incoming sensation that arouses it and an outgoing discharge of some sort . . .". Hence "the structural unit of the nervous system is in fact a triad" (RAAT, p. 113). The way in which he constantly shifts from physiological to mentalist language in referring to this threefold structure shows how intensively he was striving, at this formative period of his thought, to bring these two perspectives together in an integral conception of the body-mind. Thus a few pages farther on in the same essay (pp. 122–23) he says that "any mind, constructed on the triadic-reflex pattern, must first get its impression from the object which it confronts; then define what that object is, and decide what active measures its presence demands; and finally react".

This structure is found at the original level of acquaintance, which always involves a "synthesis of a passive perception with a certain tendency to reaction" (SR, p. 85). In between these, as we have noted in the *Principles*, there is the internal field of hesitation and preparation for new responses which, in man, is correlated with the complexity and instability of the brain (*cf. supra*, pp. 16–17). But with the coming of language and conceptual thought, there is a tremendous development of this second department—the working out of different schemes of interpretation in every field of behavior, and of totally different world-orders. Being comes first and its stubborn resistance to meaning, the mystic element, as we have seen, makes freedom possible. As James says, the recognition "of an ultimate opacity in things, of a dimension of being which escapes our theoretic control, may suggest a most definite practical conclusion,—this one, namely, that 'our wills are free'" (RAAT, p. 143). And, as he might have added, our minds as well.

Whether he be of the scientific or the speculative variety, the intellectualist may dream of a final system of meaning that will perfectly coincide with being. He is, of course, free to indulge in this dream and to defend it as well as he can. Such a theory will never be refuted by logical argument alone. It will be refuted by the brute facts of history as it moves on, and in particular by the existential freedom to think and to create, which is presupposed by the dream and makes it possible. A philosophy that does not lead to belief and to action is a mere game. It is a mere mask for the real philosophy that is being lived, and was prepared for by serious reflection. Whether he is aware of it or not, the philosopher is existing in the concrete world, and his thought belongs to his existence and expresses itself in action or inaction. "The thinker starts from some experience of the practical world, and asks its meaning. He launches himself upon the speculative sea, and makes a voyage long or short. He ascends into the empyrean, and communes with the eternal essences. But whatever his achievements and discoveries be while gone, the utmost result they can issue in is some new practical maxim or resolve, or the denial of some old one, with which inevitably he is sooner or later washed ashore on the *terra firma* of concrete life again" (p. 143).

If there is anything sound in this account, the task of "reason" is not less wide but much wider than is usually supposed. Of course it must follow its own internal rules and principles. It must seek for logical rigor, clarity, coherence, and completeness. James never denied that these criteria and principles apply to department two. But "reason" has other responsibilities as well. It must also recognize the brute facts that are entirely independent of its operations, and the desires and aspirations that also constitute the human situation. Hence it must learn to judge itself by three sets of independent criteria, not merely by one. First of all, it must take account of the brute facts as they are. Then it must find a place for the desires of men, and offer them a challenge. Finally, it must judge the systems of meaning it devises by the rigor, the clarity and coherence with which they mediate between the other two.

In judging any such ordering of the world, as James says, "all three departments of the mind alike have a vote in the matter, and . . . no conception will pass muster which violates any of their essential modes of activity, or which leaves them without a chance to work" (p. 125). The failure to meet any one of these sets of independent criteria will make it inadequate, and demote it, at best, to the level of "some partial sect". "Either it has dropped out of its net some of our impressions of sense,—what we call the facts of nature,—or it has left the theoretic and defining department with a lot of inconsistencies and unmediated transitions on its hands; or else, finally, it has left some one or more of our fundamental active and emotional powers with no object outside of themselves to react-on or to live for." The task of real philosophy, therefore, is much more far-ranging and difficult than has been traditionally supposed.

One final comment is perhaps in order. The three departments of the mind, or types of intention, are at least partially independent. Thus, as the history of philosophy shows, systems of meaning may be developed without due regard for the other departments, as James believes that idealism has paid insufficient attention to the facts, and materialism has paid insufficient attention to desires and aspirations. The same is true of the other two departments. But such independence leads only to partiality and error. In so far as they function adequately, the departments are mutually interdependent and take account of each other in certain ways. Hence James refers to this proper functioning as a mental cycle (p. 130) and to the cognitive power as only "one element in an organic mental whole" (p. 140).

The most original moves of James' thought are concerned with the relations of cognition to the other two independent spheres: brute fact and desire. With respect to the former, the relation of meaning to fact, his ideas remain consistent and clear. The realm of fact is much wider than has been supposed in the past, and this realm comes first. Meanings must fit with the facts, and not the reverse. This is the gist of his radical empiricism. With respect to the second, the relation of cognition to desire, the situation, as we shall see, is more complex. With respect to the relation between desire, or will, and fact, in his doctrine of the freedom, or right, to believe, he is more clear. But even though he certainly did not say the last word on all the questions he opened up, his opening of them was an achievement of the first importance, and the questions still remain. In sharply distinguishing cognition from the realms of pre-reflective fact and human desire, and in exploring its relations to these independent realms, he achieved novel insights of real significance.

Chapter Nine

Abstract Concepts versus
Concrete Thinking

The last chapter of the *Psychology* (XXVIII), in which James speaks of ideal systems of relations and of necessary truths, has struck many readers as a whimsical aberration in flagrant contradiction with his radical empiricism. A rationalistic philosophy can justify truths of this kind. But they have no legitimate place in any consistent empiricism, which must restrict itself to the observation of events after the fact. In this case, as in so many others, James' thought refuses to be bound by traditional oppositions and antimonies, and breaks into new ground. This makes it impossible to think of him, as of other phenomenologists, as falling under the categories of rationalism or empiricism as these terms have been understood in the past. His *radical* empiricism is neither one nor the other, and in this chapter, I shall try to single out, and to clarify the most original features of this theory of meaning and his ideas about a testable *a priori*.

Conceptual Thinking

In the two preceding chapters we have examined the world of sense with which we are directly but vaguely acquainted, and the acts of discrimination and comparison which are made at the prelinguistic and pre-reflective level. We also considered the nature of language and some of its distinctive features. Let us now turn to the conceptual thought which language makes possible, and the radical changes it brings with it when it enters into the sensory world.

Our actual perceptions (i.e. feelings) are always of some object surrounded by "fringes and halos, inarticulate perceptions, whereof the objects are as yet unnamed, mere nascencies of cognition, premonitions, awarenesses of direction . . ." (PR, I, 478, note). The conceptual analyst rules out these intuitions as vague, and, therefore, delusive. His aim is clarity, which he achieves by singling out one aspect of this blur, and sharply focusing it in separation from all else. But though they may be suppressed, some fringes still remain, and though they may be vague, they include a synthetic, cognitive element which constitutes the beginning and the end of all analysis. Whatever our result may be, it must find its final place in the fringes of some comprehensive world horizon.

The vague revealing of something is still a revealing, and its cognitive value must not be ignored. As James says, "the vague" has "its psychological [i.e. phenomenological] rights" which need to be recognized. The analytic clarification of what is first only vaguely felt is essential, but if any genuine advance is to be made, the analysis must be placed in a synthesis which is surrounded in its turn by further fringes. As James puts it (p. 550), "analysis and synthesis are thus the incessantly alternating mental activities, a stroke of the one preparing the way for a stroke of the other, much as, in walking, a man's two legs are alternately brought into use, both being indispensable for any orderly advance".

Analysis means singling out, abstraction, the sharp focusing of one thing at a time in separation from all else. This must occur if full knowledge is to be attained. Synthesis means feeling the vague fringes of an ultimate world horizon, which is also subject to its peculiar mode of clarification, as James is showing in his writings. Both have their proper roles to play. As we have already pointed out, we know directly and vaguely by acquaintance our own existence in the world of life. Here, as James says in a letter to F. H. Bradley,[1] knowledge, truth, and being coincide. This knowing belongs to our being, and no human agent can exist without it. But though certain, it is vague, confused, and mixed with over-simple and distorted interpretations. If these deficiencies are to be corrected, conceptual clarification, or what James calls *knowledge about* both things and relations in the world, as well as the world itself, must be achieved. Both are essential.

This is not merely an eclectic combination of elements taken from opposed views, but an original conception which James worked out in many diverse contexts, and never abandoned from the beginning of his thinking to the very end. He summarizes it well in the letter to Bradley: "The immediation of the mediate is just as indispensable as the mediation of the immediate." Conceptual analysis, which has been emphasized as the only reliable path to knowledge, misses the world horizon. James was acutely aware of this danger. Hence he called his own position *radical empiricism*. But without conceptual analysis, we are restricted to a narrow range of isolated objects surrounded by a vast confusion of fringes. This easily falls prey to one-sided dogmatism and fanaticism. Hence he devotes almost one-quarter of his *Psychology* to the phenomenology of the intellectual life and its origins in the world of sense (Chaps. XII, XIII, XXII, and XXVIII), and the phrase *radical conceptualism* would have been an appropriate name for his final position. Our

---

[1] Dated Nov. 23, 1909, Merton College Library, Oxford.

lived existence in the world must be mediatized and clarified by conceptual analysis which, in turn, must be immediatized by being placed in the world horizon. Both are essential, if genuine insight is to be achieved.

We have taken note of James' view that consciousness makes a difference, that it brings something new into the world. According to him, this is even more true of conceptual than of perceptual meaning. Neither one nor the other can be reduced to mere copies of what already exists. But conception is even more original. We can conceive of pure fictions (PR, I, 461) perpetual motion machines, golden mountains and round squares (p. 463). None of these conceived beings exists, and some of them never can. Nevertheless they can be conceived. This is enough to show the basic difference between meaning and being.

All through the history of epistemological discussion, we find realists, nominalists, and other schools insisting that "a thought must *be* what it means, and mean what it *is*" (p. 471). This identification lies at the root of the notion that the mind must somehow "include its objects", or "that an idea must *be* a duplicate edition of what it knows". According to James, this reduction of meaning to being implies "that knowledge in any strict sense of the word, as a self-transcendent function, is impossible". If we stick to the phenomena, we find that knowledge always involves a self-transcendent reference of the knowing act to something other than itself. This reference does not have to be a copy, or repetition, of what is known, so that, for example, our knowing of a universal must itself be universal. "Of course this is nonsense. An idea neither is what it knows, nor knows what it is; nor will swarms of copies of the same 'idea', recurring in stereotyped form, or 'by the irresistible laws of association formed into one idea', ever be the same thing as a thought of *all the possible members* of a class" (p. 477). Our meanings are quite different from the real, fictive, or ideal beings which they mean. The being of two different ideas is not the same as the idea of their difference which need "not *be* these terms with their difference, nor *contain* them". Indeed, as James goes on to say: "man's thought can know and mean all sorts of things without those things getting bodily into it—the distant, for example, the future, and the past" (p. 501).

Ideal Objects and Systems

The conception of ideal objects not found in the world of perception, and the discovery of changeless relations between them is of special importance for James. Very often these ideal objects are extrapolations of tendencies and directions found in experience. Thus in his account of discrimination, James shows in detail how the analysis of different wholes into their elements can roll out a common element found in them all. One may be found for example to consist of *abcd*, another of *aefg*. This may lead us to pay attention to *a*, apart from its divergent associates. The element *a*, however, will not be the same in its divergent settings. But by noting the way in which it continues to differ from them, "we come to form a pretty good notion of the *direction* in which each element differs from the rest" (p. 508). Then by a creative act of meaning, we carry this direction to its limit, and conceive of an ideal *a*, by itself alone. Since "*all* our abstracts must be confessed to be but imperfectly imaginable things", we must conclude that there is an ideal, creative element in all abstraction.

In the last chapter of the *Psychology* (XXVIII), James sharply rejects the empiricist theory that all our basic concepts are passively received from experience. In radical opposition to this, he asks why basic categories, like "consciousness, sensation, time, space", and novel scientific conceptions may "not, in short, be pure *idiosyncrasies*, spontaneous variations, fitted by good luck (those of them which have survived) to take cognizance of objects (that is, to steer us in our active dealings with them), without being in any intelligible sense immediate derivatives from them?" (II, 631).

We have already noted how the mind, in its activity of comparing, can observe a series of growing differences which point towards an ideal limit. Thus, in comparison with a standard white object, a set of darkening shades point towards an ideal black that is never observed. An opposite direction of differences can be observed in a series of lighter objects, departing from one that is black and moving towards an ideal white. We also noted how a set of ideal objects of this kind, like the natural colors, can be compared and ordered into a system of ideal terms and relations which can clarify and help us to understand our color experiences.

The new point that emerges in this last chapter is that these relational systems, at least in the cases of the sciences, are not mere copies of experiences passively received by the mind. They are the expression of a spontaneous "free play" of the mind. Like basic categories and metaphysical principles (pp. 669 ff.), they are rather, in James' picturesque language, "born in the house" (pp. 627 ff.). The white wood may become blackened by fire and smoke. But, as we have noted, what I mean by *black* will never change into *white*. In fact, once this difference is conceptualized and meant by the mind, it will maintain itself just as it is, whether any black or white things are found in experience or not. Such changeless relations of ideal entities are, therefore, necessarily true for all minds that go through the operations. They become independent of experience. In this sense they are *a priori*, and James actually uses this term.

He calls logic and mathematics "pure sciences" and he says that these sciences "EXPRESS RESULTS OF COMPARISON *exclusively; comparison is not a conceivable effect of the order in which outer impressions are experienced—it is one of the house-born portions of our mental structure . . .*" (p. 641). James attaches great importance to the notion of serial or transitive relations, like subsumption, or predication. Thus "*whatever has an attribute has all the attributes of that attribute*" (p. 648). Such a relation is the result of comparison, first in finding similarities between the members of a given class, and then in discovering the serial differences in a group of classes. In so far as logic studies these serial relations, including that of implication, with no attention to their special content, it is an *a priori* science concerned with the results of mental comparison only.

The same is true of arithmetic and geometry. Mill's attempt to prove the contrary showed conclusively that numbers and arithmetical relations are not gained by induction from experience. One plus one necessarily makes two. But in the world of experience when we add one drop of water to another, we get that one again, *not* two, and when we add it to a drop of quicklime, we get twelve or more. Hence the laws of number are not empirical laws of nature. They do not primarily refer to concrete things which are in constant change, and at any given moment can always be divided and numbered in different ways. According to James, "*number* seems to signify primarily the strokes of our attention in discriminating things" (p. 653), and applies to things only in so far as they are objects of this discriminaton, and thus not as they actually exist, but as the ideal correlates of mental acts. These ideal objects remain in memory as groups, large or small, and there can be compared. As a result of this comparison, we find that they fall into a transitive series in which the more than the more, is more than the less. We also find that our various pauses and regroupings in a total process of counting make no difference in the final result. Thus, whether we count continuously up to twelve, or pause after four, or pause after five and then resume, the result will be the same: $4+8=5+7=12$.

This number series also turns out to be congruent with things in nature which, at least approximately, hold to the numbers we give them (p. 656). Such congruence, however, is always unstable, and cannot explain the origin of what we mean by numbers, which are ideal meanings based on mental operations. Hence these numbers and their relations would remain exactly the same even in a world where the laws of nature were entirely different. One and one would still mean two, and, therefore, make two, even if, whenever we put two things together, a third thing appeared. This would have no effect on our *a priori* number system. It would be merely a peculiarity of the behavior of the matter involved.

James takes a similar position with respect to geometry. We have never seen a line that is perfectly straight, nor a perfect plane. "Straight lines, planes, and parallels, as they figure in geometry, are mere inventions of our faculty for apprehending serial increase. The farther continuations of these forms, we say, *shall* bear the same relation to their last visible parts which these did to still earlier parts" (p. 657). With the help of our spatial imagination, we can construct many ideal figures of this kind, and through comparison, we can find many changeless relations between them, thus setting up a system of ideal figures and relations "with which the space of our experience seems to agree" (p. 658). But not necessarily, and other spaces can be imagined. For example, movement through space might warp geometric forms in certain ways that could be exactly known. In this case, we could imagine a different type of space. "A geometry as absolutely certain as ours could be invented on the supposition of such a space, if the laws of its warping and deformation were fixed" (p. 658). James uses the term *a priori* for these "house-born" ideas and systems. But it is flexible and testable and, therefore, quite different from the Kantian conception.

A Testable *A Priori*

This *a priori* factor in knowing is an indication of the fact that in certain respects we are the "masters of our meanings" (p. 655), and that we can develop new systems of meaning to fit new situations and discoveries. As a matter of fact, such developments constitute turning points in the history of science, which shows that it also includes a constructive *a priori* factor. "The popular notion that 'Science' is forced on the mind *ab extra* . . . is utterly absurd" (p. 667). It involves ideal constructions and systems of relations which are actively invented by the mind. This is confirmed by the fact that logic and mathematics are essential factors in their procedures. As James says: "they are all translations of sensible experiences into other forms, substitutions of items between which ideal relations of kind, number, form, equality, etc., obtain, for items between which no such relations obtain; coupled with declarations that the experienced form is false and the ideal form true, declarations which are justified by the appearance of new sensible experiences at just those times and places at which we logically infer that their ideal correlates ought to be" (p. 669).

Once we cast our conceptual network over the world, we can pass from one of its phases to another by an "inward thought-necessity" (p. 667), but much is lost. As James remarks, "the sentimental facts and relations are butchered at a blow". The amazing thing is that sub-human processes so closely approximate our *a priori* inventions. Hence these methods have given us our very considerable control over nature. But they are wholly inadequate to describe the total world, which includes vast ranges of "facts and relations" that escape through its net. Hence when science is absolutized as the only way to truth, it gives us a highly reduced and distorted view of the world. To understand a natural event or a human occurrence, we must work out new concepts and a new point of view from which we may gather its elements together in a way that makes sense.[2]

But whether our new concepts come via abstraction in the sense just explained, by the continuing of observable tendencies to their ideal limits, or by sheer invention, they are constantly arising as long as disciplined thinking is active. Once established, they enable us to discover ideal relations between them, and thus come to constitute an ideal system not copied from experience, but in so far as it can be verified, often clarifying and explaining empirical events and sequences. As James says: *"the mind is filled with necessary and eternal relations* [like the difference between black and white] *which it finds between*

[2] *Cf.* E. Husserl's similar critique of Mill's theory in *Logische Untersuchungen*, Halle, 1928, I, 71–73 and 149–50, and Merleau-Ponty, *Primacy of Perception*, pp. 69 ff.

certain of its ideal conceptions, and which form a determinate system, independent of the order of frequency in which experience may have associated the conception's originals in time and space" (p. 661).

These timeless truths do not necessarily lay hold of reality, as the ancients thought, nor do they legislate *a priori* for all possible experience, as Kant believed (p. 664). James' phenomenological view is different. "They stand waiting in the mind, forming a beautiful ideal network; and the most we can say is that we *hope* to discover realities over which the network may be flung so that ideal and real may coincide" (p. 665). This is a contingent necessity, for these systems of timeless meaning must be verified, if they are to become true. So once again the manifold array of ideal systems is contained within world history. Furthermore no such system is ever finally verified in more than a vague and approximate sense. Even after it has withstood all the tests at our disposal at a given time, we can never be sure that it will not be replaced by another of broader scope which will involve corrections and revisions, and which will, in turn, have to wait for further advances. For in the life-world all is temporal and incomplete.

We are subject to the constant temptation to use such a system, especially if it be scientific, to explain and, therefore, to assimilate the imperfect perspectives of perceptual experience. As James says, "life is one long struggle between conclusions based on abstract ways of conceiving cases, and opposite conclusions prompted by our . . . perception of them as individual facts" (p. 674). Many of these abstract conclusions are supported by the never ending flux of history, but by no means all. These timeless, finished systems are abstract and, therefore, partial. They come into being and pass away in a horizon of realities that is also passing and incomplete. It is in this horizon that they meet the final test. This is where their truth or falsity, and their final meaning, if they have one, is revealed. In the end, and against the first appearances, the timeless must be tested by the temporal, and the finished and perfect must be interpreted in the light of the unfinished and incomplete.

Hence, as we have noted, these timeless constructions differ from the Kantian *a priori*. They also differ from other traditional conceptions like the scholastic *ens rationis*. It may be of interest to examine these differences more closely. So let us now turn to them, beginning with the latter.

James' Theory and the Scholastic Notion of *Ens Rationis*

James does not frequently use the term *ens rationis* in the *Principles*. So far as I know, it occurs at only three places (I, 299 and 461, and II, 677). But the concept covers abstractions, ideal entities, and relations of various kinds which play a vital role in James' thought. Hence this idea is worthy of serious comment. In scholastic usage, from which the term is taken, *ens rationis* means a mental intention which functions in the logical operations by which we understand reality, but which has no actual counterparts in *rerum natura*. Thus, subject and predicate, genus and species, would be *entia rationis*. We cannot think about real beings without using these intentions in our thinking. But in the realm of reality there are no such things. Here there are real men. But they are never divided into subjective and predicative portions. There are individual men, but there are no genera and species. These terms, therefore, stand for mental entities, logical intentions which correspond to nothing outside the mind.

James' conception is similar enough to justify his using the traditional scholastic term. Nevertheless it is marked by certain distinctive features which must be noted. In the first place, these mental beings are sharply distinguished from fictions (I, p. 461). They are not useful fictions through which we are able to gain an understanding of reality. They are not fictions at all, because they play an important role in the actual constitution of the real world in which we exist. They are mental intentions which are not supposed to copy any real facts, and in this respect they are like the traditional *ens rationis*. But they can, to some degree, become verified or fulfilled. Through such ideal constructions of the mind, we are able to gather real things together in meaningful ways. Once the idea has been seen, the facts seem to bear it out, and fit in with it.

Thus the ideal of an absolute identity between two things is never perfectly exemplified. But it enables us to gather similar things together into classes, and to arrange these similarities in an order of lesser and greater, which approaches this identity as a limit. The same is true of the other basic categories by which our human worlds are conceptually organized. These are ideal constructions of the mind, which are in no sense passively received by an induction from real things. They enter the mind not from the outside but, as James puts it, by the backstairs way. In this sense, they are beings of reason, originating in the mind itself. They enable us to order the independent beings of the world together in ways that not only fit them but make sense to us. Hence, like the world itself, these rational intentions, so far as they are verified, are neither subjective nor objective. They are not objective, because they are human inventions. But neither are they subjective, for they fit the independent realities around us, which approximate them in their actual acts and operations.

This peculiar status of the categories is shown by James' listing of similarity and, therefore, the closely related idea of difference as *entia rationis* (p. 461). This contrasts sharply with the scholastic doctrine of the reality of these relations, which are supposed to be already existing in *rerum natura*. But there are an indefinite number of possible things to be compared, and an indefinite number of ways of comparing them. To suppose that one, and only one, system of relations exists in the world is a dogmatic projection. To suppose that the relations are all out there in *rerum natura* is to engage in a wholesale projection of mental entities. Both views forget that "in noticing the differences and resemblances of things, and their degrees, the mind feels its own activity, and has given the name of *comparison* thereto" (II, 643). They both express an imperfect self-consciousness. And yet it is equally mistaken to suppose that these relations are pure mental creations with no support from the realities. Once we single out a black and a white, and set ourselves to compare them, we find unmistakably that they are different. As James says, the mind "need not compare its materials, but if once roused to do so, it can compare them with but one result, and this is a fixed consequence of the nature of the materials themselves" (p. 643).

The same is true of the notions of nothing and its correlative, being. Once we adopt this distinction, certain necessary consequences follow, for example, the law of contradiction. The same thing in the same respect cannot both be and not be. But there are other possibilities, like the world of Hegel in which being and nothing are regarded as the same. From this view, other necessary consequences follow. There are thus a large number of necessary truths arising from different ideal entities and abstractions. Before the process of verifying begins, these are ideal meanings, or *entia rationis*. As James says, "in the first instance they express relations between merely mental terms" (p. 677). But then, as we see in the history of science and philosophy, we look at the facts from these different points of view, and the labor of confirmation and disconfirmation begins. When we do this, we find that nature seems to act more in conformity with one system than with the others, or as James puts it, "nature, however, acts as if some of her realities were identical with these mental terms. So far as she does this, we can make *a priori* propositions concerning natural fact. The aim of both science and philosophy is to make the identifiable terms more numerous" (p. 677).

This language has a Kantian sound, but James makes it clear that his conception differs radically from the German theory, as we shall now see.

James' Theory and the Kantian *A Priori*

These ordering forms originate in the mind, it is true, and not from experience. But they are neither changeless nor do they have "as Kant pretended . . . a legislating character even for all possible experience" (pp. 664–65). They exist in a vast variety of different systems and forms in different individual minds and different cultures. In this early stage, before confirmation and disconfirmation, "they are primarily interesting only as subjective facts" (p. 665). In this stage, "the most we can say is that we *hope* to discover realities over which the network may be flung so that ideal and real may coincide". Hence this is an *a priori* that is not simply laid down by the mind to rule forever. It is laid down tentatively and then subjected to an empirical test by confronting independent beings over which the mind, as such, has no control.

In so far as it meets this test, which is never finally passed, it may be said to be partially confirmed, always subject to correction, revision, and even withdrawal. In so far as this confirmation occurs, the sense-giving system may be said to legislate in a parliamentary way, not over all possible experience, but over experience as it is and has been. There are also other basic differences.

In the first place, the self that legislates for all experience in the Kantian scheme is not a concrete being in the world. It is not really a self at all. It is a formal principle of unity outside the world, that brings all objects into relation with itself through the categories. For James, on the other hand, the knowing self is a finite being in the world who, at the same time, through his reasoning, is able to develop timeless systems of meanings to interpret various areas of experience. For Kant, this ordering activity of the mind cannot be directly observed or expressed. It must be transcendentally deduced from the objects of experience as the necessary condition of their possibility. The forming of basic meanings is never directly experienced. It is rather indirectly inferred as an *a priori* power coming from a source beyond the world that it organizes.

For James and the phenomenologists of our time, on the contrary, all experience is, of course, already interpreted. But this activity of meaning formation goes on in the world where meanings come into being. Hence it can be studied as it is directly experienced, described and analyzed, as James attempts to do in these important chapters of his *Principles*. For Kant, the categories have no viable alternatives. They legislate for all possible reasoning for all time. But as James specifically says, the nets of ideal meanings and the categories, as he conceives them, do not have "as Kant pretended . . . a legislating character even for all possible experience". There are always possible alternatives. New meanings, and even new categories, may arise in history. No system can ever be proved to be final and definitive. Even after it has been "confirmed", it is always subject to revision and correction, which brings us to another more basic difference.

The Kantian categories never need to be confirmed. Indeed, they already condition any process of confirmation or disconfirmation. For James, on the other hand, they must meet this test, and without it "they are primarily interesting only as subjective facts". At this preliminary stage, "the most we can say is that we *hope* to discover realities over which the network may be flung, so that ideal and real may coincide" (p. 665). For James, therefore, this rational *a priori* is not ultimate, as it is for the Kantians who believe that, apart from it, there is only a chaotic manifold of sensation. If that were true, no view of the world as a whole could ever be tested, for there is no other real order to test it.

But for James, as a radical empiricist, such a view is radically false. There are independent beings, "realities", as he calls them, which fall into a pre-reflective order that is felt, and lived, and perceived. This world is presupposed by the conceptual *a priori*, and, therefore, prior to it. Our own existence is lived through in this real world. Hence we have called it and its patterns *existentially a priori* (*cf. supra,* pp. 49 ff.). But whatever our name may be, it is in this world that our rational schemes must be tested, for until they meet this test, they may be nothing more than pretentious delusions.

The World of Existence and Its Patterns

How then are we to approach this world? How are we to understand it and clarify it, if it is prior to conceptual formulation? In the second place, how are we to think concretely about things in the world without falling into conceptual reduction and abstraction? To the traditional rationalist, this task must seem a hopeless leap into the dark. How can we get out of experience what we have not already put in? As a phenomenologist, James does not accept this Kantian formulation. The *knowledge about* that we attain through the use of concepts is not our only source. We are directly acquainted with the world in which we exist, and there are ways of disclosing this direct experience without reducing it to a conceptual scheme. James is not too explicit about these ways in his *Principles,* where he is employing them all the time. As is true of other original investigators, he prefers to use his method rather than to talk about it. Nevertheless he does give one or two hints which, in relation to what he has said before, shed a certain light on his method, and are, therefore, worthy of comment.

Can we think concretely about the world? Here we should reflect on the basic distinction between *knowledge about,* conceptual knowledge, and *knowledge by acquaintance.* It is important to recognize that James does not refer to the latter as the mere matter for knowledge, or as a condition, but as a kind of knowledge. It is in this way that we perceive and feel the concreted things around us and our own activities as they proceed and work on each other within the vague fringes of the life-world. This knowledge is pre-reflective and vague. Nevertheless, it is a positive mode of knowledge and not a mere condition. Just as our feeling for a lost name enables us to reject the wrong names when they are clearly presented (*cf. supra,* pp. 66–67), so our direct acquaintance with the fringes of the world-field enables us to reject wrong formulations of it when they are clearly and conceptually presented. In this way, it can guide us in resynthesizing the results of our conceptual analyses, or to use the words of James' letter to Bradley, in "immediatizing the mediate".

In these chapters (XII, XIII, XXII, and XXVIII) James is focusing the special operations of logical and scientific thinking, which presuppose the life-world and its concrete objects. But he leaves the way open for another kind of thinking that can work hand in hand with feeling in clarifying its dim apprehensions. Thus he says specifically that we conceive "singulars, particulars, indefinites" (I, 479). But we do not conceive of them by conception alone—only with the cooperation of sense, which first perceives them in a vague fringe of relations. These may then be brought out and clarified by conceptual analysis and comparison. Finally, with the aid of acquaintance, they can be resynthesized and assigned their proper places in the world. But how does acquaintance achieve this synthesis? Can it escape from bias?

Let us first consider the advantages of this mode of knowing. In so far as I am acquainted with my own activities and their objects, I know them directly without the mediation of any particular conceptual point of view. My active gaze, which I send out to the prickly rose bush that rejects me, is not properly described as a point of view. As I reach out with my eye and hand, I do not know the bush from a detached point of *view.* I reveal it directly by a consciousness that inhabits my hand as it reaches out and meets its object. But in this way, I become acquainted with my act and with the object in its act of rejecting me. As long as it is left in this vague, concrete state, this knowledge, so far as it goes, is both direct and certain.

A second advantage lies in its inclusive scope. I myself, other persons, and every region of our common cares, lie in the world which envelops us at every stage of our separate histories. It is not conceptually articulated, but is rather felt in the form of vague fringes which surround each field of care, like the world of finance, the world of politics, and the world of the sick. The very fact that we call them *worlds* shows the ever-present possibility of absolutizing them. But the constant need for justifying and protecting them from foreign intrusion shows that the surrounding fringes are dimly felt. This is confirmed by the sense of liberation which comes when an individual breaks through the walls of such a confining version, and steps out into the great open world where there is always room for wider horizons and development.

We may define bias in terms of these two factors as the adoption of a restricted point of view which forces us to fit many things into an alien frame. In so far as we can achieve a first-hand acquaintance with something, and can know it directly without mediation in the wider world horizon, we can, therefore, escape from the bias that comes with any clear and definite conceptual frame. This horizon is neither subjective nor objective. It has room for both. It is no single region or set of regions. It has room for them all. These advantages have led certain thinkers, like Bergson, to advocate the abandonment of conceptual thinking, in philosophy at least, and the return to an immediate intuition that would penetrate into the heart of the thing without any external mediation or reduction. James had a strong sympathy for certain aspects of Bergson's thought, which he later expressed. But he never accepted the Bergsonian theory, because he recognized certain disadvantages of knowledge by acquaintance which we may list as follows.

First of all, this knowledge is vague. It puts us in touch with whole objects whose parts are not discriminated clearly, and whose relations with other things are confused in a halo of misty fringes. As James says: "experience, from the very first, presents us with concreted objects, vaguely continuous with the rest of the world which envelops them in space and time . . ." (p. 487). The parts of such a concrete object are not carefully distinguished, and its external boundaries remain unclear. What is essential is readily confused with what is only incidental. This prepares the way for reductive interpretations of the object, in line with special desires or projects which then, though they cannot eliminate this primordial experience, set it aside and use it in a twisted form for their own purposes. We can say, in fact, that our perceptual acquaintance with ourselves and with external things in the world, unless it is given conceptual support, is peculiarly susceptible to biases of this kind. In view of the distinctive traits of conceptual thinking, as they emerge from James' description, can such support be given? While he does not analyze it in detail, he certainly implies that it can be given, and shows this by his own procedures.

In the first place, help may be given in avoiding special projects that lead to reductive interpretations of the phenomena. That rational thought can do this is shown by its capacity to attain an impartial, scientific point of view by the supression of subjective interests, and the biases attending them. In this case, however, a further step must be taken, namely the avoidance of suppressing the subjective interest in science, and the bias towards objectivity attending it. All of these special attitudes which focus certain facts by ignoring others must be set aside, or bracketed, so that we can return to our experience of the life-world in its totality. In returning to this experience, we must, in James' own language, take pains not to fall into "the psychologist's fallacy" or, as we have learned to call it, the phenomenologist's fallacy of reading his own special attitudes and purposes into the phenomena he is studying. James speaks of this (p. 196) as "*the confusion of his own standpoint with that of the mental fact* about which he is making his report". Such a bracketing of prejudice, or *epoché*, is not easy to attain. It can be closely approximated only by a special act of attention in which conceptual interpretation (knowledge about) holds itself in abeyance, so that a perceived object, and the world of perception, may come into view.

This world presents us with a vast array of concrete objects in space and time, merging into each other, and fading off into vague fringes. There are places in the spacious fringes of this world for the abstract objects of logic, mathematics, and the special sciences. But these special attitudes must be bracketed if we are to keep the outlines of the life-world in our view. And this is only one part of the story. The life-world also contains selves and their manifold acts of perceiving, feeling, desiring, imagining, and reasoning in their variegated forms. It contains gestures, linguistic expressions, and the various modes of social life and institutions which these inter-subjective communications bring forth. It includes all the events and transformations that make up human history.

Every human being is directly acquainted, in a dim way, with objects, activities, and events of these kinds, depending on his situation in history, and such acquaintance is presupposed by all the special theoretical and practical activities of man, the sciences, the arts, business, and technology. But concrete thinking, as phenomenology has now taught us, does not consist merely in vague, primordial feelings of this kind. If this were so, all of us would be concrete thinkers. As a matter of fact, it involves special modes of attention, abstraction, and reflection, which require both feeling and conception working together, as James points out, and which are fraught with peculiar difficulties and dangers. The bringing of the life-world into view is only the first step in this complex and delicately balanced activity.

The life-world must be constantly held in mind if we are to think concretely, for it is the background for all existential analysis. But, owing to the limits of human attention, we can advance in clarity only by singling out one being, or mode of being, at a time for closer examination. Among the more important patterns are those of the life-world itself, like space, time, and intentionality, which pervade it in its entirety. As we have seen, James has something to say about them, and his investigations have been greatly extended and developed by other phenomenologists since his time. Any light that can be shed on these world structures will have a clarifying effect on concrete thinking about any specific object, or region, of the world. Something analogous may be said of knowledge concerning the necessary structures of human existence like care, feeling, understanding, and freedom. "Necessary" here refers not to any logical, but rather to an existential necessity, that is, to an impossibility of living without them, which can be revealed by inter-subjective clarification and argument. Owing to the intentional pattern of experience, such structures will be reflected in all human versions of the world. Scientific theory, of course, presupposes such structures, but owing to its orientation towards objects, it is in no position to reveal them.

Beings-in-the-world

Turning now to beings in the world, we find that these fall into two groups, human beings and things, each of which may be approached in a concrete way. In order to do this, of course, we must as a first step single out some individual being, like a forest, a plant, an animal, an animal cluster, a person, a human group, or its culture. Such objects are all present to us in perception, but, as James says, this presence is vague. As he explains: "when we say that a thing is vague, we mean that it has no subdivisions *ab intra*, nor precise limitations *ab extra* . . ." (II, 343). Their parts fade into dim fringes, because we perceive each of them as a whole thing, "but", as James emphasizes, "only as a whole" (pp. 343–44). There is a type of abstract thinking which is holistic in having no eye for the parts. But analytic abstraction, which takes the whole for granted, is equally one-sided.

Hence in thinking concretely about an object, we must never lose sight of the perceptual whole. Such thinking will not ignore the parts. But it will be synthetic rather than analytic, and will resist any analysis into ideal, or independent, parts that will reduce it to a mere compound or appearance. It will also resist any identification of the essence with some part that merely fits it for some extraneous purpose. Instead of these reductive procedures, it will keep returning to the thing itself in its entirety as it is perceived or felt, seeing its essence in the style with which it expresses itself in its various perceptual perspectives.

Since this total being is found only in a temporal history, this essence will turn out to be a way of existing, with many subordinate phases that express themselves in different ways in differing situations. The external limits of any concrete being are vague because it is "concreted" together with other things that finally become its environment, and since the being is its activities, this border line is hard to draw. Thus the forest acts on the soil and the atmosphere, and merges with them for certain distances. And, to take another example, the human self exists in the various objects that constitute its *me*, and in the images and attitudes of its neighbors. So here again a fixed boundary is hard to draw.

Conceptual thinking, and the language that bears it, may help to clarify the essential style and the boundaries of the concrete being. But in doing this, constant reference must be made to feeling and perception, or misunderstanding will occur. If we do not succeed finally in expressing the feeling of the thing, all our carefully chosen words and phrases will become a mere mumbling of jargon. Hence in reading the concrete account of a fire, or a storm, we will miss the point, unless we go through the feelings suggested by the writer. The same may be said of James' description of the self, which no one will understand unless he recognizes and imaginatively repeats the warm and intimate feelings that lie within the citadel of the empirical self. In trying to think concretely about such things, the phenomenologist can learn a great deal from artists, dramatists, naturalists who have actually lived in the woods, from biographies, from literary artists, and, of course, from the poets. But if the full rightness and exactness of understanding is to be achieved, conceptual clarification and order are required.

For James, clarity, as we have seen, depends on internal analysis and distinction from other things, which "are essentially products of *intellectual discrimination*" (I, 426; *intellectual* my italics). As compared with conceptual thinking, perception is always vague. This is peculiarly true with respect to relations, which always involve at least two terms. These terms must be clearly distinguished, if the relation, or order, is to be clearly grasped. Since feeling and perception sense the relation and the terms all together, a hasty analysis is apt to confuse the two terms and to miss the relation. Thus the animal and the primitive man confuse the sign with what is signified, and common sense still confuses the intention with its object, and thus misses the intentional relation which pervades the whole of our lived experience. In this respect, the conceptual clarification of perception is peculiarly important. But an abstract analysis, which loses sight of the original feeling, is apt to leave us, after the manner of Bradley, with the two terms and *the relation* standing side by side as separate things. The cooperation of concepts and perception working together is peculiarly necessary in avoiding these common mistakes of relational analysis.

By means of language, it is possible, as we have noted, to work out conceptions of an object in its absence, and to compare these with previous ones, thus developing new perspectives, and seeing the same object in different ways. Of course, these new points of view must be verified by experience. But as James says: "our knowledge does grow and change by rational and inward processes, as well as by empirical discoveries" (p. 464), and as we have already noted, he attributes human originality and creativity to this inner ability to play freely with our ideas. Language also enables us to share our conceptions with others, and to take account of their criticism, which both sharpens and accelerates the process of verification.

James does not stress this corrective function of language in the *Principles* as much as he does in his later works. But he seems to suggest it in his long footnote on page 468 where he says that "the same A which I once meant . . . I shall now mean again, and mean it with C as its predicate (or what not) instead of B, as before". It is not enough to perceive something, or even to perceive and conceive it with a sense of certainty. Innumerable delusions are, of course, supported in this way. Hence the concrete thinker, in working out his concepts, will have to be far more careful than the scientist to refer back at

every stage to the perceptual object for an answering rever-
beration. Without this, he may be developing an ideal system of
concepts that may at best be approximated by some statistical
law. As we have seen, the scientist may be able to use such rational entities and ideals. He can afford to be more constructive,
but the concrete thinker is aiming at something quite different—a
meaningful description of the concrete mode of being, or object,
precisely as it appears.

The need for this constant reference to sense is denied by
the Hegelian theory that concepts grow of themselves towards
the truth. James attacks this theory in the section to which we
have just referred (pp. 464–68). It is true that new and truer
concepts of the same object can be formed. But "new conceptions come from new sensations, new movements, new emotions,
new associations, new acts of attention, and new comparisons of
old conceptions, and not in other ways" (p. 467). So it is false to
say "that the old conception has developed into the new", by
itself alone.

The very possibility of a close cooperation between experience
and reason is denied by two other theories of classical epistemology which are still very influential. According to the first,
which originates with Aristotle,[8] all concepts are essentially
universal, and there is no science of the individual. Since we
ourselves, and all existent beings, are individual, this means, for
James, that all concrete knowledge concerning the most precious
things for which we really care is being denied. Hence, as we
have noted, he rejects this categorically (pp. 478 ff.). Universal
characters can help us in certain ways. But their "only value" is
"that they help us, by reasoning, to know new truths about
individual things" (pp. 479–80). They can be known by the
concrete thinking we are describing, which James himself employed in the most original and interesting parts of his work.

The second theory comes from Descartes, though it has many
antecedents in previous philosophy. According to it, genuine
knowledge requires clear and distinct ideas. Hence what James

[8] *Metaphysics* VII.15.

calls *knowledge* by acquaintance is impossible, for sense knowledge is notoriously vague. Concrete conceptual knowledge is also impossible, for knowledge, as such, cannot be vague. James rejects this view on two grounds. In the first place, it ignores the intentional structure of knowing, which involves a difference between the act of conceiving and its object, *noesis* and *noema* as Husserl called them. Hence just as we may mean something universal by a singular act of thinking, so we may mean the vague by a clear conception of it, as he suggests on page 343.

In the second place, the theory of clear and distinct ideas ignores a certain peripheral vagueness that envelops the whole act of knowing, and thus enters into the knowing act itself, as well as its object. James refers to this in working out his distinction between the topic of a sentence, or discourse, and its total "object" (*cf.* I, 275–76). Thus in the sentence Columbus-discovered-America-in-1492, we may say that the topic is *Columbus*, a definite individual who can be clearly identified. But the sentence also involves the terms *discovered, America,* and *1492,* each with its own fringes of meaning. Hence no matter how clear and distinct the topic of a discourse may be, its total object involves vague fringes that fade off to the last limit of the world horizon. According to James, these fringes are felt rather than distinctly conceived (p. 275), but they will be found on the borders of any discourse that is actually expressed by a living person—no matter how abstract and precise it may be.

If we are to grasp the full meaning of the sentence to the individual uttering it, with its special shading and "its delicate idiosyncrasy", we "must reproduce the thought as it was uttered, with every word fringed and the whole sentence bathed in that original halo of obscure relations which, like an horizon, then spread about its meaning" (pp. 275–76). Every act of knowing takes place in a world horizon which, even though it may not be conceived, is dimly felt. We may push back these dim fringes, and even follow James in working out a clearer conception of them. But we cannot get rid of them altogether. This means that there is an element of vagueness involved in all knowledge of whatever kind, and that the Cartesian view is in error.

Concrete Thinking

Whether we choose to recognize it or not, we cannot lift ourselves out of the perceptual world, even in our most abstract thought and our most soaring speculations. Instead of trying to evade or suppress this fact, the radical empiricist, following James, will rather choose to recognize it. Instead of seeking to escape from the limitations of sense experience and feeling, and to negate them so far as possible, he will try rather to return to them, and to think concretely in harmony with them.

Using his concepts in this way, he will try first of all to develop and to clarify the meanings which are implicit in experience, and where this is impossible, to think clearly about the irreducible vaguenesses and ambiguities. In pursuing this endless task, he will hope to advance towards a clearer and truer insight into the patterns of the world as a whole, and the basic regions within it. Then, as he turns his attention to the concrete beings which are of special interest to him in his situation, he will hope to place them more soundly and firmly in this network of meaning.

James followed this procedure in his phenomenological and psychological writings, where he is constantly using concrete illustrations and examples, and illuminating pieces of abstract analysis with pungent flashes of concrete insight. His own practice shows us his concrete method more clearly than his theoretical remarks, and in the interpretation we have given, we have followed the former where the latter is often only ambiguous and incomplete. We have shown that this interpretation of his radical empiricism is supported by many detailed analyses to which we have referred. That its general direction is also correct, is indicated by many summary statements, with one of which we shall now end. It is from the letter written to his friend Bradley, in 1909, cited earlier, and shows, I believe, that the ideal of concrete thinking, as we have interpreted it, was a central concern of James' thought not only during the formative period of the *Psychology*, but through the whole of his career up to the very end.

"You," he says to Bradley, "loyal to the original rationalist direction which turns its back on feeling to pursue understanding through ideas, never fall back [on feeling] but continue *beyond ideas* (since they only work incomprehensibly when radically used as by you) to the supra-relational absolute in which the unity of feeling wakes up again." Turning to the dividing point where the basic issue lies, he gives the following statement: "where the roads divide, I fall back on feeling to interpret conception . . . (just as conception has to interpret feeling), and get what seems to me the fullness of knowledge out of *both*". In my opinion, the nature of concrete thinking has never been more pithily put.

Chapter Ten

❊

Instinct, Emotion, and Action

We have now reached the end. The whole second volume of
James' *Psychology* is divided into three parts in accordance with
his theory of the reflex arc; 1, incoming stimuli, sensations and
perceptions; 2, inward processes of adjustment and direction
with which we have just been concerned; and 3, bodily activities "and the forms of consciousness connected therewith" (II,
372). We have completed our consideration of 1 and 2, and will
now turn to 3, expression and action; James is concerned with
this central topic in four chapters, XXIII–XXVI, one chapter
being devoted to each of the following topics: Movement, Instinct, Emotion, and Will. We shall, therefore, begin with a
brief consideration of points in these chapters that are of special
interest from a phenomenological point of view. But during the
time when he was writing the *Psychology* and some time after,
James also wrote several essays concerned with this central topic
of action. So we shall conclude with additional points concerning
action and belief, which he deals with in these philosophical
essays.

Instinct

James thinks of instincts as "the functional correlatives of structure" (p. 383). An animal that possesses an organ will also possess an inborn tendency to use it. He defines instinct in general as "*the faculty of acting in such a way as to produce certain ends, without foresight of the ends, and without previous education in the performance*" (p. 383). In the first instance, such an instinctive act is an automatic reflex. But in man and the higher animals with memory, there is a growing flexibility. What happens on the second occasion will be affected by what happened the first time. Such instincts are flexible, and with different experiences will lead to different results. According to a widespread view, man has only a very few instincts and reflexes. On the contrary, James holds that "man has a far greater variety of *impulses* than any lower animal; and any one of these impulses, taken in itself, is as 'blind' as the lowest instinct can be . . ." (p. 390). Hence in his sense, they are instinctive. Originally, they are blind responses excited by relevant stimuli. Since two of these impulses, like shyness and sociability, may often conflict, this leads, in man, to "hesitation and choice", and further flexibility, not because he has only a few instincts, but "*rather because he has so many that they block each other's path*" (p. 393).

This brings us to the relation between instinct and habit, about which James makes a point that is worthy of serious attention. An instinctive act may be modified after being repeated one or more times. Now James develops this further (p. 390), and says that "*every instinctive act, in an animal with memory, must cease to be 'blind' after being once repeated,* and must be accompanied with foresight of its 'end' just so far as that end may have fallen under the animal's cognizance". That is, in the forming of a habit, the impulse becomes meaningful and purposive. James believes that this happens in the higher animals endowed with memory. It certainly happens in man. Furthermore "a habit, once grafted on an instinctive tendency, restricts the range of the tendency itself, and keeps us from reacting on any but the habitual object, although other objects might just as well have been chosen had they been the first-comers" (p. 395). James even suggests (p. 402) that *"most instincts are implanted for the sake of giving rise to habits"*, and that once this is accomplished, many such impulses tend to fade away.

He is speaking here not of natural teleology but of survival value. What he is suggesting is that there are different levels of behavior, in this case blind impulse and habit, one of which can get control of the other and even replace it. James bases this on phenomenological evidence, and gives many examples, like the initial interest of students which is gradually taken over by prolonged and exact training. Thus habit takes over the original interest, which is maintained, but in ever-developing forms. The action becomes purposive, its objects ordered, and its operations enormously enriched and refined. This idea has been worked out much further by Scheler in his study of higher and lower levels of behavior, and the control of the latter by the former. We have already noted James' use of this idea of appropriation in his study of self-identity (*supra*, pp. 102 ff.), and we shall see how he uses it again in his interpretation of the will.

He then gives a phenomenological review of several human impulses which he believes to be original and instinctive. Of these, his descriptions of imitation, sympathy, *Schadenfreude*, fear, miserliness, and shyness, are perhaps the most interesting. He emphasizes the point that reflex impulses often seem to be purely accidental and have no survival value. They lie at the lowest level of human action, and for the most part never become autonomous. In the normal course of development, they are taken over by higher levels, which may replace them. But ordinarily they remain as a constant, but incomplete, factor in more complex types of behavior.

Emotion and Feeling

In the next chapter (XXV), James considers the topic of emotion and feeling. It seems that he was very bored by the vast semi-literary and descriptive literature on this subject. It is certainly true that such classifications and descriptions are singularly tedious and unenlightening. This leads him to speak of the need for raising questions of genesis, and to remark that "classification and description are the lowest stage of science" (II, 454). Fortunately for us, however, James did not take these remarks too seriously, and continued with his own revealing descriptions, which now constitute the living portion of his work. They are always, even when wrong, guided by a sense for possible meaning that often leads him to qualify an original position, and even to change his mind in the light of what he finds in the facts.

This is true of his famous theory of the emotions, which he first states at the beginning of this chapter in a crude and over-simplified form, which has been widely discussed but which he is forced to qualify in the light of the evidence before the chapter is over, and in later works.[1] James begins with what he calls "the coarser emotions" in which bodily changes are more evident. He first suggests that such an emotion "follows upon the bodily expression". But he then says that our feeling of the bodily changes *as they occur* is *the emotion*" (p. 449), and that "each emotion is the resultant of a sum of elements, and each element is caused by a physiological process of a sort already well known" (p. 453). The theory then takes on a causal form which leads James to say that "we feel sorry because we cry, angry because we strike, afraid because we tremble, and not that we cry, strike, or tremble, because we are sorry, angry, or fearful, as the case may be" (p. 450). These statements in the

[1] Cf. "The Physical Basis of Emotion," *Psychological Review* (1894), pp. 516 ff.; and *Talks to Teachers* (TT), pp. 229 ff.

text can readily be interpreted in a purely physicalist sense. Certain stimuli cause a bodily response, say weeping, which is attended by certain internal feelings called *grief*.

We have already noted, however, that James rejects any such epiphenomenalist theory (*supra*, pp. 12 ff.). He is basically concerned to show the primacy of bodily response in feeling. And this can be defended. But in this case, his interest in the body leads him to give it a causal priority, and to eliminate meaning from emotion in an indefensible way, which he is soon forced to qualify. The Dutch phenomenologist Linschoten, in his study of James' *Principles*[2] has clearly revealed these qualifications, and the direction towards which they are moving.

First of all, we must not forget the context, and at the very beginning of the chapter, James makes it clear that emotions are often excited by objects with which we have no practical dealings. "A ludicrous object, for example, or a beautiful object are not necessarily objects to which we *do* anything; we simply laugh, or stand in admiration, as the case may be" (II, 442). Such objects are not bare stimuli. They bear a meaning. This is also true of the objects of memory and imagination, which "may suffice to liberate the excitement. One may get angrier in thinking over one's insult than at the moment of receiving it; and we melt more over a mother who is dead than we ever did when she was living" (pp. 442–43). He also says that when the object is physically present, it must be first perceived before the bodily changes (p. 449), and we have just seen (*supra*, pp. 188 ff. and 235 ff.) that we perceive things that are discriminated and compared in a field of meaning. We cannot feel a situation that bears no meaning.

All this is implicit in the causal language James uses in first outlining his theory of the coarse emotions. It is true that when we perceive, or imagine, two keen knife blades with their edges in contact moving to and fro, it sets "our whole nervous organization . . . 'on-edge' ". This immediate bodily reaction may be a

---

[2] J. Linschoten, *Auf dem Wege zu einer phänomenologischen Psychologie*, Berlin, 1961, pp. 217–24.

"senseless bodily effect" (II, 458). But "the mental emotion follows" (p. 461). It is the way in which we take over the bodily change and feel the edginess of the situation in which it is involved. This becomes clearer when James turns to the moral, intellectual, and aesthetic feelings, or the "subtler emotions", as he calls them (p. 468).

Here he distinguishes between a perceptual, or "cognitive", element and the following feeling of the situation with bodily reverberations. Without this bodily feeling there may be cognition, but no vital assimilation, which requires something more. Thus "unless we actually laugh at the neatness of the demonstration or witticism; unless we thrill at the case of justice, or tingle at the act of magnanimity; our state of mind can hardly be called emotion at all" (p. 471). This element of feeling, as James has said, is subjective. It "stains" or "tinges" every mental act as belonging to the living stream of thought. This feeling is vague, but it gives us their fringes, and places them in our world. For any definite object "this tinging is its sensitive body, the *wie ihm zu Muthe ist*, the way it feels whilst passing" (I, 478, note). Feeling gives us "premonitions, awarenesses of direction", and that vague sense of ultimate meaning which finally guides us in our endeavors.

This is borne out by a significant passage from his *Talks to Teachers*, written in 1892, two years after the publication of the *Principles*. He says here (TT, p. 229): "where we judge a thing to be precious in consequence of the *idea* we frame of it, this is only because the idea is itself associated already with a feeling. If we were radically feelingless, and if ideas were the only things our minds could entertain, we should lose all our likes and dislikes at a stroke, and be unable to point to any one situation or experience in life more valuable or significant than any other". We may sense specific qualities and specific objects one by one. But the value of the total situation is felt by a feeling which has the last word, or rather the last expression, on these things and persons as they pass by. In this aspect of his theory, James is very close to Max Scheler, who also held that value is apprehended not by thought but rather by feeling.[3] Further-more, these feelings are corporeal, and this central aspect of his hypothesis James never qualifies or retracts. "If our hypothesis is true", he says, "it makes us realize more deeply than ever how much our mental life is knit up with our corporeal frame, in the strictest sense of the term" (II, 467). The feeling cannot exist apart from its expression. "Whatever moods, affections, and passions I have are in very truth constituted by, and made up of, those bodily changes which we ordinarily call their expression . . ." (p. 452). Without the living body which is the centre of my world, "I should be excluded from the life of the affections, harsh and tender alike, and drag out an existence of merely cognitive or intellectual form" (pp. 452–53). I would, in short, become a computer with no inherent sense of ultimate direction or value.

James was especially anxious to make this point against the spiritualism and transcendentalism of his time. So he chose to begin with emotions, since, in them, the bodily element is more evident, and he sometimes speaks of feeling as though it were a species under this genus. That this is not his real meaning is shown by his choice of feeling as a general name for all psychic states (I, 185–86), and, as against thought, for the whole of what we know by direct acquaintance. Linschoten is therefore right in holding that, for James, feeling is the more general term. Emotion is the name for a special kind of feeling in which bodily changes are peculiarly evident. In extreme situations, like that of panic, as Strasser has shown,[4] these changes, and the feelings attending them, become blind, and lead to breakdown and paralysis. But for the most part, feelings are not blind. They give us a knowledge that is vague and inclusive, but original and direct. This knowledge by acquaintance is not exclusively objective but relates these objects to the bodily subject. It gives us a sense of transition, of direction, and of the

[3] *Der Formalismus in der Ethik und die materiale Wertethik*, Halle, 1927, pp. 260 ff.
[4] *Cf.* S. Strasser, *Das Gemüt*, Utrecht, 1956, pp. 179 ff.

fringes and meanings of things. As we have seen, it is prior to thought (*supra,* pp. 49 ff.). But the third member of the traditional trilogy, thought, will, and feeling, has not yet been considered. So let us now turn to the topic of will.

Will

According to James, the living organism is a selective agency, and the welcoming of certain objects, together with the rejection of others, is an essential aspect of the stream of consciousness (I, 284 ff.). Of the myriad possible stimuli in the world, our sense organs select only a relatively few for response. Then the formation of habits leads us to select a few of these for organized response. Of these simpler habits, certain ones are then selected for higher habits of a more complex order, and so on. James often uses the term *choice* as a synonym for this selective activity. Thus even at the pre-linguistic levels of perception, he speaks of all the visual shapes of the table which appear. Out of these, we select certain ones as the real shape, and James speaks of this as the "choice of the visual reality" (II, 237).

A living organism could not exist unless it selected certain objects and avoided others. Its very existence is a selective choice among possible alternatives. Hence it is not surprising to find that James rejects the traditional view of voluntary choice as the activity of a special faculty, marked off from the other human parts. He regards it rather as the highest level of a vital autonomy that is deeply rooted in the human body and, indeed, in life itself. This does not lead him to deny human freedom. The empirical evidence for this experience is too strong. But the freedom in which he believes is a freedom of the living body and, after examining the phenomena of experience, he is constantly trying to show that they can be reconciled with what is known of the central nervous system.

Underlying his whole consideration of the will is his conception of the reflex arc, and the principle of ideo-motor action.

Every incoming current must eventually find a release in bodily movement of some kind. Hence every sensation, perception, or idea in the brain, must have a tendency to produce such action. Consciousness is not a useless epiphenomenon. It always tends to action, and different modes of consciousness lead to different types of activity. Hence according to James' theory, as we have seen (*supra*, pp. 15 ff.), consciousness makes a difference. In answer to the question as to why then we seem to have so many ideas that remain sterile and inefficacious, James replies that this is because they are inhibited by other ideas with other tendencies. If the idea is to be fulfilled, we must either forget or overcome these inhibiting tendencies. To illustrate this, James gives the following description, which has often been quoted.

"We know what it is to get out of bed on a freezing morning in a room without a fire, and how the very vital principle within us protests against the ordeal. Probably most people have lain on certain mornings for an hour at a time unable to brace themselves to the resolve. We think how late we shall be, how the duties of the day will suffer; we say, 'I *must* get up, this is ignominious', etc.; but still the warm couch feels too delicious, the cold outside too cruel, and resolution faints away and postpones itself again and again just as it seemed on the verge of bursting the resistance and passing over into the decisive act. Now how do we *ever* get up under such circumstances? If I may generalize from my own experience, we more often than not get up without any struggle or decision at all. We suddenly find that we *have* got up. A fortunate lapse of consciousness occurs; we forget both the warmth and the cold; we fall into some revery connected with the day's life, in the course of which the idea flashes across us, 'Hollo! I must lie here no longer'—an idea which at that lucky instant awakens no contradictory or paralyzing suggestions, and consequently produces immediately its appropriate motor effects. It was our acute consciousness of both the warmth and the cold during the period of struggle, which paralyzed our activity then and kept our idea of rising in the condition of *wish* and not of *will*. The moment these inhibitory ideas ceased, the original idea exerted its effects" (II, 524-52).

Of course, we cannot will without willing to do something. In this case, it is the act of rising, with which we are already familiar as having been often repeated before, which can be released by the proper cue. Voluntary acts are, therefore, higher level acts which order and regulate those of a lower level already learned. Without such habits at our disposal, we would not be able to anticipate the consequences of any bodily motion, and a voluntary purposive act would be impossible. This is an internal self-regulative process in which established habits are selected and recombined by action at a higher level. James believes that this is made possible by the complexity and instability of the connections in the brain. Thus at times of conflict and hesitation when nervous discharge is temporarily blocked, new selections and combinations can be made by nervous processes we feel as deliberation and concentration of attention. For James holds that these "drainage currents and discharges of the brain are not purely physical facts. They are *psycho-physical* . . ." (p. 583).

Five Types of Decision

The major types of decision which we find in experience are described in the section entitled "Five Types of Decision" (pp. 531 ff.). The first is what James calls "the *reasonable type.*" In this, all the possible ways of conceiving the doing or not doing of an act are carefully run through and turned over in the mind. But there is an easy transition from doubt to assurance, for we soon find a familiar way of conceiving the situation which applies to the case at hand, and doubt comes to an end. We seem almost passive, for the decisive reasons seem to flow in from the nature of things, owing nothing to our will. Nevertheless we feel perfectly free, and under no compulsion. When we recognize a situation as unprecedented, it is more difficult. But the wise man is one who has a store of stable and worthy ends. And even in one of these indeterminate situations, after careful review, he will find it possible to bring it under an end, and to devise ways of acting which are ministerial to it. For James, the reasonable man has made his basic decisions already. His ends are chosen, and his character is essentially fixed. Decision means, for him, only a prudent selection of effective means.

In the next two types, the evidence seems indecisive. There are goods involved in each of the alternatives before us, and we cannot make a reasonable choice between them. Finally, after prolonged brooding, we become restless, and feel that even a bad decision may be better than none. In such a condition, it may often happen that some accident may upset the balance and incline us towards the one path or the other. In the second type, this accident is external. In the third, it is some chance feeling that may release the flow along habitual paths. For a time, we may feel that we are acting almost automatically. But then, weary of the fears and scruples that have pent us in, we simply go along with the stream as it bursts unexpectedly through the dam. Both types of fiat may give us a sense of being swept on by forces over which we have little control, but in James' analysis, it is the third type especially that gives rise to the feeling of fatalism. And as he says: "the fatalistic mood itself is sure to reinforce the strength of the energy just started on its exciting path of discharge" (p. 533). His whole mode of speech and the metaphors he uses make it clear that James is thinking of deliberation as a mutual inhibition of nervous currents leading in different directions, and of fiat as the conquest of one nervous pathway over another. These are the physical correlates of the psychisms we experience.

In the fourth type, the period of deliberation and conflict comes to an equally abrupt end, which may arise from external or internal changes. But here there is a basic change of heart which involves a change of motive and scheme of values. This is similar to one of the basic shifts in attitude which James later considered in his chapters on conversion in *The Varieties of Religious Experience* and which he there calls "involuntary and unconscious" (p. 202). In nervous terms, a new set of attitudes and habits has been prepared and lies ready to assume control, but has been inhibited and forced into the subconscious and sub-verbal by a previously dominant condition of mind. Then all of a sudden, the shock of grief or fear brings these subliminal patterns into the open, and they assume control. The second mode of conversion, which James calls "conscious and voluntary", occurs more gradually and reflectively. It corresponds to the fifth type of decision which James considers here.

The fifth type is clearly the only one which, according to James' view, really deserves the name of authentic decision. We may have a sense that all the rational evidence is in, and that it points in one direction. But something more is necessary. We must believe in this evidence, and relate it to ourselves before we can act. By adding this element of belief, we weigh down the beam, and make the decision ours. Or we may believe that the evidence is still incomplete. But we may still take this evidence up into a complete interpretation which does justice to it, and believe in this as the background of our action. In this case, we have made a "creative contribution of something instead of a reason which does a reason's work" (PR, II, 534).

In both cases, we have a feeling, lacking in the other four types, that the decision is ours. As James says, there is a "slow dead heave of the will", which distinguishes this from all the other types. In these, also, the other alternatives sink away and fade from our view. But in this last type, we are aware of the good which they contain. Nevertheless, in spite of the loss, we continue to make the sacrifice. This deliberate sacrifice gives us a sense of *"inward effort"* (p. 534) which is lacking in the other types. According to James, it may involve a focusing of attention in a certain direction that may achieve a nervous release down certain paths that may change an act, and ultimately a whole way of life. As he sees it, this is the heart of our human freedom, and deserves a special comment.

Freedom of Belief and Fatalism

Two ever-present tendencies stand in freedom's way, which we may call diseases of the will. The first is the "explosive" temperament which gives way to momentary impulse, without sufficient inhibition and concentration of attention. The second and opposite tendency James calls the "obstructed" will. In cases of this kind, the period of deliberation calls forth so many inhibitions and scruples that the remote goals and ideals, which may be thoroughly worked out as possibilities are never expressed in action. Such intellectual reflections become a mere game, and their authors do not believe in the endless possibilities which they constantly explore. The explosive temperament loses itself in incessant activity, with little stable meaning; the obstructed will in endless possibilities with no reality. Both lack what James calls "vision" (pp. 536, 546–47)—belief in the reality of a broad field of meaning that can elicit action. This comes only with an effort which inhibits impulses of the moment for the sake of concentration on abstract and distant goals that are hard to achieve.

James sometimes talks as if sheer occupancy of the mind were enough for voluntary decision. But as we have just seen in the case of the obstructed will, this is not his meaning. If the meaning is to become real for us, it must not be focused only at certain expected intervals and as a mere, abstract possibility out of any relation to our factual situation in the world. This is only a bare beginning. The idea must be brought into relation with the agent, and believed in as not only real in itself, but as real for him. Only then will it come to fill the mind permanently and with ease, so as to inhibit other contradictory ideas during periods of conflict and tension. When the meaning is found in something we recognize as existent, we say, it is so. When we see it to be something in the future, depending on our effort, we say let it be. In either case it "stings" us with a sense of reality that is expressed by the indicative and imperative moods, which are "ultimate categories of thinking" as well as forms of grammar.

In both cases, the word reality means that the thing is taken over into our world by belief. "It is a relation to our life. It means our adoption of the things, our caring for them, our standing by them. . . . And the transition from merely considering an object as possible, to deciding or willing it to be real; the change from the fluctuating to the stable personal attitude concerning it; from the 'don't care' state of mind to that in which 'we mean business', is one of the most familiar things in life. We can partly enumerate its conditions. . . . But the change itself as a subjective phenomenon is something which we can translate into no simpler terms" (p. 569; *cf. infra,* Chapter XI, pp. 277 ff.).

The essence of this process is the ability, first of all, to pay attention to meanings that are not familiar and, therefore, abstract and remote. After this, it is also necessary to hold on to the idea steadily, until the mind becomes filled with it in what we call *conviction*, or *belief*. In James' view, this is the very heart of what we mean by freedom and responsibility, and as he says, "the whole drama is a mental drama. The whole difficulty is a mental difficulty, a difficulty with an object of our thought" (II, 564). At the beginning, these ideas are possibilities only for periods of contemplation, with no firm ground of belief. The self is under the control of impulse and external circumstance, with no ideas of his own. The only way of bridging this chasm between possibility and actuality is for the self to take over some of these meanings, to become absorbed in them until he can believe and call them his own. In this way, abstract meanings may become embodied, and existence meaningful and free. Hence James can conclude that *"the essential achievement of the will, in short, when it is most 'voluntary', is to* ATTEND *to a difficult object, and hold it fast before the mind"* (p. 561). This is also the ultimate root of our self-control and freedom, the heart of James' ethics (*cf.* next chapter).

If we turn to experience, we find that our efforts, so far as we exert them, come from us, and that we can apply ourselves with a greater or less intensity in any given case. The determinist, however, is always able to say that it is a mere function of the object. As a scientist who is concerned with objective studies of the body and the brain, the psychologist must be open to this postulate of determinism. This is why James says at one point that "the question of free-will is insoluble on strictly psychologic grounds" (II, p. 572). But the first duty of the psychologist is not to accept *a priori* postulates, but to follow the phenomena as they are lived. As in other living parts of his text, James follows this first duty here.

The phenomena lead us beyond the narrower objective frames of the sciences into a wider world where there is room for so-called subjective as well as for objective factors. "Science, however, must be constantly reminded", he says, "that her purposes are not the only purposes, and that the order of uniform causation which she has use for, and is therefore right in postulating, may be enveloped in a wider order, on which she has no claims at all" (p. 576). In this wider world, we feel ourselves directly to be making or not to be making an effort which is under our control. Here, belief takes the place of objective theory. There are a host of other phenomena, like remorse, specifically mentioned here, which lose their original meaning when placed within a deterministic frame. Nevertheless one can choose determinism and believe in it, which, according to James (p. 573), is a free choice leading us away from freedom. And at this point, he brings up a phenomenological argument which is worthy of reflection.

When determinism ceases to be more than an abstract theory and becomes an attitude of life, it turns into something else for which the theoretical philosopher has little respect. This is *fatalism*, a living attitude holding that it is hopeless to resist the great tide of forces into which we have been thrown, and denying that there is "anything really mine in the decisions which I make" (p. 574). As James says, this is a very dubious ally for the theory of determinism, for it feels the impotence of a free effort which it seems to understand very clearly. Otherwise, how could it be haunted by its absence? When we try to live out a theory of determinism, we find that our sense of freedom refuses to be completely suppressed, but continues to imagine the very possibility that the attitude denies. James is speaking here not as a strict scientist but rather as a phenomenological psychologist who recognizes that, while he must take account of the objective facts, there are also other facts of life which he must recognize, if he is to gain any understanding of human existence as it is actually lived in the world of man.

One point especially needs to be made in thinking of James' treatment of the problem of freedom in his *Psychology*. He still uses the traditional phrase "freedom of the will". But the net upshot of his discussion is a complete break with this traditional conception, which held that the mind was determined by its objects, but that the special faculty of will has a limited freedom of action. For James, on the other hand, there is no such isolated active freedom. The first source of our actual freedom is rather mental. It is in this last citadel that the human person can become aware of the vast system of habits already accumulated, and can anticipate their consequences in any given situation. By focusing his attention on certain broad patterns of meaning, the person may then reform and recombine them in new ways.

James held that the seat of this self-regulating process lay in the brain. But he also held that what goes on there must be ultimately interpreted in the light of the phenomena as they are directly lived. We have noted how our experiences of impulse, action, and self-regulation take us into the wider world of life which, in some of its distinctive manifestations, can no longer be approached by the limited methods of psychology. Let us now turn, therefore, to the essays which James wrote during and after the writing of his *Psychology*, and where he can devote himself, in a less restricted way, to certain basic problems of belief, action, and freedom.

Part Three

❀

Responsible Action and the Strenuous Life. How Beliefs Are Verified

Chapter Eleven

❈

Ethics

We have now considered James' treatment of the three basic types of intention, or departments of the mind, in the *Principles* —sensation and perception, by which facts are grasped; thought and reasoning, by which meanings are developed; and, finally, feeling and action, by which values are recognized and achieved. We must now turn to the subject of ethics, which is concerned with the nature of action and values, and the different ways in which they may be ordered and controlled. We have noted (*supra,* pp. 215–16) that James does not regard these departments as independent faculties but as mutually inter-dependent powers which can function together in an "organic" way. Hence, while ethics is perhaps more closely connected with action, it also involves the other departments as well. So we shall first consider the relation of ethics to being and factuality, then to meaning and belief, and finally to action, and the distinctive features of James' ethical views. But since human action is a response to some vision of the world, it cannot be sharply separated from the other traditional branches of philosophy. One might say that James' whole philosophy is an ethics.

Being and Mystery

We have already considered the stubborn element of brute factuality which resists our meanings and to which James, therefore, refers as a "mystic element" in being. This places a severe limit on the speculations of an empirical philosopher who, if he is to avoid mere verbalism, must take account of these alien, brute facts. He cannot simply develop a great synthetic conception, and follow the argument wherever it may lead in the manner of the Platonists. He must also recognize a set of criteria quite different from those of logic. He must constantly try to get outside of his argument in order to look at the relevant facts, where he will always find an element of "opacity" that will lead him to adopt a more hypothetical and tentative tone. He must avoid dogmatism at any cost, though this does not mean that he must fall into a sterile scepticism that blocks further inquiry.

This recognition of the opacity of being has further implications for the ethical reflections of an empirically oriented thinker, two of which we have briefly noted. In the first place, in the moral world in which we exist, there is an unmediated dialectic between being and non-being, quite different from the mediated dialectic of conceptual thinking which takes existence for granted. On this basis, which is simply assumed, it concerns itself with possibilities which may be reconciled and held together in wide-ranging syntheses. In real life, however, this is not the case, for however it may be in the field of possibilities, in the actual world, we cannot both have our cake and eat it. Here a real choice must be made with respect to being itself, which underlies all possibilities. Here the question is to be or not to be. The choice concerns existence or non-existence, life or death.

This is the supreme challenge, and the moral philosopher should recognize its presence in any appeal that he makes. Like Kierkegaard, James recognized a certain connection between the ethical and the religious. So in trying to express the strenuous urgency of the moral appeal, he finds biblical language appropriate. "'See, I have set before thee this day life and good, and death and evil; therefore, choose life that thou and thy seed may live'—when this challenge comes to us, it is simply our total character and personal genius that are on trial . . ." (MPM, p. 214). This sense of urgency carries with it the direct feeling of existence. Hence as James repeatedly emphasizes, it is discounted and ignored by abstract, theoretical science and speculation.

The same is true of freedom. The great theoretical systems that have been formulated in our Western intellectual history have wasted little time in observing the vagueness and opacity which pervade the facts of life, and lie at the root of our human freedom. Their aim has been to overcome these "irrational" elements, together with the abrupt discontinuities that stand in the way of a monistic system of meaning. And they have succeeded so well that little or no place has been left for freedom. One who has closely followed the age-old controversies between the determinists and the advocates of "free will" can hardly avoid the conclusion that, whatever the facts may be, it is the determinists who have had the better of the argument.

Thus in his essay "The Sentiment of Rationality," James considers the view of the evolutionary moralists of his own time who hold: *'that is to be called good which is destined to prevail or survive"* (SR, p. 98). As he points out, this kind of a system simply leaves out freedom and the moral situation altogether, and thus ignores its own beginning—that a moral standard is needed to help us make moral decisions. But the upshot of the theory is simply to pass over the actual situation, for it tells us simply to wait until the laws of nature, or other persons, or both together, determine what is going to survive. It leads us not into a merely logical contradiction, but into something more basic which we have called an existential self-contradiction. It is a way of acting that denies its own factual conditions, and thus refutes itself. As James says, "its general observance would lead to its practical refutation by bringing about a general deadlock. Each good man hanging back and waiting for orders from the rest, absolute stagnation would ensue. Happy, then, if a few unrighteous ones contribute an initiative which sets things moving again!" (p. 99).

As Socrates long ago pointed out in the *Gorgias,* the same holds true of any ethics of might, or a ruling dialectic of history, which brings only good into being and determines what is as right. It is futile to argue conceptually against such a theory. The only sound mode of argument lies in an appeal to the brute facts. Has the theorist ever found himself in a moral situation? Has he ever had to decide? As a result of this, has he ever acted on his own in a way that counted? If such questions elicit no affirmative sense of the facts, the situation is hopeless. Many students find James' repeated attacks against intellectualism unfounded and tedious. But they come from a basic feeling for real existence that we have already seen at work in his *Principles.* This led him to see in many different contexts the way in which philosophical theories conceal the facts.

But there are other theories that are even more dangerous. This is because they still use the language of moral experience—freedom, choice, responsibility, etc., but take them up into a system of meaning which destroys their original factual sense. James identifies two distinct types and deals with them at some length. The first is the rationalistic type of determinism which identifies freedom with the acceptance of what is deemed "necessary" or "rational" by the system, or with "the ridiculous 'freedom to do right', which in my mouth can only mean the freedom to do as *I* think right" (OSH, p. 271). Such systems result from a free choice on the part of their authors. But, like Sartre, James sees their attempts to identify their own decisions with the divine Will, or with the necessary order of the universe, as the intellectual despotism of a "closet-philosopher" seeking to evade his own responsibility. Thus he enjoys the story about the poet Heine, who "is said to have written 'Bunsen' in the place of 'Gott' in his copy of that author's work entitled 'God in History,' so as to make it read 'Bunsen in der Geschichte'" (MPM, p. 203). One cannot really escape from his responsibility by apotheosizing his views.

Soft Determinism and Freedom

"Soft determinism" is another sophisticated way of making verbal concessions to the sense of freedom, while keeping an over-arching determinism intact. This theory, which was defended by James' friend Shadworth Hodgson, is still very much alive in our time. On this view, true freedom does not refer to a real decision for one of two incompatible acts, which makes a difference in the course of history here and now. This is a delusion. Real freedom, on the contrary, is acting without external restraint in such a way that the causes of the action lie within the agent. According to James, there is only a verbal difference between this theory and the traditional hard determinism which "did not shrink from such words as fatality, bondage of the will, necessitation and the like" (DOD, p. 149). The great defenders of this view, like Spinoza, certainly recognized causal agencies internal to man. The new soft determinists are making the same factual judgments. They too deny that decisions are what they seem to be. The world is a block universe strictly determined by causal laws. The only difference lies in the avoidance of harsh words. Thus the soft determinist avoids words like *fatality* and *necessity*, and simply uses the word *freedom* in their place, so that freedom comes to mean "only necessity understood, and bondage to the highest is identical with true freedom" (p. 149). James notes how Hodgson does not hesitate to call himself a "free will determinist".

As James says, "all this is a quagmire of evasion under which the real issue of fact has been entirely smothered" (p. 149). The basic issues of philosophy are concerned with the meaning of facts, not verbal formulations. And there is a real issue of fact at stake, "an issue of the most momentous importance". Is the individual man really autonomous in any sense? Does he or does he not make real decisions? James believes that the direct evidence of lived experience justifies an affirmative answer. If so, what does this mean?

Before we turn to these questions, we must note that in his moral writings James makes use of the term *freedom* only rather rarely. This is because of the way in which philosophers have used it for special kinds of determinism, and because of the general confusion into which its original meaning has been allowed to fall, as he specifically says in "The Dilemma of Determinism" (p. 151). But we must not follow certain interpreters who have construed this absence of the term as an absence of interest in human freedom as a specifically ethical concept.[1] This freedom cannot be "proved" by any conceptual argument (DOD, pp. 150, 159). It can be shown forth by descriptions of the experience itself with which we are directly acquainted.

The references to this experience in James' moral writings are closely connected with the account of the sense of effort he has given in the *Principles,* Chapter XI. Such descriptions will make no sense to one who cannot recall the original as he has lived it through. The use of a fixed concept, like that of freedom, by no means guarantees such a recall. In fact, as we have just seen, it may become so abstract and indeterminate by habitual usage as to convey only very partial or distorted meanings, or even those that are precisely opposite to the original sense of the experience.

In this experience, one feels the presence of opposed possibilities in an ambiguous situation where either may become real. When the act of decision occurs, of these opposed "futures that offer themselves to our choice" (DOD, p. 157), one is "mur-

---

[1] Thus R. B. Perry in his work, *The Thought and Character of William James* (Boston, 1935), deals with freedom and with ethics in widely separated chapters, and hardly mentions freedom in the latter. This, I believe, is a misunderstanding, for, in James' mind, freedom is not merely a metaphysical condition for the possibility of moral experience. It is itself an experience which lies at the centre of ethics as he understands it, and bears an intrinsic value of the highest order. Furthermore, he is able to use other terms to refer to this experience, such as *chance* and *decision* in *The Dilemma of Determinism,* decision (DOD, p. 183), *pluralism,* and even *the moral universe* (SR, p. 103).

dered", and the other realized in the present so as "to transform an equivocal and double future into an inalterable and
simple past" (p. 158). If the situation is of any importance and
the stakes are high, one is aware of a concentration of attention,
a sense of effort in which something is being decided for well
or ill here and now. It is by choices of this kind, that characters
are reformed, whole destinies changed, and new worlds brought
into being. Of course one may raise the question of evidence,
for which, as an empiricist, James is well prepared. Why, one
may ask, is this not a subjective delusion? To this, the reply
will take the form of another question. What evidence is
firmer than that of direct experience, expressed through a description of the experience as it is lived? If such evidence is to be
discounted, what else can possibly stand?

In this connection, it is important to note that the only other
"argument" presented in "The Dilemma of Determinism" follows
a similar, empirical form. It is not based on an uncritical use
of abstract concepts. It is rather a "critical", empirical argument,
which refers to a feeling with which most men are directly
acquainted. The argument simply shows forth the sense of the
feeling of remorse, or regret, and brings out some of its fringe
relations. The experience of free choice is central to our human
existence. Hence many other feelings lie on its fringes, and are
closely connected with it. Regret is one of these, for I feel no
remorse over what is necessary, but only for what was ambiguous, and freely chosen—for what really might have been otherwise.

Hence the determinist, who denies the reality of free choice,
has trouble in accounting for this feeling and the sense it bears.
If in contemplating a sordid murder in Brockton, we feel regret,
or the murderer perhaps feels remorse, then it is hard for the
determinist who accepts the feeling, to avoid a negative judgment on the whole block universe which necessarily produced
such an occurrence. If, on the other hand, he rejects the feeling
as a mere delusion, this also becomes a defect for which the
whole block universe is responsible. So in either case, he is led
to a cosmic pessimism which tends to dilute the exercise of effort

by making all action futile in the end. This is the dilemma of determinism, into which it falls as a result of ignoring a basic fact of life.

Another fact, which tends to confirm James' view that freedom is a basic character of human existence, is the phenomenon of "forced options", as he calls them in "The Will to Believe."[2] This is connected with the selective activity, which, as we have seen, belongs to pre-reflective life (cf. supra, pp. 16–17 ff.). Just as the organism is forced by its nature to select the stimuli to which it will respond, so, after the coming of language, the free man is forced to select some pattern of habit rather than others to dominate his waking existence. James refers to these selections as options rather than as free decisions because of the seemingly passive and half-concealed form that they often may take.

The logic of abstract reason, which pays no attention to the distinctive qualities of our active nature, tells us that we may avoid the risks of decision by postponing judgment until decisive evidence is found. This waiting logic may apply to less important, "trivial" options which do not directly concern our vital interests. But it does not apply to the momentous over-all issues of life. Here time is short and the attitude of doubt is equivalent to a negative stand against belief. "Scepticism . . . is not avoidance of option; it is option of a certain particular kind of risk" (EFM, p. 57), namely that evidence, sufficient to make real decision on our part unnecessary, will eventually come in. In the light of our intellectual history to date, this risk would seem to be very great indeed. In any case, we cannot avoid taking a stand on such questions, for the universe will not allow us to be neutral in real life. ". . . Dodge, or hedge, or talk as we like about a wise scepticism, we are really doing volunteer military service for one side or the other" (SR, p. 109). But instead of evading these choices and trying to conceal them, is it not more honest for us to face them and to choose that direction of action where the greatest challenge seems to lie? As we shall

---

[2] The first essay in WBA, appearing on pp. 1–31, "The Will to Believe" is published in EFM on pp. 32–62. Page references will be to EFM.

see, such an argument lies at the heart of James' appeal for the "strenuous mood", as he calls it, which lies at the heart of his ethics.

Thus even though we try to escape from it, or at least conceal it from ourselves, freedom remains an inescapable fact of human existence. This notion seems to be confirmed by another fact which impressed James very deeply, and to which he devoted serious attention in several of his moral essays: the vast diversity of differing aims and ideals that is found among different groups and among individual members of the same societies. This philosophic pluralism, which is found not only in the history of philosophy but also in the philosophies of living men, is carefully described and analyzed in "The Moral Philosopher and the Moral Life" (MPM, pp. 198 ff.). James argues that this vast diversity of ideals cannot be explained solely by the influence of diverse environments on passive minds. He concludes that in part, at least, they are the "brain-born" expressions of a native originality peculiar to man (cf. PR, II, 639 ff.).

Then he underlines the massive variety of what is actually found. ". . . In spite of the presence of a large number of ideals in which human beings agree, there are a mass of others about which no general consensus obtains" (MPM, p. 198). The traditional, philosophical attitude to this great cloud of conflicting views, which are constantly arising from the stresses of history, is disapproving disparagement, for there can be only one truth. Hence, this confusion of divergent attitudes, each fighting with the rest for a place in the sun, must be due to a lack of intellectual discipline, and to the obnoxious influence of subjective prejudice and desire.

But perhaps philosophy is not rightly understood as the attempt to find a single solution to an objective problem. Perhaps it has something to do with the roots of freedom. So looking at the matter in this way, James takes a very unconventional position. "Think of Zeno", he says, "and of Epicurus, think of Calvin and of Paley, think of Kant and Schopenhauer, of Herbert Spencer and John Henry Newman, no longer as one-sided champions of special ideals, but as schoolmasters deciding what all must think,—and what more grotesque topic could a satirist wish for on which to exercise his pen? The fabled attempt of Mrs. Partington to arrest the rising tide of the North Atlantic with her broom was a reasonable spectacle compared with their effort to substitute the content of their clean-shaven systems for that exuberant mass of goods with which all human nature is in travail, and groaning to bring to the light of day" (MPM, p. 204). As James then suggests, our slumbering revolutionary instincts are awakened even by the thought of such a tyranny.

"Better chaos forever than an order based on any closet-philosopher's rule." Mental freedom is too precious. So James welcomes the diversity. Does this mean, then, that for the sake of freedom, the empirical philosopher must pay an equal respect to all claims made by any individual, no matter how fantastic and tyrannical they may be? Must he then fall into a relativistic scepticism, and thus "give up the notion of being a philosopher at all?" (p. 204).

James gives a negative answer to these questions, which lies at the heart of his moral thinking. But the answer takes a twofold form that has often been reduced to its former part at the cost of what I believe to be a basic and widespread misunderstanding. This first part of the answer takes the form of what Professor Perry has called the "principle of inclusiveness". James develops this on pages 205–8 of his essay. We should try always "to satisfy at all times *as many demands as we can*", so that "the victory to be philosophically prayed for is that of the more inclusive side" (p. 205). Many influential commentators have identified this more or less utilitarian answer with James' final ethical position.[3] All ethical demands are on the same

---

[3] Thus Dewey, in a letter to James, says about "*The Moral Philosopher and the Moral Life*": "the article rejoiced me greatly . . . two things more than others . . . your statement that any desire, as such, constitutes a claim and any claim an obligation, and your discussion of rules" (R. B. Perry, *Thought and Character of William James*, Boston, 1935, II, 517), and takes no notice of the latter part of the essay. E. C. Moore in his book *American Pragmatism* (Columbia University Press, 1961) quotes Dewey's statement concerning the right, that "its authority is the exigency of their [other per-

qualitative level. Those, however, which can be reconciled with more of the others are to be preferred.

I do not believe that this is James' final moral position, even if we look exclusively at *The Moral Philosopher and the Moral Life*. If we consider his other moral writings, the case becomes much stronger. But in order to understand his moral philosophy as a whole, we must first look at his account of human aims, and in particular his distinction between the "strenuous" and the "easy-going" types (MPM, pp. 211 ff.). In order to understand this distinction, we must again consider the phenomenological description of belief and action.

It is clear that, for James, action, the third department of the mind, is the final member of the reflex arc triad and necessarily involves the other two. At the lower organic levels, there is first the reception of a stimulus, then internal hesitation and preparation in the nervous system, and finally the active response. In man, the situation is much more complex, but a similar pattern can be recognized. Attention must first be paid to the relevant facts as they are, both where they are opaque as well as where they are clear. Then a pattern of action must be prepared and chosen. Only then will a meaningful and autonomous response be achieved. But while the department of action necessarily involves the other two, it nevertheless possesses certain distinctive features of its own.

In the first place, it is through this part of the mind that we can see facts as such to be always open to different possibilities

<hr />

sons'] demands, the efficacy of their insistencies", p. 244. Then he says: "the reader who is familiar with William James' essay "The Moral Philosopher and the Moral Life" will recognize the identity of Dewey's interpretation with the view put forth by James in the latter part of that essay", not mentioning James' discussion of "the strenuous mood" (MPM, pp. 211–15). Perry also has identified James' "systematic ethics" with this doctrine of inclusiveness, which resembles his own point of view, and never considers James' ideas of *seriousness* and *freedom* in an ethical context. Indeed, according to him, "this heroic motive in James was connected with his neurasthenia" (*Thought and Character*, II, 271).

and, therefore, indifferent. A similar remark may be made about rational reflection, at least in its abstract, or isolated, state. In this abstract condition, it tends to regard everything, including desire, from a detached point of view, and to weave them together into a continuous system of meaning which is simply there as a fact. All partial points of view then become relative. While the whole system may be judged to be absolutely good, no one part is better than any other. The essence of reason is to be impartial and, therefore, beyond any partial commitment to anything really within our reach.

In spite of its totalitarian claims, James saw that something essentially human is missing from this absolutism, which is always implicit in the operations of reason. This is the believing, active element in our human nature, which is concerned for this rather than that, and is moving in one direction rather than another. It is this active element which chooses A rather than B, becomes committed, and even devoted to it. The theorist, however, in his proper place, is preparing for belief and choice, not choosing. So he rightly remains uncommitted—with a view towards commitment and devotion. But if he absolutizes this detached point of view, which is a point of view, then his absolute position becomes relative. His theoretical completeness becomes incomplete, because the realm of action has been forgotten. So his impartiality becomes partial and biased. This is the point of James' critique of intellectualism. He is aiming at a less abstract and broader point of view. It is only by recognizing the partiality of belief and engagement that we find a place for pluralism and for freedom in the world.

The facts about me are now true of me as I have been. They are oriented towards my past. The meanings guiding my acts are either timeless, or oriented towards the future. But the acts themselves take place in the moving present. It is only in this present that I insert myself into the real world with a chance of becoming myself. It is only in this present that the past is remembered or forgotten, and the future projected or rejected. We live only in the present, and there is a very special sense in which we *are* these present acts. I am always at a distance from my past and from my future. It is only in the present that this distance may be overcome and the three ecstasies of time held together in the full reality of an act. Thus, as James constantly emphasizes, action is the test of the reality of a belief. This leads to a third distinctive feature of the active element in man. I am more intimately and directly acquainted with my own acts than with the facts about me and the meanings I entertain, for these lie at a distance from me. But with the being of my own acts I directly coincide. Here knowing by acquaintance and being are one. Furthermore, it is only through this direct acquaintance with myself that I become acquainted with other things and persons. So James refers to this self-knowledge of acts as the "central part of the *me*" (PR, I, 371; *cf.* pp. 338 ff.), though he does not mean that it is an isolated mind.

In any case, my beliefs and acts are biased and directed. They occur in the present, and are fully real. They are also known with a peculiar intimacy and directness. These distinctive traits belong to all acts. But are they all on the same plane? Or can we distinguish different qualitative levels? James believes that we can, and the one to which we have referred is of peculiar importance. Let us now try to clarify its meaning. What is the strenuous mood?

The Strenuous Mood

First of all, a word as to its importance in James' thought. "The Moral Philosopher and the Moral Life" was written before 1891 in the full maturity of his powers, and most commentators rightly agree that James is here expressing the substance of his moral philosophy. The final pages (MPM, pp. 211–15) are devoted to a consideration of *the strenuous mood.* This is enough to justify the opinion that it must be taken seriously, though few commentators have singled it out for special attention. This opinion, however, is confirmed by the fact that, under different names, the same theme comes up again and again in other essays as well as in *The Varieties of Religious Experience,* and at central points where James seems to be expressing his own deepest views, and speaking from his heart. When we fit these various passages together, we find a view of the strenuous mood that may be summarized as follows.

James is too keenly aware of the ranges of human intellectual freedom to take moral choice, or ethics itself, for granted. Many men seem to be able to do without both of them, at least in their professed attitudes and philosophies. There is the moral sceptic who, in the absence of rational grounds of justification, believes that all choices are equally futile. And there is the fatalist who arrives at the same conclusion, because all our acts are pre-determined. Many other official and unofficial philosophies, like materialism and certain forms of idealism offer other grounds for those who seek them. ". . . Seriousness is but a superficial glaze upon a world of fundamentally trivial import. You and your acts and the nature of things will be alike enveloped in a single formula, a universal *vanitas vanitatum*" (SR, p. 107). This lies at the root of what James calls "the don't-care attitude", and there is no way of theoretically demonstrating its falsehood.

But the first act of one who is to follow the strenuous way is a free choice to break with that attitude, to believe in the reality of a moral universe. It is important to note that this basic choice, underlying all the rest, is not a choice to do this or to do that. These are matters of less importance, as Kierkegaard has said. The first choice is the choosing to really choose. Nothing constrains us to be moral in this sense. We can certainly live without it, and probably become much happier by following the easy-going way. Such an easy-goer will, in the main, treat things "with a degree of good-natured scepticism and radical levity", and he may find "that the practical fruits of his epicurean hypothesis verify it more and more, and not only save him from pain but do honor to his sagacity" (SR, p. 106). This is not James' view. But there is no strict demonstration that it is not so.

The man who believes that choices really matter will take life seriously. He will believe that the mysterious world in which we exist has "the right to claim from us the particular mood called seriousness" (SR, p. 86). What we freely choose to do makes a difference; real issues are at stake. This means "the willingness to live with energy, though energy bring pain" (SR, p. 86). Energy is a theme to which James constantly returns in his moral writings. If we are to make the most of our chance at life, every human power must be strained to the highest pitch. Only then will the richest results be achieved. "The richness lies", James says, "in the energy of all three departments of the mental cycle. Not a sensible 'fact' of department One must be left in the cold, not a faculty of department Three be paralyzed; and department Two must form an indestructible bridge" (RAAT, p. 130).

Towards the end of his life, in 1906, James devoted his presidential address to the American Philosophical Association to this theme—"The Energies of Men."[4] In this address, he makes it clear that he is not thinking of energy in purely quantitative terms. As acts become more autonomous and freely chosen, they reach higher qualitative levels, and more "inner work" is involved. "Writing is higher than walking, thinking is higher than writing, deciding higher than thinking, deciding 'no' higher than deciding 'yes'—at least the man who passes from one of these activities to another will usually say that each later one involves a greater element of *inner work* than the earlier ones, even though the total heat given out, or the foot-pounds expended by the organism, may be less" (EFM, p. 219). It takes more energy to say no than to say yes, and negative action is higher in quality. Hence the free man will tend to be rebellious and even revolutionary (MPM, p. 204) in opposing every form of intellectual or practical tyranny. The "*highest* ethical life", James says (p. 209), "however few may be called to bear its burdens—consists at all times in the breaking of rules which have grown too narrow for the actual case."

In our own time, the free man will reject the bland pressures of mass conformism which come with technological efficiency and success. Thus after his visit to Chautauqua in 1898, James reacted violently against the levelled-down "flatness" of this mass

4 This essay is reprinted in EFM on pp. 216–37.

Utopia, which he recognized as epitomizing tendencies that were more and more "coming over the world" EFM, p. 290).[5] What he found utterly lacking in "this Sabbatical city" was precisely the atmosphere of freedom and the strenuous mood. As he says (p. 289) "it was the element that gives to the wicked outer world all its moral style, expressiveness and picturesqueness,—the element of precipitousness, so to call it, of strength and strenuousness, intensity and danger".

When it is really lived, life "*feels* like a real fight", and it is only by throwing ourselves into it that life may become worth living (EFM, pp. 30–31).[6] Of course a price has to be paid. For one thing, the free man who thinks and acts for himself will be isolated and alone. "It is only in the lonely emergencies of life that our creed is tested: then routine maxims fail, and we fall back on our gods" (SR, p. 105). The strenuous life confronts us with hardship, pain, and, as James says, "tragedy" (MPM, p. 213). For those who are weak and dependent, these trials may prove to be unbearable. In order to bear them, "every sort of energy and endurance, of courage and capacity for handling life's evils" is required (p. 213). But those who are free and strenuously independent can summon up this courage, which has an intrinsic moral quality of its own (SR, p. 101).

James was not content to remain within the limits of a purely humanist perspective. As he explains in "The Moral Philosopher and the Moral Life" (pp. 212–13), the strenuous mood cannot be aroused by prospects of endless technological and utilitarian advance, though these are fine as far as they go. This is a world that has been levelled off, "where all the mountains are brought down and all the valleys are exalted" (MPM, pp. 211–12). In this horizon, one feels the absence of "infinitude and mystery" (p. 212), which alone are capable of bringing forth "the wilder passions . . . the big fears, loves, and indignations" (p. 211). For James, it is primarily in religion that "the infinite perspective

---

[5] From the essay "What Makes Life Significant?" in EFM on pp. 285–310.
[6] See "Is Life Worth Living?" pp. 1–31 in EFM, pp. 32–62 in WBA.

opens out" (p. 212), in spite of his professed belief in a finite God. But he uses the term *religion* in an unorthodox way, and so broadly as to cover any authentic sense of mystery and transcendence—any feeling, in fact, "for such a half-wild, half-saved universe" as that which we inhabit (EFM, p. 30).

The don't-care attitude is impersonal. It can be satisfied with a materialistic philosophy which "denies reality to the objects of almost all the impulses which we most cherish" (SR, p. 83). These are only subjective projections. But "a nameless *unheimlichkeit* comes over us at the thought of there being nothing eternal in our final purposes, in the objects of those loves and aspirations which are our deepest engeries" (p. 83). So the life in us is constantly seeking for "the real *meaning*", the independent value beyond us which will justify our real sacrifice and "hope" and "rapture" (p. 84). Unless it can find such a transcendent object, our freedom wastes away and our autonomy disintegrates. This is the last aim of our active nature—to find some independent being that will challenge its powers and keep it alive and working (*cf.* next chapter). But this requires the cooperation of department Two of the mind in interpreting the facts provided by department One. In a moment we shall turn to this second department, whose task it is to formulate real patterns of meaning and thus to mediate between departments One and Three.

But I emphasize now certain points concerning "the strenuous mood", which have been largely neglected by the more influential commentators. The ethics of inclusiveness often attributed to James levels down all desires and claims to the same qualitative level, so that only quantitative considerations remain. This levelling process is characteristic of the don't-care attitude, and corresponds on the practical plane to theoretical impartiality. It certainly has its place, especially in matters of social policy where strong stands are to be avoided and compromise should rule. But the free individual person is not bound by such an ethics of compromise. He is open to a higher type of action, that of the strenuous mood. The ethics of "the easy-going mood" is essentially utilitarian, and the avoidance of present evil is the ruling consideration. On the other hand, the strenuous ethics is "quite indifferent to present ill, if only the greater ideal [in quality] be attained" (MPM, p. 211). This is a radical difference. As James puts it "the deepest difference practically in the moral life of man is the difference between the easy-going and the strenuous mood" (p. 211). In "The Moral Philosopher and the Moral Life", the strenuous ethics comes after, and supersedes the utilitarian ethics.

To anyone carefully reading the many passages from different essays that we have just reviewed, it is clear that, under this name, James is expressing his own ethical point of view. Inclusiveness may be *a* principle in James' ethics, but it is not the ultimate principle. As we have noted, this principle is rather to be found in freedom of choice and autonomy, which involve a radically distinctive qualitative level. If James had been confronted with recent versions of utilitarianism, like that of his student, R. B. Perry, he would have identified them with what he calls "the easy-going mood". His most basic criticism of them would be that they have taken the whole notion of choice for granted, without carefully analyzing it in the light of painstaking, phenomenological description. As a result of this, many have implicitly denied any real freedom of choice, and have fallen into different versions of soft determinism. Even the best of them have failed to recognize this freedom as the most basic intrinsic, moral value, underlying all the different levels of moral autonomy, the most distinctive moral values, and, indeed, the whole moral world, which is not a mere fact of life to be passively accepted, but a contingent consequence of the choice to be moral.

If James' moral essays had been recently written, they would be readily identified as expressing an existential ethics of freedom and engagement. Thus his distinction between the "easy-going" and the "strenuous" bears marked resemblances to Kierkegaard's distinction between the aesthetic and the ethical, though there are also differences. But whatever we may call it, his ethics is not based on logical or factual constraint, or natural necessities of any kind. James sharply distinguishes the worlds of freedom from the realm of nature, which is dominated by regular tendencies and laws. The moral world, on the other hand, satisfies no natural want or need. It may lead to the sacrifice of life. It does not bring us happiness or pleasure, but rather hardship, suffering, and pain. It is a free creation of man that is brought forth by an unforced choice that wells up spontaneously from the depths of human existence.

If we are to become moral, we must choose this by a real choice that persists and endures through the history it initiates. When this choice really take place and stirs up others to embark on the strenuous path, it brings other aims and values in its train. Among these are serious engagement, the most intensive and highest energies of man including those of inner work, negative decisions, and "the breaking of rules which have grown too narrow for the actual case" (p. 209), hardship, loneliness, tragedy, and the courage to overcome these obstacles, transcendent ideals, the passionate devotion that these inspire, and, finally, the real meanings which alone can support this devotion.

As James says, "the capacity for the strenuous mood probably lies slumbering in every man" (p. 211), but only seldom does it become alive and awake. Still most of us have a vague feeling for it by direct acquaintance. We may call it the ethos of our active nature. By itself reason, the second department of the mind, has no understanding of it whatsoever. If left to itself, it will tend rather to produce closed and inclusive systems of determinism. But we have seen how, by using the methods of phenomenology, reason may go outside itself and gain a clarifying understanding of the opacities and ambiguities of brute facts. In a similar way, it may go outside of itself and penetrate into the active ethos to work with it, and thus to gain a synthetic understanding. Attempts of this sort usually end in a deepening of confusion. But they may serve to arouse and to strengthen our moral nature. When this happens, what we call *reason* also is transformed, and James developed some very original ideas about this transformation, to which we shall now turn.

Freedom of the Mind

This transformation is usually thought of by James' critics as an intrusion of subjective desire into the proper territory of reason. He is supposed to be arguing that in certain cases at least, we are entitled to believe anything that we happen to want, and that in certain cases, successful acts can prove that some theory connected with them is true. Both are generally held to be illegitimate invasions of subjective desire into the field of objective reason, which should remain impartial. Even commentators generally sympathetic to James have usually stated the issue in this way. Is reason to be influenced by desire, or is it to remain separate and unbiased?

Now it is true that James denies the separation of reason from active engagement in any concrete thinker. But this does not mean that he is defending the determination of belief by random desires. Such wants, of course, may be determined by natural or cultural influences over which the individual may have no control, and this is the very opposite of James' thesis in his essay "The Will to Believe". He is here arguing that there is an important place in the intellectual life, not for any un-criticized desire, but for freely chosen desires open to a certain kind of verification. In other words, he is defending a certain active freedom of the mind, a "freedom to 'believe what we will'", as he refers to it (EFM, p. 60), which is denied by those who hold that all justifiable belief must be determined by constraining factual or logical evidence. On such a view, there can be no place for freedom in the mind, nor for biased and impassioned thinking.

According to James, this is false, for action arises from belief, and this is especially true of the highest levels of free action. No one is going to act freely unless he believes in freedom, nor responsibly unless he believes in responsibility. Hence, since, as we have just seen, strenuous action is called for, there must be a place for strenuous thinking to prepare the way. Let us now try to show this by examining the two central theses in James' theory of moral belief—freedom to believe and self-verification. These theses belong together, and they cannot be disjoined without dismembering and distorting the whole position.

Since the time of the *Principles*, belief remained a basic theme of James' philosophy and at the beginning of "The Will to Believe" he says that he is going to present a "justification *of* faith", or belief (EFM, p. 32). By *belief* he here means the acceptance of some idea "in spite of the fact that our merely logical intellect may not have been coerced" (pp. 32–33). This makes it clear that he is concerned with intellectual freedom. Do we have the right to believe in something for which as yet no constraining evidence can be presented? If so, the mind must be presented with opportunities for intellectual choices, or options, as James calls them. We do not often think of the mind as a choice-making power, associating this rather with the faculty of "will". But he now proceeds to show that there are three types of option to which the mind is always open, and with which it is concerned in its serious thinking.

In the first place, options may be alive or dead. A live option touches our real interests and is of deep concern. We are willing to act on the outcome of our decision, and "the maximum of liveness in a hypothesis means willingness to act irrevocably" (p. 34). A dead option, on the other hand, does not touch us deeply. It concerns something objective from which we can remain detached. However the issue is decided, our action will remain intact. Hence we do not have to take it seriously, and we can be indifferent.

Second, options may be "forced" or "avoidable". An option is avoidable if there is a way of escape from the decision. Thus if you say " 'Either love me or hate me', 'Either call my theory true or call it false' ", I may adopt an indifferent attitude, and simply refuse to take a stand either way. But if you say accept my offer or go without it, a decision is required, for to say *I am indifferent* is equivalent to a negative choice, and the offer is rejected. In ordinary English, the phrase *take it or leave it* expresses a strong disjunction of this kind.

Finally, intellectual options may be "trivial" or "momentous". A momentous option is "live" to the highest degree. It is of over-arching importance, and touches the depths of our existence. But in addition, it presents us with a "unique opportunity". The decision I make here and now cannot be reversed in the future. As we say, it is *now or never*. A trivial option, on the other hand, is of minor importance, and lacks the element of uniqueness. Furthermore, the decision is not irrevocable. If the choice I now make turns out to be unwise, I may take it back later on.

From what James has said of the strenuous, free way of life, it is clear that it involves options that are live, forced, and momentous. The easy-going way, on the other hand, tries to avoid such serious choices, and to substitute those that are less living, avoidable, and trivial. The next step in James' argument is to show that science, and objective thought in general, are concerned with options that are of this latter kind.

First, as he says (p. 51), "in our dealings with objective nature, we obviously are recorders, not makers, of the truth . . .". Our original choice to engage in such activity was no doubt free. But once we are involved in enterprises of this kind, the decisions are not primarily in our own hands. As it is sometimes said, we prepare the way and ask the questions. But it is nature, or the objective universe, that gives the answers, which we then record. While the results of such investigation may lead us to make important decisions, we engage in them rather as spectators than as active agents. So with respect to these objective issues of pure theory, we may remain indifferent and detached. "What difference, indeed, does it make to most of us whether we have or have not a theory of the Röntgen rays, whether we believe or not in mind-stuff, or have a conviction about the causality of conscious states?" (p. 51). As James points out (p. 52), the individual investigator may become personally involved in the success or failure of his project, but not in the abstract question itself apart from its implications for the world of life, which always brings up further questions of a different kind.

Theorizing of this sort is like the playing of a game which requires a certain detachment. He is likely to play best who does not become too deeply involved in winning, but who loves the game as such, and plays simply for the sake of playing. If his losses become too great, he may always withdraw, and the results are not irreversible. He may return again and win another time. So as James says of our scientific thinking, "the questions here are always trivial options, the hypotheses are hardly living (at any rate not living for us spectators), the choice between believing truth or falsehood is seldom forced" (p. 51). Here it is always better to wait until further evidence comes in, without plunging into premature decisions.

Of course this game has to be played, and in its place James respects it. Indeed, for many early years of his life he played it himself. But when it claims to be a final philosophy of life, it becomes a justification for the escape from freedom and the easy-going way. As James sees it, this will cut us off from the strenuous life, and the higher possibilities of man. It is in this light that we may now get an understanding of his two well-known doctrines, the right to believe and the self-verifying of moral truth. Both are essentially involved in the attainment of a finite, human freedom of the mind, as we shall now try to show.

According to James, the intrinsic values of the free and strenuous life—freedom, seriousness, responsibility, energy, courage, meaning and devotion—cannot be attained without free choices of the mind. They present us with options that are living, forced, and momentous. They are alive, because they are real possibilities of life which lie "slumbering in every man", even though repressed and submerged. Since to remain indifferent is to reject them, they are forced. We must either take them or leave them. Since life is short and we have only one life to live, the opportunity is unique, and they are momentous. They involve the most intense energies and the highest value levels of which we are capable.

In questions of this kind: Is man free? Is there a real moral universe? Is there something divine transcending us? the objective evidence open to reason is ambiguous. Weighty speculative arguments can be found on both sides. Reason alone cannot decide. Hence in genuine options, which are alive, forced, and momentous, reason must go outside itself and allow our passional nature to make the ultimate choice. As James says: *"Our passional nature not only lawfully may, but must, decide an option between propositions, whenever it is a genuine option that cannot by its nature be decided on intellectual grounds . . ."* (p. 42).

But this does not mean that our cognitive powers will simply abdicate and cease to function. The meaning of what is chosen must be worked out and clarified, if the act is to be soundly guided. But when reason works *with* passion, it functions in a new manner, and, as Pascal said, it develops reasons of its own which are not those of pure reason. It also develops a peculiar freedom of its own which James calls "mental freedom" (p. 61). But after all, it is the whole man who becomes free and responsible through the contributions made by the different human powers, each in its own way. But freedom and the momentous choices of existence come primarily from passion, and from reason only in so far as it reaches out to participate. This union of reason with passion is what James means by "heart", reasons of the heart, and moral convictions.

These beliefs are freely arrived at because they are not determined by the facts, nor by logical constraint. But, on the other hand, neither are they determined by physical accidents nor by cultural conditioning, though all these factors may be recognized. No one can be conditioned to be free. We choose to become free only through the strenuous urges of our active nature, working in accordance with an over-arching pattern of meaning. The two support each other without logical constraint.

Self-verification

Does this mean that such radical choices are made blindly with no possible verification in view? James makes it very clear that it does not. This is because there are many different modes of verification, of which verification by objective facts and deductions from them is only one. Once again, James is forced by the empirical evidence concerning action to broaden a traditional conception. Hypotheses concerning external objects and things quite distinct from ourselves can be verified objectively in the traditional manner by factual observation and deduction. In this process, we play only a minor role. We ask the questions. The things decide for us, and we record their answers.

But in the case of living, forced and momentous options, which touch our innermost existence and concern us deeply, the situation is very different. Such a hypothesis cannot be verified by factual observation, for our existence is unfinished, and the facts are not all there. And yet the option is forced. We must decide either for the strenuous way or against it. Anything we know about human existence and its history is relevant. But this knowledge is vast in scope and ambiguous. It can be read in many ways. So we must allow our passional nature, indeed, every aspect of our being to enter in. But not without regard to the future! As James says of these choices—above all things man wants to be right. The hypothesis ought to be true. But if it is verified, what kind of a verification will this be?

We cannot expect things to verify a hypothesis of this sort for us, since it concerns primarily ourselves and the world in which we live. It does concern other people, but, if it is to be my hypothesis, there is a primary sense in which it concerns me. Therefore, if it is in any respect to be accepted by others, it must first of all be verified by me, for myself. I must apply it to myself, live it through with the last drop of my power, and judge the results as I go along. This is not a game in which I can be reduced to a spectator. I must choose the hypothesis in the first place, and formulate it as clearly as I can. But this is only a beginning. After this, I must really believe it with the greatest possible intensity and clarity, for belief, unlike theory, is the beginning of action, and weakness of belief will lead to weakness of action (EFM, p. 34). Then I must try to verify it by living it through, for only then will the theory have had a fair test. This is what James means by "self-verification".

As he has said, *"the essence of good is simply to satisfy demand.* The demand may be for anything under the sun" (MPM, p. 201). Most of these demands, like the need for food and shelter, are determined by forces independent of our belief. The child does not have to believe in hunger to feel hungry. Hence in the process of obtaining food, we are passively accepting an external control, and are not autonomous. The same is true of our arbitrary likes and dislikes. We have not freely chosen them. They are due rather to the accidents of conditioning. They too are passively accepted.

But strenuous values show a different pattern. They are not imposed on us by natural forces. No one has to be free or to take life seriously. One can certainly live, and perhaps more happily, without them. Nor are they imposed on us by the accidents of history. They lie "slumbering" in every man. They must first be chosen and firmly believed in before they constitute a claim. And in the process of bringing them into existence, establishing them, or "verifying" them, as James calls it, I must act of my own volition, under the control of my own free choice. So as he says, in so far as we act in this way, "we show a curious autonomy, as if we were small active centres on our own account" (EFM, p. 59).

I believe that James has here identified a distinctive type of value which represents the claim of a freely chosen belief not under constraint, and in which the action takes place with risk, but, at least for a time, without external support. Let us look at some of James' examples. Take freedom itself. My own freedom does not first exist as a fact which I can observe, and then believe in. Here, the order is reversed. I must first choose to be free, and believe that I am free before the facts will appear through my own action. So James can say, following Renouvier, (DOD, p. 146), "It [freedom] ought to be freely espoused by men who can equally well turn their backs upon it. In other words, our first act of freedom, if we are free, ought in all inward propriety to be to affirm that we are free."

The same is true of the trust in others that lies at the root of free social life. Here too the individual who will not accept the word of another without proof, who will never act on belief, and will take no risks, contributes little or nothing to the common good. "Wherever a desired result is achieved by the cooperation of many independent persons, its existence as a fact is a pure consequence of the precursive faith in one another of those immediately concerned" (EFM, p. 55). Here, too, the facts are a consequence of a belief that comes first. If genuine cooperation is achieved, it will be the result of a belief that verifies itself through its own independent action.

The same is also true of the existence of a free moral world, and the strenuous values involved in these beliefs when they are genuine. Here also factual argument is inconclusive. The hypotheses cannot be verified in this way. If it is to be proved, the individual must prove it for himself by his own existential action. This existential proof will depend on the energy of his action, and this on the clarity and strength of his belief that he is right. "For again and again success depends on energy of act; energy again depends on faith that we shall not fail; and that faith in turn on the faith that we are right,—which faith thus verifies itself" (SR, p. 100).

Freedom cannot be coerced. Hence James' argument in "The Will to Believe" does not take the form of a logical demonstration. But neither is it a mere statement of emotive approval. He makes it clear that he recognizes the high intrinsic value of freedom and the other attitudes attending the strenuous life. He claims that they should be chosen by others. But he also presents a "justification", a "defence" (EFM, p. 32). This takes the form of a clarifying description of these beliefs and attitudes as they arise and operate in the concrete, as well as a comparison of them with other values. But one may know what they are and still reject them. So they have no coercive force. We cannot force human freedom. But we may strengthen the latent freedom that may be slumbering within men by bringing their attention to bear on relevant evidence. James calls such an argument, directed towards the human heart, that is, the rational and passional natures working in union, an *appeal*. It is the appeal of one freedom to another. James calls it "personal", and acknowledges it as his own method in moral debate (DOD, p. 176). "This personal method of appeal", he says, "seems to be among the very conditions of the problem; and the most any one can do is to confess as candidly as he can the grounds for the faith that is in him, and leave his example to work on others as it may."

I have tried in this chapter to show how, in facing moral and religious questions, James, like Kant, is forced to go beyond the sphere of pure reason, and to engage in empirical studies of the active life, together with its various qualitative levels. He is especially concerned with what he takes to be the highest level, that of freedom and the strenuous life. I have also tried to show that it is this strenuous element, not the arbitrary demand, that plays a decisive role in the moral life as he conceives it. Hence the major emphasis of his ethics is on freedom and autonomy rather than on inclusiveness and tolerance, which play an important but secondary role.

According to James ethics is centered in man and what acts are better for him to perform from a human perspective. Religion is concerned with ultimate "cosmical matters" (EFM, p. 56), first and last things. These are the ultimate questions, and according to James they confront us with options that are both forced and momentous. Hence for one who thinks radically, ethics will lead to religion, and "The Will to Believe" ends with a quote from Fitz-James Stephen in which these ultimate questions are raised. "What do you think of yourself? What do you think of the world?" (p. 62).

James devoted himself during the next ten years to what he called "The religious hypothesis", and the result was his well known text, *The Varieties of Religious Experience*, published in 1902. It is to this text and to its descriptions and interpretations of religious experience *as directly lived* that we must now turn in the following chapter.

Chapter Twelve

❋

Religion and the
Strenuous Life

James is not much interested in the theories of ethics and religion. He is interested in them as *ways of life,* and regarding them in this way, he sees them as closely related, for both are expressions of what he has called "the strenuous" mood. Both involve elements of feeling as well as cognition. From the standpoint of feeling and action, we can say that the ethical way is less developed. For the highest examples of sacrifice and devotion we must turn to the religious life. From this point of view, we may think of the moral way as an inferior level which leads on to something further, saintliness, to which James devotes two chapters of his *Varieties.* But since the object of religious devotion transcends our understanding, its manifestations are more variable and it stands in constant need of moral criticism. So each requires support from the other. In view of this close relation of inter-dependence, it is important to note James' emphatic identification of religion with *"the genuinely strenuous life"* (*VA,* p. 254, my italics). This offers further confirmation of the view we presented in the last chapter that James' ethics also is centered on the strenuous way.

In this chapter, we shall not try to consider every topic dealt with in James' classic text, *The Varieties of Religious Experience*. In accordance with our past procedure, we shall single out basic topics, four of which we believe are of contemporary interest, for careful analysis. First, we shall consider the empirical method James uses in examining religious phenomena and some of its implications for philosophy; second, his distinction between the healthy-minded and the twice-born and the process of becoming a self; third, his conception of religion as the strenuous life *par excellence;* and finally, fourth, prayer and the mystical experience.

Religion and the Empirical Method

If we are going to think or speak about religion, we must already have some direct acquaintance with it. Then, if our method is to be truly empirical, we must return to these original experiences, steep ourselves in them, and find ways of verbally clarifying and describing them. It is only in the light of such research that we may finally hope to engage in speculative interpretation and evaluation that are not reductive and irrelevant. But what are these religious experiences? Ordinary language may give us some preliminary help, and James refers to it in the definition he gives near the beginning of Lecture II (VA, pp. 31–32).[1] Religion, he says, shall mean for us *"the feelings, acts, and experiences of individual men in their solitude, so far as they apprehend themselves to stand in relation to whatever they may consider the divine".*

The two major features of this definition are both open to serious question. In the first place, does it not lay undue weight

---

[1] *The Varieties of Religious Experience* were the Gifford Lectures that James delivered at Edinburgh University in 1901–2.

on solitary individual manifestations, as over against the social? There is perhaps some justice in this remark, since James had little interest in theological creeds and ecclesiastical organization. For him, individual experiences and ideas are the first sources of social change and advance. But as they radiate out to a wider social circumference, they suffer a degenerative process of hardening and decline. (Cf. WBA, p. 253.)[2] In his brief answer to this anticipated criticism (VA, p. 31) James emphasizes the distinction between the original *"founders"* of world religions and churches who "owed their power originally to the fact of their direct personal communion with the divine", as over against the churches which "once established, live at second-hand upon tradition". "So", as he says, "personal religion should still seem the primordial thing, even to those who continue to esteem it incomplete."

The second criticism is that "the divine" is too vague and too broad. But our pre-reflective experience is usually vague and broad in scope. So this did not bother James. He refers to the Buddhist religion which "in strictness" is "atheistic" (p. 32), and to Emerson's "divine soul of order" (p. 33), which implies no personal consciousness. He does not wish to rule them out as non-religious. As he says, "gods are conceived to be first things in the way of being and power" (p. 35), "and a man's religion might thus be identified with his attitude, whatever it might be, toward what he felt to be the primal truth". It is "a man's total reaction upon life" (p. 35). This is close to Paul Tillich's notion of "ultimate concern". In fact James inaugurates his discussion of the religion of healthy-mindedness (p. 77), by raising the religious question: "What is human life's chief concern?" But he feels the need of narrowing it down in certain ways (pp. 35 ff.), without, however, denying its generic truth.

While humor lies at the borderline of religion, the religious attitude is serious and "solemn" rather than frivolous (pp. 36–38). "At its highest flights" it is something "infinitely passionate"

[2] Reference is to the essay "Great Men and their Environment" published in WBA on pp. 216–54.

(p. 47), and involves the sense of a gift coming from some power beyond ourselves (pp. 47–48). But this power need not be identified with the God of orthodox faith. The service of this higher power, however it may be conceived, is free, and "never is felt as a yoke" (p. 41). But though he recognizes these distinctive features in special forms of religion, James' discussions of basic aspects of the religious life are often concerned with what is "religious in the wider sense" (p. 48, note). In this wider usage "the divine shall mean for us only such a primal reality as the individual feels impelled to respond to solemnly and gravely, and neither by a curse nor a jest" (p. 39).

How do we get into touch with this divine power? James makes it very clear that it is not primarily through rational argument and speculation. The *Varieties* was published twelve years after the *Principles*. It was written much later, and by that time James had developed a deeper respect for what he calls the subconscious and the subliminal regions of the mind. There are, in fact, passages in the later text where he suggests that if there is a divine, and whatever it may be, it is through these subliminal regions that it first touches us. In so far as this contact becomes conscious, it is felt by direct acquaintance rather than understood by verbal discourse and argument. Such argument may elucidate and expand what we know by direct acquaintance, but it cannot make any alien thing or person present to us. It is rather by sensation and perception that we feel such presences.

So it is not surprising that those who have claimed some contact with a power transcending us have felt it as an alien presence. James gives examples of experiences of this kind, and says that "they are as convincing to those who have them as any direct sensible experiences can be, and they are, as a rule, much more convincing than results established by mere logic ever are" (p. 72). These feelings and intuitions are the primary source of religious belief, and they are presupposed by the dogmatic systems and creeds that are built upon them. James strongly believes "that feeling is the deeper source of religion, and that philosophic and theological formulas are secondary products, like translations of a text into another tongue" (p. 422). Our primary religious thinking is quite distinct from the "over-beliefs, buildings-out performed by the intellect into directions of which feeling originally supplied the hint" (p. 422). But as he then points out, "feeling is private and dumb, and unable to give an account of itself. It allows that its results are mysteries and enigmas, declines to justify them rationally, and, on occasion is willing that they should even pass for paradoxical and absurd" (pp. 422–23). So rational criticism is required. "To redeem religion from unwholesome privacy, and to give public status and universal right of way to its deliverances, has been reason's task" (p. 423). But when the original feelings become diluted and pass away, conviction also will die. Rational argument alone will never lead to faith, nor even maintain it. As James says, "it hardly ever engenders it [faith]; it cannot now secure it" (p. 427). Feeling and reason must work together in harmony, if confusion and frustration are to be avoided.

What then are the implications of this distinction for the empirical investigator of religious phenomena in our own time? James' empiricism is now becoming radical. So in answering this question, he stresses the need of digging down to the primary roots of religious thought in the lived experience with which we are directly acquainted. These primary roots are found in the solitary feelings of the individual. Then having steeped himself in these original feelings as they are expressed by the individual sources themselves, the empirical investigator will compare and contrast them in the effort to arrive at generalizations which bring out their implicit meaning. First, the lived experiences, and then, from them, the sense, or as James puts it in describing his own procedure (p. 423): "a laborious attempt to extract from the privacies of religious experience some general facts which can be defined in formulas upon which everybody may agree".

Only after this arduous work has been completed will the empirical investigator be in a position to make an evaluation. Those who read James today are usually interested only in his final judgments, and pass over the detailed factual analysis, and the case histories on which they are based. As philosophers, we would rather speculate and argue than go through the grinding labor of carefully examining the facts. But it is the detailed factual analysis that distinguishes James' text from numberless other ventures with the same aim, and which have kept it alive to the present time.

But what of the final judgment? How does the radical empiricist proceed when he reaches this critical point? We shall not examine James' final judgments until we have considered his empirical studies of conversion, saintliness, mysticism and prayer. But in the text he gives us two warnings, one against the objectivist attitude of "intellectualism", and one against the related framework of scientism, as we may call it, in religious studies. These warnings, I think, are relevant to our own time in which these tendencies are ever growing and, as many believe, traditional forms of religion are passing away. The attitudes of which we have spoken were actively at work in James' time, though weaker, and he goes out of his way in urging both himself and his readers to resist them. In spite of their emphasis upon scientific facts, and their "empirical" tone, they stand in the way of sound empirical investigation in the field of religion as well as in the other human fields. Why?

First of all, the radical empiricist must recognize the basic difference between life as it is carried on "subjectively" from the inside, and as it is regarded as an object from the outside. As we have seen, James was already aware of this difference. But his studies of religious phenomena have sharpened this awareness, and have given him a deeper sense of its importance. His words have an almost Kierkegaardian ring when he says that "he who lives the life of it [religion] . . . is a better servant than he who merely knows about it, however much. Knowledge about life is one thing; effective occupation of a place in life, with its dynamic currents passing through your being, is another" (p. 479). The detached, impersonal attitude which turns everything, including human existence, into an object, and prides itself on being impartial, all-inclusive, and unbiased, as a matter of fact is terribly partial, abstract, and biased in its all-inclusive claims. The facts that we see in this way are highly abstract, for a great deal is omitted—for example, the world-field in which these objects appear, the feeling and thought of the object in the thinker, his attitude, and the self to whom this attitude belongs.

As long as we leave out all this, we are contenting ourselves with the surfaces of things, and ignoring the real "existence" with which we are directly acquainted in ourselves. As James says (p. 489): "a conscious field *plus* its object as felt or thought of *plus* an attitude towards the object *plus* the sense of a self to whom the attitude belongs—such a concrete bit of personal experience may be a small bit, but it is a solid bit as long as it lasts; not hollow, not a mere abstract element of experience, such as the 'object' is when taken all alone. It is a *full* fact, even though it be an insignificant fact; it is of the *kind* to which all realities whatsoever must belong; the motor currents of the world run through the like of it. . . ." The genuine empiricist will not be content with mere abstractions. He will try to dig down into their roots in the concrete actuality as a whole. And he will never think that he can replace it by his thoughts about it, or absorb it into a conceptual system. He will engage in a humbler and less pretentious task—to clarify it by conceptual thought, and to bring it into a brighter light.

The same general point is made from another angle in the many passages in which James criticizes the growing scientism of his time. In the most cogent of these, he warns the empiricist against confusing the objective perspective of the natural sciences with the wider and richer horizon of the life-world. This shows that his study of the "world of sense", in the *Principles*, Chapter XXI, has been strongly confirmed in his own mind. He is no longer worried by the question concerning causal determinism of concrete experience by the brain. He now sees that this arises from a mistaken attempt to absorb the life-world into the narrower perspective of objective thought. Of course, these causal facts are not to be denied. But there is room for them, and for the whole perspective to which they belong, in the wider horizon of the life-world.

Thus he says in his concluding chapter (VA, p. 509) "I *can*, of course, put myself into the sectarian scientist's attitude, and imagine vividly that the world of sensations and of scientific laws and objects may be all. But whenever I do this, I hear that inward monitor of which W. K. Clifford once wrote, whispering the word 'bosh!' Humbug is humbug, even though it bear the scientific name, and the total expression of human experience, as I view it objectively, invincibly urges me beyond the narrow 'scientific' bounds. Assuredly the real world is of a different temperament—more intricately built than physical science allows. So my objective and my subjective conscience both hold me to the over-belief which I express." James is here saying that the life-world, which has room for objects of religious devotion, is objectively wider in range than the perspectives of the sciences, which have no place for them. In addition to this, it also has a place for feelings, thoughts, active intentions, and the whole array of "subjective", or *lived*, phenomena to which observational science, in the strict sense, has no access by the nature of its methods.

These warnings certainly had an influence on James' final evaluation of religious experiences. But before turning to this, we must first review his account of the actual phenomena. What are these phenomena? Aside from abstract theological speculation and argument, how is it that religion appears in the world? What changes does it make in our lived existence? It is in these changes, lived through by existing individuals, that James is primarily interested, for without them, there would have been no religious philosophy nor theology. These are real events that have happened in history, and have actually changed the lives of men. James deals with them under the headings of the divided self and conversion. So let us now turn to them. After a brief review of these chapters, we shall turn to his discussion of saintliness, the highest form of the strenuous life, mysticism, and finally to James' evaluation of these phenomena of the unseen.

James' Theory of Self-becoming[3]

In his account of conversion (lectures IX and X), James refers to striking examples of basic personality change whose religious features are clearly marked. But he is also interested in studying the change itself for its own sake, as a purely "natural" process which may or may not involve transcendent factors. As he says (VA, p. 225), "were we writing the story of the mind from the purely natural-history point of view, with no religious interest whatever, we should still have to write down man's liability to sudden and complete conversion as one of his most curious peculiarities". And a little later he points out (p. 233) that "converted men as a class are indistinguishable from natural men" and "that there is no unmistakable class-mark distinctive of all true converts". The visions, ideas, and feelings "connected with the crisis of change, may all come by way of nature". Let us now turn to James' account of this critical change, of which religious conversion is one specific type, from "an unreal life" to "the real life" (p. 162). In order to bring it into relation with recent existential thought, I shall compare it at certain points with Heidegger's account of self-becoming in Sein und Zeit.[4]

We must begin with James' concept of healthy-mindedness, which underlies his account of the religion of healthy-mindedness (lectures IV and V). In contrast to the "sick soul" (lectures VI and VII) who undergoes a second birth, the healthy-minded man is "once-born" (p. 79). He accepts the whole situation into which he is first thrown, and his life is manifested as a continuous development, not interrupted by critical turning points or major discontinuities. He is an optimist who "looks on all things and sees that they are good" (p. 86). In so far as his thought becomes

[3] Parts of this section are taken from my article, "William James and Existential Authenticity," which appeared in *The Journal of Existentialism,* V, 19 (New York, 1965), 243–56.
[4] Sections 25–60. Cf. *Being and Time,* tr. Macquarrie/Robinson, pp. 150–341.

systematic, he conceives of "good as the essential and universal aspect of being", and excludes evil from his field of vision (pp. 86–87). Like Heidegger's conception of oneness (*das Man*), healthy-mindedness is by no means a rare or exceptional phenomenon. It is "consonant with important currents in human nature" and "we all do cultivate it more or less, even when our professed theology should in consistency forbid it" (p. 89).

This universal tendency of our nature leads us to think of ourselves as basically sound and suppresses the thought of death. "We divert our attention from disease and death as much as we can; and the slaughter-houses and indecencies without end on which our life is founded are huddled out of sight and never mentioned . . ." (p. 89). All forms of fear and anxiety are to be suppressed. "Evil is a disease; and worry over disease is itself an additional form of disease, which only adds to the original complaint" (p. 125). As over against the sick soul who thinks of evil as "a wrongness or vice in his essential nature" (p. 132), the healthy-minded "are people for whom evil means only a maladjustment with *things*, a wrong correspondence of one's life with the environment" (p. 131). Such evil can be readily cured by technical means.

James suggests (p. 92) that the whole attitude of natural science is oriented "towards healthy-mindedness", and he shows how "the idea of a universal evolution lends itself to a doctrine of general meliorism and progress which fits the religious needs of the healthy-minded so well that it seems almost as if it might have been created for their use" (p. 90). Like Kierkegaard's aesthetic person, the healthy-minded individual lives only in short spans of time, and ignores the remoter schemes and hopes to which they may be related. Thus James speaks of his "strange power of living in the moment and ignoring and forgetting" (p. 138). In his final judgment (pp. 159 ff.) he clearly brings out certain deficiencies of the healthy-minded attitude as over against what he calls "morbid-mindedness".

First of all, it is a subjective construction which is simply untrue to the evil facts of life. As he says (p. 160), these "evil facts which it refuses positively to account for are a genuine portion of reality; and they may after all be the best key to life's significance, and possibly the only openers of our eyes to the deepest levels of truth". Then he goes on to say: "our civilization is founded on the shambles, and every individual existence goes out in a lonely spasm of helpless agony. If you protest, my friend, wait till you arrive there yourself!" It is certainly clear that James did not think of himself as healthy-minded, though later commentators have often interpreted his pragmatic theory of truth as a naturalistic or healthy-minded theory. But as James sees it, healthy-mindedness is at best partial and "formally less complete" (p. 162).

Furthermore, this optimistic posture tends to be fixed and closed to real change, which is certainly required if man is to approach his highest possibilities. "The man must die to an un-real life before he can be born into the real life" (ibid.). The healthy-minded live in a world of apparent happiness which is good as it is, and therefore resistant to morbid anxiety and criticism. James does not develop the point. But he notes this tendency to dogmatism and fanaticism. "If religious intolerance and hanging and burning could again become the order of the day, there is little doubt that, however it may have been in the past, the healthy-minded would at present show themselves the less indulgent party of the two" (pp. 159–60).

So far we have restricted ourselves to healthy-mindedness as such, a general tendency of the natural man in which all of us, to some degree, share. Now we must turn our attention briefly to the conceptual development of this attitude into a comprehensive system of thought which James calls "the religion of healthy-mindedness". According to this system, evil either is unreal or is dialectically overcome in an absolute whole that is basically good in its entirety. He makes it clear that, for the reasons just indicated, he has little sympathy with such a monistic scheme in its Spinozan and Hegelian forms. But he has many kind things to say about "the mind-cure movement" of his time in a long section (pp. 92–107), which has puzzled many readers.

He admits that there is a pantheistic and monistic element in the thought of its members. But in its actual practice of mental therapy, he maintains that it recognizes the existence of evil, at least as an incidental aspect of reality which needs to be overcome, and is therefore pluralistic. In so far as this evil is regarded as only incidental, and surely to be overcome, the movement's attitude can perhaps be called healthy-minded. But as James admits in a significant footnote (pp. 477–78), this makes the border line between the healthy and the morbid rather vague. He is prepared to make this admission by his sensitiveness to concrete cases where divergent patterns are often confused and mixed.

In spite of these empirical concessions, I see no reason to question the basic importance of the distinction between the healthy-minded and the sick soul in James' thought, and the superiority of the latter over the former, which is clearly expressed in his final summary (pp. 159–62) and throughout the book. His kindly remarks about the former, as manifested in certain examples, is to be explained by his concern to avoid a dogmatic defense of his own attitude, as well as by a recognition of certain strong points not in healthy-mindedness itself, but in the religious attitude to which it is open. One of these is its openness to an abandonment of the self as it is, and its self-centered world, for the sake of a new possibility. In its purest form, however, this creative openness is found in the sick soul, and to it we shall now turn.

For James, as for Heidegger, the process of becoming "myself" originates in anxiety, and is the allied feeling of melancholy to which he refers more often, though in an equivalent sense. All men are to some degree familiar with pain, sickness, failure, and death. But our ordinary animal excitements are not concerned with them. The healthy-minded man who devotes himself to such natural interests soon develops an immunity to the negative factors of life and never broods over them. But with many of us "a little cooling down of animal excitability and instinct, a little loss of animal toughness, a little irritable weakness and descent of the pain-threshold, will bring the worm at the core of all our usual springs of delight into full view, and turn us into melancholy metaphysicians" (pp. 137–38). The sicksouled person is one whose threshold is low, who reflects on his suffering, and who finds the dark side of his world suddenly revealed to him through the feeling of anxiety.

For Heidegger, a new and more authentic world is already emerging in this feeling, which not only threatens the attitudes of *das Man* but is beginning to replace them. To James, on the other hand, this would seem to be an over-simple analysis. The attitudes of oneness, or healthy-mindedness, are being threatened, it is true. But the new life that is threatening them exists as yet only in a germinal form on the semiconscious margins of the world. Hence, for him, anxiety is essentially negative in its import, and certain other stages must be passed through before the real self emerges. Nevertheless the distinctive traits that Heidegger attributes to this feeling are also found in James' analysis.

Ever since his formulation of the notion of "fringes" in the *Psychology* (*cf.* PR, I, pp. 258 ff.), James had been aware of the conscious world, or field, on which all definite objects appear as a background (*cf.* VA, pp. 226–29). It was only later that he recognized the way in which certain moods and feelings pervade this world-field as a whole. Thus, in the case of melancholy, he points out in *The Varieties of Religious Experience* that the whole field is revealed as strange and uncanny. In his own words, "the world now looks remote, strange, sinister, uncanny . . ." (p. 149). This world is temporally moving, and the sick soul can no longer lose itself in momentary successes and joys. "Can things whose end is always dust and disappointment be the real goods which our souls require?" (p. 136). So death comes into the picture. "Back of everything is the great spectre of universal death, the all-encompassing blackness" (p. 136; *cf.* pp. 137–39). It is essentially involved in "existence" (p. 137), and its nothingness undermines all healthy-minded happiness and, as James often indicates, makes it false.

The individual feels his own melancholy by himself alone. As James put its, "these experiences of melancholy are in the first instance absolutely private and individual" (p. 142). In his account of the shattering dread that struck him after seeing the "epileptic patient" in the asylum he visited at the age of twenty-seven, the main emphasis is placed on his sense of the insecurity of his "existence", which lasted for days and days. "I awoke morning after morning", he says (p. 157), "with a horrible dread at the pit of my stomach, and with a sense of the insecurity of life that I never knew before. . . ." The feeling was not a mere internal disturbance; it conveyed a sense. "It was like a revelation," and "after this, the universe was changed for me altogether" (pp. 157–58). But the way in which this experience isolated him and made him seek company is also underlined. "In general", he says (p. 158), "I dreaded to be left alone."[5]

These aspects of anxiety are found in Heidegger's descriptions in *Sein und Zeit*. But there are other aspects that distinguish James' analysis. As he sees it, anxiety and the allied feelings of melancholy and despair express a divided condition of the self (*cf.* VA, Lecture VIII, "The Divided Self"). Of course, there may be retrograde changes, or "counter-conversions" as James calls them (p. 173), but in those cases in which James is primarily interested, it is a wider and profounder self-field, in germinal form, which is threatening another ruling one that is narrower, healthy-minded, and superficial. The two are in conflict. This can be resolved only by a "new birth" in which unity together with "firmness, stability, and equilibrium succeeding a period of storm and stress and inconsistency" (pp. 172–73), is achieved.

According to James' conception, anxiety, self-condemnation, and guilt belong to this period of storm and stress. At this stage, attention is still centered, though in the mode of revulsion, on the old life and its world, which occupy the centre of the stage. The new life is found only in negative feelings and criticisms, and in other half-formed projects and attitudes still only marginal, or even below the level of consciousness. As long as these hazy projects are not clearly perceived, and as long as we are

[5] In the *Varieties*, James attributes this account to a French correspondent. It is now known, from his diary and from statements of his son, Henry, that he was here describing his own experience. *Cf.* G. W. Allen, *William James*, New York, 1967, pp. 161–66.

simply propelled negatively away from where we are, the situation, in James' terminology, is apt to become *"jammed"* (p. 202). The person is beginning to reorder his life. But this "rearrangement" of the world may "be actually interfered with (*jammed,* as it were, like the lost word when we seek too energetically to recall it), by his voluntary efforts slanting from the true direction" (p. 206). In this *jamming,* the old life, and the obsessive anxieties and guilt which negate it, may become frozen in a vicious circle of self-condemnation that can find no release.

In order to get on the real way, this obsessive self-consciousness must be abandoned. Or, as James put it (p. 163), "there are two lives, the natural and the spiritual, and we must lose the one before we can participate in the other". There is an element of self-abandonment, self-sacrifice, in the life of the spirit. This may come through a religious abandonment to powers beyond ourselves, through a reflective exploration of other worlds quite different from our own, and sometimes through sheer exhaustion (pp. 208, 210). This recognition of the need for self-abandonment is not found in Heidegger's early work, but it is a distinctive feature of James' analysis. It is also connected with other peculiar features to which we shall now turn.

James thinks of conscience, in accordance with ordinary English usage, primarily in negative terms of self-condemnation and guilt. Thus he says (p. 167), "if the individual be of tender conscience and religiously quickened, the unhappiness [of self-development] will take the form of moral remorse and compunction, of feeling inwardly vile and wrong . . .". But this is only the negative aspect of becoming a real, or authentic, self. In speaking of the twice-born (p. 163), he says, "natural good is not simply insufficient in amount and transient, there lurks a falsity in its very being". Both authors agree on this. Heidegger merges the negative and the positive aspects of this process and, under the heading of "conscience", he deals with both. James distinguishes them more sharply, and deals with the positive aspect under the heading of "conversion" to a new way of life and understanding. But while most of the points noted by Heidegger in his analysis of conscience can be readily fitted into James' account of conversion, the latter interpretation is quite different, and the differences are worthy of attention.

As we have already noted, the American is far more aware of the diverse types into which these processes of conversion fall, and he carefully distinguishes the "conscious and voluntary way" from the "involuntary and unconscious way" (p. 202). If he had read Heidegger's analysis of conscience in *Sein und Zeit*, he would say, I believe, that it applies rather to the latter than to the former of these ways. Here the long preparation for the new world about to emerge develops in slight changes of interest and small decisions in the ordinary course of life. But these are never verbalized, and remain on the indeterminate fringes of the conscious field. New interests, new feelings, new habits, a new way of arranging the world are here being formed largely below the margin of consciousness. But as they grow stronger, they express themselves above this margin by a gradually intensifying sense of frustration, emptiness, and self-condemnation.

From this point of view, many of the phenomena which Heidegger identifies with "conscience" become understandable, but in a different way. This conscience is self-centered and may become jammed, because it arises from new attitudes that are developing in me from the submarginal depths of my conscious field, rather than from conscious reflection on the world. It tells me that I am guilty—that the self I am and have been is not what it might be, that it does not measure up to the standards of the new self forming within me. It is my own self, and yet it calls to me from beyond me in the future, because it is as yet in a wholly incipient and potential condition. From beyond me, from this future ahead of myself, it calls me to become what I really am. James calls this "the divided self". Since it attacks my whole way of thought and life, for the most part I evade it and suppress it. But the anxiety that attends this state of division may at rare moments lead me to listen.

When this happens, I find that it speaks in the peculiar mode of silence, for it has developed subconsciously and without verbal articulation. It is not curious, and I cannot argue with it, for it already lives sub-verbally in another world beyond the version I call my own. And yet I always understand its meaning, since it expresses my own deepest meanings and aspirations. It demands action rather than words, for it exists as yet only in the form of unverbalized, uncriticized tendencies. Hence the *voluntaristic* character of Heidegger's analysis of conscience.[6] The answer to this sort of subliminal conversion must take the form of a radical "resolute choice" (*Entschlossenheit*), which will work out its own mode of rationalization after the fact, in accordance with its aim. This would be James' interpretation of Heidegger's account. On the surface it seems to be *voluntaristic*, since it ends in a sudden break-through which looks like a conscious "choice". James, however, calls it "involuntary and sub-conscious", since it has been subliminally prepared, and has erupted without prolonged reflection or criticism.

Over against this subconscious way, whose results are more sensational (*cf.* pp. 203–4, 212), James finds a different voluntary and conscious way, which is exemplified in the cases of Wordsworth, John Stuart Mill, and Tolstoy, to the last of whom he devotes many pages (pp. 146–54, 180–84). This way to a new world is far more lengthy and gradual. The whole process is "intellectual as well as emotional" (p. 153), and hence above the conscious threshold, though, as James stresses in the case of such a person, "his conscious strainings are letting loose subconscious allies behind the scenes, which in their way work towards rearrangement" (p. 206). James at times refers to this rearrangement as "objective", since it is not necessarily centered in the self. The whole world including not only the self, but all its independent beings and agencies, is involved. But it is consciously recognized as being empty, strange, and meaningless, and the mind is stimulated to "a gnawing, carking questioning and effort for philosophic relief" (p. 147). Since questioning of this kind already requires a certain distance from the present

[6] *Cf. Sein und Zeit*, secs. 54–60. *Cf. Being and Time*, tr. Macquarrie/Robinson, pp. 312–41.

self, the need for self-abandonment is not so pronounced as in the self-centered, subconscious way.

Of course no real answer may ever be found. If it is, it comes as a vision of a new world and a new way of life. The man is born anew. But the old way is not simply abandoned. In the case of Tolstoy, for example, his "perceptions of evil appear within their sphere to have remained unmodified" (p. 184). But this sphere has been taken up intact into a larger world of meaning which can now give them sense. There are, of course, many overlapping and borderline cases. But James makes it quite clear that, in his judgment, this second conscious and voluntary way is less apt to fall into dangerous self-obsessions and delusions, and is more open to real possibilities. There is little doubt that he is here speaking of his own experience.

But even though he calls this second way "voluntary", nothing more is said here concerning decision and choice than in connection with the first, subconscious way. In view of the major emphasis placed on this voluntaristic factor by Heidegger and other existential authors, this omission is worthy of note. It is basically due to James' scepticism concerning a special faculty of will, and his view that what has been called "freedom of the will" is really concentration of attention (*cf. supra*, Chapter V). This noetic view of freedom is rooted in two other conceptions which play a basic role in his thought.

The first concerns the close connection between consciousness and bodily impulses or motions. Thus, according to James, "*consciousness* (or the neural process which goes with it) *is in its very nature impulsive*" (PR, II, 535). If a new movement towards an unfamiliar object is to occur, this object must first be focused somehow in consciousness. Then "with his consciousness, his action changes, for the new object, once stably in possession of the field of his thoughts, infallibly produces its own motor effects" (p. 564). No special faculty of will is required. Consciousness is so intimately fused with bodily movement that a conscious object will at once awaken a mobile impulse, "*whenever it is not kept from so doing by an antagonistic representa-*

tion present simultaneously to the mind" (II, 526). This brings us to the second source, James' field-conception of consciousness. He developed his notion of the conscious field (*cf.* VA, pp. 226–29) in strong reaction against the atomistic theories of Hume and the British empiricists. We ourselves exist in this world-field which contains not only all the present interests and objects of which we are aware, but the whole past store of memories and projections of the future. We ourselves and our living bodies are at the centre of these fields, and the objects in which we are really interested are warmer and more real (*cf.* VA, pp. 147–49, and PR, II, Chap. XXI). But these objects are surrounded by less real fringes of which we are only dimly aware, and which fade into subconsciousness at the horizon. "As our mental fields succeed one another, each has its centre of interest, around which the objects of which we are less and less attentively conscious fade to a margin so faint that its limits are unassignable" (VA, p. 226). This is the second reason for James' identification of will-power with "the effort of attention".

New projects with wider world-fields begin to form at these semi-conscious borders. If left to themselves, as we have noted, they may mature without rational criticism, and burst forth in a moment of crisis as one-sided patterns which may have a disruptive effect on life. If they are to be sound and comprehensive enough to take over the past without disintegration, they must be subjected to reflective criticism during the period of growth. This will not happen through a mere fiat of the so-called will, but only through a disciplined effort which enables the mind to pay attention to unattractive objects still on the fringes of consciousness and, therefore, still vague and confused. Thus, as James says, "*the essential achievement of the will in short, when it is most 'voluntary' is to* ATTEND *to a difficult object and hold it fast before the mind*" (PR, II, 561). This control of attention by effort is the very heart of human freedom.

The intimate fusion of consciousness with action has often been interpreted by American commentators in a pragmatic, or voluntaristic, sense, as though ideas, according to James, were only instruments for action. This is a misunderstanding. The two factors are fused, it is true. But it is the conscious vision which guides, not the action. As James puts it (p. 531), *"in action as in reasoning, then, the great thing is the quest of the right conception"*. It is in forging such conceptions, and in attending to them while they oppose the normal currents of life that our noetic freedom lies (*cf*. pp. 569 ff.). As over against Heidegger's theory of "resolute choice" by fiat, James' view of noetic freedom can justifiably be called *intellectualist* by contrast.

This is borne out by three characteristics James finds in the experience of the sick soul who manages to be born again (VA, pp. 242–43). Of these three characteristics, the first is ambiguous. He refers to it as "the sense that all is ultimately well with one, the peace, the harmony, the *willingness to be*, even though the outer conditions should remain the same". This might be primarily a matter either of conscious vision or of active trend. But the other two characteristics are unmistakably intellectual in tone. The second is "the sense of perceiving truths not known before"; and the third is "the objective change which the world often appears to undergo", a "sense of clean and beautiful newness within and without". The new life cannot be achieved without action. But even more basically it requires a new vision of the world.

We may end this comparative study of Heidegger and James with the following summary. The thought of *Sein und Zeit* is far more strictly organized and systematic than any major work of the American philosopher. James' writings, on the other hand, while looser in structure, are more far-ranging and wider in scope. They are full of suggestive gaps that are open to further development without requiring any basic change or "turning". Thus in this open frame there is room for Heidegger's precise analyses of the call of conscience, the evasion of death, and many other penetrating observations of *Sein und Zeit*. It is a flexible pattern of independent insights, still retaining a basic coherence of its own. As an example of its greater comprehensiveness, we may mention the factor of religion with which James was always concerned, but from which Heidegger abstracts in *Sein und Zeit*, and which he continues to regard, apparently, as beyond the scope of strict philosophy.[7] But according to James, philosophy should have something to say about every dimension of our lived experience.

Both would agree that philosophical description and analysis are concerned with a lived existence which they can clarify, but never replace. James is deeply interested in finding stable meanings and patterns in this flux of experience. But he is also aware of the danger of reading fixed structures into it in such a way as to reduce its enormous richness and variety. Hence after "finding" an idea that seems to be sound, he feels the need of returning again and again to individual cases where it can be tested in the concrete. Hence his thinking is more *ontic* and less *ontological*, more radically empirical and less abstract from beginning to end.

James' account of self-becoming is less anthropocentric and self-centered than that of *Sein und Zeit*. Thus he clearly sees the dangers of obsession with the self, and the need for self-sacrifice and self-abandonment at certain times. And yet he is never near the opposite extreme of a fatalistic emphasis on an independent Being which imposes its meanings upon us with little or no room for creative response. All through his active career he was aware, on the one hand, of independent beings and facts which must simply be recognized and, on the other hand, of meanings within our control. On the whole, in spite of many twists and turnings, he was able to achieve a stable equilibrium between the two, and to maintain a direction of thought that avoided both idealism and realism in a one-sided form.

Religion and the Strenuous Life

If we read these accounts of the divided self, the sick soul, the twice-born, and the precarious process of self-becoming with James' earlier essays in mind, we cannot help but perceive a

[7] *Cf. Introduction to Metaphysics*, tr. Manheim, Yale University Press, 1959, pp. 7–8.

close connection with this ethical views. This connection has often been ignored because of the widespread tendency to think of James' ethics as a version of utilitarianism based on the principle of inclusiveness. If, however, we are right in rejecting this notion, and in taking seriously his own emphasis on the importance of moral freedom and the strenuous life, we can see a continuity between his moral philosophy and his philosophy of religion. For religion also, as it appears in the numerous case histories of the *Varieties*, is a special development of the strenuous life.

Thus in commenting on conversion (p. 236), James says: "what is attained is often an altogether new level of spiritual vitality, a relatively heroic level, in which impossible things have become possible, and new energies and endurances are shown." He is interested not so much in religious creeds and doctrines as in the radical transformations of life which religion has elicited in the concrete case histories he reviews. In such a transformation, "the inner man rolls over into an entirely different position of equilibrium, lives in a new centre of energy from this time on" (p. 314). This new life is no longer centered in the self, since "the outlines of the confining selfhood melt down" (p. 267). But the sacrifice is freely made, and there is in the experience itself no sense of external coercion. On the contrary, there is "an immense elation and freedom" (p. 267).

In an existential change of this kind, and in the new way of life to which it leads, every human power must be strained to the highest pitch, and the most intensive effort is required. It is in this condition that "the greatest deeds" are performed, for "the best fruits of religious experience are the best things that history has to show" (p. 254). James leaves no doubt in our minds that, as he sees it, this is the highest level of what he has called the "strenuous life" (p. 254). Its characteristic traits at the moral level—seriousness, the finding of over-arching meaning, courage in withstanding hardship, sacrifice, and devotion—are all found here, though in a different order, as we shall see.

As we have already noted, these experiences are "solemn" and serious (pp. 38–39), for unless one is seriously engaged, one cannot be open to them. The mind is able to attend to over-arching meanings which are usually present only on the fringes of our everyday experiences. They give us "a feeling of being in a wider life than that of this world's selfish little interests" (p. 266). James is clearly aware of the risks involved in trusting such mystical feelings. They may appear in many deceptive and often pathological forms. But this is also true of our everyday experience, which has its tempting and its saving moments, its sound and its counterfeit manifestations. Although it often deceives us, we do not abandon our faith in it altogether. We become more critical, and see the need for constant empirical testing. Why should we not take a similar view of the wider world opened up by mystical experience in the broad sense of this term which is characteristic of James' usage. So, as he says, "the wider world would in that case prove to have a mixed constitution like that of this world. . . . It would have its celestial and its infernal regions, its tempting and its saving moments, its valid experiences and its counterfeit ones, just as our world has them; but it would be a wider world all the same" (p. 419).

Thus James thinks of religion as a strenuous way of life, in fact, the most strenuous possible for man. As we have seen, it is a radical transformation of existence, the breaking of old habits, attention to wider meanings, and the formation of a new way of life. Such transformations require not only intensive effort but sacrifice as well, "the sacrifices which life, whenever it is taken strenuously, calls for" (p. 452). The individual whose life has been enlarged by religious vision will have the courage to face hardships and obstacles that would break down most of us who take the easy-going way. "The sense of enlargement of life may be so uplifting that personal motives and inhibitions, commonly omnipotent, become too insignificant for notice, and new reaches of patience and fortitude open out. Fears and anxieties go . . ." (p. 268).

Furthermore, the loss of comforts and material possessions, which many of us would regard as hardships, will be regarded by those following the strenuous way as enhancing human freedom. For "only those who have no private interests can follow an ideal straight away" (p. 313). In this wider horizon opened up by a sense of transcendence, private interests in things and material possessions will seem increasingly insignificant. They pin us down and make us less free. This leads James to make a distinction between being and having which reminds us of a similar contrast in the thought of Gabriel Marcel. "In short", James says, "lives based on having are less free than lives based either on doing or on being, and in the interest of action people subject to spiritual excitement throw away possessions as so many clogs" (p. 313; cf. p. 360).

The religious life, when lived, is, therefore, the life of freedom, and seems to possess the other traits distinguishing the strenuous life from the easy-going way at the moral level. What then marks off the religious from the moral? The most distinctive mark which lies at the root of all the rest is the sense of the presence of a power beyond us and transcending man. As one of the authors James quotes in commenting on the Book of Job remarks: "It is *transcendent* everywhere" (p. 75). James gives this the first place in his list of the peculiar qualities of saintliness (pp. 266–67), and calls it "a conviction, not merely intellectual, but as it were sensible, of the existence of an Ideal Power".

He then points out that in Western religion, and in many others, this power is crystallized in the form of a personal God. But "abstract moral ideals, civic or patriotic utopias, or inner versions of holiness or right may also be felt as the true lords and enlargers of our life . . ." (p. 267). This shows the very wide meaning that James is attaching to the term religion, and his attempt to escape from the limits of any provincial orthodoxy. What is essential is to feel the presence of a power transcending us, with which we are somehow in touch, and with which, or with whom, further communication is possible. James speaks of this transcendence as a "power", and in this respect, his analysis resembles that of later phenomenologists of religion.[8]

The world horizon is expanded, and all its objects and regions

---

[8] *Cf.* G. Van der Leeuw, *Phänomenologie der Religion*, Tübingen, 1956, pp. 3–10.

are reordered with reference to this trans-human centre. Whoever possesses this sense to a high degree "comes naturally to think that the smallest details of this world derive infinite significance from their relation to an unseen divine order" (p. 361). A direct correlate of this first mark is the removal of the self from the central position, and what we may call self-surrender. As one of James' subjects states (pp. 281–82): "there appeared to be in me then, as I find it to be in me now, such an entire loss of what regards myself, that any of my own interests gave me little pain or pleasure . . .". Frets and fears tend to vanish as the self is surrendered to something higher and more important. "In deeply religious men the abandonment of self to this power is passionate. Whoever not only says, but *feels*, 'God's will be done' is mailed against every weakness; and the whole historic array of martyrs, missionaries, and religious reformers is there to prove the tranquil-mindedness, under naturally agitating or distressing circumstances, which self-surrender brings" (p. 280).

But there are two ways in which the self may be surrendered. In the first, this self may simply yield to external pressures. As James says, such people "live on smiles and the word 'yes' forever" (p. 293). This is the easy-going way that produces a "passive happiness" which "is slack and insipid, and soon grows mawkish and intolerable" (p. 293). On the other hand, there is the active strenuous way in which "some austerity and wintry negativity, some roughness, danger, stringency, and effort, some 'no! no!' must be mixed in to produce the sense of an existence with character and texture and power" (p. 293). Here the self does not merely yield and adapt itself to external pressures. It yields what it now is for the sake of something higher and transcendent. This is the heart of the religious life when it is really lived.

In the last chapter, we noted how the integral cooperation of all three departments of the mind, as James called them, is required for authentic moral action. There the dangers of an exclusive emphasis on intellectual detachment were especially emphasized. But the same balanced cooperation of feeling, will, and intellect is also required for the more heroic dimensions of religious existence. This strenuous devotion has its roots in feeling and the active side of our human nature. But unless it is supported by a "strong intellect", it becomes narrow, intolerant, and aggressive.

According to James, this narrowing of the world of devotion is what we mean by *fanaticism,* and he makes some discerning remarks on this distinctive perversion of the religious life. Intensive devotion to what transcends us can be the source of freedom from petty self-interest, and of high-level achievement in every walk of life. But unless it is purified by intellectual discernment and self-criticism, many distortions arise. The chief of these is a tendency to confuse the attitude with its object, and then, as James says, "it idealizes the devotion itself" (p. 333). The acts of worship become divine, and are regarded as merits of the worshipper. Exaggerated paeans of praise are lavished upon the divine object as though they increased his honor and glory. Those who refuse these human forms of adoration, or criticize them, are taken to be enemies of the Deity.

This absence of self-consciousness leads to intolerance and persecution of every kind. "Between his own and Jehovah's enemies a David knows no difference; a Catherine of Siena, panting to stop the warfare among Christians which was the scandal of her epoch, can think of no better method of union among them than a crusade to massacre the Turks; Luther finds no word of protest or regret over the atrocious tortures with which the Anabaptist leaders were put to death; and a Cromwell praises the Lord for delivering his enemies into his hands for 'execution'" (p. 335). In the absence of intellectual criticism and widening, all the "saintly virtues of the strenuous life" may become similarly corrupted. Thus purity may lead to escapism and the endless monotony of extreme forms of the monastic life (pp. 341 ff.); charity may turn the world over to unscrupulous aggression and the enemies of mankind (pp. 347 ff.); and asceticism may jeopardize health for the sake of an unlimited mortification (pp. 352 ff.).

Nevertheless, when supported by an intellectual vision which gives them a specific meaning and purpose, all these, including purity, are "splendid excellencies, and the saint of all men shows them in the completest possible measure" (pp. 361-62). James is especially interested in this syndrome as a way of life ordered to what transcends the individual and his present condition, both inner and outer. He is indifferent to the various forms of sectarian organization and ritual. The particular church to which a saint belongs is of no concern to him, nor, indeed, whether he belongs to any (pp. 328-31). The saint is moved by the sense of a divine order lying beyond him, and to bring some part of this into the world he is ready to sacrifice his earthly peace and comfort. "So he turns his back upon no duty, however thankless" (p. 361). When in trouble we can count upon him for assistance which is inward as well as outward, "for his sympathy reaches souls as well as bodies, and kindles unsuspected faculties therein" (p. 361). He is ready to take risks for the possibility of achieving what is really true and really good. The great critics and adventurers of our human history are saints, as James uses this word. They have lived the strenuous life *par excellence*, and have been able to inspire others to do the same.

James emphasizes this social radiance in his discussion of *caritas* (charity). "Treating those whom they met, in spite of the past, in spite of all appearances, as worthy, they have stimulated them to *be* worthy, miraculously transformed them by their radiant example, and by the challenge of their expectation" (p. 349). They are prophetic in their visions of unexplored possibilities—"nay, innumerable times they have proved themselves prophetic" (p. 349). They are the spearheads of social change, for "if things are ever to move upward, some one must be ready to take the first step, and assume the risk of it. . . . Force destroys enemies; and the best that can be said of prudence is that it keeps what we already have in safety. But nonresistance, when successful, turns enemies into friends; and charity regenerates its objects" (p. 350). These are the "creative energies" of history.

Those who are ready to take risks of this kind feel the desolate poverty of our everyday existence and the need for regeneration. According to James, this is the real meaning of "asceticism", which "stands for nothing less than for the essence of the twice-born philosophy" (p. 354). There is an element of real wrong-ness in the world, which, as we have noted, the healthy-minded seek to evade and ignore. But this healthy-mindedness "with its sentimental optimism, can hardly be regarded by any thinking man as a serious solution" (p. 356). The evil of the world must be frankly faced and fought by a creative sacrifice that James constantly identifies with the "strenuous" and the "heroic".

Thus true asceticism is derived from something "wild and . . . heroic" which is deeply rooted in human life, and felt by "man-kind's common instinct for reality, which in point of fact has always held the world to be essentially a theatre for heroism" (pp. 355–56). In comparison, "naturalistic optimism is mere syl-labub and flattery and sponge-cake" (p. 356). Modern religion has turned its back on the heroic element in traditional religion, because of the individual "egoism" with which it was associated. Hence we now think that "war is a school of strenuous life and heroism" (p. 359). But this is organized "irrationality and crime". Can we not find "something heroic that will speak to men as universally as war does, and yet will be as compatible with their spiritual selves as war has proved itself to be incompatible?" It is here (p. 359) that James first presented his idea of "the moral equivalent of war", which he later developed in his essay of that title. The voluntary acceptance of hardship in fighting not against other men, but against disease and poverty, he suggests here, "is the strenuous life". It can be manifested in these and many other ways. But in so far as they show man's capacity to give himself and all his energies to something good not yet experi-enced, and thus transcending his present condition, they involve religion, as James uses the word, and are examples of saintliness.

We may respect these acts of self-transcendence, but we may deny that they are inspired by any divine source radically tran-scending man. Why does James accept this over-belief? What evidence does he give? His answer to this question constitutes an essential portion of his work, and it is to this answer that we must now turn.

Mysticism

Is there evidence provided by direct experience that points to regions lying beyond the limits of the world of sense? The claims made for mystical experience would at least make it worthy of careful examination, and James devotes a chapter to this topic. He here defines mystical experience in terms of four primary traits. First of all, it is "directly experienced" as an imposed condition that "defies expression", so that "no adequate report of its contents can be given in words" (p. 371). In the second place, it has a *"noetic quality"*. That is, it seems to be a state of "insight into depths of truth unplumbed by the discursive intellect". Third, these experiences are transient and passing. Except for rare exceptions, "half an hour, or at most an hour or two seems to be the limit beyond which they fade into the light of common day" (p. 372). Nevertheless such insights are remembered, and "carry with them a curious sense of authority for after time" (p. 371). Finally, fourth, though the oncoming of this state "may be facilitated by preliminary voluntary operations", once it has set in, the subject usually feels "as if he were grasped and held by a superior power" (p. 372).

What then is the meaning of these experiences?

After examining many individual case histories taken from the literature of Eastern as well as Western mysticism, James then raises the question of interpretation. Mystical experiences have, of course, been placed in different philosophical and theological settings by different cultural traditions. In accordance with his empirical method, James now tries to bracket these external frames in order to find intrinsic meanings born by the experiences themselves as expressed at first hand by those who have lived them through. As he says: "in spite of their repudia-

tion of articulate self-description, mystical states in general assert a pretty distinct theoretic drift" (p. 407). The individual
feels himself taken up from the level of ordinary consciousness
"as from a less into a more, as from a smallness into a vastness,
and at the same time from an unrest to a rest" (p. 407). He
himself, and all other beings are reconciled in a nameless unity
that comes from beyond them all.

Hence the widespread use of negation in characterizing this
unifying source which is not this, nor that, nor anything. But
this is "a denial made on behalf of a deeper yes" (p. 407).
James notes the similarity with certain features of the Hegelian
dialectic, and even goes so far as to suggest that Hegel's philosophy may be an attempt to articulate a "mystical feeling" of
this kind (p. 379, note). The individual who has been touched
by such ecstatic experiences feels that he is possessed by some
higher power working in and through him. These ecstasies may
be separate and sporadic. But when the individual pays attention and prepares for them, they establish in the soul "a new
centre of spiritual energy", and when they depart, they leave it
upon a higher level of emotional excitement, ready for "heroic"
action. This seems to be generally true of mystics with "natively
strong minds and characters" (p. 404).

On the other hand, an over-abstraction from practical life is
"peculiarly liable to befall mystics in whom the character is
naturally passive and the intellect feeble" (p. 404). And there
are other graver weaknesses in any attempt to use mystical experience as support for the belief in any field of religious transcendence. In the first place, there is little doubt that "mystical"
phenomena have often involved pathological conditions such as
"imitated hypnoid states, on an intellectual basis of super-
stition, and a corporeal one of degeneration and hysteria" (p.
404). James believes that these experiences come from a "subliminal or trans-marginal" region of the mind (p. 417). But this
is also the source of other "mystical ideas" which are cited "as
characteristic symptoms of enfeebled or deluded states of mind"
(p. 417). A second weakness is the transient character that we
have already noted. This may be used to justify the sceptics'

claim that such experiences are pathological accidents, unless
they are supported by long term training in the disciplines of
"mental prayer", and are attended by a growth in the "consciousness of illumination" which, for James, is "the essential
mark" of genuinely mystical states (p. 399, n. 2). Instances of
this kind may be found. James refers to St. John of the Cross as
"one of the best of them" (p. 398). But they are very rare, which
also may be regarded as a weakness in the case for mystical
belief.

But James holds that these negative arguments can be met.
Authentic mystical experiences seem to put us into direct contact with a "wider world" (p. 419). They open up new meanings,
and incite those who live them through to a more heroic and
strenuous life. The intellectualist critic who dismisses them because of the pathological symptoms with which they are often
associated is in the weaker position, for any significant, lived
experience might be discredited in this way. He is expressing
a special metaphysical bias of his own. If he does not mix them
with extraneous interpretations, and penetrates to their common
and vague root meanings, the empiricist must respect them.
These lived experiences do not contradict any fact or pattern
that is felt or perceived in the world of sense. They appear to
give us access to other regions, to a "wider world" beyond the
limits of sense. This world may have its "celestial and infernal
regions" just as the ordinary world of every day has them. We
should have to select certain manifestations as more significant,
and reject others, just as we do with those of our "natural" experience.

"We should be liable to error just as we are now; yet the
counting in of that wider world of meanings, and the serious
dealing with it, might, in spite of all the perplexity, be indispensable stages in our approach to the final fullness of the truth"
(*ibid.*). The empiricist cannot consistently reject broad ranges
of evidence that are directly experienced by anyone, no matter
how temporary and infrequent these experiences may be. Hence
for James these mystical experiences are "inviolable", and he felt
himself obliged to struggle with the many problems they suggest.

On his view, they are a special manifestation of the more general experience of prayer, and confirm its general sense. The empiricist must always be on guard against imposing arbitrary interpretations on the manifold data of experience. Hence he must bracket all such theories as he turns to phenomena, held together by vague linguistic usage, and tries to describe them as they are lived. James has followed this procedure in analyzing the religious case-histories which constitute the central core of his text. But he is profoundly interested in finding patterns in these histories, and in clarifying them by conceptual analysis. It is not surprising, therefore, that in his concluding chapter (Lecture XX), he raises the question as to whether there is a common empirical pattern underlying all the warring creeds and theological interpretations. "Is there", he asks, "under all the discrepancies of the creeds, a common nucleus to which they bear their testimony unanimously" (pp. 497-98).

According to James, there is such a common pattern, or "essence", which can be found in the case histories of "those more developed minds which alone we are studying" (p. 498). This pattern has two parts: first, an "uneasiness", and second, a distinctive type of "solution". Then he says "we formulate the essence of their religious experience in terms like these" (p. 498). First of all, there is a sense of restlessness—"that there is *something wrong about us as we naturally stand*". We are not satisfied with the natural state in which we find ourselves. We strive to get beyond it, and, as James explains, we are already beyond it, for "the individual, so far as he suffers from his wrongness and criticises it, is to that extent consciously beyond it, and in at least possible touch with something higher, if there is anything higher. Along with the wrong part, there is thus a better part of him, even though it may be but a most helpless germ" (p. 498). At first, it is not clear "with which part he should identify his real being".

But if he decides to become responsible, he identifies with this higher self, and strives for it as an ideal. All this, of course, occurs at the moral level. The experience becomes religious only when the striving agent is pervaded by a feeling of helplessness and the threat of ultimate shipwreck. Then "*he becomes con-scious that this higher part is conterminous and continuous with a MORE of the same quality, which is operative in the universe outside of him, and which he can keep in working touch with, and in a fashion get on board of and save himself when all his lower being has gone to pieces in the wreck*" (pp. 498–99). As James sees it this is not a constructive interpretation. It is a common pattern, or "essence", that is actually found in the case histories of those who have lived through a genuine religious experience. As we have noted, this may give rise to profound "psychological" changes. The whole meaning of the world and the individual's way of life may be transformed. But is this only "his subjective way of feeling things, a mood of his own fancy, in spite of the effects produced"? (p. 499). Is the belief in this wider world well-founded? Is it objectively true?

The affirmative answer which James gives to this question is not based on theoretical argument, nor on causal inference of any kind. It is based on the direct experiences of prayer, or "prayerful communion", which he has described and analyzed in the course of his work. He uses the term "prayer" in a very broad sense in referring to "any kind of communion" with higher powers, including so-called mystical experience. "The funda-mental religious point is that in prayer, spiritual energy, which otherwise would slumber, does become active, and spiritual work of some kind is effected really" (p. 467). James holds that there is a "trans-marginal", subconscious field around the limits of our clear consciousness, and we have noted the important role he assigns to the subconscious in conversion and mystical communion. This region contains many trivial factors like im-perfect memories now forgotten, and disintegrating factors like "inhibitive timidities" (p. 502). But it is here also that new and constructive patterns of habit are prepared, and "in it many of the performances of genius seem also to have their origin" (p. 502).

Hence James accepts the hypothesis that it is this wider, trans-marginal field which first receives higher influences that later may become conscious motives for thought and action. As he says : *"the conscious person is continuous with a wider self through which saving experiences come"* (p. 505). This would explain several characteristic marks of the religious life—the sense of intimate union with a transcendent power, while the conscious integrity of the person remains intact. But is this power that seems to be coming from beyond us real, or is it a mere delusion with ideal being only? Having laid the necessary ground, James is now ready with a clear and succinct answer.

The Reality of the Unseen

The unseen region, whose presence we feel in the experience of prayer, has more than an ideal being for which we are responsible, since it produces real effects on us, and may change our whole way of existing. As James puts it: "the unseen region in question is not merely ideal, for it produces effects in this world. When we commune with it, work is actually done upon our finite personality, for we are turned into new men, and consequences in the way of conduct follow in the natural world upon our regenerative change. But that which produces effects within another reality must be termed a reality itself, so I feel as if we had no philosophic excuse for calling the unseen or mystical world unreal" (pp. 506–7). Several comments need to be made to bring out the meaning of James' conception, which has been subject to serious misunderstandings.

The human activities involved in prayer are not based upon inferences from subjective or psychological experiences. As James explains in his Lecture III on "The Reality of the Unseen," they are based rather on a *"sense of reality, a feeling of objective presence, a perception* of what we may call 'something there', more deep and more general than any of the special and particular 'senses' by which the current psychology supposes existent realities to be originally revealed" (p. 58). This "sense of reality" is broader in range than any of the special senses. Furthermore, its object may be extremely vague and obscure, as when a dying man feels himself in the presence of death.

This type of feeling lies at the pre-reflective, *a priori* level (*cf. supra*, Chapter II, pp. 40–41), and calls forth belief in spite of rational criticism and argument. As James says: "so far as religious conceptions were able to touch this reality-feeling, they would be believed in in spite of criticism, even though they might be so vague and remote as to be almost unimaginable . . ." (VA, p. 58). To one who has never experienced anything of this kind, these descriptions will mean nothing. Hence in this part of his text, James does not engage in conceptual argument. He simply quotes first hand accounts, and lets them speak for themselves to those who may understand. We need give here only one such account, which he takes from Thoreau's *Walden* (VA, pp. 269–70).

> Once, a few weeks after I came to the woods, for an hour I doubted whether a near neighborhood of man was not essential to a serene and healthy life. To be alone was somewhat unpleasant. But, in the midst of a gentle rain, while these thoughts prevailed, I was suddenly sensible of such sweet and beneficent society in Nature, in the very pattering of the drops, and in every sight and sound around my house, an infinite and unaccountable friendliness all at once, like an atmosphere, sustaining me, as made the fancied advantages of human neighborhood insignificant, and I have never thought of them since. Every little pine-needle expanded and swelled with sympathy and befriended me. I was so distinctly made aware of the presence of something kindred to me, that I thought no place could ever be strange to me again.

According to James, this feeling of an "enveloping friendliness" is an example of that direct mystical experience on which all the different theological interpretations and creeds are empirically based. Of course, the independent reality of what is appearing in such feelings may be doubted by the sceptical critic. But this may be supported by other considerations worked out by James in his Chapter XXI on "The Perception of Reality" in his *Principles of Psychology.*

As we have noted (*cf. supra,* Chapter VI), it is my direct acquaintance with my own existence which is the ground of my most indubitable beliefs. *"Whatever things have intimate and continuous connection with my life are things of whose reality I cannot doubt"* (PR, II, 298). The object with which we are concerned in prayer meets this criterion, for it penetrates into the most intimate depths of my conscious and subconscious being. It also meets other conditions for grounded belief which James describes in this important chapter (*cf. supra,* pp. 152 ff.). The presence we feel in mystical experiences stimulates the will, and is able "to arouse active impulses" (PR, II, 300). It also awakens "emotional interest", and feelings of "love, dread, admiration, desire etc.". We feel this presence to be working on us and in us, and to have "its own causal importance" (p. 300).

This belief is not grounded in any particular sensation, or group of sensations, which often call forth belief in their object. And yet, though this presence, like that of space, is more pervasive and closer than any such object, it is not something that is merely being thought about, but something directly felt that belongs to the sensory order. Hence as James says in commenting on these concrete cases: "many persons (how many we cannot tell) possess the objects of their belief, not in the form of mere conceptions which their intellectual accepts as true, but rather in the form of quasi-sensible realities directly apprehended" (VA, p. 63). Since it is characterized by marks which usually justify belief, James concludes that this object is real, and not a mere mental construction.

It is important to note, however, that this presence, as directly experienced, is vague and obscure. It is neither a personal God, nor a pantheistic deity, nor a stream of ideal tendency. Each of these, and many more, are special interpretations freely worked out by individuals and groups to meet their special needs and backgrounds. The experience of prayer points not to *another* world beyond, but rather to a "wider world", as James calls it, another "dimension" (p. 507) of this world here and now, in which we actually exist. If we follow the concrete experiences as described by those who have lived them through, "the appearance is that in this phenomenon something ideal, which in one sense is part of ourselves, and in another sense is not ourselves, actually exerts an influence, raises our centre of personal energy, and produces regenerative effects unattainable in other ways" (p. 513).

The objectively oriented positivistic mind will reject this hypothesis on the ground that "the world of sensations and of scientific laws and objects may be all" (p. 509). But this is a reductive theory. It ignores the sense of our own existence and everything connected with it, as we know them by direct acquaintance. "The total expression of human experience", as James says, "urges me beyond the narrow 'scientific' bounds. Assuredly the real world is of a different temperament—more intricately built than physical science allows" (p. 509).

Chapter Thirteen

❀

Pragmatism

We have noted the early roots of James' pragmatic theory in the *Principles*, and its close connection with his empirical method (*supra*, pp. 43 ff.). Of all his doctrines, pragmatism was the one which became best known, and involved him in the most heated controversy. For the sake of simplifying the issue, James was led to assert that his pragmatic theory was entirely separate from and independent of his radical empiricism (PRAG, p. 14).[1] But these statements were made for special purposes, and cannot be taken too seriously. They have a biographic rather than a systematic significance. In his pragmatic writings, James himself clearly indicates the empirical background of his theory of truth, and this certainly becomes clear to the careful reader, as we shall try to show. We shall also try to point out the connection with James' views of mental freedom and independence which we have just considered. In the following discussion, we shall first give a general account of the pragmatic theory. Then we shall consider its weak points, its strong points, and, finally, the general direction in which it is moving.

[1] From the author's preface to *Pragmatism*, 1907.

The Pragmatic Theory of Truth

The first thing to get clear is the empirical theory of meaning on which the pragmatic view is based. As we have seen, in the *Principles*, James makes a sharp distinction between meaning and being (*cf. supra*, pp. 221–23) which he never abandoned, and which underlines his whole pragmatic theory. The mind has the capacity to develop "brain-born" ideas of its own, but until they are verified by experience, they have only a mental being, and may be merely verbal constructions. It is only by direct acquaintance that we make a noetic contact with our own existence, and the independent being of other things and persons. He often uses the vague term "experience" for this direct acquaintance, with results that have often confused his interpreters, and sometimes even himself. One reason for this confusion lies in the subjectivist implications carried by the word (experience) in ordinary English. Thus by his constant use of this term, James often found himself involved in subjectivist views that he had not intended.

He often refers to direct acquaintance as sense experience, or perception, which, to many minds, still suggests a mere appearance of the thing perceived, or a sense-datum. But as we have seen (*supra*, pp. 180–81), perception, for James, involves the actual physical presence of being, brute fact. And this is still true of his pragmatic writings. Thus my present idea of my dog is true, if it is capable of leading me to "vivid sense-perceptions of a jumping, barking, hairy body. Those *are* the real dog, the dog's full presence . . ."[2]. James does not agree with common sense that any one or any set of such percepts gives us the "full" presence of the dog, for any such independent being has further depths and relations that are as yet unknown to us. So further investigation is always justified to make our knowledge

---

[2] *The Meaning of Truth* (MT), p. 129.

more complete. Nevertheless it is only through direct acquaintance that we are brought into the real presence of the thing, or
person, and are actually confronted with facts.

Even though perception and feeling do not constitute a
"*total conflux of the mind with the reality*" (MT, p. 156),[3] they
come as close to this as we can get. Hence all hypotheses must be
tested by such facts, for even though the object is presented in
a form that is very vague and incomplete, it is still present in the
flesh. It is only through the conceptual clarification of such brute
facts that we can arrive at a result that is really meaningful.
". . . Then that result", James says (p. 158), "being the next
thing to conflux, would make the idea true in the maximal degree
that might be supposed practically attainable in the world which
we inhabit."

But the ideal truth would be the complete coincidence of
meaning with being, or the "total conflux of the mind with the
reality". James makes this very clear. "If an idea should ever
lead us not only *towards,* or *up to,* or *against* a reality, but so
close that we and the reality should *melt together,* it would be
made absolutely true, according to me, by that performance"
(p. 157). He repeats this notion again and again in his pragmatic
texts. Thus he accepts the general notion that truth stands for
the agreement, or conformity, of our ideas and beliefs with real
being, though he wishes to stress the independence of these two
factors more than do traditional formulations.

The union of meaning and being cannot be guaranteed by any
a priori demonstration. We may have to hope for it, but we have
no right to assume that it must be so. It must be shown step
by step in each particular case by painstaking empirical procedures. We have no access to any idea that is necessarily real,
nor to any brute fact that is necessarily meaningful. In each
case, we must reveal that they are so. Generalities are insufficient. We must show by empirical investigation which meaning
fits which fact. In the beginning, realities and beliefs are completely independent so far as we know. Knowing is the active

[3] From the essay "A Word More about Truth" in MT.

attempt to bring the two together. But there is no guarantee. This is pragmatism. "If there is to be truth, it says, both realities and beliefs about them must conspire to make it" (MT, pp. 196–97).

Some of James' critics held that there was a necessary connection between meaning and being, but few of them would reject the notion that the truth of an idea lies in its agreement, or conformity, with reality. So far, then, there is no major difference of opinion. The real issue concerns the nature of verification. According to many of his critics, truth is an objective relation that attaches to any idea, or meaning, whether it is recognized or not. Thus as soon as any idea comes into a mind, it either agrees, or disagrees with its object. Verification then consists in certain activities of observation and experiment which bring this relation and its object into view. By such processes of reasoning and clarification, the truth, or falsity, of the proposition may be discovered. These operations of the mind in no sense constitute the truth. They are merely ways of bringing it, as already existent, into the light. Hence many critics accused James of committing the genetic fallacy, and of subjectivism when they found him identifying these processes of verification with the truth.

What does he mean by this?

We must here remember that department Two of the mind, the cognitive power, is able to combine ideas, derived from acquaintance, in new ways, and to develop new meanings. Once they are formulated, such meanings, of course, have a certain reality as objects of thought. Verification is concerned with their *full* reality. Do they conform with something actually existing? This is the kind of truth in which pragmatism is interested, and at one point, James refers to it as *"existential* truth" (p. 205). In order to find this truth, we must go outside of department Two, and turn either to department One, which is concerned with the facts of perception, or to department Three, which is concerned with actions, or to a combination of the two, which is usually the case.

In order to ascertain whether a certain meaning pertains to

some distant fact, I must first act in certain ways to bring the fact into the range of my sensory acquaintance. "The idea, for example, may be that a certain door opens into a room where a glass of beer may be bought. If opening the door leads to the actual sight and taste of the beer, the man calls the idea true" (p. 236). The same applies to one's idea of an abstract relation, as that between the sides and the hypothenuse of a triangle, which has a being independent of the mind. "If the thought of such a relation leads him to draw auxiliary lines and to compare the figures they make, he may at last, perceiving one equality after another, *see* the relation thought of, to be a vision quite as particular and direct as was the taste of the beer" (p. 237). On James' view, these operations and perceptions verify the idea, and constitute its truth.

The idea points to, or intends, some reality to which we have direct access in some realm of being, and attributes some meaning to it. To verify the idea means to proceed further in the direction of this pointing, either by other ideas, by concrete operations, or by both. These are called the "workings", or "consequences", of the idea. If direct access is finally achieved and the meaning is found in the reality, then it is true. As James says, "through these consequences the man's relations to surrounding realities are modified. He is carried nearer to some of them and farther from others, and gets now the feeling that the idea has worked satisfactorily, now that it has not. The idea has put him in touch with something that fulfills its intent, or it has not" (p. 236). It is through this direct familiarity, or acquaintance with the thing that it is most adequately revealed. But the idea that points to it, and the intermediate steps leading up to this direct contact, belong to a single act that achieves either the satisfaction of fulfillment, or the disappointment of falsification. Because of the darkness and opacity of real beings, no verification is ever final; there is always more to be learned, and further corrections to be made. The idea of complete verification, of full knowledge of a thing and its place in the world, is a Kantian regulative ideal that can never be fully attained. To take it as a relation already in existence but not yet known

by us is an unwarranted supposition that leads only to dogmatism. It is rather an ideal that performs its task in leading us on
to further effort and exploration.

James' constant use of the term *practical*, and his choice of
the word *pragmatism* to characterize his whole epistemological
point of view gave many critics the idea that he was repudiating
all purely theoretical activity and truth. But James sharply denies
that this was ever his meaning. In speaking of the practical nature
of truth, he meant that it concerns individual, particular things
which actively resist us, as opposed to what is abstract, general,
and inactive. "'Pragmata'", he says, "are things in their plurality"; and when he speaks of "practical experience", the point
lies "rather in the fact that the experience must be particular
than in the fact that it must be active,—by 'active' meaning here
'practical' in the narrow literal sense" (p. 210). But because it
has led to so much misunderstanding of this kind, James came
to feel that "the name 'pragmatism', with its suggestions of action, has been an unfortunate choice . . ." (p. 184).

Even when he uses the term *action*, James uses it in a very
wide sense, and not in a narrow one, which would oppose it to
what we call theory. Thus in his *Talks to Teachers*, who think
of themselves as being concerned primarily with "unpractical",
intellectual operations, James reminds them of the reflex-arc
theory, and the biological origins of hesitation and reflection. One
of the first things he suggests to them is: "no truth, however
abstract, is ever perceived, that will not probably, at some time
influence our earthly action" (TT, pp. 26–27).

Theorizing itself is a way of acting. "You must remember", he
says, "that, when I talk of action here, I mean action in the
widest sense. I mean speech, I mean writing, I mean yeses and
noes, and tendencies 'from' things, and tendencies 'toward' things,
and emotional determinations; and I mean them in the future as
well as in the immediate present. As I talk here and you listen, it might seem as if no action followed. You might call it a
purely theoretic process with no practical result. But it *must*
have a practical result. It cannot take place at all and leave
your conduct unaffected" (p. 27). As he goes on to say, this idea

that they are now thinking may lead them to ask new questions. It may lead them to answer a question somewhat differently at some future time. It may lead them to form new attitudes which are already preparations for action. Even if they remain indifferent or reject everything that he is saying, this also is a meaningful response, leading to negative action. "*Not* to speak, *not* to move, is one of the most important of our duties, in certain practical emergencies" (p. 28).

It is important to notice how James is here undercutting the traditional separation of theory from practise. No matter how detached and objective our theorizing may be, it is still a mode of action with essential negative elements of hesitation and abstention. Or, as the existential philosophers now say, it is a project with a style of its own, a way of being in the world, with its own norms and patterns. This is the direction in which James' thought is moving. Furthermore, while he bitterly attacked the tendency to absolutize theory, as though it were the end to which life itself were subordinate, he never denied theory's essential and basic importance.

Whatever may be said of other "pragmatists", James never criticized any project of pure theory, even that of speculative metaphysics, as long as it was demythologized, and kept to its proper task of providing life with a meaning. Thus, as he says in *The Meaning of Truth* (p. 256), the general questions: "Is life worth while at all? Is there any general meaning in all this cosmic weather?" are "so significant", that is, so important for the sake of action, that one way or another, either consciously and critically, or subconsciously and dogmatically, some answer must be given to them by every living individual and culture. James' critics attacked this position as anti-rational and anti-intellectual. Theorizing must not be subordinated to existence. It is an end in itself—the end. James could see in this attitude only the expression of a speculative *hubris* ready to ride rough shod over the facts of life. It is department Two of the mind, failing to see beyond, and substituting itself for the integral existence of man, discounting this, and even denying it alto-gether.

James' view is that by theorizing, we may invent and develop systems of meaning, but we cannot verify them. To find out whether a meaning is true, or not, we must go beyond depart-ment Two to departments Three and One. Any meaning ulti-mately points to a reality in some region of the world which is supposed to bear this meaning. If I move by appropriate actions in this direction, and, by a continuous series of steps, finally find myself in the vicinity of a real being which I then find by direct perception, feeling, and response, to have this meaning, it is verified. If, on the other hand, my steps are interrupted by un-bridgable discontinuities and chasms which separate me from the assumed reality, then the meaning is not an adequate guide, and is disconfirmed. Thus if, in reaching for the black pen I seem to see before me, my hand encounters a solid pane of glass separating me from it, my belief was really mistaken, and I was probably seeing only a reflection of the pen.

I may find myself believing in a general, philosophical pat-tern of meaning which tells me that power over things and persons will lead me to a certain peace and security yielding me all the satisfaction I need. Since such a theory directly concerns me, in order to test it, I must act along the lines it suggests. I must seek to gain power, and then find out, by direct ac-quaintance, if I actually have the security and happiness I should expect, and if "the general drift of experience" confirms this view. If so, it is, at least to some degree, confirmed. Then I will feel some satisfaction, not in general, but *in* the theory, and its partial verification through my existence.

But while this satisfaction is a necessary condition for such verification, it is by no means a sufficient one. The crucial factor is the finding of the meaning of reality. Without this, the theory is false. "The pragmatist calls satisfactions indispensable for truth-building, but I have everywhere called them insufficient unless reality be also incidentally led to. If the reality assumed were cancelled from the pragmatist's universe of discourse, he would straightway give the name of falsehoods to the beliefs remaining, in spite of all their satisfactoriness" (MT, p. 195).[4] Each different theory that is actually held in the concrete, demands different acts to be continuously carried out in what James calls an "ambulatory" manner (pp. 139 ff.), that is, without breaks requiring discontinuous leaps or saltations.

The theorist becomes dissatisfied if, after all goes smoothly for a while, he is suddenly confronted with an obstacle that he cannot clearly surmount or see through, except by an imaginative leap or supposition. In the same way, the practical man, in moving towards his goal, if opposed by a difficulty, or discontinuity, in his path, will seek for another way. James' emphasis is on the actual theories of real life and technology. He takes his pragmatic theory to be a description of what takes place when such particular theories, or beliefs, are actually falsified or partially verified in real life.

After a theory has been verified by specific acts and observations, it may be verbally formulated and stored up in books and written documents whereby it can be transmitted to others. These readers may then come to believe in the theory without going through the original processes of verification. James is well aware of the fact that innumerable truths that we accept and live by are believed in this way "on credit". We have never verified them ourselves, but we believe in them as "virtually true" in the sense that they can be verified. He recognizes the practical necessity for such believing on credit (p. 205). "No one", James says, "attributes more importance than the pragmatist" to this time- and labor-saving practise.

But at the same time he recognizes that it has certain dangers. When formulated as fixed propositions in a "storage-vault of essential timeless agreements", these "truths" become inactive, and develop a certain "sleeping quality", as James calls it (p. 204). Freed from the "panting struggle" for verification, they now become "static, impotent, and relatively spectral". They are simply obvious. One accepts them without any understanding of

4 From the essay "*The Pragmatist Account of Truth and Its Misunderstanders*" in MT.

how they might be verified, and even without any sense of such a need. They are not even consciously asserted, but simply taken for granted in the background of the mind. Unless they are carefully examined, consciously "asserted or questioned or contradicted", they cannot be kept alive (p. 206).

James now notes an even more serious danger. When a vast number of verified truths are formulated as propositions and stored up in books and manuals, we are apt to forget that truths exist only in the minds of living men, and in the particular acts of verification. These acts lead to an experience of contact in which the meaning is found to coalesce with the reality. But in the process of verbal formulation, the statements become separated from the revealing acts, and seem to achieve an independent status of their own. Then we have the idea on the one hand and a distant reality on the other, with an epistemological gulf between. In James' own words, in "A Word More about Truth": "the intermediaries which in their concrete particularity form a bridge, evaporate ideally into an empty interval to cross, and then, the relation of the end-terms having become saltatory, the whole hocus-pocus of *erkenntnisstheorie* begins, and goes on unrestrained by further concrete considerations" (p. 143).

Instead of belonging to the concrete, verifying acts, truth is now attributed to the ideal meanings of propositions in a separated, immaterial mind. It is a relation of pure agreement with distant realities, which simply "obtains" whether anyone ever actually thinks of it or not. "The actual workings of our ideas in verification-processes are as naught in comparison with the 'obtainings' of this discarnate truth within them" (p. 204). James rejects this whole picture as the illegitimate reification of abstractions. We have to use propositions on credit as if they agreed with reality, even though we do not verify them. But in so far as it is legitimate, this credit system is a later development which presupposes the real "workings" of active verification processes, and it is well to have their general patterns in mind, even when we take them on trust. If not, our thinking will lose touch with concrete reality, and will fall into those wastelands of ungrounded abstraction, which James calls "intellectualism".

If we are to avoid these errors, we must remember the nature of the actual verifying process, and the world of sense in which it takes place. We must not place the potential before the existential. We do not start with mental meanings which already have relations of likeness or unlikeness with distant things outside, and which may be established by purely intellectual operations in the mind. This condition, or something like it, presupposes the actual "workings" of pragmatic verification. "Intellectualist truth is then only pragmatist truth *in posse*" (p. 205). If our credit is to be sound, it must be based on something already in our possession. If I am justified in supposing that a proposition is true, this presupposes that actual "working" verifications have been made. "Truth in posse *means* only truths in act; and he [the pragmatist] insists that these latter take precedence in the order of logic as well as in that of being" (p. 206).

For James, existence is prior to possibility. Any question concerning the possibility of something presupposes the existence of a real questioner in the life-world, for thinking and questioning are ways of being-in-the-world. The thinking person is never separated from this world in which he lives. He becomes directly familiar with it as a child, before the coming of language. And linguistic propositions also must be verified in the same way by definite acts of approach and contact that make us directly familiar with the thing, as it works and responds to our advances. As James says in "A Word More about Truth", "our idea brings us into the object's neighborhood, practical or ideal, gets us into commerce with it, helps us towards its closer acquaintance, enables us to foresee it, class it, compare it, deduce it,—in short, to deal with it as we could not were the idea not in our possession" (p. 140).

By such an active contact with the thing, which may include verbal usage, we can discover something about what it means, and its place in the real world. This is to know it and reveal it, by working with it, not merely speculating about it from a distance. The whole active process is "ambulatory", and goes on within the real world without the need for crossing any epistemological gulf. The true idea, or theory, is the one which enables us to pass continuously from one thing, or region, to another without sudden breaks that impede our action. It thus gives us a meaningful map of an area, showing the place of different things and persons in relation to one another. ". . . The concrete truth *for us* will always be that way of thinking in which our various experiences most profitably combine." (p. 73).

By "most profitable" James does not mean an isolated, subjective feeling of "profit" or "satisfaction" that is not a satisfaction *in* something. The true idea is profitable in enabling me to orient myself properly in dealing with real beings independent of me. "Can we imagine a man absolutely satisfied with an idea and with all its relations to his other ideas and to his sensible experiences, who should yet *not* take its content as a true account of reality?" (p. 159). A true idea must fit reality. So James can say "this is why, as a pragmatist, I have so carefully posited 'reality' *ab initio,* and why, throughout my whole discussion, I remain an epistemological realist" (p. 195). But if the realist holds that ideas have of themselves a relation of agreement or disagreement, without any need for definite acts of approach and testing in the concrete, he is mistaken. He has separated the result from the "workings" which alone can establish it.

These "workings" are indispensable. "Surely for understanding what the word 'true' means as applied to a statement, the mention of such workings is indispensable" (p. 219). If we leave them out, the meaning and the reality are torn asunder, and the mysterious relation of truth remains an unmediated, ungrounded supposition. "Surely if we leave them out, the subject and the object of the cognitive relation float—in the same universe, 'tis true—but vaguely, and ignorantly, and without mutual contact or mediation" (p. 219). By these "workings", which achieve "cash values", James never meant an exclusive preoccupation with practical goods, leading to subjective feelings of pleasure along utilitarian lines. By the use of such terms, he was opposing not pure theory, nor rational understanding. They were directed rather against the abstract and passive forms of intellectualism which he found in the various schools of his time.

These seemed to agree that truth could be attributed to propositions rather than to the living thought of man, and that it could be valid, or hold, of them, apart from the concrete acts of approach and contact which work with the thing, and find out how it responds. James is attacking not reason, but intellectual abstraction and inertia, and the speculative *hubris* to which they lead.

If we are thinking of the ultimate context of meaning which is involved in James' use of the term *satisfaction*, we should think not of a levelling utilitarianism, but rather of those distinctive values of the strenuous life which we have just considered (*supra*, pp. 277 ff.). It is the satisfaction that comes from real freedom, the taking of risks, and the facing of real hardships that James has in mind, though in moral contexts, he often specifies it further by using the term *joy*. Thus he speaks of the "joy of responsibility" (EFM, p. 300) that goes with meaningful achievement and the "wonderful joy" that is derived from the real facing of dangers (EFM, p. 29).[5] Here again the attack is not so much against reason, which may go outside of itself and thus become strenuous, as against the inactivity of a spectatorial reason which remains indifferent, and levels down all conflicting desires and meanings to a single common plane.

James often speaks of the verifying process in general as actually "making the truth" (PRAG, pp. 133, 146; MT, pp. 120, 141). These statements were often attacked by his critics as manifestations of an unabashed subjectivism. As a matter of fact such criticisms rested on a misunderstanding, for James is thinking here primarily of those existential beliefs which concern ourselves and which, as we have seen (*supra*, pp. 288 ff.) are self-falsifying or self-verifying. Thus there is the case of the lone mountaineer, lost on a glacial valley in the midst of a storm, which James loved to cite (SR, pp. 96–97; EFM, pp. 28–29). He is faced with a crevasse of uncertain width. After he has made the most careful investigation possible, the evidence turns out to

[5] This and the three immediately following references from EFM are to the essay "Is Life Worth Living?"

be ambiguous. The side facing him is covered with snow, and reaches out towards him over the abyss. But its solidity is uncertain. He is faced with a forced option. Should he believe that he can make it? Or should he avoid the risk, and wait for death? Two possible universes wait for his decision. In which one should he now believe? How will this belief be proven or disproved? Surely not without the contribution of his own strenuous action here and now. For if he accepts the theory that the jump is impossible for him, and simply waits and dies, he will not have proved that he could not have made it. He will have proved only his own conservatism and unwillingness to take a momentous risk. He might have made it if he had tried, which leaves the issue still open. The only way he can prove whether he can make the jump here and now, or disprove it, is by making the attempt with the expenditure of all his powers. If he makes the attempt in this way and fails, he will have shown others that his belief in his capacity is false. If he makes the attempt and succeeds, he will have proved the belief to be true by his own actions.

But this does not reach the root of what James means by the example (EFM, p. 28). Let us suppose that the situation is really uncertain to the highest degree, as is true of the philosophical issues confronting us in real life. Suppose that success or failure will depend not only on our physical energy but on our "mental" poise and confidence as well, that the least amount of trembling and hesitation in the act will lead to disaster. Then the strength and courage of our belief will be a decisive factor. If we allow ourselves, at the beginning of the act, to falter and waver, we will not only have proved that we could not do it at the time. We will have been *responsible for* the failure. We will have *made it untrue* by a weakening of belief that we might have avoided. On the other hand, if we maintain the strength of our belief to the highest degree, and keep all our powers under control and working at the highest pitch, we will not only have proved to a general observer in the abstract that the leap could be made. We would now be responsible for this self-verification.

We would have *made the belief come true* by a free decision. So in cases of this kind, which resemble overarching, philosophic decisions in many respects, James can say: "you make one or the other of two possible universes true by your trust or mistrust" (EFM, p. 28).

In the case of the trivial options of science and objective speculation, which do not concern our total existence, it is not we ourselves, but the objective facts, that make a theory true or false (EFM, p. 51). Nevertheless a free choice on our part is necessary to ask the right questions, to set up the situation, and let the thing show what it is, among other alternative possibilities. Such a showing, or proving, of the truth is not the cognitive reception of a relation already in existence. It is an "event", a real "happening" in the history of science, which is a part of human history. Hence James can say: "Truth *happens* to an idea. It *becomes* true, is *made* true by events. Its verity *is* in fact an event, a process: the process namely of its verifying itself" (PRAG, p. 133).

James tended to look at this event from the side of the idea or meaning, though he also admits that it has a real, or objective, side (*cf.* MT, pp. 233 ff.). The meaning ceases to be a mere mental intention. It is found to be rooted in real being, and is able to lead us to this being and to relate it to others. So James can speak of an idea as "verifying itself" (PRAG, *loc. cit.*). In using the phrase "verifying itself", he is, no doubt, thinking primarily of existential theories and beliefs which are self-verified in the Alpine style.

But in generalizing here, as though it could also cover the scientific verification of purely objective truths, where the facts decide, he was going too far. This is perhaps due to his preoccupation at the end of his life with moral and religious questions. But as we have seen (*supra*, p. 286), James was aware of the distinction between these questions and scientific ones, and by emphasizing it, instead of slurring over it in his pragmatic writings, he might have avoided much unnecessary criticism. In verifying objective truths, as James himself knew, it is not our actions that must finally decide; it is the facts.

But he is right in holding that active operations are required for the verification of any hypothesis. He does not deny that the idea must agree with the static, formal properties of a thing. In this sense, it is correct to think of the mental conception as a copy, and as James says, "our true ideas of sensible things do indeed copy them" (PRAG, p. 132). In order to understand what a clock is, we must know what the dial looks like, from the outside, by forming appropriate images, or pictures, in the mind. But this formal knowledge is insufficient. In order to gain a real understanding of the clock, we must know something about its inner "works", what makes it tick, how it functions. Such knowledge also involves formal elements, but something more as well. As James says (p. 132), it "is much less of a copy". We cannot gain this merely by looking. We must move into the works, operate on them, and bring them into relation with our own acts. For example, the elasticity of the spring is not a static, visual property; it describes a mode of active response to stretching. In order to gain knowledge of this kind, we must approach the thing, get in touch with it, act on it, and grasp how it responds. This is not adequately expressed by the language of mental copies in the mind.

Our cognition must become congruent not only with the properties (the essence) of the thing, but with its activity (its existence) as well. An idea that is true in this sense not only corresponds with an external object. It is acquainted with its being, so that it can be related to our own existence, and, as James says (p. 133), "assimilated". The same holds also for the philosophical conceptions which apply to our existence in the world. In order to be true, these over-arching patterns must formally correspond with the patterns of existence. But to become really true, they must call forth our active concern. To find out what a philosophy means, we must live with it and in it. This is why James distrusted verbalism in philosophy, and speculative theories that are never verified in this way. The true philosophy again is the one that can be taken over and "assimilated" into real life by belief. In this sense, we can speak of

James' epistemology as existential (*cf. supra*, pp. 49 ff. and 259–60).

Two great systems that would make no difference in our experience, or conduct, if they were really lived, are not really different, and any debate between them "becomes quite idle and insignificant" (PRAG, p. 73). This is the pragmatic test, which is basically empirical in character. James is very clear about this in his pragmatic writings. Thus a scientific hypothesis is true if it corresponds with the stable structures of the facts, and if it leads to action on our part which is congruent with the behavior of the thing, so that we can use it and control it. A philosophical hypothesis is true if it corresponds to the patterns of the world, and if it leads to action on our part which is congruent with the behavior of other things and persons and with the general drift of history.

"Pragmatism represents a perfectly familiar attitude in philosophy, the empiricist attitude, but it represents it, as it seems to me, both in a more radical and in a less objectionable form than it has ever yet assumed. A pragmatist turns his back resolutely once and for all upon a lot of inveterate habits dear to professional philosophers. He turns away from abstraction and insufficiency, from verbal solutions, from bad *a priori* reasons, from fixed principles, closed systems and pretended absolutes and origins" (p. 45). This pragmatic theory presupposes a noetic freedom of the mind to pay attention to unnoticed aspects of experience, and to create new patterns of meaning to take account of the new as well as the old.

James often brings this up in connection with his criticism of the notion that the mind is chiefly engaged in copying, and repeating over within itself something that was already there. Thus, he refers to Rudolf Lotze in criticizing the widely held view that "reality, we naturally think, stands ready-made and complete" (p. 166), so that the mind can only repeat it over as it is. Then on the next page (p. 167), he sharply contrasts this traditional conception with the pragmatic view that "in our cognitive as well as in our active life we are creative" in a universe that "*is still in the making, and awaits part of its com-*

plexion from the future". And in "Humanism and Truth" (1904)[6] he asks, "Why may not thought's mission be to increase and elevate, rather than simply to imitate and reduplicate existence" (PRAG, p. 244).

I believe that James is thinking of two things, at least, in speaking of this creative power of free cognition. In the first place, while the brute facts must be recognized as they are, they may always be taken account of in different ways. This happens at the level of science. But at the level of human history, new beliefs may be made true by human acts that lead to new facts, and thus increase existence. Thus by believing in freedom, a man may become free, and by his new thoughts and acts, as they become related to other facts, he may help to usher in a new development of history. The world in which we live is ambiguous and "malleable" to new choices and beliefs. The spatio-temporal field that is subject to such self-verifying change, from age to age, is what we call the world of history, which James distinguished sharply from the world of nature, as we have seen (*supra*, pp. 288–92).

Criticism

We have now given a review of James' pragmatic theory of truth, based primarily on his own words in *Pragmatism* and in the later essays of *The Meaning of Truth*. Let us now turn to criticism. We shall first take up certain objections which we believe to be well-founded, and then others which arise from bias and misunderstanding. Finally, we shall compare and contrast James' pragmatism with certain common elements which can be found in recent existential and phenomenological writers.

Let us turn, first of all, to the objection we have already mentioned that James focuses primarily on the process by which historic truth, as we have called it, is self-verified, and has paid

[6] Reprinted in MT and as an addition in the Meridian edition of PRAG, pp. 229–56.

insufficient attention, in his pragmatic writings, to the verification of scientific theories concerning objective fact. These are certainly not self-verifying in the same sense, though I believe that James was right in denying that they could be properly understood as a mere copying of given facts, or as a result of *induction*, in the sense of John Stuart Mill. As we have indicated, James was aware of the difference, but he slurred over it in his pragmatic texts. This is a serious defect, and opened him to many criticisms which might have been avoided if he had made the distinction clearly, and had emphasized it in the exposition of his pragmatic theory.

James makes it clear that a true theory concerning facts, or actions, must agree with the independent realities involved. But we may then ask how this agreement, or disagreement, is ascertained? To this question, James usually gives an answer that emphasizes direct sensation in the case of facts, and feeling in the case of actions, especially the feeling of *satisfaction* that terminates a successful act. There is hardly any mention of the need for conceptual clarification except in *The Meaning of Truth* (p. 206), where he mentions the importance of "asserting", and "questioning", and "contradicting", and presumably of clarifying our beliefs, in order to keep them alive.

We have seen how, in other places, he stressed the need for genuine cooperation between perception and conceptual thought, if lived experience is to be adequately understood (*supra*, pp. 234 ff.). But in the pragmatic writings, ideas seem to be assigned only a guiding function. They lead us up to the reality with which we are concerned. But the task of final verification is handed over, apparently, to sense and feeling, as if verbal clarification, and even insight, as he elsewhere speaks of it, had no role to play. This also is a serious defect in his exposition, which fails to do justice to his more considered and less one-sided views.

James' theory is commonly criticized as being too subjective in its orientation and neglecting the objective pole of the knowing relation. Thus he is concerned with the invention of the meaning or idea, in following through, in detail, what happens to it in the process of becoming true, and in the satisfaction that attends this culmination. But little is said about the independent being, and what happens to it as it is being revealed. In this connection, he seems to have been influenced by the realistic conception of knowing as a purely mental change which leaves the object known completely changeless and intact (*cf.* PR, I, 219). This leads him to speak of being and of facts as though they were not known at all. "The 'facts' themselves", he says, "meanwhile are not true. They simply *are*. Truth is the function of the beliefs that start and terminate among them" (PRAG, p. 147). It is here that the *"mental content"*, or meaning, and the *"object"* are identical (p. 228),[7] and the thing is revealed as it is.

I think that James is groping for an important new conception that will enable him to dispense with the notion of a thing in itself, lying back of the appearances which are presented to us. It is precisely the things in themselves as they are, independent of us, that appear at these moments. He is moving towards the view that the being of a thing is its being revealed. But this view is never clearly expressed, and is left in an unfinished form which is open to serious objections. If the being appears in experience, then it must be known in some way, and cannot be reduced to sheer being, or fact, as he often calls it. He still speaks of "acquaintance or familiarity" as a form of "knowledge" (PRAG, p. 209), but then how can it escape from being true? James does not consider these questions. In the *Essays in Radical Empiricism,* as we shall see (*infra,* pp. 360 ff.), he does try to do so but not without further confusion and difficulty.

For most people, pragmatism means that we can believe in the truth of a theory if our believing in it turns out to be satisfactory to us. This "subjectivism" was often brought up against the theory during James' lifetime. But as he often pointed out, it rests on a misunderstanding. No belief can be justified, or verified, by merely believing in it and feeling

---

[7] From the essay "The Tigers of India" (1895) reprinted in MT and as an addition in the Meridian edition of PRAG, pp. 225–28.

"satisfied". The real test lies in working with the idea, acting on its basis, and this includes acts of understanding as well as overt dealings with the real being involved. This being must turn out to be as the theory indicates, and enable us to establish working relations with it. In so far as we achieve this, we will feel not a mere subjective satisfaction, but a real satisfaction *in* this specific fulfillment of existence.

The emphasis on action opened James to many charges of voluntarism and anti-intellectualism. While it must be granted that his language, taken out of context, sometimes may have given an excuse for them, these attacks hardly do justice to his integral theory. He consistently rejected a faculty psychology, and did not believe in an isolated faculty of will. He does speak of the active phase of human life, and distinguishes it from the other two "departments", concerned with the recognition of fact and the elaboration of meaning. He speaks of it as the "final" phase (RAAT, p. 123) for without it, the other two remain incomplete. We cannot act in a human way unless we make a meaningful effort in a factual situation. So James refers to it as the last phase of the mental cycle.

Does this mean that the other two departments, and especially the second, the search for meaning, are to be regarded as instruments for action, which lies at a higher normative level of intrinsic value?

James sometimes uses language of this kind (PRAG, pp. 127, 134; MT, p. 207), and he speaks favorably of the "instrumental view" of the Chicago School (PRAG, p. 49). But I do not believe that it represents the drift of his considered thought on the matter. Unless it is supported by the other two departments, the active element in man will "sicken and die", or burst forth in one-sided "convulsions" that will jeopardize life (RAAT, p. 127). The full energy and proper functioning of each department is required for any real project of life. The facts of the situation must be recognized, a meaningful pattern must be developed, and then carried out. A failure of any one function may lead to disaster. "Any one of these defects is fatal to its complete success" (PRAG, p. 125).

There is no attempt here to subordinate one as a mere means to the other as an end. An act without vision is as defective as a mere wishful vision with no act. As we have seen, (*supra,* p. 310) James speaks of "vision" in *The Varieties of Religious Experience* as having a special priority and pertinence. So, in the end, I do not believe that we can properly characterize James' basic attitude as either intellectualist or anti-intellectualist. The whole man is more than the sum of these three "departments". And it is the integral action of this whole man that finally counts.

Let us now conclude by noting some similarities between James' theory of knowledge and certain aspects of recent phenomenology. There is good reason for accepting the widespread opinion that modern existentialism began with Kierkegaard's criticism of the great speculative system of Hegel on the ground that it had no place for the contingent facts and patterns of lived existence. One might say that Kierkegaard was more concerned with this active existence, and its conditions in the concrete, than in far-reaching speculation about it. Similarly one might say that Marx, in his reaction to Hegel, was more concerned with social action in the concrete, or as he put it, with changing the world rather than speculating about it. If this is the underlying sense of existentialism, we can say that James also belonged to this movement of thought. He also found past philosophy, and Hegel in particular, too speculative and remote from the facts of life, as we are directly acquainted with them. This is, in fact, the basis of his radical empiricism.

By turning his attention to the world of sense, as he called it, he was led to a theory of knowledge which understands knowing not as the transcendental activity of a worldless mind, but rather as an essential phase of human existing. As Kierkegaard might have put it, instead of existence being included in knowing, it is rather knowing that is included in existing. Thus, according to James,[8] every man is a philosopher (PRAG, p. 17),

[8] In "The Present Dilemma in Philosophy," the opening lecture in *Pragmatism.*

and he is anxious to bring academic thought into closer touch with the actual philosophical process that is going on constantly in living individuals and groups. The philosopher has much to learn from literature and the arts, and from those engaged in statecraft and political reform. "His books on ethics", James says, "therefore, so far as they truly touch the moral life, must more and more ally themselves with a literature that is confessedly tentative and suggestive rather than dogmatic—I mean with novels and dramas of the deeper sort, with sermons, with books on statecraft and philanthropy, and social and economic reform . . . and they must more and more abandon the old-fashioned, clear-cut, and would-be 'scientific' form" (MPM, p. 210).

As a matter of fact, since the time of Kierkegaard, existential thinkers have expressed their ideas in this style. Like James himself, many of them have been able to write in the first person singular, like a living person rather than an impersonal observer or computer. They have been tentative, because they are aware of human freedom, and the vast range of options that are open to human choice. They have sometimes been best able to express their ideas in the form of novels and plays, because they wish to get closer to the drama of life in the concrete.

But if all men have some understanding of their existence in the world and of its basic patterns, on which the playwright and the novelist can draw, it is not a conceptual understanding that is clearly formulated in words and propositions. It does not give us a sharply focused knowledge about ourselves conceived as objects, from a detached point of view. It is a direct self-knowing that is vague but certain, and makes us acquainted with our being in the world, as we hesitate, choose, and act. James called this *knowledge by acquaintance,* and sharply contrasted it with *conceptual knowledge about,* which necessarily presupposes the former and leads to it so far as the latter is true. Hence this direct awareness lies at the root of his whole pragmatic theory of truth.

Since this direct familiarity with our existence in the world is distinct from and prior to science and to objective knowledge in general, we have referred to it as an *existential a priori* (*supra*, pp. 49 ff.). James did not use this terminology. But he had the relevant facts in mind, and this, indeed, is why he hesitated to call it true or false. It is a peculiar mode of revealing that is prior to the later, derived modes which must be tested and are, therefore, true or false. This prior mode of direct revealing (acquaintance), while it requires further clarity and precision to become communicable, requires no further test. Hence as James keeps saying, it is neither true nor false, but simply *is so*. This is not because *being familiar with* is not a way of knowing. It is the ultimate way that is presupposed by the others. Thus, if you ask how do you know that being is not nothing? that the true is not the false? James would say not by defending your answer as a true theory. Rather by direct acquaintance, for it is here that questioning comes to an end, and we find what is simply so. This is the radical, *a priori* empiricism which is the foundation of his pragmatic theory of truth.

In identifying this direct empirical awareness, which is presupposed by science and by linguistic understanding in general, James was anticipating a development in which many phenomenologists, coming from different traditions, have participated. Thus, Husserl was interested in "pre-predicative" consciousness, and in *Sein und Zeit*, Heidegger constantly refers to the "pre-thematic" understanding of being which all men share, and which he is trying to clarify and make explicit in his "fundamental ontology". In his early works, Sartre was deeply concerned with what he calls the "non-reflective cogito" that gives us a direct, "non-thetic" awareness (of?) being,[9] and in his recent *Critique de la raison dialectique*, he describes that "comprehensive non-knowledge" by which a man grasps his concrete situation, and which lies at the root of intellectual understanding.[10] Can we find ways of gaining access to this vague and im-

---

[9] *Transcendence of the Ego*, tr. Williams/Kirkpatrick, New York, 1957, pp. 32–54.
[10] *Cf. Search for a Method*, tr. Barnes, New York, 1963, pp. 171 ff.

plicit awareness by the use of conceptual thought? Can it be described and analyzed without reduction and distortion? The French phenomenologist, Merleau-Ponty, has gone farthest in working out a disciplined answer to these questions. His notion of a pre-objective consciousness is certainly an important development of a line of investigation already inaugurated by James. We need not hesitate to think of this phase of his empiricism as phenomenological and existential as well.

In one of his first pragmatic essays, "The Function of Cognition" (1885),[11] James clearly rejected the notion of an "epistemological gulf" separating the knower from the known. "The whole truth-relation", he says, "falls inside of the continuities of concrete experience . . ." (PRAG, pp. 223–24, note). In the light of the phenomena, there is no need for supposing a transcendental knower beyond the world (cf. supra, pp. 110 ff.). Knowing is a way of being-in-the-world, which may be phenomenologically described and analyzed. This is a basic thesis of James' pragmatism. There is also no need for the supposition of unknown things in themselves, lying back of the empirical phenomena (PRAG, pp. 170–71). This means, as he clearly recognized (p. 239) that the distinction between appearance and reality must be explained in empirical terms. As he constantly emphasized, it is being itself, hard resistant fact, which shows itself to us, if we are prepared to grasp it. Merleau-Ponty has called it the in-itself for us.[12]

At the most basic levels of his epistemology, James is also thinking along these phenomenological and existential lines.

---

[11] Reprinted in MT and as an addition in the Meridian edition of PRAG, pp. 204–24.
[12] Phenomenology of Perception, p. 322.

Part Four

*Radical Empiricism
and Existence*

Chapter Fourteen

✿

Radical Empiricism—The Last Phase

Let us now turn to the *Essays in Radical Empiricism* (ERE), written in the years 1904–7, towards the end of James' life. He is now ready to use the phrase *radical empiricism* to characterize his whole philosophical position, and to deal with certain basic issues that he had passed over in his earlier works. The most important of these is the question of psycho-physical dualism. In *The Principles of Psychology*, as we noted, James accepted a vague dualism according to which bodily events, especially those of the brain, are accompanied by conscious experiences. But there is abundant evidence to show that he was not satisfied with this traditional solution as, for example, his criticisms of epiphenomenalism, interaction, and the theory of a separate soul substance. There is further evidence to show that he was devoting serious attention to this question in the years immediately preceding the publication of the *Essays*. One written statement dated April 10, 1898[1] is especially worthy of comment.

"It obviously contradicts logic to say that a portion of a field

---

[1] Cf. Perry, *Thought and Character of William James*, II, p. 369.

is the cause (in the ordinary sense of that word) of the entire field itself, or rather such words seem quite devoid of any intelligible meaning. By what discrimination, then, might the matter be cleared up? Will the distinction between object in its sensational immediacy and object *qua* remote terminus help? . . . The brain thought-*of* is not entitatively the brain thought-*with*. But if diverse entitatively, in what sense are they the same? The one thought *of* potentially terminates in the one thought *with*. It is as terminus that it *causes* the thought field of which entitatively it forms a portion. . . ."

The brain that the physiologist thinks about and tests in various ways is a single object in a world-field that is taken for granted by him. This is entitatively very different from the active brain of the living body with which he is himself thinking and working in the field constituted by this living body and its living brain. James now realizes that the brain he was talking about in the *Principles* was the former, not the latter. But the physiologist, of course, is ultimately interested in the active, living brain, towards which his investigations are moving, or in which they terminate. The processes of this living brain do not run parallel to my conscious thoughts. They belong to these thoughts, for I think *with* them, as I throw the baseball *with* my arm, and speak *with* my tongue.

It is now possible to say that I *am* these bodily processes with which I think. For James, this opens up a new approach to the mind-body problem which he had not carefully explored, though in the *Principles* he was moving in this direction. In the *Essays* he takes up this new approach and actually explores the strange territory to which it leads him. Sometimes, as we shall see, he is lost and falls into confusion. But here and there he emerges with a sense of meaningful patterns he has not seen before. In this chapter, we shall first of all give a summary statement of the general doctrine. Then we shall offer some criticisms from a phenomenological point of view, and finally, we shall comment on the novel insights which take James beyond the position of the *Principles,* and, indeed, the whole of his earlier writings.

The Doctrine of Radical Empiricism

In order to overcome the psycho-physical dualism of traditional philosophy which has strongly influenced common language and what we call common sense, James maintains that it is necessary to return to what he calls *pure experience*, that is, to life as it is actually lived through. This means an abandonment of theoretical constructions that may have become habitual, and even incorporated in accepted modes of speech, like the terms *mind* and *body*. We must make an effort to place these interpretations in suspense, in order to regain the feeling of a lived situation.

Thus I am now sitting with my typewriter on the table before me, struggling with the question of how to make James' thinking clear, and where to strike the next key on the board. When we make such a return to pure experience, we find, according to James, that we cannot describe it in terms that are exclusively objective or exclusively subjective. As he says (ERE, p. 10): "we have every right to speak of it as subjective and objective both at once". That is, my lived experience involves both factors together, my inner struggle with my problem, and the objective machine here before me. As in the *Principles*, the life-world has room in it for both the subjective and the objective.

There is no doubt that James sometimes speaks of pure experience in this way. But if it has room for both the subjective and the objective, it is easy to infer that in itself, as pure experience, it must be neither the one nor the other, and in itself neutral. Now this differs from the former conception, and there is no doubt that James often adopted it, with unfortunate consequences for his own consistency and descriptive clarity. On the former view, experience may have an over-arching structure that is neither purely subjective nor purely objective but with a place for both of these phenomena. On the latter view, pure experience itself is composed of units which are themselves neither the one nor the other, but neutral to the whole distinction. Thus James says "by the adjective 'pure' prefixed to the word 'experience' I mean to denote a form of being which is as yet neutral or ambiguous, and prior to the object and subject distinction. I mean to show that the attribution either of mental or physical being to an experience is due to nothing in the immediate stuff of which the experience is composed—for the same stuff will serve for either attribution. . .".[2]

On this view, James would have to say that my situation before the typewriter is a neutral unit of experience in which it is impossible originally to distinguish my inner doubt and searching from the objective keyboard in front of me. But this is clearly in error, for it ignores the distinction between my intentional confusion and its object, the keyboard. Furthermore, it raises a general question concerning the meaning of the general term *experience*. In the *Principles*, James definitely stated that every experience belongs to a personal self. There is no thought, or experience, "which is nobody's thought" (PR, I, 226). Our experience is always "dualistic", or intentional in structure. "It supposes two elements, mind knowing and thing known, and treats them as irreducible. Neither gets out of itself or into the other, neither in any way *is* the other, neither *makes* the other" (ERE, p. 218). Now in his effort to overcome psycho-physical dualism, James is denying this intentional structure of experience, which he had clearly recognized and expressed. We may sympathize with his basic purpose. The dualism of mind and body needs to be overcome. But this is too high a price to pay.

There are no free floating experiences that are not centered in a subjective being of some kind. The intentional structure of experience is not merely an "external" relation that is found to hold between certain objects within it. It is a stretching out towards the world that is presupposed by any things or objects whatever. Without this world-field, there would be no objects nor relations within it. As we have seen, in the *Principles* James recognized this world-field as existing. But he had not recognized its *a priori* necessity. His reduction of world intentionality to a set of neutral experiences is, therefore, a relapse into traditional empiricism. The most that one can say of this lapse is that James did not consistently stay with it, and in spite of it, he often continues to refer in the *Essays* to "the world of pure experience".

One finds certain illustrations of this tendency to confuse experiencing with its object in the *Principles*. But it plays a central role in the argument of the *Essays*. Once having identified these neutral "units" of experience, it is easy for James to suggest that they may be ordered together with different associates in different contexts to become what we call the physical and the psychical. Thus the room in which I am now working may be regarded in two different ways (ERE, pp. 13 ff.). On the one hand, as a room, it has occupied the same geographic place for more than thirty years. It will take an earthquake, or a gang of men, and in any case, a certain length of time to destroy it. Fire will consume it, and in order to inhabit it, you must pay so much a month. On the other hand, as a mental reference, or state, the very same room may have just come into existence as you began to think of it, you may destroy it in an instant by closing your eyes or shifting your attention, you may let fire play over it without effect, and you may inhabit it as long as you like, rent-free.

The first room, we say, really exists in physical reality, whereas the second is only a mental being in the mind. But as a matter of fact, James says, these two rooms are "numerically the same" (p. 23). It gets counted twice when placed in different contexts with different associates. But in itself, as an item of pure experience, it is not two but one. Here it is not some mental representation that I experience, but the room itself. "In its pure state, or when isolated, there is no self-splitting of it into consciousness and what the consciousness is of" (p. 23).

Furthermore if I think of this room when I am far away, it is the same real room to which I am referring directly and not through the mediation of some mental state. James now categorically rejects all representative theories of perception or conception. When I am presently perceiving it, the room itself is directly present before me, and when I think of it, when far away, it is the same real room of which I am thinking, not some mental image. James himself held such a theory of images in the *Principles*. Now, he says, they "violate the reader's sense of life, which knows no intervening mental image but seems to see the room and the book immediately just as they physically exist" (p. 12). As we shall see, this is a significant development of James' thought.

With a disregard for the notion of intentionality—that consciousness is always *of* some object, James now speaks of consciousness and its "content" (*cf.* pp. 6, 18) as of a container and what it contains. It is this merging of *noesis* with *noema* which enables him to deny consciousness as something distinct from its objects. It is, therefore, no separate thing or substance, nor any kind of stuff from which mental operations emerge. Hence, as a mode of being, radically distinct from physical being, it is denied. This does not mean, of course, that James is denying concrete thoughts. These activities are experienced, and they are just what they are experienced to be—anticipations and transitional experiences, ending in fulfillment or disconfirmation.

As he has suggested in his pragmatic theory of knowledge, a thought first anticipates a perception of some kind, and then embarks on a procedure of discovery to see if it can be found. If, by gradual transitions, this procedure finally leads to the experience exactly as it was anticipated, then the theory, or anticipation, was true. But in this relational experience of fulfillment, no epistemological chasm between a mind thing and a physical thing has to be bridged. The whole procedure occurs *within* the experienced world. "Knowledge of sensible realities thus comes to life inside the tissue of experience. It is *made;* and made by relations that unroll themselves in time" (p. 57). The perception (pure experience) is simply there. As it comes before us "in its passing", it "is always truth" (p. 24).

As is usual with James, in expounding his theory, he develops it as he goes along, and often arrives at *aperçus* which are worked out for their own sake, apart from the general theory to which they are only vaguely relevant. Some of these we shall consider later on. One of them, however, because of its basic importance, deserves to be mentioned here. This concerns the notion of the lived body which is found in the *Principles*, but is now considered in new contexts, and developed in new ways at certain points in the *Essays*. It is worthy of note that in these passages, it is not the brain alone that attracts James' attention, but the lived body as a whole. This body is the centre of the individual's world. As James puts it (ERE, p. 170, note): "everything circles round it, and is felt from its point of view". This body is not only an object in the world, but also its subjective centre (pp. 65, 153). Here, at least, the objective and the subjective coincide. Finally, it is because of our ability to follow the expressive gestures of the living body of another and to mesh our actions with his, that solipsism is no problem for us in real life (pp. 77 ff.).

In the *Essays*, it is really the meaningful behavior of this living body that takes the place of a separated consciousness as traditionally interpreted. It would be an inexcusable error to think of James as a behaviorist in the Watsonian sense of this term. He never dreamed of denying or evading the factual existence of thoughts, ideas, and the meaningful search for knowledge. His radical empiricism stood in the way of any such move. He is prepared to admit even the subjective as a legitimate relational or contextual concept. But in his notion of the living body as presented in the *Principles*, and further developed in the *Essays*, James is rightly regarded as one of the founders of that modern behaviorism which sees no need for a separated consciousness, and which is found in writers like Merleau-Ponty.

Such then is the general doctrine presented in James' *Essays in Radical Empiricism*. Let us now give it a critical examination.

Defects of the Doctrine

In order to understand the nature of these new developments, we must remember that, since the time of the *Principles*, James has developed his pragmatic theory of truth (*cf. supra*, Chapter XIII). It is an essential part of this theory, as we have seen, to regard the knowing process not as the transcending of an ontological gulf between the knower and the known, but rather as the movement towards a verifying perception which takes place *in* experience, as James constantly says. It is possible to see, therefore, why this should lead him to question the intentional relation of subject to object which he had so clearly recognized in the *Principles* (*cf.* I, 184, 197, 275 ff. *et passim*).

Hence in certain expositions of his pragmatic theory, he falls into idealistic language and speaks of the original idea, the intermediate stages leading to the verifying perception, and this perception itself as being *in* experience, as in a mental container (PRAG, pp. 169 ff., 200 ff.). This language brought forth many criticisms of pragmatism as a new sort of subjectivism. In his replies (*cf.* PRAG, pp. 201 ff.; MT, Chap. XII, pp. 230 ff.) James is surprised at these interpretations, and denies that he has ever abandoned his belief that real beings, independent of our cognition, are perceived and known. This was certainly the view of the *Psychology* (*cf.* I, 271 ff.), where it was closely connected with the intentional structure of experience. Does he still hold to this view in his pragmatic writings? The answer, I think, is probably yes, but in a somewhat weakened form (*cf.* MT, pp. 190 ff.).

In the *Essays*, it is still further weakened by his theory of a neutral experience which, as he now hopes, will enable him to find a solution to the traditional dualism of mind and body. A rereading of the British empiricists, and especially Berkeley, seems to have played an important role in these new developments (*cf.* ERE, pp. 10 ff.). It may have strengthened his tendency to lapse into the traditional language of consciousness as a container, as Berkeley spoke of ideas as being *in* the mind. But James' notion of neutral units of experience, belonging to no one, is radically unBerkeleyan, and also, I am afraid, radically unsound. But in the passage to which we have referred (ERE, 10 ff.), it is something else that James draws from Berkeley— the absence of any representative ideas standing between us and the real things we perceive. For Berkeley, the ideas are not mere intermediaries. They are the realities themselves, as he shows by saying "that what common sense means by realities is exactly what the philosopher means by ideas" (p. 10). As James reads Berkeley, it is not so much that *esse est percipi* as that *percipi est esse*. In perception, it is not merely some sign but the actual thing that is directly present.

James is now fascinated with this conception, which is only hesitantly and restrictedly defended in the *Principles*. He now takes it over without serious qualifications, and extends it not only to perception but also to our references to absent beings. By imagination and linguistic conception, I can refer directly to my absent friend without the mediation of an image. In this part of his doctrine, James is clarifying and strengthening a position only suggested in the *Principles*. But in other parts, he is making radical changes which are not only dubious but inconsistent with views that he continues to hold. Thus he speaks of "mere bits of pure experience" (ERE, p. 15), and "a unit of pure experience" (p. 127) which is neither a physical nor a mental fact, and which, in itself, is not even perceived. At one point, he even refers to these pure experiences as "so many little absolutes" (p. 134) without relations to anything outside.

But such a conception would seem to violate several basic principles of James' empiricism. Is this not falling into that abstract atomism, or "mind-stuff" theory, which he attacked so vigorously in the *Principles*, and still rejects (ERE, p. 43)? How can this be reconciled with the field theory, according to which every focused experience is surrounded by a halo of fringes from which it cannot be separated except by a reductive abstraction? And James has not abandoned this field theory (*cf.* pp. 74 and 170). Indeed, he still speaks of it as a basic aspect of experience, referring to "the world experienced (otherwise called the 'field of consciousness')" (p. 170, note), and to "a world of pure experience" (pp. 39–91).

He also speaks of these atomic units as though they share something in common. Thus he refers to them as units of experience in the singular. But in what sense are they one? Furthermore, in what sense do we apply the term experience to something which involves no element of perception? How can anything be given, or presented, without being given, or presented, to a receiver? These "little absolutes" have no centre, for each is centered in itself. As a matter of fact, they are reified abstractions, never found in the concrete life which James claims to be describing. They represent a speculative venture on his part, which he cannot assimilate into the main body of his radical empiricism. This is shown by the fact that, in a passage we have already noted, he speaks of the living body as the "centre" of the field of consciousness, the "centre of vision, centre of action, centre of interest" (p. 170, note).

Another set of difficulties, associated with James' first formulations of the pragmatic theory of truth, arises in connection with his reductive view of perception. We have observed in the *Principles* how sensory experience is identified with a kind of *knowledge* (by acquaintance). This *knowledge* is pervaded with vagueness, but is, nevertheless, a form of genuine knowledge. It is intentional in structure, always involving an approach of the living subject to an object of some kind. Thus I become acquainted with things by desiring, seeking, finding, enjoying, hating, and exploring them by my bodily movements. It is in this way that I come to perceive the spatio-temporal things around me, together with the hazy world-field that always lies around both them and me. Perceptual illusions and hallucinations are always possible. Hence this perceptual *knowledge by acquaintance* has its own mode of truth and falsity (PR, II, 85; *cf.* I, 191–92).

In the formulation of his pragmatic theory, however, James, influenced by traditional rationalism and the atmosphere around him, was primarily concerned with conceptual thought, and its verification by perception. It was always clear to him, as an empiricist, that the ultimate test of such theories must be found in sense experience. Here we are directly confronted with objects of our concern, of which we can be as certain as we are of our own existence (II, 297–98). Of course, this certainty is not infallible, and in the *Principles*, James shows that it is subject to certain deformations which may upset our whole sense of reality, or dilute it to almost nothing (II, 284–85; *cf.* p. 298).

But in defending his theory of truth, it was easier to pass over the intentionality of sense experience and its illusions, and to consider it exclusively in its authentic mode as mere sensory fact. This change is facilitated by the fact that the disinterested attitude of sensory observation is lost in its object, and, therefore, inconspicuous (*cf.* PR, I, 194–95). But when, in dealing with the topic of conceptual truth, James slurred over this intentionality, the role of the object became dominant. That which verifies knowledge in the strict sense, i.e. conceptual knowledge, does not have to be known. It is a bare fact that is simply given.

This aberrant feature of James' theory of knowledge has been taken over by later pragmatists. Thus C. I. Lewis, for example, restricts the term *cognition* to theoretical formulations which refer to experience. This experience, however, is a bare given which is neither true nor false. What James called *knowledge by acquaintance* simply is not knowledge at all. In the *Essays*, he does not abandon this insight, which played a central role in his psychology, and still refers to a knowledge of "direct acquaintance" where "we and the object are . . . face to face" (ERE, p. 73). But then, in developing his answer to psycho-physical dualism, as if by inadvertence, he himself falls into the pathway of his pragmatic successors, and speaks of the perceptual object as if it could occur alone without coming face to face with anyone or anything.

In thus denying the intentional structure of direct acquaintance, he refers to "the sensible percept, which is the object" (p. 60). Having gone this far, it is easy for him to move on to his notion of a "unit", or a "field", of pure experience which "is only virtually or potentially, either object or subject as yet".

For the time being, "it is plain unqualified actuality, or existence, a simple *that*" (p. 23). In this condition, one cannot say it exists for a subject, but only "it is *there*" (p. 24). Such a pure actuality, which is still an "experience" is, of course, ideally fitted to verify theoretical constructions.

Since it is, in itself, neither subject nor object, neither mind nor body, it also seems to offer a solution to the mind-body dualism. But unfortunately there is no percept without a perceiver, and no "field" without a centre of some kind. Direct acquaintance, as he had insisted, is a mode of knowledge with an intentional structure and a truth or falsity of its own, quite distinct from that of theoretical knowledge. Someone, or something in us, gets acquainted with something. But in pushing his new adventure, James has to deny this. As an absolute without relations, we cannot ask whether a pure experience, as such, is true or false. "No more ought the question of its *truth* to be asked" (p. 134). But James knows better than this. Even in its immediate passing, the pure experience is true for someone. So even here, he says, it "is always 'truth'", though not theoretical truth. The word truth is put in quotes. But even the barest fact is recognized as such. Therefore it is not merely given as an abstract actuality. It is given to *something* in some way, and is, therefore, in some sense "true". James' mind cannot come to rest in this adventure.

We have noted the difficulties which it faces and the contradictions into which it falls.

But in spite of these mistakes and inconsistencies which make his new proposals as a whole unacceptable, and which have been seen by many critics, there is another side that has not been so widely seen. In pursuing his new project—which finally shattered—as is often the case with a genuinely original mind, he developed new insights which confirmed and strengthened the phenomenology of human existence that he outlined in his psychology. His attempt to solve the problem of psycho-physical dualism at one fell swoop, by finding neutral units of pure experience everywhere, was unsuccessful. But in the course of his investigations, he did find one such unit, the lived body, which is both psychical and physical at the same time, and, therefore, neutral in the sense of not being exclusively one or the other. This does offer a new approach to the mind-body problem already indicated in the *Principles*. James did not follow this up in great detail. But he arrived at certain conclusions which go far beyond his earlier theory, and which are worthy of serious attention on the part of empirically oriented thinkers of our own time.[3]

It is to these insights and suggestions that we must now turn.

A New Approach to the Mind-Body Problem

In dealing with James' *Principles*, we noted his acute dissatisfaction with the "vague parallelism" which he adopted unwillingly as a heuristic device, but which ran counter to many facts and, indeed, to the whole drift of his argument. Take, for example, his firm stand at the very beginning of the text (PR, I, 6–11) that consciousness is not an inactive accompaniment to bodily changes but makes an actual difference in the course of events that actually happen in the world. This might have led him into some form of dualistic interactionism. He could not accept that because of the total lack of evidence for any violation of the principle of the conservation of energy in physical nature. And yet our conscious states of mind are clearly not the same as neural motions in the brain. So he is forced back again to that vague parallelism which he reluctantly and very tentatively accepts for the time being.

Now, however, all is different. The distinction between the physical and the psychical is no longer ultimate and ontological. It is secondary and, in part, epistemological—two different ways of reading the same phenomena. These phenomena are related in many different ways to form different groupings or contexts.

[3] J. Linschoten has made some penetrating comments on James' views concerning the living body in his book, *Auf dem Wege zu einer phänomenologischen Psychologie*, Chaps. VIII and IX, pp. 175 ff.

What we call *physical nature* is one such context related together by the laws of physics. It is useful for certain purposes
to look at everything that happens from this point of view.
Then the relational contexts of personal biography and history
sink to secondary importance. On the other hand, the very same
facts are linked together in psychical contexts. It is more natural
for us to focus these, and to look at everything from the standpoint of human history. In this case, physical nature falls into
the background. But in the world of experience there is room
for both.

James does not say specifically which is the broader and richer
horizon, and this is a defect in his analysis, which is far from
perfect. Nevertheless it enables him to avoid any ontological
dualism of a mental stuff over against a physical stuff, any
form of interactionism between mind and matter, and any psycho-physical parallelism. This does not mean a denial of the
distinction which involves, not two kinds of thing, but rather
two relational systems, each of which is found in the very same
world. In spite of its inadequacies, this formulation represents
an advance in coherence and clarity over the confusion and
indefiniteness of his earlier position.

James does not have to deny the distinction between the
knowing subject and the object known, nor the intentional relation between them. But he is now able to see them in a
new perspective. Subjectivity is not a thing, nor a source of
synthesis which knows the world from the outside. It is not a
substance of any kind. It is a pattern of relations, which develops
and opposes itself to the things it knows within the world. Within
this world, it not only knows these objects in an abstract way.
As a concrete person with a biographical history, it seeks after
them and flees them, enjoys and suffers them, loves and hates
them. Hence, in the *Essays*, James moves away from the abstract
terminology of subject and object, preferring to speak of human
biography and history on the one side, and of impersonal nature
on the other (ERE, p. 16). The difference between the subjective and the objective is founded on this relational distinc-

tion between the personal and the impersonal. But it is also a difference between two perspectives, each of which can regard everything that happens from its point of view, as the room in which I am working can be regarded either as a part of my biography or a part of the physical house in *rerum natura*.

Knowing without Representation

We have noted how, in the *Principles,* James attacked the traditional notion of a soul substance and the transcendental theories of German philosophy (*cf.* PR, I, 360 ff.). He was struggling at this time to work out an empirical theory of knowing as an activity taking place within experience. But he did not yet possess the requisite categories and perspectives. Now, as a result of his formulation of a pragmatic theory of truth, he has worked them out. Knowing is a relational activity that happens within experience, a sequence of transitions through which an anticipatory intention leads up to perceptual experiences that either fulfill it or fail to do so. No epistemological gap has to be bridged over. Every phase of the process may be described without the introduction of transcendental entities.

Knowing is not the only way in which man is related to things. He also cares for them in many different ways, or forgets and becomes indifferent to them. But knowing is a crucially important activity of man, a special way of being in the world. The world itself is not an object, nor any set of objects. Neither is it a subject. The world is an over-arching horizon that transcends this distinction. It is not something known, but rather the condition for all such knowing. Hence, like the idealistic absolute, it is neither true nor false, since knowing and failures to know occur "inside", and are conditioned by it (ERE, p. 134).

But in so far as I attain the truth, and I always attain it to some degree, it is the real thing that I know, not some appearance, or representative, of it in the mind. In the *Principles,* James had striven to get rid of substitute things and copies of things in a psychic substance. But because of the dualism from which he could not free himself, these efforts left him short of the goal. How could a physical thing be present face to face with an immaterial mind? Hence James failed to free himself from the notion that sensations were somehow "similar" to their objects (cf. PR, I, 217, 471, and II, 619, 632), and that in imagining an absent object, some little image, or picture of the thing, must be present in the mind. Now, as we have seen, his forthright rejection of dualism has enabled him to get rid of this mentalist paraphernalia. It is true that in the *Essays,* he does this only by denying the fact of intentional reference, and by merging the sensation with its object in a so-called "unit of pure experience". This was a mistake. But his purging the mind of spurious copies and representative entities is certainly a step in the right direction.

In pure experience, we now meet the reality face to face, not some appearance that is similar to it. The real object *is* these appearances, and there is nothing behind. Similarly, when in Paris James thinks of his home three thousand miles away, it is the real home in Cambridge he thinks of directly. He needs no "little interior fact", no image thing to project across the sea (ERE, p. 214).[4] The image thing is a reification, a falsification of a direct relational reference to the absent thing. This is a significant advance over his previous point of view. But in so far as it is genuine, it depends on another supposed advance towards a solution of the mind-body problem—which seems subject to serious question, as we have seen, in that it involves a wholesale merging of the subjective and the objective in every "unit" of pure experience.

Is there any reason to believe that, aside from this dubious theory, James made any real progress in working out a new approach to the dualism of mind and body, which is the nub of the whole matter? There is such a reason, and it lies in a further development of James' conception of the living body.

---

[4] In Chap. VIII, "La notion de conscience"; the chapter, too, is written in French.

The Living Body

In the *Principles,* James had followed the accepted opinion of his time in singling out brain changes as the direct correlates of conscious experiences. This was, indeed, natural when the first results of modern brain physiology and pathology were becoming widely known. Hence for every basic type of conscious experience, he is constantly speculating about the corresponding brain changes that must be going on, without paying much attention to the rest of the human body (*cf.* PR, I, 101–3, 141–43, 234–36 *et passim*). This concentration on the brain made it impossible for James to identify consciousness with these physical changes, since men have been conscious for thousands of years without having any exact knowledge of what was going on in their brains. When conceived in this way, body and mind are two separate fields of change, and the relation between them is highly external and secret. This leaves open only such alternatives as a vague interactionism, or the vague parallelism which James reluctantly accepted in the *Principles.*

In the *Essays,* his interest in the human body was not weakened. But it is not the brain alone which now focuses his attention. It is the living body as a whole (*cf.* ERE, pp. 37, 153, 170, note, and 221). Men have never been totally ignorant of their bodies, and of the close relation between these bodies and themselves. This is reflected in such modes of ordinary speech as, *I weigh 196 pounds, I am thin, I am lying down,* and *I fell downstairs.* These expressions suggest a more radical possibility. The separated consciousness of traditional philosophy is a fiction, but the concrete thoughts which I actually think are physical motions and expressions. As James says, *"thoughts in the concrete are fully real. But thoughts in the concrete are made of the same stuff as things are"* (p. 37).

When he says this, he does not mean, of course, that these thoughts and feelings are the motions that one finds in inorganic matter or in a corpse. It is the living, breathing, sentient body which is the self. "Its sensorial adjustments are my 'attention', its kinesthetic alterations are my 'efforts,' its visceral perturbations are my 'emotions'" (p. 153). In other words, I *am* this living, sensing, active body. My consciousness does not run parallel with these vital activities. It is incarnated in them, and manifested by them. In the *Principles,* he was tending towards a position of this kind, as we have seen (*supra,* pp. 87–89), and even expressed it in certain isolated passages, but not firmly as a position he can back with relevant categories and constraining evidence. His official position is that of a vague parallelism (PR, I, 182). But now in the *Essays* it is put forth boldly not only as his own *view,* but as one that he has a right to hold.

The most interesting passage of this sort is the long note (ERE, pp. 168–71) to which we have already referred, in which James is answering a criticism of his view that "*our entire feeling of spiritual activity, or what commonly passes by that name, is really a feeling of bodily activities*" (PR, I, 301–2) by Stout. In the text of the *Principles,* this view is put forth as a "hypothesis" which James merely considers without pledging himself "in any way to adopt" (I, 302). But there is nothing hypothetical about his answer to Stout in this long note. "So far as we are 'persons'", he says, "and contrasted and opposed to an 'environment', movements in our body figure as our activities; and I am unable to find any other activities that are ours in this strictly personal sense" (ERE, p. 170).

In the *Principles* he certainly arrived at the notion of fringes (I, 281, 471–72), and in *The Varieties of Religious Experience* at that of a field of consciousness (*cf.* VA, pp. 226–28), but he was vague as to the exact nature of its center. Now (ERE, p. 170) his words are precise and clear. "The world experienced . . . comes at all times with our body as its centre, centre of vision, centre of action, centre of interest. Where the body is is 'here'; when the body acts is 'now'; what the body touches is 'this'; all other things are 'there' and 'then' and 'that'. . . . Everything circles round it, and is felt from its point of view". I am not a self-enclosed substance apart from the world. I am the movements of a living body that exists within this world. It is worthy of attention in this connection that James is now abandoning the term "field of consciousness" because of its dualistic connotations, and prefers to use the term *world* or "world experienced (otherwise called the 'field of consciousness')", a term previously used extensively by him in *The Varieties of Religious Experience,* but now placed in quotes.

Furthermore, this living body is not a static centre. The various things and regions of the world are "systematized" in relation to the acts and interests of this vital centre, which is always here and now. "These words of emphasized position imply a systematization of things with reference to a focus of action and interest which lies in the body." This ordering of the life-world becomes taken for granted and 'instinctive', but whether we are fully conscious of it or not, it underlies all our organized and developed behavior, including that of conceptual thinking. As James says, "the systematization is now so instinctive (was it ever not so?) that no developed or active experience exists for us at all except in that ordered form" (ERE, p. 170).

It is the conscious, living body that lays down this general structure of the life-world in relation to its needs and possible acts. But in spite of this constitutive function, as a body it is also a mere object, or thing, in the world, or as James says, "a part of the content of the world experienced". At the same time, it "is the storm centre, the origin of co-ordinates, the constant place of stress in all that experience-train", and it has "its point of view". This living body which exists as a finite thing in the world, and which can be objectively measured and examined, plays a major role in the constitution of the very same world. This "paradox", as we have already seen, (*supra,* p. 111) is a basic element in James' thought. I do not merely accompany this living, sentient body in its various activities and wanderings. I am it and them.

No one who is familiar with the literature of recent post-Husserlian phenomenology can miss the parallels with James' radical empiricism as it emerges in this last mature statement, which nevertheless presupposes the whole of his earlier *Psychology* to be properly understood. To those who are unfamiliar with this literature, suffice it to say that in the living phenomenology of our time, both in Europe and in this country, James' conceptions of what he called "the world of life" (ERE, p. 187) and of an embodied self are very much alive. These ideas, and the empirical evidence on which they are based, have become common property, and are now being further developed and explored. This is particularly true of the thought of Merleau-Ponty, whose work is now beginning to become better known in the Anglo-Saxon countries.

World Facts

Am I then a mere being in the world, or a conscious source of meaning? Which am I? The answer is in a sense both, and in a sense neither. But in their accepted usage, they are exclusive. The same thing cannot be both physical and psychical all at once. Hence the answer must be *neither*. In other words, these categories are inadequate to grasp human existence. Or we can put the situation in another way. Is an existing person physical or non-physical? Which do we say? We have to say neither. Is he psychical or non-psychical? Again we must say neither. When in our thinking we are faced with seemingly exclusive alternatives a *or* b, and in the light of the evidence we have to say both and neither, this means that our categories (a and b) are inadequate. The evidence is as yet ambiguous, and until we find a new structure of meaning, it must remain so.

Hence in times of intellectual change and ferment, ambiguities pop up everywhere, and one whose thought is moving sees them. It is from these ambiguities that new meanings grow. James was a creative thinker of this type who is constantly seeing ambiguities, that is, the inadequacies of the concepts at his disposal to grasp the sense of experience in the concrete. Thus he speaks of "appreciations" as "an ambiguous sphere of being, belonging with emotion on the one hand, and having objective 'value' on the other, yet seeming not quite inner nor quite outer . . ." (ERE, p. 34). In his essay "The Place of Affectional

Facts,"[5] he goes further, and says that "all our adjectives of worth are similarly ambiguous" (pp. 142–43).

In the text, he refers to many experiences which belong to "this equivocal realm". When we speak of them, it remains unclear whether we are expressing a quality in the independent thing, or "a feeling in our mind". Thus we say that "the man is really hateful; the action really mean; the situation really tragic —all in themselves and quite apart from our opinion. We even go so far as to talk of a weary road, a giddy height, a jocund morning or a sullen sky . . ." (p. 144). In such expressions, are we referring to a real fact or to a subjective feeling? Surely not both, for this would destroy the unity of our meaning. I am saying *the act is mean*, not *there is an act* and *I feel mean*. As James says, in terms of these "exact" interpretations, the affectional fact is essentially ambiguous. "We can treat it as physical or as non-physical . . . and conversely, of course, we must treat it as non-mental or as mental" (p. 153). That is, if the category of mental really applies to the fact, "we must treat it as non-mental or as mental". But it is neither. Nor is it either physical or non-physical (p. 153). These concepts, as we are now using them, do not apply to the fact we are expressing. It escapes through the holes of our conceptual net, and remains still alive and swimming in the great ocean of ambiguity.

What kind of a fact then is it, and how are we to approach it? James gives us no systematic answer to these questions. He has shown us the ambiguity, and the need for new concepts closer to our pure experience. Then he gives us a few suggestions, for he is feeling his way in a strange territory. One of these is the very title of the essay "The Place of Affectional Facts." According to our accepted conceptual schemes, the diamond's being precious is not a fact. Its weight, composition, and measurements are objective facts. But its value, its being precious, is a subjective judgment added on from the outside. First of all, there is the physical thing as it really is, the fact, and then later on, its

[5] Chapter V, "The Place of Affectional Facts in a World of Pure Experience," ERE, pp. 137–54.

endowment with preciousness and other value properties by separated and subjective minds.

Now in his essay, James is questioning this whole interpretation. The diamond is really precious. This is a fact, as hard and recalcitrant as any scientific fact. But it is a fact of a different order, belonging to a different world, the "world of life", in which our bodily selves exist. Hence he calls it an *affectional fact*, endowed with human meaning and value, the basic type of human meaning. But these meanings are not projected into valueless things by a separated mind. They are in the world. They actually pervade its regions, and the things within these regions.

The scornful gesture to the child is really mean, and the diamond glittering on the table is really precious. It is found to be precious, and is really precious, whatever my opinion may be. These are facts pervaded by human meaning, *world-facts* as we may call them, found in the world of life. Furthermore, so far as human history is concerned, these facts are not preceded by scientific facts. Men had to take account of such world-facts long before they knew anything of science. They still, and always will, have to take account of them, as long as men exist. These are the original and primordial *facts of life*. They did not originate from scientific facts by addition—but rather scientific facts arose from them by subtraction.

No doubt man has established many of these meaningful facts by his foresight, sweat, and labor. Without him, they would not exist, and in this sense they are relative to man. But they are still *facts* that are found in the world, and present themselves to us with constraining evidence. Many facts are conditioned by and, therefore, relative to other facts. Man is himself a fact now existing at the centre of his world. What of him? Is he to be understood as a physical thing with a meaningful mind added thereunto? Can we take account of him properly in terms of the categories of the physical, or the psychical, or both together? Or do these concepts lead us into the same ambiguity as in the case of the diamond and the sullen sky?

We can now anticipate what James will say in general to these questions. But let us listen to his own words. "Our body", he says, "is the palmary instance of the ambiguous. Sometimes I treat my body purely as a part of outer nature. Sometimes again, I think of it as 'mine', I sort it with the 'me', and then certain local changes and determinations in it pass for spiritual happenings" (ERE, p. 153). In other words, it is neither not-me nor me, neither physical nor mental, neither objective fact nor separated meaning. Neither is it any of these pairs added together. Each of these categories, no doubt, gives us some aspect that is found in man. But even when taken with its opposite, it does not do justice to human existence as we feel it and live it through in the life-world. To this, the categories do not adequately apply. They leave us with an ambiguity.

What then is man? He is an objective subjectivity, an embodied source of meaning, a meaning-originating-fact. These makeshift terms, of course, are only additive compounds, and James does not use them. But if we follow him in returning to the original data of perceptual experience, they may serve *faute de mieux* to suggest the new conceptual frame, the new sort of meaning, and the language we have in mind. It is the embodied self, thrown amongst other bodies, that pursues its projects amongst them, and orders a world around itself.

Double-intentions and Solipsism

But instead of *talking about* this world of pure experience, James prefers rather to recapture the feeling of some process that occurs within it, either by memory, or by what he calls "sympathetic imagination". Then after he feels his way through it, such a lived experience can be conceptually expressed in a way that will not only be true to the facts but will also avoid many problems artificially raised by the inadequacy of traditional concepts. One of these "problems" is concerned with our knowledge of other minds. James begins his condensed analysis (ERE, pp. 76 ff.) with a consideration of the Berkeleyan view of a separated mind.

According to this view, my mind would have its own mental field in which all the objects I perceive (ideas) have their place. My body is a set of ideas (color, shape, sound, feelings of effort, etc.) that constantly reappear on the field, following certain regular laws. Your body is another set of ideas in my field (color, shape, sound, etc., but no inner feelings) which I perceive only occasionally. In your field, your body is a different set of ideas which include inner feelings. Since you have individual peculiarities and your whole field belongs to you, no one of your ideas will be the same as any one of mine, though relational similarities may be found. In their perceptual givenness, before all rational inference, the two fields are wholly out of touch with each other. As James puts it, "our lives are a congeries of solipsisms out of which in strict logic only a God could compose a universe even of discourse. No dynamic currents run between my objects and your objects. Never can our minds meet in the *same*" (p. 77).

He finds this view "strained" and "unnatural" to an extreme degree, and doubts whether Berkeley himself could have believed, when he was walking through the streets of London, that he and his fellows were viewing a different town. But James focuses his criticism on the fantastic view of my body and your body to which this mentalistic interpretation must lead. As an active spiritual principle, I myself am separated from my body, which is a mere set of objects (ideas) in my field. This body never acts. It is a "passive" set of objects associated together. Your body is another set, associated by similar laws. When I play tennis with you, I see certain motions of your body and racket which are followed by results that are similar to those of the motions I observe in my own body and racket. On the basis of such analogies, I conclude that your motions are actuated by an unobserved spiritual principle, like myself, with feelings similar to mine.

For such a point of view, this well-known argument from analogy is the only escape, if it is an escape, from solipsism. It is also the only escape for views less extreme than Berkeley's but which hold to a separated mind. Such a disembodied mind

cannot be perceived. Hence even the parallelist who, unlike
Berkeley, believes in a real body independent of consciousness,
must use some form of this argument for the existence of other
minds. This has been very widely defended by many different
types of philosophy. All this must be held in mind, if we are
to understand James' criticism of the theory of a separated mind.
It is based on an attempt to recapture what happens in our
actual, pre-reflective experience when my body meets with yours.
It has its obscure points. But the gist of the analysis is clear.

Why do I postulate your mind, James asks. "Because I see
your body acting in a certain way" (p. 77). I do not see
objective motions. When I watch you serving the ball from the
opposite corner of the court, I see your body acting in a purposive
way with a certain inherent meaning, as I see the value of the
diamond. I see this meaningful intention, and prepare myself
to respond. The gestures, words, and conduct of your body
are not mere motions which may or may not have a meaning
attached. In themselves, they bear a meaning, and without this
meaning, they cannot be perceived or understood as they are. As
James says, they are "'expressive'" (p. 77), they put forth a
meaning.

But at this point, he makes a move that has been often
misunderstood. He speaks of this perception as an argument
from analogy. The expressive gestures I observe in another are
like those I can observe in myself. Looking back on the event,
after it has happened, I can construct this as "my *reason*".
But the experience which James is describing is pre-reflective.
It is based not on a reason but a perception. This is why he
italicizes *reason*, and proceeds at once to ask a question which
cannot be answered by any reason. If your body is only a
percept in my field, why should I ever think of it as *yours*
and not mine? Where does this original sense of otherness come
from? Later on I seek a reason for it. But in the first place,
it is a bodily fact that is perceived, as he now proceeds to show.

It is only in perceiving you to be animating and actuating
this bodily object in my field that I gain any sense of otherness
at all. This means that you cannot be elsewhere in a separated

mind or in some other body. You must be *in* the very body that I perceive in my field, or "we belong to different universes, you and I, and for me to speak of you is folly" (p. 78). Two separate consciousnesses might have imaginary meetings, each in its own world. But they could never really meet. It is your living, conscious body that I encounter. "In that perceptual part of *my* universe which I call *your* body, your mind and my mind meet. . . . Your mind actuates that body and mine sees it . . ." (p. 78). For your mind is not a separate and invisible substance. It is actively planning and projecting itself in and through your body which I see. I perceive these meaningful intentions as they play against me and try to pass me by, just as I feel my own preparing to respond.

This is a point where James differs sharply from the early Husserl and other phenomenologists who made the self only a centre of outwardly directed intentions to other things and persons. This view gave the early theory a solipsistic twist. For James, as we have noted (*supra*, pp. 83–85 ff.), the self is from the very beginning a centre of double intentionality. That is, it not only projects intentional meanings towards others, but also receives them from others and responds to them. James gives an example—"for instance, your hand lays hold of one end of a rope and my hand lays hold of the other end. We pull against each other" (ERE, pp. 78–79). Here we are not merely radiating active intentions. We are each receiving active intentions from the other and responding to them. I feel the operations of your body either opposing or meshing with mine, and this body which I feel tugging against me from the outside is the very same one you are actuating and feeling from the inside.

James also points out that this same body, which we both perceive in common, "hangs together with all our other physical percepts" (p. 78). It is a genuine body thrown amongst them, bone of their bone and flesh of their flesh. Hence "if it be our common possession, they must be so likewise" (p. 78). In the case of our pulling against each other on the rope, "Can the two hands be mutual objects in this experience, and the rope not be mutual also?" (p. 79). Any object that we can act on together is the same. But we can go further than this. Once I perceive the hand you are moving to be the same as the hand that I see, I can also perceive that towards which you are pointing as the same for you and me. "If I ask you *where* some object of yours is, our old Memorial Hall, for example, you point to *my* Memorial Hall with *your* hand which *I* see" (p. 79). In this case, I do not merely see a motion and read a meaning into it. The motion expresses a meaning which I perceive, as I see you pointing. Then, through the lived body, a distant object beyond the reach of our action may become the same for both of us.

Even when the same place is occupied by different perceptual bodies, the lived body enables us to perceive it as the same. First of all, "that body of yours which you actuate and feel from within must be in the same spot as the body of yours which I see or touch from without" (p. 84). If I reach out and touch ycur arm there, this is also there for you. "Your inner actuations of your body meet my finger *there;* it is *there* that you resist its push, or shrink back, or sweep the finger aside with your hand" (p. 85). Once these common bodily places are established, further common positions can be indicated by pointing, and common directions signified by the orientations of the body, as James has already suggested in the *Principles* (II, 36). Thus *in front* and *behind* become generalized into North and South, and left and right into West and East.

James does not go any further into the establishment of a spatio-temporal field by the possible actions of the living body, which faces ahead towards the future, and passes things by as it proceeds on its way. Thus moving towards the future, it can see ahead, prepare for what is coming, and maintain its poise. When it moves backward, however, it sees things only retrospectively after they have happened. Hence its movements become fumbling and awkward, and it is apt to be surprised and upset. Merleau-Ponty has made many acute observations and analyses of this kind, and other phenomenological investigations are now proceeding which promise to shed further light on a deeply neglected area. But it was James who first opened the door.

The Exploration of the Life-world

The world-facts that we confront in our existence are neither scientific abstractions devoid of all human meaning, nor are they meanings projected into things by a separate mind, nor any additive combination of the two. After many mistakes and wanderings, James finally came to see that they are not scientific facts but *affectional facts*, as he called them, real beings endowed with meanings produced by human reflection and toil. He also came to see that the self is neither a physical body, nor a separated consciousness, nor any combination of the two. These traditional categories are inadequate to grasp the self as a whole, and leave it ambiguous. After years of reflection and many errors, he came to see that it is a living, sentient body dependent on the things among which it has been thrown, and inseparable from the world in which it exists.

This embodied self does not live in isolation from others in a world of its own. James came to see that many of the difficulties of solipsism arise from the notion of a separated mind, or consciousness, and after abandoning these traditional conceptions, he had no trouble in dealing with them. By returning to pre-reflective experience, he finally realized that the embodied self directly perceives the meanings of other "minds" in their expressive gestures. The living bodies of men are the centres of the life-world, and they order it around themselves, not merely by their ideas but by their sweat and labor.

Monistic systems fail to do justice to the richness and complexity of this world of life with its manifold regions and relations. As we have seen, all the regions of pure mathematics and logic, the fields of the sciences, art, religion, politics, individual biography, and history—all of these, and many more, find their places within it. At present, the over-arching patterns of this world are only dimly understood by a vague common sense, almost never subjected to disciplined criticism and review.

Past philosophy having devoted the greater part of its energies to the construction of abstract systems taking little account of world facts, human opinion has been left to itself to fall into ever grosser forms of provincialism and fanaticism, which now threaten the world with total destruction.

This "world of life", as James called it, is not a static system. It is itself a history and, in fact, many histories, as he saw, none of which is as yet finished. It is neither subjective nor objective, neither physical nor psychical, neither wholly real nor wholly meaningful, though, if clearly defined and distinguished, all these qualities may be found within it, together with a pervasive vagueness and ambiguity. Nevertheless, certain patterns may also be found, and some of these James discovered, and hesitantly expressed in his radical empiricism.

His explorations are now being continued. But only a bare beginning has been made, though even this has brought forth a revolutionary transformation in philosophy. James also came to see this, for he said at the end of his life: "I saw that philosophy had been on a false scent ever since the days of Socrates and Plato, that an *intellectual* answer to the intellectualist's difficulties will never come, and that the real way out of them, far from consisting in the discovery of such an answer, consists in simply closing one's ears to the question."[6] But the remedy is not to be found in an abandonment of conceptual thinking, nor in any form of irrationalism. We must return to the pre-reflective world of pure experience to get a sense of the depths of life by burying "ourselves in the thickness of those passing moments over the surface of which they [our concepts] fly" (PU, pp. 251–52). But then we must use concepts to clarify, and to gather together these scattered insights.

As James says, "direct acquaintance and conceptual knowledge are thus complementary of each other; each remedies the other's defects" (p. 251). But the disciplined study of the facts of the life-world and their meanings will be the condition for any genuine advance. By following James in this arduous task, we

[6] A *Pluralistic Universe* (PU), p. 291.

may hope to work out a literature close to the concrete, and a critical philosophy which will help men not only to think in a more disciplined and more open way, but to build a world order that is more sound and truly human.

Chapter Fifteen

❀

Radical Empiricism
and Existence

In his article "The Productive Paradoxes of William James",[1] Gordon Allport has said: "it [radical empiricism] might have served as the foundation for an American school of phenomenology, but it did not. Instead, the examination of the intent and constitution of experience was left largely to Husserl and his associates in Germany . . .". This remark, I think, is well taken. Until recently, and even then primarily in Europe, James' work has been read as a contribution to psychology, conceived as a natural science. There is some reason for this, as between 1880 and 1890 James was certainly concerned with this aspect of the subject. His scientific contributions have now certainly been superseded by later developments. But as we have tried to show in these pages, they were not his major concern. This was rather to describe and to clarify the phenomena as they are directly experienced and lived through. As James saw it, these two interests are closely related, but as E. G. Boring

[1] *Psychological Review*, 50 (1943), 95.

has perceived, the latter is phenomenological rather than scientific in character.[2]

As we have tried to show in Chapter VI, James' phenomenology cannot be identified with that of Husserl's middle period. It is more closely related to the existential phenomenology of Merleau-Ponty, Erwin Straus and others now working in this field. But in terms of these recent developments, James is not only a phenomenologist but, first and foremost, a phenomenological philosopher who, in his later years, as we have seen, tried to work out an ethics, a theory of truth, and, indeed, a pluralistic "metaphysics" based on his empirical investigations. The range of his thought is very wide, and if we consider his earlier and later works together, they give us a total and distinctive vision of the world. It is not a system starting out from one narrow region of fact, and then excogitated in advance to show how other regions may be fitted in. This more traditional procedure is not in accord with James' radical empiricism. So he does not follow it. His aim is rather to let the facts of each region speak for themselves, without any forcing by prior categories.

One gets the impression that when he approaches a new problem, he is beginning all over again, *de novo*. This, I believe, is largely responsible for the freshness and discerning power of his descriptions. He hopes that a unity of meaning may be achieved. But this must be a *real* meaning that is found in the facts, and not imposed by any extraneous forcing or straining. Hence James' "system" is filled with many tensions, or paradoxes, which have attracted the attention of many commentators. But as Allport has pointed out in his article, these are "productive paradoxes" never left without fertile suggestions as to how they may be overcome. Thus we have noted the tension between the scientific and the phenomenological perspectives which runs through the whole of the *Principles* (*supra*, Chapter II, pp.

[2] *Cf.* "William James and the Psychology of the Present," *American Journal of Psychology*, 55 (1942), 310–27.

31–35).[3] But we have also noted his suggestion that the "world of sense" is the wider and prior horizon, in which the facts and laws of science may be included without distortion and reduction. (*Cf. supra*, Chapter VI.)

So James arrives at his vision of an "unfinished pluralistic universe" that is in flux, but still not chaotic and irrational if we let it be as it is without prior prejudice. Why, James asks (PU, p. 73) "may not the flux of sensible experience itself contain a rationality that has been overlooked, so that the real remedy would consist in harking back to it more intelligently, and not in advancing in the opposite direction away from it and even away beyond the intellectualist criticism that disintegrates it, to the pseudo-rationality of the supposed absolute point of view?" There are aspects of unity, relations which hold different members of this collection together. But there are also aspects of diversity and independence. As we live through this empirical world, it is "like one of those dried human heads with which the Dyaks of Borneo deck their lodges. The skull forms a solid nucleus; but the innumerable feathers, leaves, strings, beads, and loose appendices of every description float and dangle from it, and, save that they terminate in it, seem to have nothing to do with one another" (ERE, p. 46).

Original Meanings of the Sense-world

Real life is a vague and rich pluralism of this kind, in which numberless individual things and events are thrown together all at once in a vast array of newborn infants, helpless old age, industrial production, moving works of art, war, poverty, happiness and tragedy. To the intellectualist this seems like an unmitigated confusion with no native principles of order. Patterns of meaning come from reason alone, and, without these,

[3] *Cf.* Bruce Wilshire, "Natural Science and Phenomenology: William James' *Principles of Psychology* as a Search for Reconciliation," unpublished Ph.D. thesis, New York University, 1965.

we are immediately confronted with a mere disordered manifold, which is disparaged by the constant use of such terms as subjective, fleeting, unstable, and confused. Hegel's term for this pre-reflective disarray was "the immediate", and according to him, as James notes in quoting Hegel's *Logic* (PU, p. 51),[4] "the true knowledge of God begins when we know that things as they immediately are have no truth".

From the very beginning of his philosophical career James rebelled against this traditional disparagement of the world of sense. Before we know anything about this world through the mediation of concepts, it is known by acquaintance, and even after the coming of language, we continue to know it directly by perception and feeling. What is known in this way is not a mere jumble of individual things and events, for, from the first, they are held together by relational patterns such as space, time, consciousness, the self and the world. In fact, all our most basic categories, including being itself, refer back to this prior knowledge. This is why discursive argument ends with these ultimate principles, which are either already known from a pre-reflective source or not known at all. It is true that traditional currents of thought have invented special rational faculties, like the Aristotelian *noûs*, or the reason of modern idealism, to account for this direct, intuitive knowledge. But is not James right in rejecting these inventions so far as they ignore the prior contribution of perception and feeling?

Would the notion of being (existence) have any meaning for us, if it excluded what we feel and perceive by direct acquaintance? This is the prior and independent source of such understanding as we have of our ultimate meanings. Hence conceptual argument ends with them. We have words for these original meanings in our modern languages, but either they are used without critical examination in a way that is so vague and diffuse as to lapse into the "obvious", or if subjected to the usual mode of conceptual analysis, they become so mixed with abstract inter-

4 *Cf. The Logic of Hegel*, tr. William Wallace, Clarendon Press, Oxford 1874, p. 181.

pretation as to lose their original concreteness and certainty. The aim of radical empiricism is to avoid both these extremes by the use of concepts in cooperation with feeling and perception in such a way as to clarify the original meaning without destroying it. This requires a patient and painstaking process of elucidation in which what was at first inarticulate, floating, and untranslatable gradually becomes articulate, fixed, and communicable, without too great a loss of its original concreteness and certainty.

According to James, the most basic task of the radical empiricist is to attempt this clarification of the world of sense and its basic regions and structures, such as space, time, consciousness, and the self. But this is not its only task. Any individual thing, person, or event may be approached in this empirical way, and to be properly understood, it must be so approached by relating it to these prior structures, and finding its position in the life-world. This is true also of speculative philosophy with which James was always deeply concerned both as a human being and as a philosopher. His attack on systems to which he was opposed was empirical in character. Thus he criticized Hegel primarily for his disparagement and neglect of the immediate data of lived experience and its original structures.

Furthermore his philosophy of religion was based on a painstaking study of concrete personal experiences, and he felt that the whole subject will be revolutionized if it is ever approached more carefully and intensively in this empirical manner (VA, pp. 492–93; cf. PU, pp. 312–14). This is also true of his pluralistic "metaphysics", and in his late work on A Pluralistic Universe he goes out of his way to show how it is founded on what he took to be lasting results of his radical empiricism. His philosophical and religious speculations are in line with these results, but are not implied by them. Other alternatives are still possible. So he develops them in a very tentative way. There are certain philosophical conclusions, however, which are directly involved in any investigation that is genuinely empirical, and which he explains, as we have seen, in his essays (supra, Chapter VIII, pp. 209 ff.).

In our lived existence, we are confronted with beings which are altogether independent of us, and over which we have no direct control. This is not a conceptual theory or postulate. It is a ubiquitous pattern of pre-reflective experience where alien things and persons are presented, or given to us in the flesh, in their alien otherness, which resists not only our actions, but our efforts to know them as well. As James sees it, this is a lasting result of the method which all empiricists should take to heart. It is responsible for "the realistic element" in James' thought which he had to emphasize again and again, against the recurrent misinterpretation of it as "subjectivistic" (MT, pp. 190 ff.).

This has several further consequences of a general nature which James feels will be recognized by any sound empirical procedure. One of these is the factor of sheer givenness, or presentation, which attaches to any object of empirical inquiry. If the enquirer is to approach such an object without prior bias, he must place his own views about it in brackets, and be ready to learn from it. He must, for the moment, put his theories in brackets in order to penetrate into the being of the thing, to discover something about its own patterns which may be essentially different from his own. The idealistic argument that we cannot put our categories and theories in suspense is really an excuse for dogmatism and lethargy of mind. If one has his own categories and his own system ready at hand, he will have little difficulty verbally in finding a place for anything presented to him, without having to go through the arduous ordeal of listening, and of seriously investigating what is other.

The empirical thinker, on the other hand, is ready to listen and to learn. No doubt he has his own systems and conclusions, but no matter how well confirmed they may be, he is ready to examine carefully any new and discordant fact, and to make the necessary revisions and corrections. So he will tend to be sceptical of any great system, like that of Hegel, which claims to have absorbed all that is given into a necessary whole that is complete in itself. In the light of the negativity which urges him on, he will still be able to point to surd factors that are simply given, for example, the system itself. So he will continue to ask why it is this way and not otherwise?

This means that in such facts there is an element of opacity and "mystery", as James calls it. No matter how far his knowledge of existence may reach, there will be further depths beyond. Hence the radical empiricist should recognize that in these concrete investigations, he is not concerned with problems that can ever be solved once and for all. He is concerned rather with mysteries into which he may penetrate in various degrees, but which he will never be able to exhaust. This means that he will put forth his own conclusions in a tentative way, attempting at all costs to maintain that openness of mind which is so characteristic of James. This element of mystery that is found in the simplest and humblest things of life will suggest to the empiricist that there is a certain pluralism and free play in the universe, which would not be present in a system where everything is perfectly clear and determinate. In a world pervaded by mystery there is also room for human freedom, so that men may give justifiably different responses in their lives and in their thought. Hence the empiricist will welcome these diverse responses, so far as they take account of the known facts, and even rejoice in them, if they are put forth tentatively and with an open mind.

In opposition to traditional rationalism, as well as traditional empiricism, James maintained from the beginning that relational patterns are directly felt and perceived. Immediate experience cannot be dismissed as a set of isolated data. It involves relational structures of the most basic kind, including selective attention, consciousness, continuous transition, and the search for truth. These patterns have always been a central concern of philosophy, because it is only through them that our discrete experiences are gathered together into a meaningful world. In the past, however, they have been identified with the sense-giving activity of a separated mind. According to James, this supposition is unnecessary, for these patterns are already known by direct acquaintance independent of language and conceptual thought, and may become articulate and communicable by a certain kind of conceptual analysis.

This is the most original feature of James' radical empiricism, which he always emphasized in his careful expositions (*cf.* ERE, pp. 41 ff.). It is necessary to repeat that these relational structures are directly known by sense and feeling, which have a deeper cognitive significance than has been traditionally attributed to them. So there is no need for introducing a separate trans-empirical reason or a transcendental consciousness. This sharply distinguishes James' empiricism from Husserl's phenomenology. It is a *radical* empiricism which looks to experience for light on the most basic forms and categories that underlie our human thought. If this is true, it is not only the scientist who must check his theories by turning to empirical fact. The philosopher too, in dealing with the most basic questions of life and thought, must also look, and feel, and listen, if he is to avoid one-sided and reductive views.

James followed this method in dealing with all the questions that attracted his serious attention. It is the central thread which is found in his variegated reflections, and brings them together in a certain pluralistic unity. It leads him to a realistic view of independent realities, which we have noted, and to a sense of unfathomable but penetrable mystery. If we think of it historically, we must recognize it as a new type of empiricism. It is the key insight which underlies all of his disciplined thoughts and gives them at least a methodological unity. But we cannot separate this underlying method from the more specific results which we have been studying in these chapters. So now, in order to get some sense of the whole, let us try to gather these results together in a brief review. What does it all come to in the end?

We shall do this by following the rough chronological order of our text. This means that we shall start with the first volume of the *Principles*, in which James distinguishes between knowledge by acquaintance and conceptual knowledge about, and describes certain basic patterns of experience that are known originally in the former way. Next we shall consider his "reflex arc" conception of mental life, which underlies the second volume of the *Principles* and several essays written during this period, especially

"Sentiment of Rationality", 1879, and "Reflex Action and Theism", 1881. Finally, we shall turn to those questions concerning meaning and value with which James was especially concerned at the end of his career—his ethics, philosophy of religion, and pragmatic theory of truth. In each of these divisions, we shall try not merely to repeat what we have said before, but to bring these different theories together, and to show how they are related to his radical empiricism.

An Empirical A Priori

It is in the early chapters of the Principles that James makes the crucial distinction between knowledge by direct acquaintance and conceptual knowledge about, and shows how the former is always presupposed by the latter. In much of our sophisticated thinking, we are concerned with concepts, or meanings, that are already established. And this is apt to lead us into a sense of conceptual autonomy, as if we were moving in an already finished universe of discourse where everything we think about is covered by a clear-cut meaning. There is no need to depart into another world, and to engage in a different style of thinking. But, as we have noted, this does not seem to be true of first concepts, like that of existence. We seem to know already what it means, but when we subject it to careful examination, this meaning turns out to be so vague and general that it fails to satisfy our sense of logical clarity. And yet any attempt to define it in terms of other concepts turns out to be either verbal or circular, and we find that we are presupposing what we are trying to define. Unless we can gain help from some other source of knowledge, we are left unsatisfied.

Our other, more particular concepts presuppose the ultimate ones, and thus are subject to the same difficulties. But apart from this, it is usually clear that they eventually refer us to some feeling, or perception. It is evident, for example, that we cannot talk meaningfully about a planet, a rose, or a kitchen without referring to an object of direct perception, or to pain, joy, and sadness without referring to an experienced feeling. These meanings, therefore, cannot be understood by concepts alone. They require another mode of knowing by direct familiarity. As we have seen, (*supra*, Chapter II, pp. 46–49 and Chapter III, pp. 65–66) James also shows how any linguistic discourse occurs in a concrete situation, some knowledge of which is always presupposed and indicated by the use of pronouns and demonstratives.

All this evidence is relevant to his conclusion that conceptual knowledge *about* presupposes a prior knowledge by direct acquaintance. Without this, our words are ultimately empty and meaningless. We have called this James' theory of an existential *a priori* (*supra*, Chapter II), and in the early chapters of the *Principles* he is considering certain basic patterns of existence, the living body working for conscious ends, habit, the stream of consciousness, the self, attention, and finally the world of sense which are prior in this way.

But if these meanings are vaguely known independently of language and conception, how then may we ever come to express them in words? Feeling is one thing and conception is another! So how can the two unite?

James does not try to overcome this difficulty by dialectical argument. Instead of this, in his chapter on the stream of consciousness, he gives concrete examples from experience to show how it is actually overcome. Then in reflecting on these examples, he tries to develop suitable concepts which will really fit the facts. First, he gives the example of trying to remember a forgotten word. We do not know what the word is, in a verbal sense. And yet, we have seen, (*supra*, Chapter III, p. 66) we have a dim, non-verbal knowledge of the word which enables us to reject wrong suggestions, and to approve of those that come closer to what we already know. So here is an example of a dim, pre-verbal knowledge in operation. In this case, the full knowledge we are seeking is the exact recovery of a precise, specific word.

But our pre-reflective familiarity with patterns of life is not precise and specific in this way. It is inexact and unspecific. Can we find an example of vague knowledge of this kind, which is not radically altered when "it" becomes clarified and verbally expressed. James gives us such an example—the intention to express an idea before it is verbally expressed (*cf. supra,* pp. 66–67). In many cases such an idea, in its early stages, is vague and indeterminate. And yet it is present, and exerts a real efficacy in rejecting wrong moves and accepting those that lead us on in the right direction. The pre-reflective meanings of experience are present in the same way, and when they are clearly formulated, a definite change occurs. This should not be denied. But if the process is followed through with patience and care, and we constantly refer back to the original feeling, it is possible for us to arrive at a formulation which reverberates with it, and in which something of its vagueness is also maintained. This meaning has now become fixed, articulate, and communicable. But it is the same form that is now expressed. It is by this radical empiricism that James seeks to penetrate through the barriers of overly abstract and simple concepts to the original patterns of experience as they are lived.

Thus he tries to dig below the traditional dualism of mind and body to reveal something of the living, striving body that is neither the one nor the other, nor any mere combination of the two. This means that he must reject the concept of a detached, spectatorial consciousness, except as a derived mode, in order to disclose the consciousness that dwells in our bodily acts, for which causes become means and effects become ends. This is a consciousness with which we are directly familiar as it struggles for these ends, and makes a real difference in the world. In considering the patterns of this active consciousness, James adopts neither a purely external nor a purely internal, mentalist point of view, but brings the two together in his discussion of habit, and the periods of hesitation in which habit breaks down. The living brain then becomes more active, and its instability, as James suggests, makes it possible for conscious choice to weigh the scales.

Conceptual analysis, on the one hand, has reduced our conscious life to a mere succession of isolated states. On the other, it has turned it into a timeless unity. Penetrating through this traditional dichotomy, James seeks to disclose this life as we live it through, and the feelings of transition that maintain it as a continuous "stream". Similarly the self is neither a set of discrete episodes, nor a timeless substance (*cf.* Chapter IV). It is rather a field with several different levels, material, social, and personal, which maintains its identity through time by taking over its past pulsations and their objects, by representing them, and carrying them on in the specious present.

There are several points which are especially worth noting in James' treatment of conceptual understanding (*cf.* Chapters V, VIII, and IX). One of these we should expect from his radical empiricism. This is his interest in trying to get at the feeling, or the sentiment, of rationality as we are directly acquainted with it. He identifies this with a sense of the easy flow of meaning in any factual area, without any gaps or obstacles. But unless it is to become ungrounded fantasy, reason must take account of the given facts, and this means an interruption in the flow, a surd element that simply has to be accepted, even in the most complete system (*cf.* Chapter VIII, pp. 208 ff.). Even of Hegel's great *Encyclopedia* one may ask why this and not rather nothing? without receiving a perfectly cogent answer. But this did not lead James into a distrust of reason, when employed within its limits. To say that life involves other factors is not to say that it is irrational, and we have noted James' disagreement with Bergson on this point (Chapter IX, p. 236). He is a disciple neither of rationalism nor of irrationalism, but of something demanding another category.

As Allport has noted,[5] James, with his remarkable sense for the concrete situation, was always looking for structures precisely *there* in the concrete itself. In this respect, his radical empiricism resembles the best of what we now know as phenomenology. At the speculative levels of philosophy, he saw no sound objection to a cooperative venture of reason, together with aspiration, in working out a pattern of meaning that makes sense to us, and challenges our active powers. Is it really rational for reason to

[5] *Op. cit.,* p. 112.

absolutize itself, and to remain blind to the facts and acts of life? Anyway they are present, whether clearly recognized or not. This is James' position.

The last *a priori* pattern which James considers in the *Principles* is the world horizon of Chapter XXI. This is the vague, but ever-present background for every object of perception and feeling. It surrounds every particular world-version of an individual, or a group, with its fringes, and also the distinct sub-worlds of science, ideal relations, and mythology. While he recognizes different modes of being in the objects of these other worlds, James clearly asserts the priority of the world of sense which is pre-eminently real (*cf. supra,* Chapter VI). We exist in this world with the whole of our being, and all of our powers rather than with only a few. We do not merely observe this world from a detached point of view; we are actively engaged and inhabit it. Hence it bears the real tang of existence. It is also, in a sense, indubitable and inescapable. Hence in assigning the central position to this world, James' position is similar to that of recent phenomenologists who have rejected Husserl's transcendental reduction, and have developed an existential rather than a transcendental phenomenology (*cf. supra,* Chapter VI, pp. 159 ff.). In unhesitatingly asserting the priority of the life-world over against the world of science, this position is radically distinct from modern naturalism.

The Three Departments of the Mind

In the first part of the *Principles,* which we have just reviewed, James considers certain questions concerning the nature of psychology, and certain patterns, like consciousness, the self, and the world, which are basic to the whole of human experience. One of these is the intentional structure of experience, which he may have learned from his reading of Brentano (*cf. supra,* Chapter II). Psychic phenomena are bipolar in nature, being divisible into an intentional act of some kind and its object. Thus each desire is a desire *for* something, and each thought is a thought *about* something. Now James was deeply impressed by a fact concerning intentionality which was also noted by Husserl. Our attention is normally focused on the objects rather than on the intentions, so that our direct awareness of the latter is usually vague and peripheral (*cf. supra*, Chapters II, pp. 36 ff., and III, pp. 59 ff.). It is for this reason that we often lack specific terms for our intending acts, and have to name them after their objects, as we speak of an orange taste or a cheesy smell. This renders the psychologist's task more difficult, for his special concern is precisely with these intentional acts of feeling, thinking, believing, etc.

Hence it is not surprising that the second volume of the *Principles* is primarily concerned with these mental intentions which James divides into three distinct groups: sensation and perception whose objects are facts; conceptual understanding whose objects are ideas or meanings; and the active side of our nature whose objects are ends or values (*cf. supra*, Chapters VII–X). James refers to these as "the three departments of the mind" (RAAT, *cf.* EFM, pp. 125–33), and correlates them physiologically with the reflex-arc pattern of bodily life—the reception of external stimuli (facts), hesitation and preparation for response in the central nervous system, and the active response (value) which completes the cycle.

One fact about this scheme of classification is worthy of comment. This is its apparent omission of feeling, which is specifically recognized, for example, in the traditional scheme of thought, will, and feeling. This is somewhat surprising in view of James' emphasis on knowledge by direct acquaintance, and his constant use of the term "feeling" for such knowledge. I suggest that the omission is not due to any disparagement of feeling on James' part, but rather to his recognition of its radical and central importance. As he sees it, feeling is the most primordial phase of our conscious experience, the one that is closest to life, the common stem from which the three different branches emerge, and in which they all participate. This is why James thinks of feeling as an inclusive term covering "mental states at large, irrespective of their kind" (PR, I, 186–87). But now let us turn to what he says about the three departments one by one, and consider this in relation to his radical empiricism.

His aim is to describe the phenomena as they are lived through, and to protect them against over-simplified and reductive interpretations. In dealing with sensation and perception, we find James doing precisely this. Thus in the light of his descriptions, he rejects the atomism of traditional empiricism and the representational view of perception. I am not aware of sense-data in the mind, but of external things and persons in space, whose actual presence in the flesh I feel. The difference between such a present object and one that is imagined must be also directly felt to be understood, and apart from this, any attempt to work out theoretical criteria for making the distinction is a waste of time. A real thing is ordinarily perceived in its place in a field of meaning. But James also describes certain situations in which this meaning is largely absent, and we are presented with a brute facticity, later described by Sartre under the heading of nausea (supra, Chapter VII, pp. 190 ff.).

James rejects Berkeley's view that the depth of space is not directly seen, and, like later phenomenologists, he holds that the different distances and directions of this life space are oriented with respect to the motions of the living body. I constantly feel this body, though vaguely, as a voluminous whole "much larger than any local pulsation, pressure, or discomfort" (PR, II, 135). Avoiding unnecessary metaphysical assumptions and postulates, he simply described this field-pattern, which we feel inside us and around us, as it is found.

The same is true of his account of time, which also agrees in several respects with the views of later phenomenologists (cf. supra, Chapter VII). He was constantly trying to get back to the continuous flow of lived time, as we may now call it, and he worked out penetrating descriptions of the specious present through which this flow proceeds. He clearly distinguished lived time from the successive beats of clock time by which we measure it, and showed how an interval filled with interesting experiences is lived through as shorter than a dull interval of the same length as measured by the clock, but nevertheless seems longer in retrospect. He criticized the theory that memory could be explained by the persistence of brain traces, and pointed out that this could not account for the pastness of the past. He also distinguished between desultory, systematic, and what we may call *memory proper*, in which a past experience is remembered with all its fringes of feeling and meaning as a total object in the world.

In these investigations, James is not speculating or defending a view already taken by conceptual disputation alone. He is using concepts. This is true. But he is using them to clarify patterns of experience already known vaguely by direct acquaintance. In many cases, his observations have been confirmed by others coming from different backgrounds and traditions. So it is hard to dismiss them as "subjective" vagaries. James put forth his own views in a very tentative style. But he was thoroughly convinced that it was a primary responsibility of any philosopher worthy of the name to study these patterns of the sense-world with great care and patience. For unless they are tested in this real world, philosophical speculations and arguments will turn out to be verbal constructions, or subjective vagaries, of a most persistent kind.

This critical aspect of James' thought comes out very clearly in his consideration of the second department of the mind, concerned with conceptual thought and the elaboration of meaning (*cf. supra*, Chapters VIII and IX). He had a deep interest in this from the beginning, and five chapters of the *Principles* are specifically devoted to it. In these chapters, he stresses the interdependence of conceptual thought and language. The use of verbal symbols gives us a distance from things which enables us to regard the present as though it were absent, and the absent as though it were present, and thus frees us from subservience to the flux of events. James' whole discussion of language is dominated by this enhancement of freedom and autonomy which it brings (*cf. supra*, Chapter V, pp. 197 ff.). Thus we may refer to the same thing again and again even after it has passed, and may compare it with another thing widely separated from it in time. By noting these real similarities and differences, we may build up a "conceptual world" which is no longer dominated by mechanical association and the accidents of history.

This freedom is further amplified by our ability to invent new concepts and ideal systems which do not enter the mind through the front door from experience, but come in *by the backstairs*, as James puts it, the inner way of invention and creation (*supra*, pp. 224 ff.). He was thoroughly convinced of the vital importance of such *a priori* constructions, not only in logic and mathematics, but also in the development of ethical and aesthetic norms, and in the actual practise of science as well. In the last chapter (XXVIII) of the *Principles*, he devotes so much attention and care to this conceptual *a priori* that serious questions may be raised as to whether he can still be called an empiricist. Nevertheless, as we have seen (pp. 229 ff.), this theory is quite distinct from the Kantian conception of the *a priori*, and from other traditional versions. It has no legislative authority over the whole of experience. It is rather a tentative *a priori*, which must be tested in the world of sense and show its worth. Without such testing, the freedom of reason is apt to overstep its limits, and to develop great systems of meaning with all inclusive claims that cannot withstand empirical criticism and turn out to be unfounded verbal constructions in the end.

Having a deep grain of scepticism in his nature, James was acutely aware of this danger. It led him to make certain criticisms of "intellectualism", which became increasingly harsh as his thought matured (*cf.* PU—first published 1909—pp. 252 ff. *et passim*). But it is already expressed in outline in the essay "The Sentiment of Rationality" which was written before 1879, and in which he thinks through his radical empiricism, not merely as a method, but as an ultimate philosophy. The philosopher cannot begin to think *de novo*. At the inauguration of his reflections, he finds himself already existing in a world, and confronting alien, independent beings. In these beings, there is an element of brute fact, with depths that resist our meanings. James calls this a "mystical" factor in things, which the rationalists have not adequately recognized. But it is there nonetheless.

On the other hand, this does not mean that being is utterly

meaningless, and altogether beyond our grasp. There are implicit patterns in the world that we sense and perceive. Hence, while mysticism and scepticism have a ground, James rejects them, for empiricism is a viable alternative. Meaning is not the same as being. So, unlike the intellectualist, the empiricist will not assume *a priori* that the two must coincide. But, unlike the mystic and the sceptic, he will not abandon the search. He will recognize the brute factual element in things. He will know that existence can never be replaced by a system of concepts. But it has germs of meaning in it, which may be developed and amplified. Hence by a new use of language and concepts, working in cooperation with sense and feeling, he will try to find and to create meanings that will clarify and do justice to the facts.

Man's powers of thought and action are limited. He cannot create a world of meaning *ex nihilo*. Such attempts will lead only to verbal extravagance that will impede responsible action. But by finding the meanings already present in the real world, and then by developing them, he may be able to elicit action that will take this world over and remold it gradually into a more human form. This is the theory of meaning, the second department of the mind, which James develops in his radical empiricism.

In turning to the third department of the mind (action), James considers instinct, emotion, and will (*cf. supra*, Chapter X). He uses the term *instinct* in referring to any innate, active tendency which is correlated with an organ, or part, of the body. James holds that man has been richly endowed with a vast variety of such hereditary tendencies towards anger, curiosity, fear, affection, etc. At first they are excited by random stimuli in a more or less chaotic manner, but they do not remain in this condition. Long before the coming of language, they are taken over and regulated by the process of habit formation. Through such learning, certain stimuli are selected and others rejected. The responses become ordered together with others under the guidance of perception and feeling. Then, as we shall see, this advance in self-regulation reaches its final level in voluntary action, where habits, based on instincts, are reordered under the guidance of conceptual meanings and purposes.

In working out his well-known theory of the emotions in the *Principles,* James first uses causal language, which has led many readers to interpret his view in a physicalist and epiphenomenal sense. But when we remember his clear-cut rejection of epiphenomenalism (Chapter I), when we read his highly qualified statements more carefully, and relate them to later remarks on the same subject, we find that his thought is moving in a different direction. Feeling may sometimes follow after the beginning of a bodily response, and can never be separated from it. This is the main point James is making by his deceptive use of causal language. But it is never a blind, visceral reaction without cognitive meaning of any kind. According to James, it is through feeling that the objects of perception and thought are subjectively assimilated into the life-world and evaluated. If perception and thought could ever be completely separated from feeling, which is not the case, they would be neutral to what we call value. It is primarily through feeling that values are grasped. This is the gist of James' theory, and we noted its marked similarity to the ideas later developed by Scheler on this subject (*supra,* pp. 252–53).

As we have indicated, voluntary choice is the highest level of self-regulation of which the nervous system is capable. It is the centre of what we call human freedom, though its ultimate sources are found in the selective activities of the living organism, and especially in those that occur at the level of habit. There is no need to suppose a separate faculty of will to explain what we call rational choice. Any idea or vision will lead to action. If it does not, this is due to interference by other ideas and visions. The key to voluntary choice, therefore, lies in our ability to avoid distraction, and to attend persistently to a difficult or unfamiliar idea. James believes that a strong effort of concentration may be a decisive factor in such a case, and may lead to real choice for strenuous action.

It is true that the active department completes the reflex-arc cycle, and there is a sense in which the other two are ordered to this final phase. This has sometimes been interpreted as a kind of voluntarism in which reason is to serve as a mere instrument for the satisfaction of occasional desires. But, as we have tried to show (pp. 284 ff.), such an interpretation is not supported by a careful reading of the texts. James says that a true vision must take account of our active nature and give it something to do. It must challenge our aspirations, and stir them to strenuous effort, not merely serve them as they are. As James sees it, there is a peculiar relation of mutual interdependence between thinking and striving, and if the highest level of achievement is to be attained on both sides, each must support the other. A pattern of meaning must call forth intensive effort, which, in turn, must elicit further clarification and development of meaning. This is, in fact, true of all three departments, which as James says, constitute an "organic" unity. Hence to function at the highest level, each must operate adequately according to its own norms, and support the others to a maximum degree (RAAT, pp. 125 ff.). Hence it is hard to think of this view as either voluntaristic or intellectualistic.

Responsible Action and the Verification of Belief

In Part III, we have turned to certain later works, in which James tries to develop the implications of his empirical investigations for ethics, the philosophy of religion, and the theory of truth, and in his *Essays* of 1909, tries further to clarify and develop his radical empiricism. His ethics has often been interpreted along utilitarian lines as based on the principle of inclusiveness which he mentions in his essay, "The Moral Philosopher and the Moral Life". According to this view, all interests are on the same qualitative level, and the ethical problem is reduced to finding ways of satisfying the maximum number of desires. But when we read the essay as a whole, and other relevant texts, we find James identifying this view with what he calls "the easy-going way", which is really sub-moral in character. The "moral universe" becomes open to us only in the light of free action, and as James maintains, following Renouvier, the first act of freedom is to convince ourselves that, with effort, we are able to choose and to become free and responsible.

These "values", and the others connected with them, like willingness to take risks, and courage in facing hardships, are not so much fixed properties, or essences, as ways of existing joined together in an integral pattern which James calls *"the strenuous way of life"*. Every human power is strained to the ultimate pitch in the accomplishment of some task which makes sense to the agent. James is not concerned merely with the expenditure of energy, but rather with certain qualities of life which become accessible only through maximum effort. Freedom itself is not mere random action. It is meaningful action in a given situation which has a quality of its own that can be felt by those who are sensitive enough to discern it. The same is true of intellectual courage, devotion, sacrifice, tragedy, and the other strenuous values.

These existential values, as we have called them (Chapter XI), are in no sense forced upon us from the outside. We can be happy, no doubt happier, without them. But neither are they the result of an arbitrary fiat. They are rather the response to an appeal which slumbers in every man to make the most out of himself, and to become what he really can be. James sometimes calls this way of life "heroic", and, in *The Varieties of Religious Experience,* connects it with "the sick soul" and those who become "twice-born". This, I believe, is not only the ethics which James wrote about in print, but that which guided his own personal endeavors.

Is this anything more than a personal expression of James' subjective views? If it is seriously proposed, as it seems to be, what does it have to do with his radical empiricism? It certainly does not describe the way in which men act for the most part. This, of course, must be admitted. But it does describe a way of life that is generally respected and admired in many divergent cultures. Can we go further? Can we say that it makes more explicit that dim sense of oughtness that is present in every free person? In the depths of his being, does he not somehow desire to become himself to the fullest degree? If so, can we not say that this ethics of the strenuous life describes an imperative that, as James says, "lies slumbering in every man"? He is not telling them what they ought to do. He is rather appealing to them to recognize more clearly and sharply what, as they themselves already know, they ought to do. In this sense, then, James' ethics may be said to be descriptive and radically empirical.

The same can certainly be said of his philosophy of religion. He attacks traditional, rational theology, because of its remoteness from lived experience and its verbalism. The case for religion must rest not primarily on such abstract argument, but rather on the direct experience of individuals. Hence his whole study of religion is radically empirical in nature, and rests primarily on a detailed examination of case histories which he undertook at the end of the century. Allport is doubtless correct in his conjecture[6] that this laborious study of first-hand reports weakened James' confidence in scientific objectivity as the method for the study of man, and led him towards that further strengthening of his empiricism which was a marked phase of his later thought.

James believes that this evidence from direct experience points to a transcendent power beyond man which is able to influence us in various ways, often through the unconscious, and to give us certain powers which we would not otherwise possess. He is indifferent to sectarian creeds and dogmas, and consistently maintains that this "divine" power, though genuinely transcendent, is nevertheless finite. In our study of the *Varieties* (Chapter XII) we noted its greater concern for the phenomena of the unconscious, which he had argued against in the *Principles,* and his penetrating chapters on conversion, in which he clearly distinguishes those that are largely unconscious and involuntary from those that are conscious and voluntary.

In considering James' pragmatic writings, which were written

6 *Op. cit.,* p. 101.

after his ethical and religious investigations, we were led back to the theory of meaning on which his pragmatism is based. This theory is directed against transcendental theorizing and empty verbalism, and is radically empirical in James' sense of this phrase. According to it, any idea, or theory, which, if it were true, would make no real difference in any direct feeling, or perception, of an object, or in our way of dealing with it, is empty. There is no point in disputing about it, since such disputation would be purely verbal in character. Some false theories are still meaningful, for they would make an empirical difference if they were true. Also theories that might make an empirical difference, though no way, as yet, has been found to verify or falsify them, may be meaningful, for they might be verified.

James believes that this theory of meaning rules out certain types of metaphysical speculation as meaningless, but not all kinds. Thus the issues between his pluralistic conception and monistic conceptions of the world make a real difference in how we experience this world as a whole, and how we act towards it. Hence they are meaningful, and discussion of these issues is not empty. Thus my belief in my own freedom, and that of other men, is a meaningful issue that can be verified or falsified by my own action. In general, we may say that "metaphysical" issues concerning the nature of the empirical world as a whole and human action are meaningful, and worthy of discussion. But theories which have no conceivable relevance either to the empirical world as a whole, or to anything in the world, are empty and meaningless.

In the light of his empirical theory of meaning, we found James' pragmatic theory of truth to be defensible when certain misunderstandings are removed. Thus, as Chisholm and other critics have pointed out, James did not mean by the satisfactoriness of a theory that it would satisfy certain subjective desires, as certain European critics have maintained. He meant rather its capacity to satisfy certain expectations, and to fulfill certain intentions in the phenomenological sense. We found even his controversial conception of self-verification and the making of truth to be defensible within certain limits. But in so far as James did not sufficiently clarify these limits in his pragmatic writings, we found that he laid himself open to legitimate criticisms.

Radical Empiricism and Existence

His *Essays in Radical Empiricism* show a strengthening of his phenomenological empiricism at the end of his life, which we tried to clarify and to explain. We found that his effort to overcome the dualism of subject and object by the supposition of neutral units of experience, neither the one nor the other, was unsuccessful, and that he could not consistently carry it through. This effort, however, did lead him to focus certain phenomena where the subjective and the objective come together, and where the need for overcoming a sharp conceptual dualism is empirically evident. James now ceases to speak of the brain alone, and focuses the whole living body both as a psychic centre of intentions and an object in the world. He sees this body as expressing meanings, and uses this conception in working out an original answer to the problem of solipsism.

Also, he now sharply focuses a distinctive kind of fact, which he calls affectional fact. These facts are objective, and, as in the case of the precious stone, are just as stubborn and constraining as scientific facts. But unlike these, they embody meanings and values which are not subjective additions to a neutral stuff, but which belong to their independent, physical being. These insights are important developments of James' radical empiricism.

Let us conclude by raising certain questions concerning the meaning of this empiricism. First of all, is it a science? Are his empirical investigations to be construed as would-be contributions to the science of psychology? James often speaks in this way in his *Principles*. But as his thought matured, he came to recognize that he was doing something different at a more fundamental level where not only objective factors but also "subjective" factors are at work. The sciences may have to begin with what is known by direct acquaintance. But then each of them leaves this behind, in order to turn to the special objects of its field, and to deal with them in as objective a way as is possible. James' method, on the other hand, requires him to dwell on this direct knowledge, vague and subjective though it be, and then to use concepts for the sake of clarifying and expressing the implicit meanings that are present in it. He is concerned with experience as we live it, and with the world in which we exist. But there is no science of being, no science of the world. These are taken for granted and presupposed by the sciences. As we think we have shown, however, they are the chief objects of James' concern.

But this existence in the concrete is a vast jumble of diverse attitudes and worlds, constructed according to the subjective biases of different individuals and cultures. By immersing ourselves in this concrete, how can we fail to end in a confused relativism of some kind? In answering this question, James, I think, would refer to his works. His mind was gifted with an amazing sense for the concrete, and an ability to give us the feel of it by flashes of descriptive insight. But as Allport has noted in "Productive Paradoxes", James also had a profound sense for structure, and was always looking for patterns precisely *in* the concrete. And sometimes he actually found them. Our existence, and even our freedom, is not a structureless chaos, and the world in which we live has distinctive patterns of various kinds. These can be focused and clarified by a "reason" that is not above looking, and working in close touch with perception and feeling.

James welcomed diversity, and he encouraged his students to think for themselves. This is a distinctive mark of his philosophy of freedom. He even rejoiced in speculative diversity, but under two conditions which he made very clear. First, speculation should not be undertaken as a game. When confronted with a pattern of ideas, the philosopher should always ask: can I really believe this? and what difference will it make whether I believe it or not? The second condition is that the pattern of ideas should not ignore, or contradict, the *a priori* structures of the life-world, for such a pattern cannot be really believed by any existing individual, or group. So this philosophy does not lead to any kind of relativism.

How, then, is it to be classified? Where does it belong in the history of philosophy? Like other original thinkers, he has been classified in many different ways. He has often been called an *empiricist*, but this fails to bring out the depth and range of his criticisms of the British tradition. In this country, he has been called a *naturalist* and even a *materialist*. But these terms are inappropriate for one who recognized the priority of the life-world, and rejected any reductive physicalism. Of all these various possibilities, his own term, *pragmatism*, has stuck the closest. But this word has practical implications of a subjective kind, which James rejected, and which led him publicly to regret his original choice of the term. Furthermore, I think we have shown that in spite of certain casual statements of James', his pragmatic theory of truth is grounded on his radical empiricism.

If, as I believe, this is, in fact, the operative principle which lies at the root of his other distinctive doctrines, then his close affiliation with the general phenomenological movement becomes evident, as we have indicated in the most substantial portions of this work. But this affiliation can be defended only if phenomenology is taken in a very broad sense, and not identified exclusively with the transcendental phenomenology of Husserl. It is certainly correct to think of James as one of a large group of thinkers scattered widely over the Western world, including Bergson and the later existential philosophers in France, Husserl, Scheler, and Heidegger in Germany, and many others, who, about the turn of the century, became profoundly dissatisfied with the abstractness and artificiality of traditional, systematic philosophy, and turned to concrete experience and its real structures for firmer guidance. In this broad sense, Professor Allport is right in thinking of James primarily as a phenomenologist.

If we are to continue to use this term in our English vocabulary, we need to remember that one of our native thinkers succeeded in finding the *logos*, or meaning, of many concrete phenomena, precisely as they appear, and thus, at a very early stage in its development, helped to found this basic discipline, which he called radical empiricism. This is what we have tried to show in this work.

BIBLIOGRAPHY

I. Major works of James abbreviated in the text

Essays in Radical Empiricism (abbr. ERE), Longmans, Green & Co., New York, 1912; ed. by R. B. Perry with PU (2 vols. in 1), 1958.
Essays on Faith and Morals (abbr. EFM), ed. by R. B. Perry, Meridian Books, World Publishing Co., Cleveland, 1962.
The Meaning of Truth: A Sequel to Pragmatism (abbr. MT), Longmans, Green & Co., New York, 1909, 1911.
A Pluralistic Universe (abbr. PU), Longmans, Green & Co., New York, 1909; ed. by R. B. Perry with ERE (2 vols. in 1), 1958.
Pragmatism (abbr. PRAG), Longmans, Green & Co., New York, 1907. Edited by R. B. Perry with four essays from MT, Meridian Books, World Publishing Co., Cleveland, 1955.
The Principles of Psychology (abbr. PR), 2 vols., Henry Holt & Co., New York, 1890. Authorized, unabridged and unaltered republication, 2 vols., Dover Publications, Inc., New York, 1950.
Talks to Teachers on Psychology, and to Students on Some of Life's Ideals (abbr. TT), Henry Holt & Co., New York, 1899. Authorized, unabridged and unaltered republication, Dover Publications, Inc., New York, 1962.
The Varieties of Religious Experience (abbr. VA), Longmans, Green & Co., New York, 1902. Authorized edition, The Modern Library, New York, n.d.
The Will to Believe, and Other Essays in Popular Philosophy (abbr. WBA), Longmans, Green & Co., New York, 1897. Authorized, unabridged and unaltered republication, Dover Publications, Inc., New York, 1956.

II. Other works of James referred to in the text

Collected Essays and Reviews, Longmans, Green & Co., New York, 1920.

Human Immortality: Two Supposed Objections to the Doctrine, Houghton, Mifflin & Co., Boston, 1898.

Memories and Studies, Longmans, Green & Co., New York, 1911, 1924.

The Letters of William James, ed. by his son Henry James, 2 vols., Atlantic Monthly Press, Boston, 1920.

The Letters of William James and Théodore Flournoy, ed. by Robert C. LeClair, University of Wisconsin Press, Madison, 1966.

III. Works consulted and referred to in the text

Allen, Gay W., *William James, A Biography*, Viking Press, New York, 1967.

Allport, G. W., "The Productive Paradoxes of William James," *Psychological Review*, 50 (1943), 95 ff.

Angell, J. R., "William James," *Psychological Review*, 18 (1911), 78 ff.

Bergson, Henri, *The Creative Mind*, tr. by M. L. Andison, Philosophical Library, New York, 1945.

Boring, E. G., "William James and the Psychology of the Present," *American Journal of Psychology*, 55 (1942), 310 ff.

Bradley, F. H., Letters of James to Bradley, Merton College Library, Oxford.

Brentano, Franz, *Psychologie vom empirischen Standpunkte*, I, Meiner, Leipzig, 1874.

Capek, Milic, "The Reappearance of the Self in the Last Philosophy of William James," *Philosophical Review*, 62 (1953), 526 ff.

Dewey, John, "The Reflex Arc Concept in Psychology," *Psychological Review* (July 1896), pp. 357 ff.

——, "The Vanishing Subject in the Psychology of James," *Journal of Philosophy*, 37 (1940), 589 ff.

Gurwitsch, Aron, "On the Object of Thought," *Philosophy and Phenomenological Research*, 7 (1947), 347 ff.

——, *Studies in Phenomenology and Psychology*, Northwestern University Press, 1966 (essays on James).

Gusdorf, G., *Mémoire et Personne*, 2 vols., Presses Universitaires de France, Paris, 1957.

Heidegger, Martin, *Einführung in die Metaphysik*, Niemeyer Verlag, Tübingen, 1953. *Introduction to Metaphysics*, tr. by Ralph Manheim, Yale University Press, 1959.

——, *Sein und Zeit*, 7th ed., Neomarius Verlag, Tübingen, 1957. *Being and Time*, tr. by John Macquarrie and Edward Robinson, SCM Press, London, 1962.

Husserl, Edmund, *Cartesianische Meditationen und Pariser Vorträge*, Nijhoff, The Hague, 1954. *Cartesian Meditations: An Introduction to Phenomenology*, tr. by Dorion Cairns, Nijhoff, The Hague, 1960.

——, *Ideen zu einer reinen Phänomenologie und phänomenologischen Philosophie*, Niemeyer, Halle, 1928. *Ideas: General Introduction to Pure Phenomenology*, tr. by W. R. Boyce Gibson, Allen & Unwin, London, 1931, Collier Books, New York, 1967.

——, *Die Krisis der europäischen Wissenschaften und die transzendentale Phänomenologie*, Nijhoff, The Hague, 1954.

——, *Logische Untersuchungen*, 3 vols., 4th ed., Niemeyer, Halle, 1928.

Kallen, H. M., *The Philosophy of William James*, Modern Library, New York, 1925.

Kant, Immanuel, *Prolegomena to any Future Metaphysics*, tr. by Paul Carus, Open Court, La Salle, Ill., 1955.

Landgrebe, L., "Husserl und Cartesianismus," *Philosophische Rundschau*, 1961.

Linschoten, J., *Auf dem Wege zu einer phänomenologischen Psychologie: Die Psychologie von William James*, Gruyter, Berlin, 1961. *On the Way towards a Phenomenological Psychology*, tr. by Giorgi, Duquesne University Press, Pittsburgh, 1968.

McGilvary, E. G., "The Fringe of William James' Psychology," *Philosophical Review*, 20 (1910), 137 ff.

Merleau-Ponty, Maurice, *Phénoménologie de la perception*, Gallimard, Paris, 1945. *The Phenomenology of Perception*, tr. by Colin Smith, Humanities Press, New York, 1962.

——, *The Primacy of Perception and Other Essays* (translations from French originals edited by J. M. Edie), Northwestern University Press, 1964.

Moore, E. C., *American Pragmatism: Peirce, James, and Dewey*, Columbia University Press, 1961.

Perry, R. B., "The Philosophy of William James," *Philosophical Review*, 20 (1911), 1 ff.

——, *The Thought and Character of William James*, 2 vols., Little, Brown, Boston, 1935.

Ravaisson-Mollien, Félix, *De l'habitude*, Alcan, Paris, 1933.

Renouvier, Charles, *Essais de critique générale*, 4 vols., Librarie philosophique, de Ladrange, Paris, 1864 (esp. vols. II and III).
——, *Le personnalisme*, Alcan, Paris, 1903.
Sartre, Jean-Paul, *L'être et le néant: Essai d'ontologie phénoménologique*, Gallimard, Paris, 1943. *Being and Nothingness*, tr. by Hazel Barnes, Philosophical Library, New York, 1956.
——, *Critique de la raison dialectique*, Gallimard, Paris, 1960. *Search for a Method*, tr. by Hazel Barnes, Knopf, New York, 1965.
——, *La Nausée*, Gallimard, Paris, 1947. *Nausea*, tr. by Lloyd Alexander, New Directions, Norfolk, Conn., 1949.
——, "La transcendence de l'égo: Esquisse d'une description phénoménologique," *Recherches philosophiques*, 6 (1936), 85 ff. *The Transcendence of the Ego*, tr. by Forrest Williams and Robert Kirkpatrick, Noonday Press, New York, 1957.
Scheler, Max, *Der Formalismus in der Ethik und die materiale Wertethik*, Niemeyer, Halle, 1927.
Schuetz, Alfred, *Gesammelte Schriften*, I, Nijhoff, The Hague, 1962 (for references to and papers on James, esp. pp. 207 ff. and 340 ff.). *Collected Papers*, I, ed. by M. Natanson, Humanities Press, New York, 1962.
Smith, J. E., "Radical Empiricism," *Proceedings of the Aristotelian Society*, March 22, 1965, p. 217.
Strasser, Stephan, *Das Gemüt: Grundgedanken zu einer phänomenologischen philosophie und theorie des menschlichen Gefühlslebens*, Herder Verlag, Utrecht, 1956.
Straus, Erwin, *The Primary World of Senses*, tr. from 2nd German edition of *Vom Sinn der Sinne* by Jacob Needleman, New York, Free Press of Glencoe, 1963.
——, "The Upright Posture," *Psychiatric Quarterly*, 26 (1952), 529 ff.
Van der Leeuw, G., *Phänomenologie der Religion*, Mohr, Tübingen, 1956.
Wahl, J., *Les Philosophies pluralistes d'Angleterre et d'Amerique*, Bibliothèque de philosophie contemporaine, Paris, 1920.
Wild, John. *Existence and the World of Freedom*, Prentice-Hall, Englewood Cliffs, N.J., 1963.
Wilshire, Bruce, "Natural Science and Phenomenology: William James' *Principles of Psychology* as a Search for Reconciliation," Ph.D. thesis, New York University, June 1966, soon to be published.

Index